Keeping Found Things Found

The Morgan Kaufmann Series in Interactive Technologies

Series Editors: Stuart Card, PARC; Jonathan Grudin, Microsoft; Jakob Nielsen, Nielsen Norman Group

GUI Bloopers 2.0: Common User Interface Design Don'ts and Dos
Jeff Johnson

Visual Thinking: Design for the Brain
Colin Ware

Moderating Usability Tests: Principles and Practice for Interacting
Joseph Dumas and Beth Loring

User-Centered Design Stories: Real-World UCD Case Studies
Carol Righi and Janice James

Sketching User Experience: Getting the Design Right and the Right Design
Bill Buxton

Text Entry Systems: Mobility, Accessibility, Universality
Scott MacKenzie and Kumiko Tanaka-ishi

Letting Go of the Words: Writing Web Content that Works
Janice "Ginny" Redish

Personas and User Archetypes: A Field Guide for Interaction Designers
Jonathan Pruitt and Tamara Adlin

Cost-Justifying Usability
Edited by Randolph Bias and Deborah Mayhew

User Interface Design and Evaluation
Debbie Stone, Caroline Jarrett, Mark Woodroffe, Shailey Minocha

Rapid Contextual Design
Karen Holtzblatt, Jessamyn Burns Wendell, Shelley Wood

Voice Interaction Design: Crafting the New Conversational Speech Systems
Randy Allen Harris

Understanding Users: A Practical Guide to User Requirements: Methods, Tools, and Techniques
Catherine Courage and Kathy Baxter

The Web Application Design Handbook: Best Practices for Web-Based Software
Susan Fowler and Victor Stanwick

The Mobile Connection: The Cell Phone's Impact on Society
Richard Ling

Information Visualization: Perception for Design, 2nd Edition
Colin Ware

Interaction Design for Complex Problem Solving: Developing Useful and Usable Software
Barbara Mirel

The Craft of Information Visualization: Readings and Reflections
Written and edited by Ben Bederson and Ben Shneiderman

HCI Models, Theories, and Frameworks: Towards a Multidisciplinary Science
Edited by John M. Carroll

Web Bloopers: 60 Common Web Design Mistakes, and How to Avoid Them
Jeff Johnson

Observing the User Experience: A Practitioner's Guide to User Research
Mike Kuniavsky

Paper Prototyping: The Fast and Easy Way to Design and Refine User Interfaces
Carolyn Snyder

The Morgan Kaufmann Series in Multimedia Information and Systems

Series Editor: Edward A. Fox, Virginia Polytechnic University

Web Dragons: Inside the Myths of Search Engine Technology
Ian Witten, Maro Gori, Teresa Numerico

Introduction to Data Compression, Third Edition
Khalid Sayood

Understanding Digital Libraries, Second Edition
Michael Lesk

Bioinformatics: Managing Scientific Data
Zoe Lacroix and Terence Critchlow

How to Build a Digital Library
Ian H. Witten and David Bainbridge

Digital Watermarking
Ingemar J. Cox, Matthew L. Miller, Jeffrey A. Bloom

Readings in Multimedia Computing and Networking
Edited by Kevin Jeffay and HongJiang Zhang

Multimedia Servers: Applications, Environments, and Design
Dinkar Sitaram and Asit Dan

Managing Gigabytes: Compressing and Indexing Documents and Images, Second Edition
Ian H. Witten, Alistair Moffat, Timothy C. Bell

Digital Compression for Multimedia: Principles and Standards
Jerry D. Gibson, Toby Berger, Tom Lookabaugh, Dave Lindbergh, Richard L. Baker

Readings in Information Retrieval
Edited by Karen Sparck Jones and Peter Willett

Keeping Found Things Found

*The Study and Practice of
Personal Information
Management*

William Jones

AMSTERDAM • BOSTON • HEIDELBERG • LONDON
NEW YORK • OXFORD • PARIS • SAN DIEGO
SAN FRANCISCO • SINGAPORE • SYDNEY • TOKYO

Morgan Kaufmann is an imprint of Elsevier

MORGAN KAUFMANN PUBLISHERS

Publisher	Denise E. M. Penrose
Executive Editor	Diane Cerra
Publishing Services Manager	George Morrison
Project Manager	Marilyn E. Rash
Assistant Editor	Mary E. James
Copyeditor	Carol Leyba
Proofreader	Dianne Wood
Indexer	Keith Shostak
Interior Concept/Design	Lisa Liedgren
Interior Illustrations	Elizabeth Boling
Cover Design and Layout	Lisa Liedgren
Typesetting/Illustrations	diacriTech
Interior/Cover Printer	1010 Printing International Ltd.

Morgan Kaufmann Publishers is an imprint of Elsevier.
30 Corporate Drive, Suite 400, Burlington, MA 01803

This book is printed on acid-free paper.

Library of Congress Cataloging-in-Publication Data
Jones, William, 1952–
    Keeping found things found: the study and practice of personal information
        management/William Jones.
        p. cm.–(The Morgan Kaufmann Series in Multimedia Information and Systems)
            (The Morgan Kaufmann Series in Interactive Technologies)
    Includes bibliographical references and index.
    ISBN 978-0-12-370866-3 (alk. paper)
1. Personal information management. 2. Information retrieval. 3. Privacy. I. Title.
    HD30.2.J664 2008
    025.04–dc22   2007029784

For information on all Morgan Kaufmann publications, visit our Web site at
www.mkp.com or *www.books.elsevier.com*

Printed in China
08 09 10 11 12   10 9 8 7 6 5 4 3 2 1

I dedicate this book to my wife,
Maria Jones Staaf

Credits

Contents

Preface   xi
Contributors   xvi

FOUNDATIONS

Chapter One   *A study and a practice*

1.1 Keeping found things found   4
1.2 An ideal and the reality   7
1.3 A brief history of PIM   10
1.4 Who benefits from better PIM and how?   13
1.5 A study and a practice   14
1.6 Looking forward: A map for this book   15

Chapter Two   *A personal space of information*

2.1 Starting out   25
2.2 What is information to us?   28
2.3 How is information personal?   33
2.4 The information item and its form   36
2.5 Defining a personal space of information   40
2.6 Making sense of the PSI   45
2.7 Looking back, looking forward   50

Chapter Three   *A framework for personal information management*

3.1 Starting out   56
3.2 Perspectives on personal information management   59
3.3 PIM activities to map between information and need   60
3.4 PIM-related activities and PIM-related areas   67
3.5 Weaving PIM activities together   72
3.6 Looking back, looking forward   75

ACTIVITIES

Chapter Four   *Finding and re-finding: From need to information*

4.1 Starting out	80
4.2 Getting oriented	82
4.3 Everyday finding: Death by a thousand look-ups	89
4.4 Finding is multistep	93
4.5 The limitations in ideal dialogs of finding	105
4.6 Wayfinding through the PSI	107
4.7 Looking back, looking forward	114

Chapter Five   *Keeping and organizing: From information to need*

5.1 Starting out	122
5.2 Getting oriented	125
5.3 Everyday keeping and organizing: To each his own	126
5.4 Keeping is multifaceted	129
5.5 The limitations of future perfect visions	134
5.6 PICing our battles	138
5.7 Looking back, looking forward	150

Chapter Six   *Maintaining for now and for later*

6.1 Starting out	154
6.2 Getting oriented	156
6.3 Maintaining for now	160
6.4 Maintaining for later	166
6.5 Maintaining for our lives and beyond	171
6.6 Looking back, looking forward	176

Chapter Seven   *Managing privacy and the flow of information*

7.1 Starting out	180
7.2 Getting oriented	182
7.3 Managing the outflow	186
7.4 Managing the inflow	195
7.5 Staying in the flow	202
7.6 Looking back, looking forward	207

Chapter Eight   *Measuring and evaluating*

8.1 Starting out	212
8.2 Getting oriented	214

8.3 A yardstick for measuring PIM practice elements 216
8.4 What can research tell us about methods of measuring and evaluating in our practices PIM? 222
8.5 Measuring and evaluating in real life 230
8.6 Can self-study of PIM practices contribute to the larger study of PIM? 236
8.7 Looking back, looking forward 239

Chapter Nine *Making sense of things*

9.1 Starting out 244
9.2 Getting oriented 245
9.3 Making sense as outcome vs. activity 251
9.4 Making sense of things as a PIM activity 257
9.5 Methods for making sense 263
9.6 Looking back, looking forward 267

SOLUTIONS

Chapter Ten *Email disappears?*

10.1 Starting out: Is email a very successful failure? 272
10.2 PIM problems in email: the one-two punch 274
10.3 PIM activities in email 279
10.4 Future visions of email 284
10.5 Looking back, looking forward 296

Chapter Eleven *Search gets personal*

11.1 Starting out 300
11.2 Search as interaction 303
11.3 Search as technology 307
11.4 Making search more personal 310
11.5 Wayfinding and search 313
11.6 Looking back, looking forward 317

Chapter Twelve *PIM on the go*

12.1 Starting out 320
12.2 Getting oriented 323
12.3 A foreseeable future 325
12.4 What to expect from PIM-on-the-go? 336
12.5 Looking back, looking forward 344

Chapter Thirteen *PIM on the web*

13.1 Starting out 348
13.2 Getting oriented 349

13.3 A foreseeable future?   351
13.4 What to expect for PIM-on-the-Web?   354
13.5 Looking back, looking forward   366

CONCLUSIONS

Chapter Fourteen   *Bringing the pieces together*

14.1 Starting out   370
14.2 Getting oriented   372
14.3 Stories of synergy   374
14.4 Kinds of integration   379
14.5 Enabling unifications   380
14.6 Looking back, looking forward   385

Chapter Fifteen   *Finding our way in(to) the future*

15.1 Starting out   388
15.2 To the future   389
15.3 In the future   394
15.4 On our way   399

References   403
Index   423

Preface

This book has its origin in the Keeping Found Things Found (KFTF) project, which began in 2000 at the University of Washington Information School. Funding for the project originally came through a three-year National Science Foundation[1] grant to study how people keep web information for later use and how tools might help. As primary author of the grant proposal, I selected the working title, "Keeping found things found on the Web." It stuck and was shortened to become the name of the overall project (see *http://kftf.ischool.washington.edu/*).

Finding information is an important and well-studied problem. Communities of researchers study how people seek information and the ways in which information retrieval systems might help. But, once found, what then? We often encounter information that's useful but most likely later, not now. How do we keep and organize such information for later, and sometimes repeated, use in our lives?

In a first-year study, we observed that people used many methods to keep web pages for later use. Analysis revealed that different methods served different purposes. And no method came close to doing everything a person might like to do to keep information available for future use.

One major challenge was simply figuring out where and how to keep information. At home or at work? On which computer? In which account? In which organization? In what form? As a paper printout? An e-document? In an email message? As a web bookmark? Or perhaps, as an in-line-reference in some document?

Later, questions like these were asked again as people tried to decide where and how to re-find the information ("Where did I put it?"). And, in between keeping and re-finding, people also need to determine how best to organize and maintain all the information accessed and accumulated. Is it worth it to organize information into folders? Or maybe labels and tags could be used instead? Or maybe nothing at all, if information could be searched for? But what if basically the same information—a document being revised, for example—exists in many versions. How is one to be sure the most up-to-date or relevant version is the one retrieved?

The preceding are basic questions of *personal information management*, or *PIM*.

---

[1] National Science Foundation under Grant No. 0097855: *http://www.nsf.gov/awardsearch/showAward. do?AwardNumber=0097855*.

Mike Eisenberg, while still dean of the University of Washington Information School and also a member of the KFTF project, was the first to suggest the connection between work of the KFTF project and the larger problem of PIM. At first I balked: "Personal information management?"

I knew of Lansdale's excellent "Psychology of Personal Information Management" article written back in the 1980s (1988 to be exact). Since then, however, the phrase seemed to have become most strongly associated with "PIM tools," which combine email management with time, task, and contact management.

Leaving aside its associations, what about the phrase itself? Isn't nearly everything we do informational? Isn't "personal information management" quite broad? Can there be a meaningful area of study for something as broad and inclusive as that? Yes, yes, and yes.

Yes, nearly everything we do is informational. More to the point, in this information age, much of what we "see" and "hear" about the world is not through direct experience but rather through various forms and channels of information. We watch television, read newspapers and email messages, or surf the Internet. Likewise, many of the ways to effect change in our world are mediated by information. We complete web-based or paper-based applications, send email messages, and write reports. Some of us post information on blogs or to personal web sites. Our days are filled with many acts of information management, large and small.

Yes, personal information management is broad; but its breadth is also part of its point. As I've talked to people, formally through the KFTF studies and informally at social gatherings, my ever-growing impression is that important aspects of our personal relationship to the world—as mediated by information and information tools—have been falling through the gaps between established areas of research and development. Feature-laden cell phones, digital cameras, software applications, and various other information tools, even as they help us in some ways, often add extra stress and complications to our lives. One tool organizes and formats information in one way; another tool organizes and formats information in a completely different way. Even though each accomplishes its intended purpose, these tools don't work together in ways that make sense for our lives with respect to the things we hope to do and strive to be.

Finally, PIM can be, and is becoming, a meaningful area of study with a community of researchers. The process of building a community for the study of PIM may have begun with a Special Interest Group session on personal information management, which was organized as part of the CHI 2004 conference on human–computer interaction.[2] But perhaps the watershed event in the creation of a PIM community was PIM 2005—a special NSF-sponsored workshop[3]

---

[2] Bergman, O., Boardman, R., Gwizdka, J., and Jones, W. (2004). A special interest group session on personal information management *CHI '04 Extended Abstracts on Human Factors in Computing Systems*, Vienna, Austria. New York: ACM Press.

[3] National Science Foundation (NSF) grant # 0435134—see *http://www.nsf.gov/awardsearch/showAward. do?AwardNumber=0435134*.

held in January of 2005 in Seattle.[4] The participants formed a nexus for follow-on workshops,[5] special issues,[6] and an edited book on PIM.[7]

The community of researchers studying PIM is diverse with respect to primary discipline and technical background. For example, the PIM 2005 Workshop brought together researchers from the fields of cognitive science, human–computer interaction (HCI), information science, artificial intelligence, database management, knowledge management, and information retrieval. Participants had been doing PIM-relevant research all along. But the workshop, and other community-building events that followed its lead, have helped give common expression to PIM problems researchers had each been tackling in separate ways. Events like these have also promoted the exchange of data and ideas in support of PIM solutions.

It is my hope that this book will serve a similar purpose for each of us no matter what our professional, educational, or technical background. We are all involved in a daily struggle to make effective use of information and numerous informational tools. We have been doing PIM all along. The book can help, first of all, by giving expression to our PIM activities and the problems encountered as we try to make sense of all the information in our lives.

The book is also about solutions and approaches to take. It describes steps we can take right now to improve our PIM practices. The book also describes the PIM support we can expect to find available in the not-too-distant future. Most important, the book describes the kinds of questions we need to ask and the considerations we need to apply to a never-ending cavalcade of new tools, new technologies, new systems, new initiatives, and so on. What will work for us in our lives? How can we take charge of our information? And, in doing so, how might we also take greater charge of our lives?

Acknowledgments

The following people have helped, directly or indirectly, with the completion of this book. The ordering of names is arbitrary save for the first:

- My wife, Maria Jones Staaf, gave support at many levels and in many ways even as the process of book completion seemed to take over not only my life but hers as well. The book could not have been completed without her support, encouragement, and understanding.

---

[4] For more information on this PIM 2005 workshop and to access its final report, see *http://pim.ischool.washington.edu/pim05home.htm*.

[5] PIM 2006, a special two-day workshop, was held as part of SIG-IR 2006 (*http://pim.ischool.washington.edu/pim06/index.htm*). As of this book's writing, planning for another workshop in association with CHI 2008 is underway.

[6] The January 2006 issue of the *Communications of the ACM* included a special section on PIM—see Teevan, J., Jones, W., and Bederson, B. (eds.). (2006). *Communications of the ACM: A Special Issue on Personal Information Management*. New York: ACM Press. A special issue on PIM for *ACM Transactions on Information Systems* is planned for release in 2008.

[7] See Jones, W., and Teevan, J. (2007). *Personal Information Management*. Seattle: University of Washington Press.

A number of people provided useful feedback on matters ranging from structure and content to style and clarity. I take full responsibility for the book's remaining failings, but the book is much better for their efforts:

- Bob Boiko, John Wetherbie, and Ryen W. White gave considered, invaluable comments on nearly all chapters in the book.

- Alan Dix, Edward Fox, and Peter Morville provided extremely useful comments on numerous chapters.

- Rick Boardman, Mary Czerwinski, Alan Dix, Jonathan Grudin, Jacek Gwizdka, and one anonymous reviewer provided very useful feedback on the original book proposal that helped me set the book's direction and coverage.

- Diane Cerra was the personal face of the publisher through much of my struggle to complete the book. She arranged for reviewer feedback from the people just mentioned, as well as its interpretation. Diane was a constant, comforting source of support and guidance.

- Michael Adcock, Andrea Lisabeth Civan, and Predrag V Klasnja provided very useful feedback on several chapters.

- Olle Bälter, Susan Dumais, George Furnas, Jim Gemmell, Jane Glascock, Lars Johansson, Mike Kelly, Rod Such, and Don Webb gave very useful feedback on selected chapters in the book.

- Olle Bälter, Bob Boiko, Mike Kelly, Peter Morville, Mike Nakahara, and Dan Russell took time out of their already busy professional lives to contribute some of the book's sidebar content. The book is much better and more well-rounded because of their contributions.

- I am also grateful to Hala Annabi for the many useful references she provided me to current research about information management at the organizational level. I also thank Karen Erickson for her assistance with two of the book's figures.

- Cheyenne Maria Roduin provided constant, often short-notice, assistance throughout the book's completion, ranging from research on various topics to copyediting and proofreading. Other people to help me directly with copyediting and proofreading include: Andrea Lisbeth Civan, Glenda Claborne, Marguerite Finnigan, Beth Fournier, Shelley K. Minden, and anonymous editors at Morgan Kaufmann/Elsevier.

Other people have provided support without which the book's completion would have been much more difficult:

- Harry Bruce, as my long-time colleague and co-manager of the Keeping Found Things Found project, provided invaluable support for the project during the book's completion, even as he also worked to meet the considerable demands of his new position as dean of the University of Washington Information School.

- Kerstin Severinson Eklundh and Olle Bälter were excellent, understanding hosts during my extended springtime visit to the Royal Institute of Technology (KTH) in Stockholm, even though the final stages of the book's completion were a dominant presence throughout the visit.

- Maria Zemankova, as a program officer at the National Science Foundation, deserves great credit for her vision in seeing the potential of personal information management. Many of the community-building activities listed previously in this preface can be traced, directly or indirectly, to her support and guidance.

Acknowledgments include things as well as people and are a testament to the transforming power of the informational tools and technologies that are a primary topic of this book. For example, the reliable use of email (only occasionally supplemented by the phone) meant that book-related communication could happen over time and across great distances.

The Web greatly increased my reach to relevant material. I was especially grateful for the use of Google's search service and the Wikipedia to provide useful points of disembarkation into the Web in all its vastness.

Information sources must always be qualified and information validated. This is perhaps especially true for information found on the Web. But the qualification of sources and the validation of information was itself greatly facilitated by the online, Web-mediated access to information collections in the extensive University of Washington Libraries system.

The book was done in its entirety on an aging but very reliable IBM Thinkpad X30 laptop computer. With the benefit of wireless access, large portions of it were completed at home, in my favorite coffee shop, and even at the Kirkland Public Library.

The Web provided me with access not only to information but also to people. For example, I first "discovered" Elizabeth Boling, whose illustrations appear in every chapter of the book, through her work on a professional web site. As of this writing, I have not yet met Elizabeth in person. Our interactions have been entirely through email with the exception of one phone call. Similarly, my interactions with Cheyenne Roduin were exclusively via email (including an email introduction) for a period of nearly seven months before I finally met her in person—even though, for much of this period, we were both in the greater Seattle area.

But even as my work on the book was greatly facilitated by new modes of communication, the serendipitous networking enabled by old-fashioned "face-to-face" contact still played an essential role in its completion. Lisa Liedgren, as noted on the copyright page, did the concept work for the book's overall design and layout, including its cover and chapter opener spreads. Lisa is a well-known, Seattle-area artist and also a family friend. At the very beginning of my work on this book, I happened to mention my plans to her as we talked to each other at a dinner party. Lisa is interested in PIM and was the one to say, "Let me design your book." It would not have occurred to me to ask. I have been grateful ever since for Lisa's involvement; the book would not be the book it is without her.

Finally, it is important to acknowledge the underlying support of the National Science Foundation for the KFTF project and for the efforts by its principle researchers to facilitate an exchange of information among people doing PIM-relevant research. Descriptions of the project and these efforts are based on work supported by the NSF under Grant Nos. 0097855, 0334623, 0435134, and 0534386. Any opinions, findings and conclusions, or recommendations expressed in this material are those of the author and contributors and do not necessarily reflect the views of the National Science Foundation.

Contributors

Olle Bälter
Royal Institute of Technology, Stockholm, Sweden

Olle Bälter became known as "Mr. Email" in Sweden in 2002 after a popular book based on his doctoral thesis was published. It has advice on how people can improve their email situation. Olle is currently an associate professor and vice dean of education in the School of Computer Science and Communication at the Royal Institute of Technology.

Bob Boiko
University of Washington, Seattle, WA

Bob Boiko is the author of *The Content Management Bible* and the new book *Laughing at the CIO: A Parable and Prescription of IT Leadership*. He has almost 20 years of experience designing and building web, hypertext, and multimedia systems and tools for some of the world's top technology corporations, including Microsoft, Motorola, and Boeing. Bob is founder and president of Metatorial Services Inc. and is also a faculty member at the University of Washington.

Mike Kelly
Microsoft Corporation, Redmond, WA

Mike Kelly is the director of the Emerging Practices team within Microsoft's Engineering Excellence group. This team investigates and promotes new software development practices that the company's product teams can leverage to improve their engineering efficiency and quality. Before joining Engineering Excellence in 2006, Mike worked for 12 years in various development roles on the Microsoft Office team.

Peter Morville
Semantic Studios, Ann Arbor, MI

Peter Morville is the best-selling author of *Ambient Findability* and *Information Architecture for the World Wide Web*. He is president of Semantic Studios, a leading information architecture and user experience consulting firm, and he is a founder and past president of the Information Architecture Institute. Peter is also an adjunct faculty member at the University of Michigan. He blogs at findability.org.

Mike Nakahara

Avocent, Redmond, WA

Mike Nakahara is a director at Avocent, a leader in connectivity and IT infrastructure management. Previously, Mike was a program manager in the Smart Personal Object Technology (SPOT) group at Microsoft. In his years there, he worked on a new class of mobile products including Smart Watches and portable weather stations.

Dan Russell

Google, Mountain View, CA

Daniel M. Russell is a research scientist at Google where he works on search quality, with a focus on understanding what makes the company's users happy when they use the web search engine. From early 2000 until mid-2005, he was a senior research scientist in the User Sciences and Experience Research (USER) lab at IBM's Almaden Research Center. Dan is perhaps best known for his recent work on the large, interactive IBM BlueBoard system for simple collaboration and for his studies of people's sensemaking activities.

A study and a practice

Keeping found information found is an essential challenge of personal information management or PIM. More generally, PIM is about taking charge of the information in our lives. Are we managing our information, or is it managing us? Can we weave an informational fabric that has a strength, utility, and beauty that is far greater than a simple jumble of its component threads? Better PIM starts by asking the right questions. Better PIM means that each of us becomes a student of our practice of PIM.

Chapter One

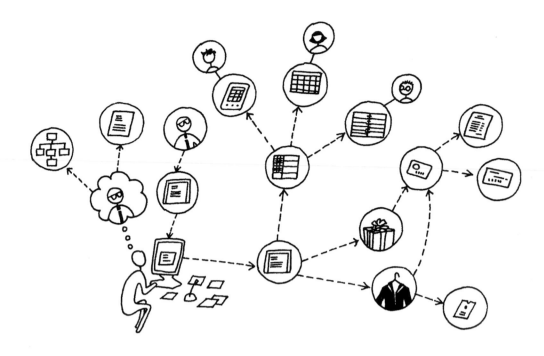

Where is the Life we have lost in living? Where is the wisdom we have lost in knowledge? Where is the knowledge we have lost in information?

T. S. Eliot (1888–1965)

1.1 Keeping found things found

Much of our lives is spent in the finding of things. Find a house that's just right for you. Find a computer or "build" your own. Find your dream job. Find your dream mate. But, once found, what then?

Keeping found things found presents its own set of challenges. You invest your time, your money, your hopes and dreams—your self—in the things you find. Now what? Now that you have found the house that's just right for you, how do you pay for it? How do you maintain it? How do you make it a home? Your computer comes with lots of processing power, memory, and disk storage. It's loaded with software. But how do you make it work for you in your life? Similarly with a dream job or even a dream mate. How do you balance the demands of work and love?

As with other things, so it is with our information. We find information with difficulty or sometimes we find too much information, too easily. Regardless, finding is just the first step. How do we keep this information so that it's there later when we need it? How do we organize it in ways that make sense for us in the lives we lead and want to lead? Information found does us little good if we misplace it or forget about it before we have a chance to use it. And just as we must maintain a house or a car, we need to maintain our information—backing it up, archiving or deleting old information, updating or correcting information that is no longer accurate.

Keeping found information found is an essential challenge of personal information management or PIM.

PIM is about finding, keeping, organizing, and maintaining information. PIM is also about managing privacy and the flow of information. We need to keep other people from getting at our information without our permission. We need to protect our time and attention against an onslaught of information from telephone calls, email messages, the television, radio, and the Web. PIM is also about measurement and evaluation: Is this new tool worth the trouble? Should we change a current strategy (e.g., a strategy for getting through the email inbox or for organizing web references)? And PIM also includes efforts to make sense of our information. What is it telling us about our world? About ourselves? In a larger sense, PIM is about the use of information to keep ourselves "found"—on track to fulfill our life's goals and our life's roles and responsibilities.

Here is a more formal definition for PIM:

> *Personal information management* (PIM) refers to both the practice and the study of the activities a person performs in order to acquire or create, store, organize, maintain, retrieve, use and distribute the information needed to meet life's many goals (everyday and long-term, work-related and not) and to fulfill life's many roles and responsibilities (as parent, spouse, friend, employee, member of community, etc.). PIM places special emphasis on the organization and maintenance of personal information collections in which information items, such as paper documents, electronic documents, email messages, web references, handwritten notes, etc., are stored for later use and repeated re-use.[1]

I notice, though, that when I describe PIM in these terms to people in casual conversation, their eyes glaze over. When I talk instead about "keeping found things found," people invariably say something like "that's my problem" or "let me know when you figure this one out." Is this a problem for you too?

PIM is about finding answers to questions such as these:

- What should I do with all my digital photographs and videos? Will I still be able to see these in thirty or forty years or will they disappear like all the data on my first PC disappeared?
- Why do I seem to practically live in my email inbox? (—if you can call this living). I try to keep up with email but then I don't seem to get anything else done.
- How should I organize my hard drive? I know what to do with paper documents but my computer files are a mess! Sometimes I think I'd be better off reformatting my hard drive and starting all over again.

---

[1] This definition for personal information management is a small variation on a definition provided by Jones (2006).

But PIM is also about finding answers to this question:

- How can I get smarter about the way I manage my information so that I have more time for my family, friends and the things I really care about in life?

By way of introducing PIM and the remainder of this book, discussion in this introductory chapter moves through the following sections:

☑ *An ideal and the reality*. One ideal of PIM is that we always have the right information (in the right place, in the right form, in the right quantity, etc.) to meet our current need. The reality, however, may well be that we spend significant amounts of time overcoming a pervasive problem of information fragmentation made worse by the very tools that are designed to help us.

☑ *A brief history of PIM*. PIM is a new field with ancient roots. The development of a community of people doing PIM-related research is in response to several observations: (1) Analogous to a personal problem of information fragmentation, research relating to PIM is scattered across a number of different disciplines ranging from cognitive psychology to database management. PIM as a field of study provides a productive meeting ground for researchers from these disciplines. (2) PIM concerns—such as the importance of understanding the life cycle of personal information—easily fall in the spaces between other disciplines. (3) PIM is an area of intense interest, both scholarly and popular.

☑ *Who benefits from better PIM and how?* We all do and in several ways. Better PIM also has the potential to provide broad societal benefits.

☑ *A study and a practice*. Better PIM starts by asking the right questions. We can all become better students of our own practices of PIM. The book, through its exploration of PIM foundations, research into PIM activities, and developments in PIM-related technologies, can help by providing concepts and a framework in which to express PIM problems and solutions.

☑ *Looking forward*. The concluding section to this chapter maps out the remainder of the book. The book begins with PIM foundations and then reviews PIM activities we all do (or avoid doing). PIM solutions follow (for email, from search, on PDAs, on the Web), before concluding with a look to the future and to the ways we can "bring the pieces together."

Let's get started.

Information is a source of learning. But unless it is organized, processed, and available to the right people in a format for decision making, it is a burden, not a benefit.

William Pollard (1938–)

1.2 An ideal and the reality

We depend on information to understand our world, to get things done, to make good decisions, to learn and gain better mastery of the world, to understand what we can affect and what we must learn to live with.

One ideal of PIM is that we always have the right information in the right place, in the right form and of sufficient completeness and quality to meet our current need. Tools and technologies help so that we spend less time with time-consuming and error-prone actions of information management. We then have more time to make creative, intelligent use of the information at hand in order to get things done.

This ideal is far from reality for most of us.

In the real world, we do not always find the right information in time to meet our current needs. The necessary information is never found, or it arrives too late to be useful. Or information enters our lives too soon and is misplaced or forgotten entirely before opportunities for its application arrive. We forget to use information even when (or sometimes because) we have taken pains to keep it somewhere in our lives. We fail to get the information we need even when it is directly in view.

This is not the way it was supposed to be. In an inspirational and aptly titled article, "As we may think," Vannevar Bush (1945) expressed a vision that many of us probably share. Tools of information management should provide us with a perfect complement that extends our abilities, compensates for our limitations, supports us to work and think as we need to—only better:

> Consider a future device for individual use, which is a sort of mechanized private file and library. It needs a name, and, to coin one at random, "memex" will do. A memex is a device in which an individual stores all his books, records, and communications, and which is mechanized so that it may be consulted with exceeding speed and flexibility. It is an enlarged intimate supplement to his memory. (p. 6)

The vision endures. One review not so long ago included the following:

> There's a fundamental difference between searching a universe of documents created by strangers and searching your own personal library. When you're freewheeling through ideas that you yourself have collated . . . there's something about the experience that seems uncannily like freewheeling through the corridors of your own memory. It feels like thinking. (Johnson, 2005, p. 27)

Many of us probably share the experience described in this quote: namely, that the ways of accessing and interacting with our personal information are fundamentally different from the ways of accessing and interacting with publicly available information. Less common—much as we might yearn for it—is the experience that personal collections of email messages, web references, files, paper documents, handwritten notes, etc., are a natural extension to memory or that working with these collections of personal information feels like thinking.

More common may be a feeling of being perpetually out of synch with our information. The information is "ours" in the sense that we can move, copy or delete it. But in other ways, the information is not ours and is out of our control. Inboxes are overflowing. Hard drives are encrusted with files and folders that haven't been looked at in years but that still manage to get in the way as we try to access newer information.

New tools, even as they help in some areas, often exacerbate an already pervasive problem of *information fragmentation*. The information we need may be on the wrong computer, PDA, smart phone, or other device. Information may be "here" but locked away in an application or a different format so that the hassles of extraction outweigh the benefits of its use. We may find ourselves maintaining several separate, roughly comparable but inevitably inconsistent, organizational schemes for electronic documents, paper documents, email messages, and web references. The number of organizational schemes can increase if we have several email accounts, use separate computers for home and work, use a PDA or a smart phone, or use any of a bewildering array of special-purpose PIM tools.

These are failures of PIM. Some failures of PIM are memorable. Many of us, for example, can remember the frustration of failing to find an item of information—a paper document, a digital document, an email message—that we know is "here somewhere." In an already busy day, we may spend precious minutes, sometimes hours, looking for lost information.

Other failures of PIM may go unnoticed as part of what might be called an "information friction" associated with getting things done. In his highly influential article, "Man–computer symbiosis," Licklider (1960) described his observations of his own workday:

> About 85 per cent of my "thinking" time was spent getting into a position to think, to make a decision, to learn something I needed to know. . . . [M]y choices of what to attempt and what not to attempt were determined to an embarrassingly great extent by considerations of clerical feasibility, not intellectual capability. (p. 4)

Many of us might reach similar conclusions. For example, a seemingly simple email request can often cascade into a time-consuming, error-prone chore as we seek to bring together, in coherent, consistent form, information that often lies scattered in multiple versions contained in various collections of paper documents, electronic documents, email messages, web references, and the like. Can you give a presentation at a meeting next month? That depends. What did you say in previous email messages? When is your child's soccer match? Better check the paper flyer with scheduled games. Does the meeting conflict with a conference coming up? Better check the conference web site to get dates and program information. What have you already scheduled in your calendar? And so on. In their observations of people processing email, Bellotti et al. (2005) describe instances in which a single email message initiates a task involving several different software applications and lasting an hour or more.

How do tools need to work so that their use feels more like thinking? How do we need to manipulate our information so that it is truly ours—and more like an extension of our own memories? These are long-standing questions of PIM, given new urgency with ongoing, dramatic increases in the amount and variety of information that can be stored digitally for personal use.

1.2.1 What are we really managing?

Information is a means to an end. Not always, not for everyone, but mostly. Information is rarely even a very precious resource. We usually have far too much of it. Even a document we have spent days or weeks writing is typically available in multiple locations (and, sometimes confusingly, in multiple versions). We manage our information so that we can manage our lives.

We manage information for what it represents: our world, alternatives, and the means for effecting change in this world. Information represents alternatives—alternate hotels, alternate life journeys. Information represents the means for change—information to make the hotel reservation, information concerning how to practice Zen and where.

Even if information itself is rarely a precious asset, we manage information because information is the most visible, "tangible" way to manage other resources that *are* precious.

In 1971, Herbert Simon, Nobel laureate in economics, elegantly expressed this point with respect to the resource of attention:

> What information consumes is rather obvious: it consumes the attention of its recipients. Hence, a wealth of information creates a poverty of attention and a need to allocate that attention efficiently among the overabundance of information sources that might consume it. (p. 40)

This quote still rings true if we replace "attention" with "time," "energy," or "well-being." Certainly the nagging presence of papers representing unpaid bills, unanswered email or unfiled documents can distract, enervate and demoralize. We can't see our well-being, our attention or our energy or even our time. But we can see—and manage—our paper documents, our e-documents, our email messages, our digital calendars and other forms of information. It is through the management of these personal information items that we seek to manage the precious resources of our lives.

1.2.2 More than organizing; more than just getting things done

PIM is about the use of information to manage precious resources such as our time and attention. PIM is also about the use of information to make good decisions and to get things done. But to equate PIM with decision making or time and task management is to understate its scope. We live in a world of information. Our understanding for and feelings about the world around us are increasingly a product not of direct experience but rather of the information we receive in the form of newspapers, magazines, television programs, selected slices of the Web, and so on. To manage our information is to manage our reality.

An important distinction must also be made between organizing and managing information. Many of us know people who have very disorganized collections of information and yet they manage. Some of these people may even be exceptional in their ability to manage not only themselves and their personal projects, but also the work of others. On the other hand, many of us may have had the experience that sometimes the hours we spent to "get organized" never really paid off. People who are very organized can fail in their practice of PIM; people who are very disorganized can succeed. Personal information collections can appear to be a disorganized mess. But is this mess part of a larger strategy of PIM, or not?

Bob and Ted each have email inboxes with more that two thousand email messages. To outward appearances, both inboxes are equally disorganized. When asked about his inbox, Bob expresses a guilty, fearful exasperation. "I know! It's a mess! I just don't know what to do about it!" When asked about his, Ted says, "I like having ready access to all email I've received over the past year. If an email message is really important, I'll drag a copy of it to my calendar or to the file system. But it's not worth my time to sift through and file away or delete inbox messages one by one."

Ted is managing his incoming email; Bob is not. For Ted, the disordered inbox fits into a larger strategy of PIM. For Bob, the disordered inbox is a repeated reminder of his failure to gain control of his information (and perhaps the inbox stands for a larger lack of control in his life).

1.3 A brief history of PIM

PIM is a new field with ancient roots. When the oral rather than the written word dominated, human memory was the primary means for information preservation. Various mnemonics[2] were essentially information management as applied to human memory.

As information was increasingly rendered in documents and these increased in number, so too did the challenges of managing these documents. To support the management of paper-based information, tools were developed over time. J. Yates (1989) notes, for example, that the vertical filing cabinet, now such a standard feature of home and workplace offices, was first commercially available in 1893.

The modern dialog on PIM is generally thought to have begun at the close of World War II with the publication of Vannevar Bush's "As we may think" article. Bush recognized the difficulty brought on by the sheer quantity of information being produced and by the compartmentalization of information by an increasing specialization of scientific disciplines: "The investigator is staggered by the findings and conclusions of thousands of other workers—conclusions which he cannot find time to grasp, much less to remember, as they appear." Bush expressed a hope that technology might be used to extend our collective ability to handle information and to break down barriers impeding the productive exchange of information.

The 1940s also saw the development by Shannon and Weaver (Shannon, 1948; Shannon & Weaver, 1949) of a theory of communication that lay the groundwork for a quantitative assessment of information value. Key to this theory is the notion that the information content

---

[2] See F. A. Yates (1966) for an excellent review of mnemonic techniques.

of a message can be measured for its capacity to reduce uncertainty. Although the precise definition of information with respect to uncertainty will come to be seen as overly restrictive, a larger point in the work of Shannon and Weaver remains: the value of information is not absolute but relative to a context that includes the intentions of the sender, the method of delivery, and the current state of a recipient's knowledge.

With the increasing availability of computers in the 1950s came an interest in the computer as a source of metaphors and a test bed for efforts to understand the human ability to process information and to solve problems. Newell and Simon pioneered the computer's use as a tool to model human thought (Newell, Shaw, & Simon, 1958; Simon & Newell, 1958). They produced "The Logic Theorist," generally thought to be the first running artificial intelligence (AI) program. The computer of the 1950s also inspired Donald Broadbent's development of an *information processing approach* to human behavior and performance (1958). By analogy to standard stages of information processing on a computer, people input information via their eyes, ears, and other sensory organs; they store and process this information internally; and they output the results of this processing via their motor organs, including hands and mouth.

After the 1950s research showed that the computer, as a symbol processor, could "think" (to varying degrees of fidelity) like people do, the 1960s saw an increasing interest in the use of computers to help people think better and to process information more effectively. Working with Andries van Dam and others, Ted Nelson, who coined the word "hypertext" (Nelson, 1965), developed one of the first hypertext systems, the Hypertext Editing System, in 1968 (Carmody et al., 1969). That same year, Douglas Engelbart also completed work on a hypertext system called NLS (Engelbart & English, 1994—video in 1968). Engelbart (1961, 1963) advanced the notion that the computer could be used to augment the human intellect. As heralded by the publication of Ulric Neisser's book *Cognitive Psychology* (1967), the 1960s also saw the emergence of cognitive psychology as a discipline in its own right—one focused primarily on a better understanding of the human ability to think, learn, and remember.

The term "personal information management" was itself apparently first used in the 1980s (Lansdale, 1988) in the midst of general excitement over the potential of the personal computer to greatly enhance the human ability to process and manage information. The 1980s also saw the advent of so-called PIM tools which provided limited support for the management of such things as appointments and scheduling, to-do lists, phone numbers, and addresses. And a community dedicated to the study and improvement of human–computer interaction emerged in the 1980s as well (Card, Moran, & Newell, 1983; Norman, 1988).

PIM as an area of study with its own community of practitioners has emerged more recently. This book's preface lists some of the key events of the past decade leading to the establishment of a community of people doing PIM-related research and to the publication of this book. Efforts to form a community for the exchange of PIM research have several motivations:

1. *PIM-related research is scattered across existing disciplines*. Just as the information we need to answer a question or complete a task in our lives is often scattered (by location,

application, computer, etc.), PIM-related research is scattered across a diverse set of disciplines that includes cognitive psychology, human–computer interaction, database management, artificial intelligence, information and knowledge management, information retrieval, and information science.

2. *PIM concerns often fall through the cracks between these disciplines.* PIM requires the study of and support for people as they do the work of their lives in their own informational environments over extended periods of time, as opposed to short-term, experimenter-provided tasks in a controlled laboratory setting. PIM means considering the life cycle of personal information—from the acquisition of information to its initial use, its organization for repeated use, its ongoing maintenance, and its eventual archiving or deletion.

3. *PIM continues to increase in importance and relevance.* Not only academic publications but also articles in the popular press reflect a growing interest in and concern with matters of PIM. Pick up a magazine or newspaper and you have a good chance of seeing articles on one or more PIM-related topics such as (1) information overload, (2) our kids' ability to get things (like homework) done with TV on, iPod plugged in, and several different instant messaging (IM) conversations going at the same time, (3) how to protect our digital information—especially photographs and videos, (4) how to protect our privacy, when companies keep so much information (and misinformation) about us, (5) new, cool smartphones and PDAs, and (6) meeting, dating, and doing virtually everything else on the Web.

The growing interest in PIM also has two sides. On one side, the pace of improvements in various PIM-relevant technologies suggests that earlier ideals of PIM may actually be realized in the near future. Digital storage is cheap and plentiful. Why not keep a record of everything we have encountered?[3] Digital storage can hold not only conventional kinds of information, but also pictures, photographs, music, and even films and full-motion video. In this vision, better search support can make it easy to pinpoint information. The ubiquity of computing and the miniaturization of computing devices can make it possible for us to take our information with us wherever we go and stay connected to a much larger world of information. Improvements in technologies of information input and output (e.g., better voice recognition, voice synthesis, integrated displays of information) can free us from the mouse, keyboard, and monitor of a conventional computer.

This is all very exciting. But the current, growing interest in PIM is also spurred by the awareness that technology and tool development, for all their promise, invariably create new problems and sometimes exacerbate old problems. Information that was once only in paper form is now scattered around in multiple paper and digital versions. Digital information further scatters into "information islands" when each is supported by a separate application or device. This other side of current interest in PIM recognizes that new tools and new applications—for all the targeted help they provide—can still end up further complicating a person's overall information management challenge.

---

[3] See Czerwinski et al. (2006) for a recent review of digital memory initiatives.

1.4 Who benefits from better PIM and how?

PIM may involve the "personal," but better PIM promises to bring broad societal benefit:

- Within organizations, better PIM can mean *better employee productivity*. Better PIM can mean that employees have a clearer understanding of their information and their needs. Such an understanding can also facilitate better teamwork and better group information management.[4] Longer-term, PIM is key to the management and leveraging of employee expertise. (See Chapter 3's discussion of knowledge management.)

- Progress in PIM is evidenced not only by better tools but also by new teachable strategies of information management of direct relevance to education programs of information literacy.[5]

- As people age, their working memory (the number of things they can keep in mind at one time) generally decreases. Better PIM can translate to compensating tools and strategies of support.

- The challenges of PIM are especially felt by people who are battling a life-threatening illness such as cancer as they try to maintain their jobs and profession-related activities while living their lives and fulfilling their various roles (as parent, spouse, friend, member of a community, etc.). Better PIM can help patients better manage their treatments and their lives overall.[6]

But certainly better PIM benefits you, regardless of your special circumstances. There is little chance you could be reading these lines were information and external forms of information (email messages, web pages, newspapers, this book) not of great importance to your world-view and the way you lead your life.

Consider two kinds of people, *information warriors* and *information worriers*. Information warriors see their information and their information tools as strategic assets. Information warriors are wiling to invest time and money to keep up with the latest in PDAs, smartphones, operating systems and application software, and anything new on the Web. For an information warrior, information technology is, so to speak, a profit center.

By contrast, information technology for information worriers is a cost center. New offerings in PDAs and smartphones, new releases of operating system and application software, new developments in the alphabet soup of Web-based initiatives—these and other developments in information technology represent more time and money that need to be spent just to keep up with everyone else. Information worriers may have a nagging feeling they could do better in their choice of supporting tools and strategies. But they don't know where to begin.

Even if these descriptions are stereotyped, many of us can probably think of people we know who come close to fitting each description. Perhaps you are an information warrior or an information worrier. Or perhaps, like me, you are a little of both.

The simple fact is that even if we embrace new developments in information technology, we must recognize that we don't always have the time to learn about all the latest developments.

---

[4] See Lutters, Ackerman, and Zhou (2007) for a discussion of connections between PIM and group information management.

[5] For more on recent initiatives in information literacy, see Eisenberg, Lowe, and Spitzer (2004).

[6] For more on special considerations of PIM that apply to patients, see Moen (in press) and Pratt et al. (2006).

We need a basis for deciding whether a new tool or a new way of doing things is likely to work for us. We'd like to avoid investing money and, more important, time to learn to use a new tool or strategy only to conclude belatedly that it won't work for us.

Better PIM starts by asking the right questions. Better PIM means that each of us becomes a student of our practice of PIM.

Just because it's common sense, doesn't mean it's common practice.

U.S. actor, lecturer, and humorist Will Rogers (1879–1935)

1.5 A study and a practice

Occasionally I teach half- and whole-day seminars on PIM. After one such course a few years ago, an attendee approached me with the comment: "The course made me realize that I know more than I thought I knew." Was the course too basic for him? No, he explained, the course helped him a great deal and especially by giving credence to and words to express vaguely felt intuitions he had already.

Let this be a purpose of this book too. We each know a great deal already concerning our ways of managing our information. We know what seems to work and what doesn't. Although this book reviews research that relates to PIM, research alone can't tell you how to practice PIM. Use the concepts, framework, and examples of this book to become a better student of your own PIM practice. There is little about PIM that can be studied in a laboratory. PIM needs to be studied in situations of actual information management and used over extended periods. Who better to study your own practice of PIM than you?

In the other direction, your experiences and the insights you have gained from your practice of PIM can inform the overall study of PIM. Our practices of PIM are each uniquely tailored to our own unique circumstances—our education, our familiarity with computers, our jobs, our tolerance for risk, and many other factors. But our circumstances also overlap. We can learn from each other. Toward this end, a Web-based "Tales of PIM" discussion forum has been established as a means for researchers and practitioners (that's all of us) alike to share our experiences with PIM. What problems have we encountered? What solutions have we developed? Please share your experiences too.[7]

To become an able and successful man in any profession, three things are necessary, nature, study and practice.

U.S. clergyman and abolitionist Henry Ward Beecher (1813–1887)

---

[7] For more, you can read the experiences of others at *http://talesofpim.org./* without registering. Registration takes only two minutes, and then you can share your experiences as well.

1.6 Looking forward: A map for this book

The book moves through the following sections:

- ☑ Foundations of PIM are established in this chapter and the next two (Chapters 1 through 3).

- ☑ Activities of PIM are described in Chapters 4 through 9. How do we practice PIM? What essential challenges must be faced? What problems arise? And what does this say for the supporting tools we need?

- ☑ Solutions of PIM are described in Chapters 10 through 13. Email, search, PDAs and other portable devices, and the Web are all assessed for their impact, current and potential, on our practices of PIM.

- ☑ Conclusions about PIM are discussed in Chapters 14 and 15. How should the pieces of a PIM practice fit together? How can our tools help? What does the future hold?

Think of this book as a journey—a shared exploration of matters relating to PIM, ranging from academic research, to technical development, to everyday practicalities. Topics in each of the remaining chapters are introduced in a "Starting out" section. Each chapter concludes with a "Looking back, looking forward" section, with a summary of the chapter's main points and a brief preview of the chapter to follow. And now a little more about each section and its chapters.

1.6.1 Foundations

This part sets the stage with an introductory chapter and two others.

Chapter 1. *A study and a practice.*

Chapter 2. *A personal space of information.* What is information to us, and what does "personal" mean in this context? Personal information and informational tools combine to form a personal space of information that is just as real—sometimes more real—than the physical space we occupy.

Chapter 3. *A framework for personal information management.* PIM activities are an effort to establish, use, and maintain a mapping between information and need. Kinds of PIM activities are situated with respect to this mapping. Explanations for what PIM is and is not are developed through a comparison with related areas of study.

1.6.2 Activities

This part explores key kinds of PIM activities in greater detail.

Chapter 4. *Finding and re-finding: From need to information.* Finding is a multistep process, each step of which may entail some stumbling around. Various small acts of finding happen throughout a day and can easily consume much of the time in a day. Different finding activities have in common an essential movement from a current need toward information that will meet this need.

Chapter 5. *Keeping and organizing: From information to need.* The essential challenge of keeping stems from the multifaceted nature of the decisions concerning anticipated need. Is the information useful? Do special actions need to be taken to keep it for later use?

Where? When? In what form? On which device? With no crystal ball to see into the future, answering these questions is difficult and error-prone. Like finding, small acts of keeping occur throughout a day and can likewise consume much of a day's time. With keeping, the focus is on individual information items such as a web page, an email message, or a proffered business card. With organizing, the focus is on a collection of such items. With both keeping and organizing, the movement is from information at hand to anticipated need.

Chapter 6. *Maintaining information for now and for later.* Do you know where your information is? Is it safeguarded against hard-drive failure? Fire? Theft? What about those digital photos you took that can never ever be replaced if lost? Information needs to be backed up. Support for older digital formats—especially for media items such as photographs and videos—may disappear as newer formats emerge. Old information needs to be deleted, archived, or otherwise moved out of the way so that we don't keep tripping over it as we try to access current, working information. Document duplicates and near-duplicates may create havoc later if they are not removed or reconciled with one another. Information needs to be corrected or updated (perhaps in several different places). These and other maintenance activities are discussed here.

Chapter 7. *Managing privacy and the flow of information.* A discussion of privacy and security brings us to a consideration not only of "our" information but also information "about us" and the large overlap between these two kinds of personal information. If our first reaction is to say that "personal information is personal and no one else can see it," we are likely to realize later that some distribution of our personal information can be very useful. We want the travel agent to know about our seating preferences. We want colleagues and friends to know about our schedule. We may want close friends and family to know about our current condition if we are battling a serious illness. The proliferation in the ways to project our personal information onto the Web naturally brings out a desire for technology that can support a personal privacy policy with finer distinctions concerning who can access what under which circumstances. Similarly, we want to control the flow of incoming information so that, for example, our dinner hour is not interrupted by telephone calls that can wait or our inboxes do not fill up with spam. Activities to manage the flow of information (to us, about us) are discussed here.

Chapter 8. *Measuring and evaluating.* We should periodically ask ourselves: Is it working? Are our schemes for organizing information maintainable? Are the strategies we try to follow sustainable? Is this tool really helping, or is it more trouble than it's worth? For paper documents, the evidence that things aren't working is sometimes all too clear. For example, if paper documents continue to pile up in a to-be-filed stack and we never have time to actually file these documents away, this may be a sign that our great new organizational scheme, for all its promise, is simply not sustainable. As we look for efficient, accurate, objective ways to evaluate our own practice of PIM, we run into many of the same problems, at an individual level, that are also in evidence for the field of PIM. Activities to measure and evaluate are discussed here.

Chapter 9. *Making sense of things.* We try to understand our information and its implications for our lives. What does the information mean? How should it inform our decisions? Efforts to make sense of information are often facilitated by piling, sorting, and otherwise manipulating information items so that key patterns and relationships are more apparent and, literally, more visible.

Each chapter in the PIM activities part of the book includes the following three sidebars meant to make more explicit some of the implications for a chapter's discussion:

- *What now for IT?* PIM issues are organizational as well as personal. Good PIM can improve employee productivity and job satisfaction in ways that directly impact the bottom line of a company or other organization. Managers of information technology departments know this. But they also know that letting in the wrong tools and promoting the wrong practices of information management can have the opposite effect.

- *What next in tool development?* How can software developers apply the lessons of a chapter in their development of tools? PIM-relevant technologies are numerous, quickly advancing, and still greatly underutilized. Many opportunities to improve PIM tool support are missed for the simple reason that people with an understanding of PIM problems and opportunities don't talk with the people best able to make better tools to address problems and exploit opportunities.

- *What now for you and me?* We should not hold ourselves and our practices of PIM captive to future tools that may or may not fulfill their marketing brochure promises. What can we do now with what we have in available tools and techniques? With a particular kind of PIM activity in mind, what considerations apply no matter what the available tools?

1.6.3 Solutions

This part includes chapters on four distinct solution areas, each of which has had and will continue to have a profound impact on our practices of PIM:

Chapter 10. *Email disappears?* The title provocatively suggests that email, as we know it, may need to change profoundly and in ways that mean we no longer recognize it as email. Two necessary improvements in email will require its radical transformation: (1) Email, as one mode of communication, will need to integrate with other modes of communication such as the telephone and instant messaging. This process of integration is already underway. (2) Email conversations need to be situated within the collaborative informational contexts in which we work. Support for wikis, for example, though basic now, points to the possibility that people working together might communicate more directly through a shared representation that greatly reduces the need for email exchange and that also improves the efficiency of such exchanges when they do occur. This chapter reviews email challenges with respect to each of the seven kinds of PIM activity.

Chapter 11. *Search gets personal.* Each of the six ways that information can be personal (see Chapter 2) also points to a way that search can get more personal. This chapter considers new opportunities to personalize search both as interaction and as technology. Making search-as-interaction more personal means using personal information to improve both the initial processing of a search request and the quality of results returned. Making search-as-technology more personal means leveraging a process of content analysis, done in any case to create an index, in order to support PIM activities in new ways that have little, visibly, to do with search-as-interaction.

Chapter 12. *PIM on the go.* A near future is described in which a single gadget—call it a PDA— that we carry in a pocket or a purse can store nearly all the information most of us are likely to need and can also come equipped with sufficient processing power—exceeding that of current laptops—for its management and use. We consider it a devil's irony that all our information could be "there" in a single gadget and yet still be deeply fragmented in informational space by information tool and form. Features of a PDA can, and should, be analyzed with respect to their support for each of the seven kinds of PIM activities. A consideration of PIM activities suggests ways to better leverage and integrate the features of a PDA.

Chapter 13. *PIM on the Web*. A near future is described in which nearly all of life's activities—schooling, shopping, job search, working at a job, dating—are mediated by the Web. We use the Web as an extension of ourselves, projecting our preferences, interests, opinions, availability, abilities, and services. Between our PDA as one focus and the Web as another, many of us may decide to dispense with our traditional personal computer (desktop or laptop) altogether. Just as with features of a PDA, we can analyze a confusion of Web services and initiatives with respect to their support for each of the seven kinds of PIM activity.

1.6.4 Conclusions

This part has just two chapters:

Chapter 14. *Bringing the pieces together*. There is a large difference between simple convergence of information and its integration into a larger whole in which pieces are mutually supporting. How can we achieve better levels of integration for the information in our lives, and how can our tools help?

Chapter 15. *Finding our way in (to) the future*. The book concludes with a return to PIM as a study and practice we each do now and can do better. We're doing our best to find our way with respect to the management of information in our lives. What about the future? Finding our way into the future can be approached from two perspectives. How do we find our way to the future? Which future? What must we be certain to plan for? Second, how do we find our way *in* the future? How do we keep our life's purpose and values foremost when we're sure to be pulled in many directions by new tools and new forms of information?

1.6.5 Other PIM topics covered throughout this book

In a book that is already long, many other topics of PIM are perhaps deserving of their own chapters, but will be discussed instead, throughout the book, as the opportunity arises. Topics covered in this distributed fashion include:

- *Individual and group differences in PIM*. Each practice of PIM is unique. People also differ in their approach to PIM and their needs for PIM by age group (e.g., teens vs. college students vs. elderly people) and special circumstance (e.g. patients fighting a life-threatening illness such as cancer). Implications of individual and group differences for PIM practice and the design of supporting tools are discussed at various points in the book, albeit all too briefly.[8]

- *Techniques of PIM*, which might be incorporated into program of PIM training or a larger program of information literacy, are also discussed in Chapters 4 through 9 (see, especially, the "What now for you and me?" sections).

---

[8] But for a much more complete discussion of individual differences in PIM, see Gwizdka and Chignell (2007); and for a discussion of patient needs for PIM, see Moen (2007).

- *Considerations of PIM* vary for different forms of information, such as paper documents, email messages, digital music, photographs, and videos. Paper printouts, for example, can be easily taken wherever we go, marked up, and then discarded when "used up" (with the assurance that the digital original remains). Email messages carry an expectation of response. Digital photographs and videos representing events in our lives are irreplaceable. Variations in PIM for different forms of information will be covered—especially in Chapter 6's discussion of maintenance. Just as important, however, are the common considerations of PIM that apply regardless of information form.

- *Digital memories* and the possibility to record all of a life's experiences (to some level of fidelity) are discussed as part of Chapter 12's discussion of "PIM on the go."[9]

- *Good and bad futures enabled by PIM technologies.* So many visions of a future made better by technology tend to be picture perfect. But for every picture there is a negative. Across chapters, there is an attempt to explore PIM potentials both good and bad as enabled by the technologies covered. Armed with an understanding of the ways that technology can go right and wrong, there is the hope that we—collectively and in the small daily decisions we make in our individual lives—can take a more active hand in determining how technologies are used in the management of our information and our lives.

1.6.6 Themes and metaphors

One of the book's themes is explicit in its title: PIM is a study and practice that each of us does and can do better. Two other themes help to weave together the book's content: (1) information use and information management are inextricably interwoven; and (2) we need tools to help us situate our interactions with our information.

One model of PIM has it that information management is what we do before and after information use. Many actions taken with paper-based information seem to be consistent with this model. When we visit our doctor, for example, she is still likely to talk to us with reference to a paper chart documenting our medical history. She may ask questions. "Are you still experiencing pain in your lower back?" Certainly this is information use. And the actions to retrieve our file from a filing cabinet and to place it back again when our visit is over are actions of information management.

But look closer and we might notice that our doctor underlines or circles some information. She may make notes in the margin. Are these actions information use or information management? Later, the chart may go into a stack of other charts to be processed for insurance reimbursement. Is this use or management?

The boundaries between use and management blur further for digital information. Information use and information management are inextricably interwoven. To separate the two is to risk missing important opportunities for a synergy between and integration of different activities. Certainly management should facilitate use. But, conversely, the impressions made by our use of information should facilitate its management and subsequent use.

---

[9] But see Tan et al. (2007) for a much more complete discussion of digital memories in the context of PIM.

Many of us, for example, follow a kind of hub-and-spoke approach when browsing the Web. From one page as a starting point, we click first on one hyperlink to go to another page; then we go back, and then click through to another page. This action is greatly facilitated when the web browser changes the appearance (through font or color) of hyperlinks we've already clicked. The change in hyperlink appearance is a kind of automated management of information based on use, which facilitates subsequent use.

Information is used to complete tasks such as "book a hotel" or "make airplane reservations" and to complete larger projects such as "plan a trip to Stockholm." Therefore, the position that information use and information management are interwoven might be alternately stated as information management and task/project management are interwoven—two sides of the same coin.

Throughout this book, considerations of task and project management are often used as lenses for assessing PIM activities. How does information management help us to manage and complete tasks and projects in our lives—the things we want to get done? Conversely, how can activities of task and project management that we must do be leveraged in support of better PIM?

But information use is about more than tasks and projects or is equated with these only if they are given very broad definitions. We sometimes need to manage information—digital photographs or videos or even life-affirming anecdotes, for example—with no clearly defined end in mind. We may manage information for the possibility of a use at some unspecified point in the future—to share with our future selves when we need an emotional lift or to share with future grandchildren who haven't yet been born.

A second theme of this book—essentially a restatement of the first—is that better PIM depends on and follows from tool support that situates our information and the use of informational tools with respect to both the physical and informational contexts of their use. A basic example of support for situating information would be Vannevar Bush's description of a memex able to associate, on command and by current use, two pieces of information that happen to co-occur in time or space so that, thereafter, with retrieval of one piece, the other piece can follow.

A larger point is that access to an item of information or the use of a tool does not occur in isolation. Access and use occur at a place and a time—possibly as part of an event involving other people. Access and use also occur in an informational context that includes other items currently in view or recently accessed. Access and use occur in the context of tasks or projects we need to complete.

Many of our tools do not make provision for this larger context but instead seem to be designed as worlds unto themselves, with an assumption that their use is our primary purpose. The consequences for our workflow are often disruptive. For example, as we're working in one context—to complete a document, research information on the Web or review a budget—we may experience a need that can be met by an email exchange (e.g., "Does this number include equipment rental?"). But if doing so means going to an email application, with its inbox in view by default, we pay double for the resulting disruption in context. We must leave the context that prompted us to send the email and may pay a price later to reconnect with the earlier context. Worse, we are drawn into a new context defined by the email application, not by us. Who can see email messages newly arrived and not be tempted to look and perhaps send a quick response?

We may say things like "this shouldn't take long" or "I'm just gonna. . . ." An hour or more may pass before we manage to return to our original context.

We move continuously through a day from need to information and from information to need. Tools built with an awareness of this basic "warp and weft"[10] of informational interactions can help us to weave an informational fabric with a strength, utility, and beauty far greater than a simple jumble of its component threads. Keeping our information found means situating this information in our lives—in the contexts of daily use and also in the contexts of our goals, our roles and responsibilities, our hopes and our dreams.

Metaphors help to facilitate our exploration of PIM. As an alternative to the metaphor of PIM as a weaving of a fabric, activities and supporting tools of PIM can be viewed as the structural elements of a bridge or a building. If these are mutually supporting, then the resulting structure is much stronger even as the costs of construction and the final weight of the structure are greatly reduced.

But first, in Chapter 2, we explore another metaphor. Our information and our informational tools combine to form a vast sea. We do not have good control of this sea—not even in the home waters of our office or the hard drive of our computer. Farther out are pirates intent on stealing our information and robbing us of our time and money. And farther out . . . thar be dragons.

---

[10] From the online version of the *Oxford English Dictionary*, warp means "the threads which are extended lengthwise in the loom, usually twisted harder than the weft or woof, with which these threads are crossed." Warp and weft together weave a fabric. Interestingly, this end result is sometimes referred to as the "web."

A personal space
of information

We're each awash in an informational sea that we do not control, not even in the home waters of our offices or the hard drives of our computers. Farther out there are pirates who will steal our information and rob us of our time and money. Farther still "thar be dragons" of offensive material and viruses intent on wreaking havoc. PIM means projecting our control where we can and making allowances for regions we can't control. PIM means using information to have things our way.

Chapter
Two

repli..tion, tas
defined activities
digest, processan
error, bookmark, a n face   ies, objects,
news, stacking, photo   classifies,   yes, read, wi
gem, approach, thinking, brain, reflect tickts, bank,   izization, goal
resistance, travel, elect, physical, abstract, hidden, paper   echmology, glob
ing, seek, curiosity, absorb, return, waves, pattern, depth, ear, Overlap   ty, search gadge
explore, conceptua;, connect, conclude, fields of inquiry, information, exchange, keeping, inbox,
files, documents, paper. Web, alias, shortcuts, stored, moved, transported, copied, out, newspaper
uted, deleted, tools, paperclips, staples, filing, desktop, digital, filing, browser,   flow, overwhelm
framework,interaction, islands, continents, boundaries, oceans, sea, map, time, processing,
personal space, collection, organization, structures, keeping, finding, mapping, action,
calendar, date/time, folder, phone, MPRs, torage, virtual, physical objects, anticipation,
making choices, intuition, screen, sort, select, manipulating, eyes, read, writing, repiti-
tion, task, orientation, refrences, access, problemsolving, categorization, goal defined
activities, explorer, discover, region, human, personalization, techmology, global, instant
faster than the speed of light, the M-levels, structures, priority, search gadgets, digest,
processing, gadgets, memories, data, rules, chaos, fluid, solid, keeping, inbox, error,
bookmark, flag, multifaceted, logic, classification, going in, going out, newspaper, news,
stacking, photos, everyday, invitations, rituals, information as a means to an end, goal,
approach, thinking, brain, reflect, tickts, bank, work, everyday life, integrating, resistance, travel, select, physical, abstract, practical, hidden, pocket, flow, overwhelming,
seek, curiosity, absorb, return, waves, pattern, depth, , ear,Overlap, definition, explore,
conceptua;, connect, conclude, fields of inquiry, information, exchange, paper, files, documents, paper. Web, alias, shortcuts, stored, moved, transported, copied, distributed,
deleted, tools, paperclips, staples, filing, desktop, digital, filing, browser,,
ramework,interaction, islands, continents, boundaries, oceans, sea, map, time, processing,
ersonal space, collection, organization, structures, keeping, finding, mapping, action,
lendar, date/time, folder, phone, MPRs, torage, virtual, physical objects, anticipation,
king choices, intuition, screen, sort, select, manipulating, eyes, read, writing, repiti-
n, task, orientation, refrences, access, problemsolving, categorization, goal defined
ivities, explorer, discover, region, human, personalization, techmology, global, instant
er than the speed of light, the M-levels, structures, priority, search gadgets, digest,
ssing, gadgets, memories, data, rules, chaos, fluid, solid, keeping, inbox, error,
ark, flag, multifaceted, logic, classification, going in, going out, newspaper, news,
ch, photos, everyday, invitations, rituals, information as a means to an end, goal,
ch, thinking, brain, reflect, tickts, bank, work, everyday life, integrating, resis-
travel, select, physical, abstract, practical, hidden, pocket, flow, overwhelming,
uriosity, absorb, return, waves, pattern, depth, ear, Overlap, definition, explore,
ua;, connect, conclude, fields of inquiry, information, exchange, paper, files, docu
aper. Web, alias, shortcuts, stored, moved, transported, copied, distributed,
tools, paperclips, staples, filing, desktop, digital, filing, browser,
,interaction, islands, continents, boundaries, oceans, sea, map, time, processing,
pace, collection, organization, structures, keeping, finding, mapping, action,
date/time, folder, phone, MPRs, torage, virtual, physical objects, anticipation,
ces, intuition, screen, sort, select, manipulating, eyes, read, writing, repiti-
orientation, refrences, access, problemsolving, categorization, goal defined
explorer, discover, region, human, personalization, techmology, global, instant
the speed of light, the M-levels, structures, priority, search gadgets, digest,
adgets, memories, data, rules, chaos, fluid, solid, keeping, inbox, error,
g, multifaceted, logic, classification, going in, going out, newspaper, news,
os, everyday, invitations, rituals, information as a means to an end, goal,
king, brain, reflect, tickts, bank, work, everyday life, integrating, resis-

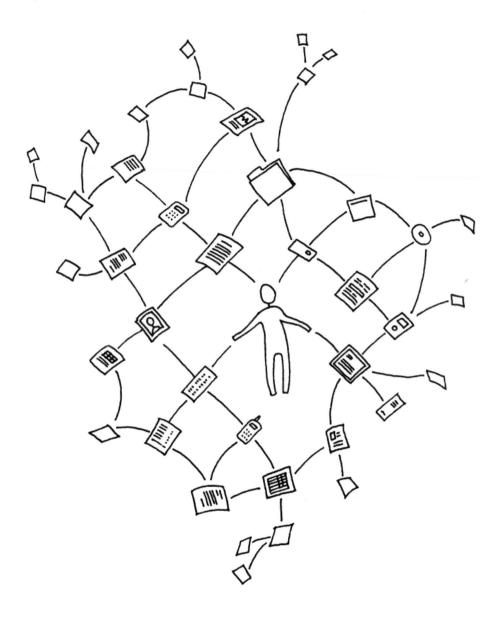

Men's private self-worlds are rather like our geographical world's seasons, storm, and sun, deserts, oases, mountains and abysses, the endless-seeming plateaus, darkness and light, and always the sowing and the reaping.

U.S. novelist Faith Baldwin (1893–1978)

2.1 Starting out

A person preoccupied is described as "in his own world." People who stay that way most of the time are considered odd or eccentric—or crazy. Can our information and our information tools make it so? Consider these examples:

A man approaches from the distance on the street. He is talking to himself. He gestures. He laughs. He even shouts . . . for no apparent reason. How do you feel? Maybe you look around for the reassuring presence of other people. Or maybe you think about crossing to the other side of the street. And then, on closer observation, you see that the man is talking on his mobile phone. Of course! So he's normal after all. As normal as the rest of us.

I work at home a lot. I especially like the opportunity to share a physical space with my eight-year-old son even as we do different things. He plays or does his homework; I work through email. With my notebook computer and a wireless connection, I can work virtually anywhere. I once had dreamy thoughts that modern technology might thus enable a return to a situation where families were closer knit on account of the time they spent together in work and play. As a boy at the turn of the last century, for example, my grand-father spent lots of time with his father doing the daily chores of a Wisconsin farm. Contrast this with the situation many of us who grew up in the 1950s and 1960s faced when parents (still mostly fathers) came home from a distant office at the end of a long day, often too tired to do more than fall asleep in front of the TV. But the situation with my son is like neither of these scenarios. My emotions can range widely from happy to frustrated or angry as I work, completely absorbed, through email correspondence. My son can't see the reality I experience. He has told me "you're here but not really here. You're kind of like a decoration."

Those of us who travel have seen a major transformation in commercial airline entertainment systems. Once a single movie played for everyone in the cabin. Passengers who didn't know one another would still laugh out loud in unison to a funny part of the movie. A shared experience, a shared reality. But now passengers on many flights can customize their reality—picking from several available movies and deciding when to view the movie. Some may even view movies on devices they have brought. The person sitting next to you on a flight may burst out in laughter like a crazy person. The person is "there" but very much in a reality separate from yours.

Four young men, by prior arrangement, converge to meet one another in a popular coffee shop in downtown Stockholm, Sweden. One man arrives, picks a table, sits down, and begins talking on his mobile phone while waiting. A second man arrives, already engrossed in a conversation on his mobile phone, gives a gesture of greeting to the first, sits down, and continues talking on his phone. A third man arrives and a fourth, and they each do the same. For several long minutes each person, while physically sitting at the same table, is in a world of his own as he speaks into his phone. (All four ignore a sign nearby asking people not to use their mobile phones while in the coffee shop.)

Civilization and the development of technology can be seen as an effort to "have it our way" by freeing us from the dictates of the immediate environment. We store away food so that we can eat when we're hungry, whether or not there is game to be hunted or berries to be gathered. We build houses so that we can stay warm and dry even when it's cold and wet outside. Mobile phones and email and personalized passenger entertainment systems are simply a recent manifestation of this enduring desire to have things our own way.

We won't go back. Even as mobile phones draw us away from full participation in our current physical environment, these enable and enrich other realities. How nice to be able to talk with friends or loved ones even though they are a continent away. How nice to see the movie we want to see, when we want to see it, and not be yoked with a hundred or more strangers to the same B-grade movie displayed in grainy resolution on a distant screen.[1] And if information tools occasionally distract us or compromise our participation in the physical world—well, this is often a fair trade, given the alternatives. At least my son can interrupt me from time to time with a question about his homework or a comment about his day at school.

If we won't go back, personal information management starts with a belief that we can—we must—do better. The growth of available information—and in the technologies for its creation, storage, retrieval, distribution, and use—is astonishing and sometimes bewildering. How can there be comparable growth in our understanding of this information, its impact on our lives, and the ways in which tools can help us, and sometimes hinder us, in our attempts to gain mastery of our lives? How can we better use information and information technologies so that we can have things our way?

Later chapters will consider several essential kinds of activity that make up a practice of PIM. But first, it is important to better understand the object of this PIM activity. What is personal information? What does it mean for information to be personal? How do we come to have—to inhabit—a personal space of information, and what does this mean for us in our daily lives?

This chapter is organized into the following sections:

✓ *What is information to us?* "Information" is an overloaded term, with uses that range from the physical—information as a document or some other "thing"—to the abstract—information as a means of reducing uncertainty. This section takes a practical survey of some ways information is used by and impacts us in our daily lives.

✓ *How is information personal?* What does it mean for information to be "mine"? Look for the "me" in "mine." From any given person's perspective, information can be owned by, experienced by, about, sent by, sent to, or (potentially) relevant to "me." Each relationship defines a kind of personal information. Each is relevant to a general discussion of PIM.

✓ *The information item and its form* are defined as essential terms for an analysis of personal information management. Information comes packaged in many different ways. People still

---

[1] Of course good books have offered us a similar "escape" into other realities for centuries now—as made accessible by technologies of printing and mass distribution and by a civilization that teaches us to read.

receive conventional letters, account statements, magazines, and junk mail in paper form via postal, or snail, mail. People also work with email messages, electronic documents, web pages (and pointers to these), digital photographs, downloaded music, and so on. The collection of tools and techniques for working with information vary widely with its form. But, regardless of information form, we can speak of information items for which the same basic operations, the same basic decisions, apply.

☑ *Defining a personal space of information (PSI).* A PSI includes personal information in each of its senses. The PSI also includes various tools and other objects (virtual and visible) affecting the flow of information to, from, and through a PSI. An ordinary office door affects the flow of information in a personal space. A PSI includes regions of information over which a person has very little direct control but ought to have. People have very little control over "their" medical information as kept by their doctor. But achieving greater control—the ability to correct serious errors, for example—can be a matter of life or death. People, by broadly defining their PSI to include regions that ought to be under their control, take an important conceptual step toward making it so. The PSI is central in discussions of personal information management throughout this book.

☑ *Making sense of the PSI* is aided through concepts introduced in a final section of this chapter. Concepts help to carve a large, amorphous PSI into more manageable regions. Across different forms of information, for example, we can follow Sellen and Harper's (2002) distinction between small *hot* regions of daily use, larger *warm* regions of less frequent use (relating to active projects and ongoing roles and relationships), and large *cold* regions where information is accessed infrequently or not at all.

2.2 What is information to us?

What is information? This question has been a repeated topic of discussion in its own right.[2] Buckland (1991) provides an analysis illustrating that the word "information" alternately denotes a process (the act of informing), a result (a state of being informed or the knowledge imparted), or a thing (such as a document that contains and communicates information). In reaction to the definitional inclusiveness of "information" and the many senses in which the word is used, Buckland concludes that "we are unable to say confidently of anything that it could not be information" (p. 356).

Even so, for any given event or item, each of us can make an assessment of information value, as in "I knew that already" or "That was incomprehensible; I learned nothing," or (we can hope) "that was really useful; I learned a lot and now know better what to do." This second sense of information in Buckland's analysis—as understanding or knowledge imparted—makes contact with the seminal work of Shannon and Weaver (Shannon, 1948; Shannon & Weaver, 1949). Key to their work was the notion that the information content of a message can be measured for its capacity to reduce uncertainty. The information value of a message depends on the recipient of the message and his/her state of knowledge. The message that "Bob is coming to the meeting" has no information value, for example, if its intended recipient knows this already or if the message is given to the recipient in a language she does not understand. In neither case does the message do anything to reduce the recipient's "uncertainty" concerning who will be attending the meeting.

Making information exclusively about the reduction of uncertainty has come to be seen as overly restrictive.[3] An exchange of information has a sender as well as a recipient, for example, and the exchange is not always collaborative. It's nice to think that the sender is trying to reduce the recipient's uncertainty, but of course the sender may have many other intentions. The sender may want to impress or persuade. The sender may want to increase the recipient's uncertainty ("have you considered these other possibilities?"). The sender may even want to confuse or deceive.

Nevertheless, a larger point in the work of Shannon and Weaver remains: The value of information is not absolute but relative to a context that includes the intentions of the sender and the current state of a recipient's knowledge. What is information to us? We might better ask, What is information without us? Table 2.1 provides a sampling of the ways in which information is used by and impacts us.

---

[2] For discussions of what information is, see Braman (1989), Buckland (1991, 1997), Capurro and Hjørland (2003), Cornelius (2002), and Machlup (1983).

[3] See Aftab et al. (2001), Capurro and Hjørland (2003), and Cornelius (2002); each considers the need for alternate measures of information and the impact that information can have.

Table 2.1 Information can mean many different things

Information is . . .	As in . . .
Information is what people process to understand their world.	We are processors of information. Information comes in sights, sounds, touches, tastes, and smells. Information helps us to understand, predict, and even control outcomes in the world that matter to us.
Information is what's in documents, email messages, web pages, MP3 files, photographs (digital and paper-based), videos, etc.	This is Buckland's sense of information as "thing."
Information is what can be stored, retrieved, copied, transformed, and distributed.	As an alternate perspective on "information as thing," information is defined by what we can do with it.
Information is how other worlds are represented to us: past and present, possible and pretend.	For example, information helps people to imagine (1) their summer vacation, (2) how people live in Mongolia, or (3) what the world will be like in 50 years.
Information is how we are represented to the outside world, accurately or not, for better or worse.	Information represents our medical histories, our financial status, our purchasing patterns, and even our airplane seating preferences. But information can be nearly impossible to update or correct. Statements we made 10, even 20, years ago may persist on the Web even though these no longer reflect the "us" of today.
Information is what people use to get things done.	People send email messages to make reservations, fill in forms to order things, write reports to influence people, etc.
Information is an extension of us.	Take the getting-things-done perspective a step further. Information can persist in printed documents, and now on personal web sites, blogs, and the like, to serve as an extension of ourselves.
Information is a drain on a person's money, energy, attention, and time.	Advertisements convince us to buy things. Email messages can distract us and take up all our time and energy. Even small changes—the red squiggly line under a misspelled word inside a document we're writing, for example—can distract.

Continued

Information is . . .	As in . . .
Information is what we can use to have things "our way."	Information and information technologies can work as a cushion to free us from the immediate demands of our environment so that we can set our own timetable of work and play.

Information is what people process to understand their world

The efforts people make to understand their world have long been characterized as acts of information processing.[4] According to this view, our intelligence comes from our ability to process the raw information received through our senses into concepts, patterns, and implications. Everything coming in through our senses is information waiting to be processed and understood. The world is a confusing and uncertain place. Information helps us to understand, predict, and even control outcomes in the world that matter to us. More important, information should help us to understand its own limits and the limits of our ability to understand our world.

We also provide information, in our actions and appearance, for others to process. We send information in the clothes we wear, the car we drive, and in the way we act. We send information (often more than we intend) with every sentence we speak or write. It is with respect to the information we send that it is most clearly necessary to go beyond Shannon's original notions of information as a collaborative exchange between sender and recipient. As Machiavelli might have said, we send information, or try to send it, to serve our own purposes.

Information is what's in documents, email messages, and web pages

This is the case for everything that we send and receive. Information is also, these days, what's in files containing digital photographs, music, and videos. This invokes Buckland's sense of "information as thing." As a thing, like other things, information can be stored, retrieved, and moved. However, information has certain properties not inherent in most other things (a kitchen table, for example). That is, information can be easily copied, transformed, and distributed. Information—especially digital information—is malleable. A recipe for cookies may start out in a paper document which is then scanned into a computer, converted from image to text, and then sent via email to appear eventually on a web page. We're likely to judge the information to be the same across these transformations—providing, of course, that we can still follow the recipe to make the cookies.[5]

---

[4] See Broadbent (1958).

[5] The cookie recipe example can be taken further. We may judge the information to be the same even as it's copied and transformed. However, it does not necessarily follow that the information's impact is unaltered. Following a recipe on a computer screen is a very different experience from following a paper-based version. The mistakes we make are likely to be distinctive as well. An important step may be missed with the first form because it has scrolled off the screen or, in the second, because ink on the paper has gotten smudged.

Because information as a thing can be stored and retrieved later, its processing can often be deferred—pending, for example, the arrival of other information or the time to process. Because information can be transformed and distributed, it has a "reach" over time and space. Information, in the ease with which it can be stored, retrieved, moved, copied, transformed, and distributed, differs from a person's internalized knowledge. Knowledge in one's head can be well integrated in ways that make its separate articulation very difficult, even as the knowledge has a subtle, pervasive impact on a person's beliefs, viewpoints, rules of thumb, and decision making.

Information represents other worlds—past and present, possible, and pretend

Information is also what we get from photographs, videos, voice recordings, books, and letters. Information evokes memories of past worlds we once lived in. Information can also be made to represent other worlds far away in time and place—worlds we may never be able to, or want to, experience in person. Information can even be made to stand for future worlds that have yet to be realized. The picture of a vacation cottage stands for a summer vacation we hope to experience with our family. The associated to-do list stands for things that must still be done in order for the vacation to be a success.

PIM focuses on the capacity of information to effect change in our lives. The information we receive influences the actions we take and the choices we make. A minor decision such as which hotel to book is made depending on the information we are able to gather concerning price, location, availability, and so on. Major decisions, such as what job to accept or what person to marry, are also heavily influenced by the available information. To quote one person about her failed first marriage to her small-town high-school sweetheart, "We looked around and decided there was nothing else to do and no one else around. We didn't know any better."

Information is what we use to get things done

My grandfather and grandmother milked cows. They sowed and harvested corn, alfalfa, and oats. Information-as-thing arrived with the newspaper, letters, and a monthly subscription to the *Reader's Digest*. They sent letters too and mailed in orders to get items from a warehouse hundreds of miles away as advertised in the Sears catalog. In these ways, their world was mediated by information items. But in most other ways, even as their farm became increasingly mechanized, their involvement with their world was hands-on. Things did not get done except by their own direct physical involvement.

What a different world most of us live in! On the input side, we consult the newspaper or a web page to read the headlines of the day and to find out what the weather will be like (perhaps before we even bother to look outside). We learn of meetings via email messages. We receive the documents we are supposed to read for a meeting via email as well. On the output side, we fill out web-based forms. We send email messages. We create and send out reports in paper and digital form. Technology enables new forms of information (email messages, web pages, blogs) through which we project ourselves and our desires across time and space in ways that would never have occurred to our forebears.

Information is an extension of us

The information we send out doesn't simply disappear after it has reached its intended destination. For better, and sometimes worse, information about us persists. Travel agents keep information concerning our credit card, our preferences in airlines and seats. Doctors and health maintenance organizations (HMOs) keep our medical information. For some of us, documents we wrote 20 years ago linger on the Web somewhere, providing at least one view of us regardless of whether it is currently accurate. Many of us now have personal web sites that operate 24/7 to represent us, our accomplishments, skills, histories, likes and dislikes, to the rest of the world.

Information gets us to spend our money, energy, attention, and time

Even as we send information outward to effect change in our world, we face an onslaught of incoming information from others designed to get us to pay attention and to do things. Information grabs our attention in ways that are nearly impossible for us to control. Who among us can see the red squiggly line under a typed word and not make an immediate effort to correct the misspelling so indicated? Who can ignore the incessant changes in sounds and scenery emanating from our television sets? We're wired to attend. As Simon noted in the quote of Chapter 1, information "consumes" our attention. And a good deal more.

An old saying nicely relates three other precious resources in our lives: "When you're young you have lots of time and energy but no money. When you're middle-aged, you have lots of money and you still have energy too but no time. When you're old, you have lots of time and you still have money but you have no energy."

The resources of money, energy, and time differ from one another in many respects and our relative supply of each may vary with age. But each of these resources, like attention, is limited. And, like attention, each is also consumed by our information:

Money. Advertisements bring us beautiful pictures of an expensive, fuel-guzzling, sport utility vehicle (SUV) up above the world atop some mountain. We buy the vehicle and use it instead to drive around town, for which we could have bought a much smaller car that would have cost less to buy and to use.

Energy. Energy itself may come in different forms—physical and creative, for example. For some of us, the morning's first cup of coffee gives us the energy we need to tackle especially difficult and challenging assignments that require us to be at our very best.

Time. Once information has our attention, it consumes our time as well. Web pages draw us to information we don't really need to read. Email messages draw us into lengthy responses we don't really need to make. And the time goes by. . . .

Of course, this is not to say that incoming information is always bad or that there aren't good uses of our money, energy, attention, and time which we wouldn't know about were it not for the incoming information. But too often the uses of these precious resources seem to be controlled by our information world and not by us.

An irony is that information is also our means to represent and better control our life's resources. Most of us don't keep our money in a mattress. We track the money we have and our solvency through financial statements we receive from banks and brokerages.

Similarly, time is an abstract concept made more real to us through its representation in clocks and calendars and Gantt charts. What about attention and energy? Some day soon these too may become more real as resources to monitor and control. When this happens, it will of course be through information. A graphical rendition of eye movement patterns, for example, may tell us where our attention goes as we try to get work done. Biorhythm charts may tell us what time of the day we're at our peaks and valleys with respect to different kinds of energy. When is it generally best to go jogging? When is it generally best to get creative work done? When should we plan to do more routine clerical work?

Information lets us have things our way

We can conclude on a more positive note concerning what information is to us. Information is power, of course, in the conventional sense that what we know that others do not can give us a real advantage in a variety of situations. But in our everyday existence, information can be a cushion between us and our immediate environment. Information, properly managed, can free us from the need to take every twist and turn presented by our day's events so that we can instead stay more focused on our life's most important goals and roles. The essential point of personal information management is to make information our ally and not our enemy.

2.3 How is information personal?

What does it mean for information to be personal? As summarized in Table 2.2, there are several ways in which information can be "personal." Information can be owned by, about, directed toward, sent by, experienced by, or relevant to "me." Each kind of personal information is briefly described below.

Table 2.2 How information can be personal

	Relation to "me"	Examples	Issues
1	Controlled by (owned by) me	Email messages in our email accounts; files on our computer's hard drive.	Security against break-ins or theft, backups, virus protection, etc.
2	About me	Credit history, medical, web browsing, library books checked out.	Who sees what when (under what circumstances)? How is information corrected or updated? Does it ever go away?
3	Directed toward me	Phone calls, drop-ins, TV ads, web ads, pop-ups.	Protection of me and my money, energy, attention, and time.
4	Sent (posted, provided) by me	Email, personal web sites, published reports and articles.	Who sees what when? Did the message get through?
5	(Already) experienced by me	Web pages that remain on the Web. Books that remain in a library. TV and radio programs that remain somewhere in "broadcast ether."	How to get back to information later?
6	Relevant (useful) to me	Somewhere "out there" is the perfect vacation, house, job, lifelong mate. If only I could find the right information!	If only I knew (had some idea of) what I don't know. How to filter out or otherwise avoid information we don't wish to see? (How to do likewise for our children?)

1. *Controlled by (owned by) me*. The information a person keeps, directly or indirectly (e.g., via software applications), for personal use is personal information. Included are email messages in an email account, files on the hard drive of a personal computer, and also the papers kept on surfaces and inside conventional filing cabinets. Although information is, at least nominally, under the person's control, the rights of ownership for portions of this information are sometimes in dispute. In the context of a person's work inside a company or in collaboration with others, for example, it is often unclear who owns what information.

2. *About me*. Information about a person but available to and possibly under the control of others is personal information. Personal information in this category includes the information about a person kept by doctors and health organizations, for example, or the information kept by tax agencies and credit bureaus.

3. *Directed toward me*. Included in this category is the email that arrives in the inbox and also the pop-up notifications that this new email has arrived. Alerts raised by a person's computer, the "push" of advertisements on a visited web page or the television or the radio, and the ringing telephone are all examples of information directed toward a person. The information itself may not be personally relevant. But the intended impacts of directed information certainly are personal. For better or worse, information directed to a person can distract the person from a current task, consume a person's attention, and convince the person to spend time, spend money, change an opinion, or take an action.

4. *Sent (posted, provided) by me*. Information sent by the person (or posted or published) is personal information. We often try to control, albeit imperfectly, who sees what (and when) for the information we send, post, or otherwise provide. We do this with email, for example, through distribution lists and notices on the email messages such as "Confidential, please do not distribute." Or we may hide information on a disconnected web page and then selectively distribute the address to this web page.

5. *Experienced by me*. Information experienced by a person is also personal information. Some of this information is under the person's control and so is also personal in the first sense of personal. Other information is not under the person's control: the book a person browses (but puts back) in a traditional library, for example, or the pages a person views on the Web. This fifth sense of personal information is especially important since we rarely consume all of an item's information in one or even several readings. Over a period of time we may return to an information item—a document, a web page, or even an email message—several different times. One major challenge of PIM is to support re-finding—the return to information previously experienced.

6. *Relevant (useful) to me*. A final sense in which information can be personal is determined by whether this information is relevant or useful to us. This category cuts across others to include subsets of the information we control, information we've experienced before, and also new information we've never seen before. Out there, somewhere, is an article that is perfect for a report we're writing or an advertisement for a vacation package that perfectly fits our needs. This final sense of personal information can be expanded to include information that we or our family would find offensive and that we definitely would *not* want to see. As noted in the conclusion to Chapter 1, "thar be dragons" out there—especially if we surf the Web, but even in the junk mail of our inbox. With respect to this expanded "sixth sense" of personal, we depend on filters both to filter in the information we'd like to see and to filter out the information we do not want to see.

These broad categories have value not for what they exclude—in their union, they exclude very little. Rather, each category in its turn provides an important focal point for this book's discussion of PIM. Much of that discussion relates to the first sense of personal information—information a person keeps for later use and repeated reuse. The book also considers the second sense of personal information—information about the person kept by others—especially in Chapter 7's discussion of privacy, distribution, and the flow of information. Chapter 7 also considers the third kind of personal information—information directed toward "me." Considerations surrounding the fourth sense of personal information—information sent or posted or otherwise provided by "me" are discussed especially in Chapter 10's coverage of email and Chapter 13's coverage of web-based PIM. The fifth sense of personal information—information experienced by "me" (to which we might like to return)—and the sixth sense of personal information—information that is relevant or useful to "me"—are discussed as part of Chapter 4's coverage of finding and re-finding and in Chapter 11's coverage of search.

Note that distinctions between the different senses of personal information can quickly blur. For example, a session of web browsing can be recorded by a history facility in the person's web browser so that this record becomes a part of the information kept by (for) the person. The person may also, knowingly or unknowingly, provide identifying information to a visited web site which can then go into a record about the person (his or her web site visits) that is maintained by others (e.g., the webmaster of the web site or the employer's IT department).

2.4 The information item and its form

When Buckland wrote of "information-as-thing," one thing he spoke of first and that likely comes first to our minds too is the document. However, the word "document" has resisted easy definition. Levy provides an introductory meditation, in his book *Scrolling Forward* (2001), on an ordinary cash receipt as a document. He observes that the receipt, in its use of letters, numerals, punctuation, and layout, reflects a shared convention that is the result of centuries of development and innovation. Levy concludes that "there is something remarkable about the receipt's ability to preserve or freeze some aspect of the world" (p. 19).

Buckland notes that a document need not be either textual or paper-based:

> A printed book is a document. A page of hand-writing is a document. A diagram is a document. A map is a document. If a map is a document, why should not a three-dimensional contour map also be a document? Why should not a globe also be considered a document since it is, after all, a physical description of something? (1991, p. 354)

In a subsequent article, Buckland (1997) further explores the issues that arise when trying to answer the question, What is a document? Briet (1951), for example, considers an animal in a zoo—she gives the example of an antelope—to be a document. An animal in captivity (but not in the wild) has been selected (captured) to represent something beyond its physical self. A captured antelope represents a whole species of antelope, for example, as well as a specific ecosystem in Africa. Otlet (1934) asserts that any object can be considered a document, provided we are informed by observing it. By this expansive definition, it would seem that anything could serve as a document. A tree stump as document tells us, by its number of rings, how old the tree was when cut. For that matter, a standing tree is a document telling us how tall it is by the shadow it casts.

These definitions are too inclusive for our purposes, but at the same time the conventional sense of "document" makes its use feel awkward when applied in reference to common objects of PIM such as email messages, web bookmarks, and downloaded music. We return, therefore, to Buckland's motivation for discussing "information-as-thing" as the only sense of information "with which information systems can deal directly" (1991, p. 359).

Information-as-thing gives us something tangible to be manipulated—to be created, copied, stored, retrieved; given a name, tags, and other properties; and moved, copied, distributed, deleted, and otherwise transformed. In this spirit, it is useful in discussions of PIM to speak of an information item and its associated form:

> An information item is a packaging of information. Examples of information items include (1) paper documents, (2) electronic documents, digital photographs, digital music, digital film, and other files, (3) email messages, (4) web pages, and (5) references (e.g., shortcuts, aliases) to any of the above. Items encapsulate information in a persistent form that can be created, modified, stored, retrieved, given a name, tags, and other properties, moved, copied, distributed, deleted, and otherwise manipulated. An information item has an associated information form that is determined by the tools and applications that support these operations. Common forms of information include paper documents, e-documents and other files, email messages, and web bookmarks.

Consider the example given earlier of a cookie recipe. The recipe itself can be considered information. The representation of this information—typed on a piece of paper or displayed on a web page—is an information item. An information item can contain other information items. An email message as an information item might contain as an attached item the scanned image for the recipe. Similarly a paper envelope as an item can contain the letter as an item. Once the letter is taken out of the envelope or the attachment saved separately from the email message, these items can be stored, retrieved, moved, copied, distributed, and deleted independently of and in the same way as their containing items can be stored, retrieved, moved, copied, distributed, and deleted independently.

The ways in which an item is manipulated will vary depending on its form and the tools available for this form. The tools used for interaction with paper-based information items include, for example, paper clips, staplers, filing cabinets, and the flat surfaces of a desktop. In interactions with digital information items, we depend on the support of various computer-based tools and applications such as email applications, file managers, and web browsers. The ways we delete a paper document differ from the ways we delete an electronic document (e.g., tossing in the trash or shredding vs. using the commands "Cut" or "Delete"), but some notion of deleting applies to each (a similarity the Macintosh reinforces through its metaphorical "trash can").

The information item establishes a manageable level of abstraction for the consideration of PIM. Certainly, a person's interactions with an information item vary greatly depending on its form. Interactions with incoming email messages, for example, are often driven by the expectation of a timely response and perhaps also by the awareness that, when an email message scrolls out of view without some processing, it is apt to be quickly forgotten. A person may make a paper printout of the same email message, to be folded, carried in a briefcase, marked up, and ultimately discarded when its information has been consumed.

But there are many essential similarities in the way people interact with information items, regardless of their form. Whether people are looking at a new email message in their inbox, a newly discovered web site, or the business card they have just been handed at a conference, many of the same basic decisions must be made: Is this relevant (to me)? To what does it relate? Do I need to act now or can I wait? If I wait, can I get back to this item later? Where should I put it? Will I remember to look?

At the same time, the category of information item does not blur to include all things informational. A hallway conversation between two people, for example, conveys information but is not itself a packaging of information. A conversation is not an information item. A cassette recording of this same conversation is an information item. The recording can be stored away, sent, copied, and so on. A person's memory of a pending doctor's appointment is not an information item. The scrap of paper containing a written reminder of this appointment is an information item.

Essential to the management of any collection of information items are operations to copy, move, retrieve,[6] and delete these items. At the risk of getting overly (and perhaps prematurely) precise, we must then consider "semi-items" to which some operations can be applied but not others. Table 2.3 compares various objects with respect to the four essential operations.

Table 2.3 Which objects qualify as information items?

Object	Copy?	Move?	Retrieve?	Delete?	Information item?
Computer file folder	Copy & paste	Drag & drop	"Open"	"Delete"	Yes
Computer file	Copy & paste	Drag & drop	"Open"	"Delete"	Yes
Paper bank statement	Photocopy	"Pick up and place"	Open	Toss or Shred	Yes
Email message	Copy & paste	Drag & drop	"Open"	"Delete"	Yes
Web bookmark	Copy & paste	Drag & drop	"Open"	"Delete"	Yes
Web page	Save as file(s)	No	"Open"	No	No (semi-item)
Wiki	Save as file(s)	No	"Open"	No	No (semi-item)
Human "engram"[7]	No	No	Remember	No	No
Antelope in zoo	Cloning?	Carefully…	Walk to the cage	Kill, cook, and eat?	No

---

[6] The abiltiy to store is not considered an essential operation here since storage is implicit in the existence of most items; a file folder, file, or email message is stored if it exists at all. Moreover, it makes little sense to speak of storage without speaking of retrieval.

[7] The term is misleading since there appears to be nothing item-like about an engram in human memory. For a discussion of the difficulty in treating human memories as items (which then might be deleted), see Lashley (1950).

By the analysis in Table 2.3, computer files, file folders, paper bank statements, email messages, and web bookmarks all qualify as information items. Each can be copied, moved, retrieved, and deleted.[8] By this analysis, a page we encounter on the Web is a semi-item. We can retrieve it ("Open"), but we can't move it and we certainly can't delete it. The information on the web page can easily be copied, but doing so effectively represents a transformation. If we "Save As," for example, we create a new file or files—another form of information. A web page is subject to dynamic changes controlled by its author/owner. The file copy will not participate in subsequent changes. Alternatively, we could create a bookmark pointing to the web page. The bookmark is certainly ours to copy, move, retrieve, and delete. But the bookmark is not the web page. The bookmark is a separate form of information (with separate tools for its management).

What about wikis? Unlike a typical web page, a wiki by design can be modified by a group of people—potentially a very large group of people. But in other ways, the wiki is much like a standard web page. If we acquire an account, we can modify the wiki but we cannot (or should not try to) move it or delete it.

A wiki can be likened to the field in a public park after a snowfall. We can write what we like in the snow but others can too. We should not be surprised to return later and discover that what we wrote has been erased or written over. And, of course, the field of snow (or the wiki) might disappear altogether (once the weather gets warm in the case of the snow field, or if the owner decides to remove it in the case of the wiki). We have some control but not much.

Even more questionable is whether a human memory, an "engram," qualifies as an information item. Operations to copy or move are undefined and, try as we might, we cannot localize memories—in humans or animals—as something that can be deleted.[9] A consideration of an antelope as an information item becomes irresistibly tongue-in-cheek. Whatever its qualifications might be as a document, it is certainly not an information item.

In contrast to what we hear or see in our physical world, another point concerning information items is that we can often defer processing. We can, and do, accumulate large numbers of information items for a "rainy day." This is quite unlike, for example, the scenarios faced by the driver of an automobile or the pilot of an airplane. In these situations, acceptable delays in processing information are short, and there is no option to "look at this later when I have time."[10]

---

[8] The semantics of each operation can vary greatly, of course. This is a topic of discussion in its own right. If "delete" means "no longer visible to me," then each of these items can be deleted. If "delete" means "no longer visible to anyone," then additional steps must be taken. And, for email and the files of a network drive, deletion so that no one else can see the item may be impossible.

[9] Lashley (1950), for example, conducted experiments in which rats had various portions of their brains removed after learning to run a maze. No surprisingly, rats did worse on the maze after the operation than before. But performance degradation was always gradual, never complete. Memory for how to run the maze was distributed throughout the brain rather than localized.

[10] See Durso and Gronlund (1999) for a review of research on situation awareness.

Table 2.4 A sampling of objects that bear information or control information flow

Object	Options and operations	Comments
Office door	Wide open, slightly open, shut.	Shut to say, "Don't bother me"; leave open a little to say "I'm here but knock only if it's important."
Word-processing application	Spell checking on or off. View as printed document or as draft.	In early stages of a document's composition, it may be a waste of time to correct misspellings or to format it.
Cell phones	Mute or not; answer or not.	If only we could remember to mute our cell phone during movies and meetings!
Chair	Good for reading or writing?	Different chairs for different uses.
Dining room table	Empty, or covered with bills or information for a project (where do things go during dinner?)	Clearing the table can mean a loss of information concerning the state of the current project. Does the family eat in the kitchen instead?
Picture of special place	Frame? Place in prominent place on a wall where we will see it?	A picture or painting of a special place may give us inspiration or the strength to meet the day.

2.4.1 Other objects that bear information and control its flow

Let's reverse words and consider this differently. Rather than "information-as-thing," let's consider "things-as-information"—that is, let's consider objects other than information items for the information they carry or control. From a PIM perspective, we're still interested in how we can use these objects to better manage our information.

Table 2.4 provides only a small sampling of the objects we might want to consider from an informational perspective, together with some of the PIM-relevant options and operations supported by each object.

2.5 Defining a personal space of information

Add it all together. Add in the information that becomes personal through any of several possible relationships to us. Add in the information we keep in the form of documents, both electronic and paper. Add in the photographs we take, which can also be in digital and paper-based forms. Add in our music (whether in CDs or MP3 files) and our videos (whether on old-fashioned tape, or DVD, or in the MPEG files on a hard drive). Add in the books on our

Alice Uses Her Information for a World as She Wants It to Be

Consider the following simple progression toward a better, more effective personal space of information involving Alice. Alice gives lots of parties in connection with her consulting business, which she has had now for over 30 years and which she runs out of her house. Sometimes parties are last-minute and impromptu.

- Long ago Alice would arrange parties over the phone. She called up each guest, invited them, and—especially for new guests—gave directions on how to reach her house (which was not that easy to find).

- Alice was very happy when email gained widespread use. She could then send out invitations—even last-minute invitations—via email, which saved a lot of time. Moreover, she created a standard, tested set of directions to her house which she saved as a file to be used repeatedly across parties in attachments to email invitations. She also created various invitation lists (current clients, potential clients, colleagues, etc.) to be used and reused.

- Alice now has her own web site with information about her consulting business. The web site includes driving directions to her house. Alice's email invitations now point to the web site. People can go to the web site for driving directions, to find out more about the party, and also to note their "regrets" if they are unable to attend. The web site is a 24/7 extension of Alice.

In the near future, the web site will represent Alice in still more ways. It might, for example, include pages that tell people how Alice is doing in her battle with cancer. (Alice is happy not to have to repeat the same story of recovery with each new well-meaning friend or family member.) The web site may include other pages with information concerning Alice's preferences when she travels (airplane seating preference, hotel and room preferences), emergency medical information, food allergies, and the like.

A little further in the future, Alice will have a PSI in which distinctions between the Web, email, and local file storage are mostly irrelevant. The PSI reflects the way Alice thinks about her world—both as it is now and as Alice would like it to be in the future. Alice makes parts of her PSI public according to *what* (information is involved), *who* (needs to see), and *when/why* (under what circumstances). Public projections of Alice's information can persist as what we think of today as web pages, and projections can also attract attention and invoke an expectation of timely response in the way that email does today.

In this future, Alice uses PIM support to design her future world. Suppose, for example, that Alice wants to plan a business trip to Chicago in early October and also to use the trip to reconnect with an old friend who lives there. She describes her world as she would like it to be in early October. She wants a window seat on a nonstop flight to and from Chicago, ideally in business class. She wants a nice hotel room (non-smoking) in downtown Chicago with a view over Lake Michigan, exercise facilities, and wireless Internet access. She would like to have dinner with her friend on at least one night of the trip in a nice restaurant near her hotel.

As Alice builds her world, her system of PIM support reminds her of other details she might otherwise have overlooked. If her trip involves attending a conference in Chicago, for example, then she'll need to register—better do so now in order to qualify for the early registration fee. Reminding happens simply because Alice is able to reuse, in modified form, a plan she has already used successfully on previous trips. The plan not only reminds Alice of tasks to be completed, it also provides a structure and context in which to store incoming information (hotel confirmation, electronic airplane tickets, etc.) and in which to situate outgoing information, including "email" correspondence.

As Alice builds her world as she would like it to be, she makes parts of this description public. For example, Alice makes her preferences concerning travel dates, seating, hotels, and rooms available to travel services which then put together alternate packages as part of a competitive bid process. Alice can pick the package she likes best. Alice can do something similar later to find a new computer or a car (or a house or, even, a mate) that best meets her needs. In each case, the process begins with the creation of descriptions by Alice of things as she would like them to be.

Alice's description of her world as she would like it to be goes well beyond making travel arrangements. Alice would like to reach a period of "semi-retirement" in about ten years' time (she is now in her early 50s) so that she can work part time and travel much of the rest of the time. Her description is used by her and her financial advisor to develop a financial plan that specifies a little more work now, a little less spending, and a rebalancing of her portfolio toward a higher percentage equity position.

Alice would like to lose weight, get in better shape, and find a lifelong mate. Though she is past childbearing age, she loves children and would like to find some way of including children in her life. In developing her descriptions of a world as she would like it to be, Alice can count on PIM tool support.

Tool support gives Alice the ability to describe a virtual world—even providing her with pictures of herself as she might look under various scenarios of the future. PIM support includes the ability to download "Life Organizers" that include customizable, modifiable step-by-step plans for realizing various goals and roles in life (get a better job, plan a summer vacation, find a lifelong mate, etc.). Organizers also provide a structure and context in which to organize the information—incoming and outgoing—needed to make things happen. Organizers help Alice make effective use of her precious resources of money, energy, attention, and time. Organizers help Alice see the ways in which her dreams of the future are incomplete or inconsistent.

bookshelves and the magazines and newspapers scattered on chairs and coffee tables. Add in the email messages and the web references we keep.

Add in also the information we create and send out or publish in the form of documents, email messages, blog messages, web pages, and so on. Add in the information that others keep about us. Add in the information "out there" that we have experienced and might like to return to—in libraries, on the Web, in radio and TV programs, and even in the billboards we see on the way to work or school. Include also the information we might like to see—the information out there that we might use, the information that might entertain us, inspire us, or profoundly influence us if only we could find it. And include also the information out there we don't want to see or stumble across—offensive material on the Web, for example. Add in the various devices, gadgets, software applications, and tools that we interact with to manipulate and to control the flow of information. Add in our computers, our telephones, our personal digital assistants (PDAs), our radios, and television sets. Add in storage devices including our filing cabinets for paper, our hard drives, and the space we're given through web sites. Add in even ordinary objects like tabletops and doors for their uses in presenting and controlling the flow of information.

When all is added together, each of us has a unique personal space of information, or PSI, as depicted in Figure 2.1. We inhabit this space as surely as we inhabit a physical space. Our informational space affects the way we view and interact with the world(s) we inhabit. Our space of information also affects the way we are seen, categorized, and treated by others. By the definition given here, a person has only one PSI. The PSI lets us refer to all things informational for a person.

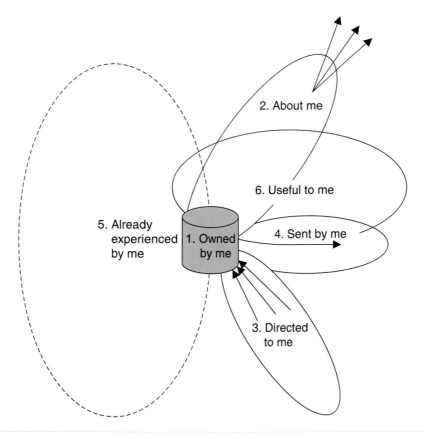

Figure 2.1 A personal space of information (PSI) contains information that is personal (in any of six senses) together with information tools, objects, and constructs used to manage this information.

At its center, a person's PSI includes all the information items that are, at least nominally, under that person's control. At its periphery, the PSI includes information that the person might like to know about and control but that is under the control of others. Included is information about the person that others keep. Also included is information in public spaces, such as a local library or the Web, that is or might be relevant to the person.

The PSI might be visualized as a vast sea of personal information. If the "home waters" represent information under the person's control, then, farther out in the PSI, are waters of information that are shared, disputed, or under exploration. This area includes information about the person, the use of which the person might like to control (or at least monitor) but which is currently under the control of others (credit agencies, tax authorities, insurance companies, etc.). At the periphery of a person's PSI are oceans of available information (on the Web, corporate intranets, public libraries, etc.), only the tiniest fractions of which the person explores in order to complete various tasks and projects and in order to fulfill various roles in the person's life.

Even in the home waters of the PSI, a person's sense of control over information is partly illusory. For example, an email message can be deleted and no longer appear. However, the message is very likely still in existence. We're adrift in a sea of information. Our own personal

spaces of information (PSI) are large, mostly unexplored, with uncertain boundaries and big areas of overlap (with the PSIs of other people and organizations).

But PIM is about extending our control, or at least our influence, out over this sea of personal information. We will never have perfect control. We do what we can. And most of us can do much more than we're doing now.

2.5.1 Characteristics of the PSI

A few aspects of a PSI can be emphasized:

- We each have only one PSI. A person's PSI is everything informational as it relates to the person.
- A PSI is defined as much by what we would like to be able to do as by what we can currently do. For example, the information others keep about us is included as a "region" of the PSI as a way of staking a claim, so to speak, on this information. We might at least like to control who sees this information, how long it's kept, and how easy it is to correct or update.
- The PSI is external to the person. A person could literally walk away from his PSI tomorrow, move to Mongolia, and have little further to do with his PSI aside from the few pieces of the PSI that can travel with him (e.g., his wallet, the notes he may have written on the palms of his hands, or the proverbial string he may have tied around one of his fingers).

2.5.2 Why "PSI"?

A simple answer to this question is that "personal information space" does not produce an attractive acronym. Some readers will also note that *PSI* is frequently used as the Roman alphabet spelling of the Greek letter Ψ which, in turn, is frequently associated with psychology. The Merriam-Webster OnLine dictionary defines "psychology" as the "science of mind and behavior."[11] *Psyche* has its origins in the ancient Greek word for breath, essence of life or soul.

One thread we explore throughout the chapters of this book is the extent to which a personal space of information can be said to reflect the mind and life of its owner. The book also explores the ways in which elements in a PSI—a calendar or a to-do list or a even a set of touchstone words of wisdom placed on the bathroom mirror—not only provide a passive reflection of a person's mind, but can also serve, more actively, to complement and facilitate the development of mind and soul—in the same way that a person's space of things reflects, complements, and facilitates the development of the body.

2.6 Making sense of the PSI

For each of us, our PSI is large and amorphous. We can't see it all at once. When we try to make a full list of just the kinds of information in our PSI, we are sure to overlook something. What about the documents relating to the car and its registration that are in the car's glove

---

[11] See *http://www.m-w.com/dictionary/psychology*.

compartment? What about the old computer in a "dead corner" of our home office? It too has information we once considered essential.

The PSI establishes an arena for the essential activities of PIM as these are listed in the next chapter. But in most discussions, we look for ways to carve the PSI into smaller, more manageable regions in order to focus and make more concrete the book's discussions of personal information management. As we do so, it is important to resist an easy reliance on distinctions that only perpetuate a state of information fragmentation all too familiar to most of us.

There is little to be gained, for example, from a focus on digital information to the exclusion of paper-based information. There is little to be gained from a focus on email to the exclusion of web-based information or e-documents and other digital files. Even if the goal is to design a better email application, focusing on email alone places artificial boundaries on an informational landscape that can cause us to overlook important opportunities for integration.

Our lives contain many forms of information. It is difficult to think of any meaningful project or regular activity that does not depend critically on several forms of information. Consider something as simple as buying food for the evening's meal. Henry is cooking dinner and wants Jill to do the shopping on the way home from work. His list of things to buy starts out in his head but is then copied to an electronic document while he works at his computer. The list grows longer as Henry consults a recipe for the meal he wants to cook. The recipe itself might come from a paper-based cookbook or from a web page.

When Henry's done, he first thinks to call Jill with the list but then decides it's faster to send Jill the list in an email message. Jill gets the email message but calls Henry for clarification on a few of the items ("How many cans of tomato sauce? What size?"). She has a mobile device which she could use to refer to the list in digital form, but past efforts to do this in the grocery store proved cumbersome. She prints out the list instead. Later Henry calls with a few more items to buy, and Jill scribbles a few more lines onto the paper printout in order to remember to get these items too.

In even this simple, everyday example—the creation of a shopping list for grocery shopping—information moves through several forms, from human memory to e-document to email message to paper printout. Along the way, information in other forms—a recipe book or a web page—is also consulted and several devices are used (the telephone, the computer, the printer) or considered for use (the mobile device).

The remainder of this section lists some concepts that aid us as we seek to explore portions of a PSI. Concepts support the creation of manageable regions in a PSI that correspond to our goals and roles as people rather than to regions defined by the happenstance of development in information tools, applications, and devices.

2.6.1 Personal information collections

Are there islands in this sea of personal information? Several researchers have discussed the importance of collections in managing personal information. Karger and Quan (2004) define a "collection" broadly to include a variety of objects, ranging from menus to portals to public taxonomies. Boardman (2004), in contrast, defines a collection of personal information to be "a self-contained set of items. Typically the members of a collection share a particular technological format and are accessed through a particular application."

This book defines *personal information collections* (PICs) by neither technical format nor application. Instead, PICs are defined by the activities people do in relation to their PSIs.

> *Personal information collections,* referred to as "PICs" or simply "*collections*" in the remainder of the book, are personally managed subsets of a PSI. PICs are "islands" in a PSI where people have made some conscious effort to control both the information that goes in and how this information is organized.

PICs can vary greatly with respect to the number, form, and content coherence of their items. Examples of a PIC include:

- The papers in a well-ordered office and their organization, including the layout of piles on a desktop and the folders in filing cabinets.
- The organized papers in a specific filing cabinet and their organizing folder where, perhaps, the office as a whole is a mess.
- Project-related information items that are initially dumped into a folder on our notebook computer and then organized over time.
- A carefully maintained collection of bookmarks to useful reference sites on the Web and their organizing structures.
- A collection of digital photographs and videos in a "family memories" album.
- A collection of digital music or a collection of CDs.
- An EndNote database of article references including custom properties added by the user.[12]

In a sea of personal information, PICs are islands of relative structure and coherence. A PIC includes not only a set of information items, but also their organizing representations, including spatial layout, properties, and containing folders. A PIC may or may not be strongly associated with a specific application (such as an application to manage digital photographs or digital music). The items in a PIC will often be of the same form—all email messages, for example, or all files. But this is not a necessary feature of a PIC. People might like to place several forms of information in a PIC, even if doing so is often difficult or impossible with current software applications.

Just as the information item is self-contained as a unit for storage and transmission of information, the PIC is self-contained with respect to the maintenance and organization of personal information. People typically refer to a PIC when they complete a sentence such as "I've got to get these [papers | emails | photographs | documents] organized!" The organization of "everything" in a PSI is a daunting, perhaps impossible, task. But people can imagine organizing a collection of web bookmarks, their email inbox, their laptop filing system (but probably only selected areas), and so on. Likewise, in the study of PIM, PICs are a tractable unit of analysis,

---

[12] In a personal communication, one researcher told me she uses 12 separate custom properties and "lives by" her EndNote database.

whereas consideration of a person's entire PSI is not. Why do people go to the trouble of creating and organizing PICs and how are these then used? Answers have implications for the larger study of PIM.

2.6.2 Tasks and projects

Tasks and projects provide a practical way to approach a person's PSI and to understand his/her practice of PIM without "falling into" existing tool-based partitions (e.g., by studying only email use or only Web use).

The terms "task" and "project" (and associated terms such as "task analysis," "task management," and "project management") mean different things to different people in different research communities.[13] Even within a single community such as the human–computer interaction (HCI) community, the term "task" takes on different meanings in phrases such as "task management"[14] and "cognitive task analysis."[15] Also, "project" and "task" are often used interchangeably.

In the context of PIM, a useful and important distinction is made between a *personal task* and a *personal project* or, simply, *task* and *project*. For *task*, we can use a simple, intuitive definition implicit in Bellotti's use of the term (Bellotti et al., 2004): A task is something we might put on a to-do list. "Check email," "Send mom flowers for Mother's Day," "Return Scott's call," and "Make plane reservations" are all examples of tasks. With respect to everyday planning, tasks are atomic. A task such as "Make plane reservations" can certainly be decomposed into smaller actions—"get travel agent's phone number," "pick up phone," "check schedule"—but there is little utility in doing so. Tasks can usually be completed in a single sitting but often stay on a to-do list of pending tasks for long periods awaiting the requisite information. We can't make hotel reservations, for example, until we know the dates of the trip and the location of the meeting.

A project, in turn, is made up of any number of tasks and subprojects. Again, the informal to-do measure is useful: While it makes sense to put tasks like "Call the real estate broker" or "Call our financial planner" on a to-do list, it makes little sense to place a containing project like "Buy a new house" or "Plan for our child's college education" into the same list (except perhaps as an exhortation to "get moving!"). A *project* has an internal structure of interdependent subprojects and tasks and can last for weeks or months. In the project depicted by the open windows in Figure 2.2, for example, a mother must contend with several different considerations when planning for her sons' summertime activity. Do activities conflict with one another? How far is the drive to and between activities? Can both sons attend the same soccer camp? And so on.

---

[13] See Grudin (1993) for a discussion on the large differences in meaning a term can have for different communities.

[14] See, for example, Bellotti et al. (2004); Bellotti et al. (2003); Czerwinski, Horvitz, and Wilhite (2004); Gwizdka (2002a, 2002b); Kaptelinin (2003); Kim and Allen (2002); Mackay (1988); Silverman (1997); Whittaker and Sidner (1996); Williamson and Bronte-Stewart (1996); Wolverton (1999); and Yiu (1997).

[15] See, for example, Card, Moran, and Newell (1983).

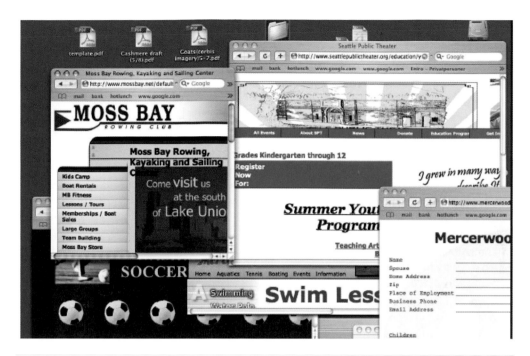

Figure 2.2 **Information relating to a mother's attempts to plan summer activities for her sons.**

Task management—as used, especially recently, in studies of human–computer interaction[16]—refers primarily to the management *between* tasks, including handling interruptions, switching tasks, and resuming an interrupted task.

Project management, on the other hand, refers primarily to the management of various components *within* a project.[17] The extended lifetime of a project and the structures that are imposed on it are perhaps an inevitable consequence of its many components and their interdependencies. For the project to be successfully completed, many or most of these components must also be completed, in the right order, at the right time. In planning a wedding, for example, it's important to set a wedding date but not before dates of availability for the preferred location of the wedding are confirmed. If the wedding cake, wedding dress, vows, bouquet, and whatever else are all selected on time, the wedding is still not likely to be considered a success if the invitations don't go out in time.

---

[16] See, for example, Bellotti et al. (2004), Bellotti et al. (2003), Czerwinski et al. (2004), Gwizdka (2002a, 2002b), Kaptelinin (2003), Kim and Allen (2002), Mackay (1988), Silverman (1997), Whittaker and Sidner (1996), Williamson and Bronte-Stewart (1996), Wolverton (1999), and Yiu (1997).

[17] See, for example, Jones, Bruce, and Foxley (2006); Jones, Bruce, Foxley, and Munat (2006); Jones, Munat, and Bruce (2005); and Jones, Phuwanartnurak, Gill, and Bruce (2005).

The project and the task are both useful units of analysis. Both provide a basis for understanding how people manage their information over time and in ways that cross the many boundaries set by current tools.

2.6.3 Hot, warm, and cold regions of personal information

Regions of a PSI can sometimes be distinguished with respect to frequency of access. Cole (1982) referred to three kinds of information: action information, personal work files, and archived information. Similarly, Barreau and Nardi (1995) referred to ephemeral, working, and archived information. Essentially the same distinction, with yet another set of terms, is used by Sellen and Harper (2002). This book mostly uses Sellen and Harper's terms, being the simplest set among alternatives. The terms are used as follows:

Hot (immediate) information is in active use now. Included are the documents opened on our computer that we're reading or editing. Also included is the notepad by the phone that we're using to take notes on a phone conversation. Hot information is generally used in some way at least once a day.

Warm (working) information is the information we are holding for use in a particular task to be completed or in a project that is active. Information may be grouped together but not necessarily. A task- or project-related grouping can take the form of a pile—physical piles for paper information or virtual piles for the files and web references on a computer desktop. Or a grouping can be accomplished through the use of folders and folder structures where these, again, can be paper-based or computer-based.

Cold information is no longer in active use. Cold information includes information that is consciously archived, that is, by placing in less accessible storage such as a warehouse for paper documents or tape for digital information. However, cold information can also include inactive paper piles on a desktop or files on a computer that we've learned to ignore but that we never seem to find time to move or delete.

> When a man undertakes to create something, he establishes a new heaven, as it were, and from it the work that he desires to create flows into him. . . . For such is the immensity of man that he is greater than heaven and earth.
>
> German-Swiss physician Philipus Aureolus Paracelsus (1493–1541)

2.7 Looking back, looking forward

In this chapter, we have looked at several perspectives on "information":

- ☑ Information is what people process to understand their world.

- ☑ Information is what's in documents, email messages, web pages, MP3 files, photographs (digital and paper-based), videos, and so on.

✓ Information is what can be stored, retrieved, copied, transformed, and distributed.

✓ Information is how other worlds are represented to us: past and present, possible and pretend.

✓ Information is how we are represented to the outside world, accurately or not, for better or worse.

✓ Information is what people use to get things done.

✓ Information is an extension of us.

✓ Information is a drain on a person's money, energy, attention, and time.

✓ Information is what we can use to have things "our way."

We then considered the six senses in which information can be said to be personal, according to our relationship with the information. Information can be:

1. Controlled by, owned by me. Examples include email messages in our email accounts and files on our computer's hard drive.

2. About me. Examples include credit history, medical, web browsing, and library books checked out.

3. Directed toward me. Examples include phone calls, drop-ins, TV ads, web ads, and pop-ups.

4. Sent (posted, provided) by me. Examples include the email we send, post to a blog or a personal web site, or publish in a report or an article.

5. (Already) experienced by me. Examples include web pages that remain on the Web or books that remain in a library, or TV and radio programs that remain somewhere in "broadcast ether."

6. Relevant (useful) to me. This sixth sense of personal information includes information "out there" that we would like to see. This sense of personal information also includes information that we do *not* want (ourselves or our family) to see, such as offensive material on the Web.

Information is sometimes packaged in information items that can be can be created, modified, stored, retrieved, given a name, tags, and other properties, moved, copied, distributed, deleted, and otherwise manipulated. However, the ways of manipulating an information item vary according to an item's form, as supported by and sometimes defined by the tools we use such as applications to manage email, music, photographs, or web browsing. Personal information is often scattered by its form into separate organizations for which we have developed distinct habits and strategies of PIM. Multiple forms of information exacerbate a situation of *information fragmentation* that is a central problem of PIM: the information we need is often widely scattered. A great deal of our time and effort is spent in managing information in different organizations on different devices and in gathering information together to get things done.

A personal space of information includes personal information in each of its senses. The PSI also includes various tools and other objects (virtual and visible) affecting the flow of information to, from, and through a PSI. The PSI can be thought of as a vast sea of personal information. If the "home waters" represent information under the person's control, then, farther out in the PSI, are waters of information that are shared, disputed, or under exploration. This region includes information about us, the use of which we might like to control (or at least monitor). In this region lurk "pirates" intent on stealing our information and, through our information, our very identities in an information world. At the periphery of our PSI are oceans of available information (on the Web, corporate intranets, public libraries, etc.) of potential relevance to us and the things we want to do or be. And, yes, at this periphery are "dragons" of various kinds, including offensive web pages we don't want to see and computer viruses that threaten to wreak havoc on the information we control.

Various concepts help us to make sense of our PSIs and to map out manageable regions of the PSI for special attention. But there are good and bad ways to divide a PSI into regions. We can give special focus on the management of paper—or email messages or web references or songs or photographs—as distinct forms of information. But in doing so, we risk perpetuating a state of information fragmentation that is a source for many problems of PIM. And we risk missing important opportunities for an integration of our personal information.

Instead, throughout this book, the *task* and *project* define manageable regions of the PSI. We have personal projects for the various things we mean to accomplish with our lives, ranging from getting a better job to having a wonderful summer vacation. Projects mean planning—whether done mostly inside our heads and by jotting down notes and to-dos, or through the use of some special-purpose tool. Projects, in their planning and execution, may last for days, months, or even years and include many subprojects and individual tasks. To complete a project, we often need lots of information in several forms. Solve the problems of information fragmentation for a project and we may have a solution for the larger problem of information fragmentation so pervasive in our practices of PIM.

This chapter began with a discussion of personal information and associated technologies as part of an enduring quest to "have things our way," free from the demands and constraints of the immediate environment. We can speak with people on the phone even though they are thousands of miles away. We can also correspond with these people via email and at a time of our choosing, not theirs. Our access to information, especially as mediated by the Web, gives us an astonishing reach to "realities" (both real and make-believe) far removed from our current time and place.

Herbert Simon, in his book *The Sciences of the Artificial* (1969), describes the zigzag path taken by an ant as it struggles across a pebble-strewn beach toward some distant goal. He concludes that "the apparent complexity of its behavior over time is largely a reflection of the complexity of the environment in which it finds itself" (p. 64). Simon goes on to consider the hypothesis that the apparent complexity of human behavior might similarly be understood to be a reflection of the environment in which people find themselves as they struggle toward their goals.

Our modern environment has been radically transformed by our tools and technologies. If we mean to understand the complexity of human behavior, we cannot do so in most cases by considering the physical environment alone. A person walking down a hilly road is observed to shorten his stride going uphill and to lengthen it going downhill. Variations in his stride

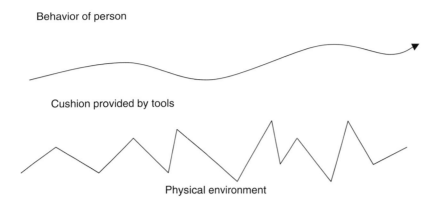

Figure 2.3   **Tools as a cushion between people and their immediate environment.**

correlate perfectly with—are attributed to—variations in the grade of the road. Similarly, if this person cycles down the road on a simple bicycle with no gears, we will see him pedaling slower on the uphill and faster on the downhill. But, if that same person cycles down the road on a 10-speed bicycle, variations in pedaling are dampened. The gears on the 10-speed enable the person to maintain a roughly constant rate of pedaling regardless of road grade. In this sense, the 10-speed lets the cyclist have things his way and not the way of the road. The use of the 10-speed to modulate the literal ups and downs in the roadway is characterized by the rough drawing of Figure 2.3.

Now shift to Alice's environment (see sidebar) as she works in her home-based consulting business. Figure 2.3 also characterizes Alice's relationship to her tools and her informational environment. Long ago, before most of her clients were on email, much of her correspondence happened over the phone. When the phone rang, Alice answered—not doing so meant possibly disgruntling or even losing a client. But now many more of her client interactions happen via email. Alice has more leeway concerning when she answers a client's inquiry. She finds she is able to work more effectively by "batching" responses so that she works through a set of inquiries at the end of the day. As Alice makes increasing use of her professional web site, she hopes that interactions with the web site will, in turn, take the place of much of her current email correspondence. If so, Alice's behavior is even less tied to the "zigzag" of individual client inquiries so that she is able to maintain more constant focus on longer-term objectives.

Having our information and our information tools work with us, in the manner shown in Figure 2.3, instead of against us is certainly one primary purpose of PIM. But what is PIM? As an area of study, how does it relate to disciplines such as human–computer interaction, information retrieval, information science, cognitive science, and artificial intelligence? More important, what is PIM in our daily practice of it? How do we do PIM, and how can we do it better? These are questions to be explored throughout the remainder of this book. The next chapter begins this journey with a framework for understanding and interrelating the essential human activities that comprise a practice of PIM.

A framework for personal information management

PIM activities are an effort to establish, use, and maintain a mapping between information and need. Finding and re-finding activities move from need to information. Keeping activities move from information to need. Meta-level activities focus on the mapping itself. In an ideal of PIM, we see everything more clearly: where we are now, where we want to be, and how we can get there. We get to our goals faster, with greater comfort—our way and not the way of the road.

Chapter
Three

Art consists of limitation. . . . The most beautiful part of every picture is the frame.

English essayist, novelist, journalist, and poet G. K. Chesterton (1874–1936)

3.1 Starting out

Chapter 2 concluded with the positive thought that our information and information tools can work with us so that we can have things our way rather than the way of our immediate physical environment. An analogy was made to a 10-speed bicycle. By using the different gears of a bicycle, a cyclist can maintain a roughly constant rate of pedaling even as the grade of the route varies. An information item can have a similar function. We see a film, listen to a song, look at a picture, read a book or article, or respond to an email message at a time and place of our choosing. Performer and audience, author and reader, information sender and receiver no longer need to be present at the same place or time for an exchange of information to happen.

Technology brings new tools which create new modes of communication. The telephone, voice mail, email, instant messaging (IM), blogs, wikis, and personal web sites made easy through services like MySpace and Facebook—these and other modes not yet invented explore a space of possibilities for audiences reached, levels of interactivity, and required synchronicity of communication.

With so many modes to choose from, and as the richness or "bandwidth" of communication increases, the disparate physical realities of people who are party to the communication become less and less relevant. You might be in a park somewhere dressed in your workout clothes. I might be at home in my bathrobe. Our conversation with each other via our avatars in a virtual space such as Second Life is unaffected by these circumstances of our physical world. Physical space is mostly irrelevant (until it rains on you or until my power goes out).

But tools are not always strictly our selfless high-tech servants letting us have things our way and not the ways of the physical world. Tools make their own demands. Tools must be maintained, upgraded, backed up, and synchronized.

Moreover, an active conversation (or channel) enabled by a mode of communication rarely provides equal benefits to each person who is a party to this conversation.[1] It's nice to call someone far away at a time of our choosing. But on the receiving end, the presence of a telephone means that no gathering—not dinner, not even a funeral service—is safe from random interruptions by a caller clueless to the situation he is calling into.

The negative counterpart to the picture of Figure 2.3 of Chapter 2 is depicted in Figure 3.1. Our rider now has a hilly ride indeed, with ups and downs of the physical world and new hills brought on by information technology. Now new tools, and the new forms of information they bring, add to and accentuate the bumpiness already present in the environment. People still stop by our office unannounced for old-fashioned face-to-face conversations. But these conversations are now interrupted by calls through the mobile and office phones and by beeps from the computer announcing the arrival of new email messages or requests for IM conversations.

Does our day ever give us a ride like that depicted in Figure 3.1? How would we know? One clear sign of trouble: We're spending too much time managing our information and

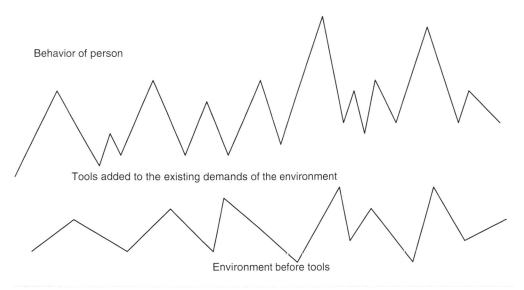

Figure 3.1 **Tools that add to and accentuate the ups and downs of the immediate environment.**

---

[1] See Grudin (1988) for a groundbreaking analysis of asymmetries often found in tools of communication and collaboration.

information tools and not enough time doing the things we want to do. Consider this description:

> I spend a lot of time working on a computer. Have four of them, two at home (there is a reason for two), one in my office at Tufts and a laptop that I take on trips. I am forever transferring files from one system to another (despite some minor incompatibilities among systems), always checking to make sure that I am using the latest version of some document or manuscript (that I didn't update it on another system and forget to put the latest version on the system I am "now" using). I correspond with a sizeable number of people, get/send thousands of emails a year, some of which I want to keep on file, many of which I don't, so I am purging files often, but not often enough to keep from feeling that things are out of control. Often looking for some scrap of prose that I know I wrote a couple of years ago for future reference, but not remembering what I labeled it or where I filed it. Etc, etc.[2]

How many of us can relate? What we're often doing instead of the things we want to do is personal information management. Getting in a position to do work is rarely as satisfying as doing the work. This "PIM overhead" may be increasing even as the apparent order of our information spaces decreases, and we may feel as if we're losing control of our information.

It doesn't have to be this way. Our tools of PIM can automate or obviate some PIM activities. In other cases, our tools can better leverage the activities we must do so that we get more benefit for the cost of our time and effort. Tools can sometimes help by simply "getting out of the way" so that, for example, needless restrictions or inconsistencies in the management of information are removed. In short, there's room for considerable improvement in our PIM tools. But before exploring this space of improvements, we need to better understand what PIM is and what it is that we do (or sometimes avoid doing) when we're doing PIM.

Toward a better understanding of PIM and PIM activities, this chapter moves through the following sections:

- ☑ The section *Perspectives on personal information management* considers various definitions of PIM and the characterization of PIM activities in relation to the management of a very large, amorphous store of personal information.

- ☑ In *PIM activities to map between information and need*, key activities are assessed for their role in helping establish, use, and maintain a mapping between information and need.

- ☑ *PIM-related activities and PIM-related areas* reviews the relationship between key PIM activities and other important human activities that are more likely to be placed on the "use" vs. "management" side of the informational coin. PIM as an area of study is also situated with respect to other fields, ranging from cognitive psychology and cognitive science to fields of database, information, and knowledge management.

- ☑ *Weaving PIM activities together* returns us to the practice of PIM through a review of two personal scenarios of information management and use.

---

[2] Descrtiption provided by Professor Raymond Nickerson of Tufts University.

3.2 Perspectives on personal information management

PIM is easy to describe and discuss. We all do it. We all have first-hand experiences with the challenges of PIM. But PIM is much harder to define. PIM is especially hard to define in ways that preserve focus on the essential challenges of PIM.

Lansdale (1988) refers to PIM as "the methods and procedures by which we handle, categorize, and retrieve information on a day-to-day basis" (p. 55). Bellotti et al. (2002) describe PIM as "the ordering of information through categorization, placement, or embellishment in a manner that makes it easier to retrieve when it is needed" (p. 182).

Barreau (1995) describes PIM as a "system developed by or created for an individual for personal use in a work environment." Such a system includes "a person's methods and rules for acquiring the information . . . the mechanisms for organizing and storing the information, the rules and procedures for maintaining the system, the mechanisms for retrieval, and procedures for producing various outputs" (p. 328).

Boardman (2004) notes that "many definitions of PIM draw from a traditional information management perspective—that information is stored so that it can be retrieved at a later date" (p. 13). In keeping with this observation, and as exemplified by Barreau's definition, PIM can be analyzed with respect to a person's interactions with the PSI, as viewed as a large, amorphous store. From the perspective of such a store, the essential operations are input, storage (including organization), and output.

In rough equivalence to the input-store-output breakdown of actions associated with a store, key PIM-related activities can be grouped as follows:

- *Keeping* activities affect the input of information into a PSI. Input can come directly as the result of a finding activity or incidentally via encounters with the environment.
- *Finding/re-finding* activities affect the output of information from a PSI.
- *Meta-level activities* include the maintenance and organization of information within the PSI.

The characterization of PIM as the management of a store of personal information (albeit a very large, amorphous store) provides a useful starting point as we try to develop a framework for PIM (Figure 3.2).

But this "input-store-output" characterization is also seriously limited. First, the characterization separates information management from information use. As noted in Chapter 1, this separation sometimes seems to make sense. We find a paper document from a filing cabinet and we read it. Perhaps later, we put the document back in the filing cabinet. Finding and keeping (putting back) are PIM actions—the steps from store to use and back again.

But in many situations, information management and information use are much more closely interweaved. If we highlight a passage in a document, for example, is this information use or information management? Perhaps both. The acts of highlighting and deciding to highlight may draw our attention to the information so that we "use" it in the sense that we understand

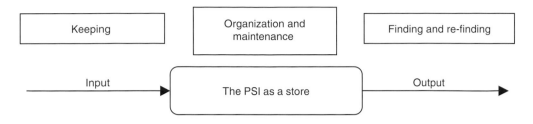

Figure 3.2 **From one traditional perspective of information management, the PSI is a store and PIM activities affect the input to, output from, and internal composition of this store.**

it better and internalize its implications. But at the same time, the highlighting is an act of information management. We're distinguishing highlighted passages from the rest of the document's content so that our attention on a second read later will go first to these highlighted passages, just as it might go first to the more visible items on a desktop when we enter our office.

To return to a main theme of the book: Good personal information management needn't and shouldn't occur as a separate activity from information use. To be effective, information management and information use must be interweaved.

A second, related point is that the input-store-output characterization of PIM leaves a lot unsaid concerning what happens inside the store. How are items of information grouped, named, labeled, and interrelated? What role do organizational elements such as folders and tags play? In what ways do tools help and sometimes hinder the process? Information items, organizing constructs, and tools are all part of intricate mapping between information and need. This mapping provides a framework for understanding PIM and key PIM activities.

3.3 PIM activities to map between information and need

The following statement will guide discussion of PIM activities for the rest of this book:

> PIM activities are an effort to establish, use, and maintain a mapping between information and need.

This simple statement can be expanded, and PIM activities interrelated, with reference to the diagram in Figure 3.3. Needs, as depicted in the leftmost column, can be expressed in several different ways. The need may come from within a person as she recalls, for example, that she needs to make plane reservations for an upcoming trip. Or it may come via the question from a colleague in the hallway or a manager's request. Needs themselves are evoked by an information item such as an email message or a web-based form.

Information, as depicted in the rightmost column, is also expressed in various ways—as spoken comments from a friend or as a billboard seen on the way to work or via any number of information items including documents, email messages, web pages, and handwritten notes.

Connecting between need and information is a mapping. Only small portions of the mapping have an observable external representation. Much of the mapping has only hypothesized existence in the memories of an individual. Large portions of the mapping are potential and not realized in any form, external or internal. A sort function or a search facility, for example, has the potential to guide one from a need to desired information.

But parts of the mapping can be observed and manipulated. The folders of a filing system (whether for paper documents, electronic documents, email messages, or web references), the layout of a desktop (physical or virtual), and the choice of names, keywords, and other properties of information items all form parts of an observable fabric helping to knit need to information.

All PIM activities we consider in this book have some relationship to the mapping in Figure 3.3.

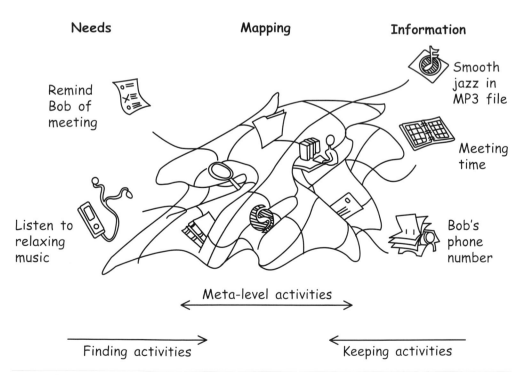

Figure 3.3 **PIM activities viewed as an effort to establish, use, and maintain a mapping between needs and information.**

3.3.1 Finding: From need to information

We have a need. We try to find information to meet that need. Needs can be large and amorphous (the need for information relating to a lifestyle change, for example) or small and simple (for example, the need for the phone number of someone we wish to call). The need may come packaged in an information item: an email request, for example, or a web-based form requesting certain information for its completion. Many needs correspond to tasks, such as "prepare for the meeting," "answer my boss's email," "return the client's call." Other needs, however, may not fit tasks except by the broadest definition: for example, "see that funny web site again" or "hear 'Five to one' for old time's sake."

In their efforts to meet a need, people seek. They search, sort, and browse. They scan through a results list or the listing of a folder's contents in an effort to recognize information items that relate to a need. These activities are all examples of finding activities. Finding is broadly defined to include both acts of new finding, where there is no previous memory of having the needed information, and acts of re-finding. More broadly still, finding includes efforts to create information "from scratch," as in "finding the right words" or "finding the right ideas."

 "Information finding" or, simply, "finding" is applied throughout this book to a class of activities that all start with a need and move to information that, somehow and in some form, meets this need.[3] In many cases, the term's use is natural. We find a magazine, or directions to someone's home, or web sites relating to a term paper.

In other cases, the term is stretched beyond its usual uses. Sending an email message, for example, is a packaging of information to meet one or several needs. Sometimes an email message is a request for information. In still other cases, the term "finding" makes sense only as shorthand for the longer expression "mapping from need to information." For example, we might send an email message to our travel agent to make airplane reservations.

When crafting an information item, we have choices concerning what information is referenced and where we look for it. For example, we will gauge whether it is faster to access a web site again via an email message we've sent or whether it is faster to simply search again using a web search service. We also have choices concerning how much of the item is "old"—composed with reference to, and perhaps copied and pasted from, other documents we have previously authored—and how much is "new"—coming directly from our own minds and through the keyboard without (conscious) reference to previous information. Our choices reflect an often complicated calculus of expected cost and expected benefit.[4]

Finding a digital information item involves many of the same steps and the same problems as finding a physical item such as the car keys or a package of walnuts needed for tonight's dinner salad. To be sure, there are differences between digital information items and physical

---

[3] For some activities, the term "information seeking" may seem more apt (Wilson, 2000, p. 49). See Chapter 4's longer discussion on information seeking and information finding.

[4] See, for example, Pirolli and Card's 1999 analysis of information gathering as an act of foraging.

objects. Digital information items may occupy a virtual space, but such a space cannot, yet, compete with the richness of our physical spaces. On the other hand, we can search for digital information using computer-based tools in ways that we cannot (yet) use in the search for physical objects.

But there are also many similarities between the finding of a physical object and the finding of an information item, whether digital or paper-based. We can fail to find the walnuts we need for a dinner salad for any of several reasons, each with its analog in the finding of a digital information item. The walnuts may not be on the shelves we look through in the kitchen. Perhaps they aren't in the kitchen at all. Or the walnuts may be right there in front of us on the shelf but in a container that we do not recognize. Or, in the midst of everything else we are doing to prepare dinner, perhaps we forget to look for the walnuts—for this, too, is a failure of finding.

Similarly, we may fail to find a web site we have bookmarked for our current project for any of several reasons. We may be looking in the wrong folders, or perhaps the bookmark is on another computer entirely, or we may fail to recognize the bookmark even though its listing is on the display. Or, in our rush to complete a project, we may forget about the bookmark altogether.

3.3.2 Keeping: From information to need

Many events of daily life are roughly the converse of finding events. Instead of having a need for which we seek information, we have information "in hand" and must determine what, if anything, we need to do with this information. Large amounts of information come to us through the searches we do or through regular channels of communication such as surface mail and email. We also encounter information by happenstance in many different ways and forms. We come across an interesting announcement for an upcoming event in the morning newspaper. A colleague at work may whisper news of an impending re-organization. While searching or surfing the Web for one need, we frequently encounter information that might be useful for some other need.

Decisions and actions relating to encountered information are referred to collectively as *keeping* activities. Is the information at all relevant, or potentially useful? Do we have an anticipated need for this information?[5] We can safely ignore much of the information we encounter, because the likelihood that we will need it is small and the cost of not having the information is small as well. Other information can be "consumed" immediately with no need to make a special effort to connect this information to need.

Then there is a middle area of encountered information. We may have a need for this information, but not now. We must then decide whether to keep this information and, if so, how. Even if we judge the information to be useful, we may still decide that no special action is required—perhaps because we already "have" this information somewhere in our PSI or because we can

---

[5] See, for example, Bruce's (2005) discussion on the importance of anticipated need.

easily return to the information—for example, by repeating the same search or the same path of hyperlinks that brought us to the information in the first place.

If we decide to keep the information we have encountered, then we must decide how. Keeping activities must address the multifaceted nature of an anticipated need. When and where will we need the information? We must also assess our own habits and anticipate our own state of mind. Will we remember to look? Will we remember to look in this particular folder? Will we recognize the information? Will we even remember why we kept it? Information kept in the wrong way may prove useless when a need arises later on.

As an example, a salesperson gives us his business card with his phone number. Do we need to keep this information at all? The answer may be no, either because we don't care to contact this person again or because we're certain we can easily access his phone number by another means. On the other hand, we may decide this information is important enough to keep in several different ways. We may write the phone number down in a notebook or in a calendar to be sure of calling him again later, and we may also enter this information into a contact database. But none of these methods of keeping will be any good to us if we're stuck in traffic and want to call him on our mobile phone to tell him we're running late for the meeting. (If only we had also entered his number into our phone!)

Consider still more variations in keeping. We keep appointments by entering a reminder into a calendar. We keep good ideas that occur to us or "things to pick up at the grocery store" by writing down a few cryptic lines in a notebook or on a loose piece of paper. We frequently re-keep information inside our PSI. For example, as we encounter a forgotten web bookmark during a spring cleaning, we may decide to move the bookmark to a new folder where we are more likely to notice it. Or, as we comb through the documents associated with a completed project, we may decide that some of these documents still have value in connection with a new project and should either be moved to a corresponding folder or assigned a label for this new project.

Just as an email sent represents one or more acts of finding, an email received invokes one or more acts of keeping. Is the message spam or "semi-spam" (announcements for conferences, meetings, or fund raising events, etc., for which we have no time or interest)? Does the message require immediate attention, or can it be dealt with later? If later, should the message be flagged or moved to a special folder? And so on.

Just as disparate acts of finding share in common a movement from need to information, disparate acts of keeping share in common a movement from information to need.

3.3.3 The meta-level and the mapping between need and information

A third set of PIM activities is focused on the mapping that connects need to information. These are collectively referred to as "meta-level activities" or, simply, "m-level" activities since, in English, many relevant terms begin with an *m*. *M* as in "mapping" or "meta." *M* also as in essential PIM activities such as *maintaining* collections of information, *managing* privacy (and, more generally, managing the flow of information into and out of a PSI), or *measuring and evaluating*.

In the coming chapters, we'll consider the following kinds of meta-level activity:

- *Organizing*. Organizing activities involve both the thinking that goes into deciding on a scheme of folder organization or tagging for an information collection and also the actions taken to implement this scheme. Keeping and organizing activities are distinct but interrelated kinds of activity. Both are covered in Chapter 5.

- *Maintaining*. Maintaining activities include information back-ups, updates and format transformations with an eye for near-term and the longer-term preservation. These and other maintenance activities are discussed in Chapter 6.

- *Managing privacy and the flow of information*. We need to manage both the outward flow of information from us and about us and the inward flow of information directed toward us. Activities to manage the inward and outward flow of information are discussed in Chapter 7.

- *Measuring and evaluating*. We need to measure the costs and benefits of current elements in our practices of PIM. And we need to assess the costs and benefits of alternatives. How well do current supporting tools, schemes of organization and overall strategies work? What should we change and how? Activities to measure and evaluate are discussed in Chapter 8.

- *Making sense*. We need to make sense of the information we have and of the needs for which this information is applied. Activities for making sense of things are discussed in Chapter 9.

Meta- is commonly used to mean "beyond" (everyday PIM activities) or "about" (the mapping or a PIM practice overall).[6] But another, more original sense is "meta-" as in "after."[7] After other PIM activities are done, which is to say, later but not now. We might say that the *m* stands for "mañana" or "maybe tomorrow but not today."

Activities of keeping and finding are triggered by many events in a typical day. Information is encountered, and keeping decisions are made (even if only the decision to do nothing). The information needed for a variety of routine activities (calling someone, planning the day's schedule, preparing for a meeting, etc.) triggers various finding activities. But there is often little in a typical day to trigger meta-level activities such as maintenance and organization. Meta-level activities can and often are postponed for weeks on end.

3.3.4 Putting more "meta" into a balanced practice of PIM

Finding and keeping activities need to complement each other. It makes little sense to take the trouble to keep information if this information can't be found again later when it's needed. Searching can dramatically improve the ease with which we find information but, as we'll explore more in Chapter 4, without some effort to keep information—at least to note its existence and relevance to projects in our lives—we may forget even to look for this information later.

---

[6] See, for example, the entry for "meta-" in the online Wikipedia (*http://en.wikipedia.org/wiki/Meta-*).

[7] See, for example, the entry for "meta-" in the Merriam-Webster Online Dictionary (*http://www.m-w.com/dictionary/Meta-*).

The effectiveness of keeping and finding activities depends, indirectly, on the effectiveness of an underlying organizational scheme and the strategies we apply to implement and maintain an organization over time. Lots of time can be wasted with bad schemes and bad strategies. Worse, information may be effectively lost even though it is right there—somewhere—neatly filed away. A bad organization can be worse than no organization at all.

Considerations of organizational schemes and strategies for keeping and organizing move us to the meta-level where the focus is more directly on the mapping between information and need. Which organizational schemes and strategies work best? How can we know? By what measurements and evaluations? Do our practices of maintenance ensure that the information, once found, is correct and current? Do we get the right version of a document? Or do we face a confusing "none of the above" choice between several document versions? Can we manage the flow of information, incoming and outgoing, in ways that reduce the occasions to find and keep information? For example, subscriptions, RSS feeds, even our friends and colleagues can provide us with useful information we might otherwise need to find on our own (if we think to look in the first place).

But the meta-level activities are the "after" activities—the activities we postpone or never seem to have time for in a typically busy day. Don't worry! This book is not a long harangue about the virtues of self-discipline and organization. With each PIM activity explored in Chapters 4 through 9, with each solution area explored in Chapters 10 through 13, we consider variations of the same theme: information management and information use should not be separated from each other. One supports the other; they are intertwined.

There are three general ways that better information management can leverage and be a part of our daily use of information.

Incidental

Given proper tool support many, if not most, measurements needed to evaluate our PIM practices can be collected automatically, as an incidental by-product of our daily use of information. For example, Chapter 2 defined an information item as a packaging of information that can be created, modified, stored, retrieved, named/tagged, moved, distributed, and deleted. Why not support the creation of repositories within the PSI where any instance of one of these events involving any information item is recorded together with a time/date stamp and a reference to the information item and other circumstances of the event (e.g., physical location, device involved, etc.)? Chapter 14 explores some of the many issues to be addressed if such an *item event log* is made.

Incremental

A meta-level activity is easier to do if it can be done in small chunks spread over time. How can we accomplish something within a few seconds here and there when we're unwilling to take a longer period of time out of an already busy day? We do one kind of meta-level activity—managing the flow of information—every time we designate that an email message is "junk." An email application should use this designation to update and fine-tune its definition of what "junk" is to us. The designation of email messages as junk is an incremental activity. We can designate as many or as few as we want, depending on our time or inclination.

With respect to management of information flow, we may ultimately want a more comprehensive privacy policy customized to our needs, with fine-grained distinctions drawn according to who wants what, when, and why (under what circumstances). But if we had to create such a policy in a single sitting, we might never do so. And the policy created might not be that good either. Questions relating to privacy are more likely to get answered (with better answers) if these are distributed over time as the occasion arises. Similarly, maintenance actions—such as moving or deleting old information, updating or correcting information, removing duplicates and near-duplicates—these can also be distributed over time so that the incremental cost of completing a maintenance action is small.

Integrative

Meta-level activities are more likely to be done if these are integrated into other activities we do anyway and perhaps even like doing. A similar argument applies to exercise. We can exercise on a treadmill or by doing something we actually like doing, such as taking a nature walk or playing Ultimate Frisbee. What about organization of information? Why do so many of us talk about "getting organized" a lot more than we actually do it? Part of the answer is that organizing is a separate activity—made separate by the well-intentioned schemes of filing and tagging that are designed to support us. We do another activity all the time and we sometimes even enjoy it: we plan.

Planning—whether planning a party, a vacation, or even a weekly meeting—can be fun and, anyway, it needs to be done. Chapter 5 considers the possibility that, given the proper tool support, an effective organization of information (based on file system folders, even) can emerge as a natural by-product of the planning we must do in any case. Chapter 9 generalizes by considering various activities that help us to make sense of our information. These activities help us understand and make better use of our information. These activities can also be a way of managing our information.

3.4 PIM-related activities and PIM-related areas

PIM shares considerable, potentially synergistic overlap with disciplines such as cognitive science, human–computer interaction, information science, artificial intelligence, database management, and information retrieval. Having explored what PIM is—its purpose and its constituent activities—it is time to explore what PIM is not or, rather, it is time to explore how PIM relates to but differs from other fields of inquiry that study the interactions between people, information, and technology.

3.4.1 Cognitive psychology and cognitive science

Cognitive psychology, simply put, is the study of how people do smart things: how people learn and remember, solve problems and make decisions, form and apply concepts and, in general, make adaptive use of available information. *Cognitive science* applies these questions more broadly to the study and simulation of intelligent behavior. Cognitive science has strong connections to—some would say, subsumes—the field of artificial intelligence.

The potential for a mutually beneficial interplay between cognitive science and PIM is considerable. Human activities that have long been a subject of basic research in psychology but that also have clear relevance to PIM include *problem solving* and *decision making*. For example, work on a big project such as "plan my wedding" can be viewed as an act of problem solving, and folders created to hold supporting information may sometimes resemble a *problem decomposition*.[8] In turn, the decision to keep or not to keep can be viewed as a *signal-detection task* and, as such, invites questions concerning the rationality of our keeping choices and our ability to estimate costs and outcome.[9]

To take another example, an important goal of cognitive psychology is to understand *categorization* and *concept formation*. How are categories and concepts learned and used? Several lines of research over the past 20 years or so have attempted to move beyond the traditional study of taxonomic categories and the study of artificially defined categories.[10] There has also been a search for more ecologically valid alternatives to the traditional experimenter-supervised, forced-choice classification paradigm.

An analysis of how people organize their information in support of a personal project and its goals could prove very useful to these efforts. For example, the folders people create in the course of completing a project may reflect internal *goal-derived categories*. If so, folders and the act of filing may have significant impact on what we notice and remember about an information item.

Or consider the activities of *reading* and *writing*. Both are areas of study in cognitive psychology with clear relevance to the study of PIM. We must read, or at least skim, an encountered information item to determine what should be done with it. In our daily interactions with information items such as email or e-documents, we must also write.

Conversely, the study of how people practice PIM may enhance a more basic understanding of the impacts that information technologies are having on our habits of reading and writing. There is evidence to suggest that ready access to vast amounts of digital information and the ability to view and work with this information on a variety of devices is changing our habits of reading in fundamental ways.[11] For example, we may be reading more superficially, counting

---

[8] See, for example, Jones et al. (2005).

[9] The signal-detection analysis was originally developed by Peterson, Birdsall, and Fox (1954). For its application to keeping decisions, see Jones (2004).

[10] See, for example, the work of Barsalou (1983, 1991), Ratneshwar et al. (2001), Ross (1999, 2000), and Ross and Murphy (1999).

[11] For more discussion on the impacts that modern tools may be having on our activities of reading and writing, see Levy (2001), Manguel (1996), and Marshall (2006).

instead on ready and repeated encounters with the same information over time. To take the standard PIM example of an incoming email message, we may quickly scan it to determine if an immediate action is required. If not, we may (or may not) perform a keeping action such as setting a reminder or placing the message in a special folder to ensure that the email is accessible to be read in more depth later on.

Access to large amounts of digital information is surely also changing our habits of writing. Legitimate reuses of information can represent a considerable savings in time. We may, for example, make small changes in a presentation to use it for a new audience. By reusing the presentation (with minor modifications), we then effectively "reuse" the hours of work it took to put the original presentation together.

Now large portions of a document may be the product of Copy & paste operations (from our previous writings) rather than a product of original writing. Certainly, management of text pieces pasted for reuse is a PIM activity, and this raises several interesting questions. How do we go about deciding when to reuse and when to write from scratch? We may sometimes spend more time chasing down a paragraph we have previously written than it would have taken to simply write a new paragraph expressing the same thoughts. Beyond this, we can wonder at what point a reliance on an increasing (and increasingly available) supply of previously written material begins to impact our creativity.

People don't do smart things like PIM in isolation from an external environment that includes other people, available technology, and organizational settings. Consequently, the study of *situated cognition, distributed cognition,* and *social cognition*[12] all have relevance to the study of PIM. Also very relevant is the study of affordances provided by the environment and by the everyday objects of a person's environment.[13] People vary greatly in their approach to PIM-relevant behaviors such as planning and with respect to personality traits such as risk-aversion—making the study of individual differences and personality also relevant. More generally still, there are emotional, motivational, and social aspects to a person's practice of PIM that engage a more general study of human psychology.

The interplay between applied research in PIM and basic research in human psychology (especially human cognition) promises to be rich and mutually beneficial. PIM provides a broad reality for the study of human cognition. Psychological study, in turn, can bring a deeper reality to our understanding of PIM.

3.4.2 Human–computer interaction/human–information interaction

Much of the work of the PIM-related research reviewed in this book originates from practitioners in the field of *human–computer interaction (HCI)*. But PIM research emphasizes the

[12] See, for example, Fiske and Taylor (1991), Hutchins (1994), and Suchman (1987).

[13] The interested reader is referred to Gibson's groundbreaking work on affordances (1977, 1979). Also very interesting and more accessible are Norman's discussions on the impact that "everyday things"—computer-based and not—can have on our ability to handle information (1988, 1990, 1993).

broader study of how people manage their information over time using a variety of tools—some computer-based, some not. PIM includes a consideration of our personal use of information in all of its various forms, including paper. Although it is difficult these days to imagine a practice of PIM that doesn't involve computers, nevertheless, computers are not a primary focus; information is.

In recent years, there has been discussion of *human–information interaction* (HII) in contrast to HCI.[14] Interest in HII is partly due to a realization that our interactions with information are much more central to our lives than are our interactions with computers. This realization is reinforced by trends toward ubiquitous computing. Success in computing and, perhaps paradoxically, in HCI may mean that the computer disappears[15] into the backdrop of our lives, much like electricity. If we move toward transparent interfaces, then we are left with our information.

However, recognition of the importance of the human–information interaction may be neither new nor recent. Fidel and Pejtersen assert that the terms "human–information interaction" and "human information behavior (HIB)" represent essentially the same concept and can be used interchangeably. As such, HII-relevant discussions have been a long-standing mainstay of the library and information science field.[16]

PIM borrows from both HCI and HII. In the spirit of HII (or HIB), the focus is on information, in all its forms, rather than on computers. At the same time, PIM is practical. When digital information dominates, we can expect that many supporting tools of PIM will be computer-based. But not all. Walk into any office and it's not uncommon to see "sticky notes"—sometimes ringing a computer display as a testament to the persistence of paper.

3.4.3 The management of data, information, knowledge, time, and tasks

The study of *information management* and *knowledge management* in organizations also has relevance to the study of PIM.[17] Issues seen first at an organizational level often migrate to the PIM domain. The merits of various schemes of classification or the use of controlled vocabularies, for example, have long been topics of discussion at the organizational level.[18] But these topics may find their way into the PIM domain, as the amounts of personally kept digital information continue to increase. This migration has already happened in the area of privacy, protection, and security.[19]

---

[14] See, for example, Fidel and Pejtersen (2004), Gershon (1995), Lucas (2000), and Pirolli (2006).

[15] See, for example, Streitz and Nixon (2005).

[16] See, for example, Belkin (1993).

[17] For more about information and knowledge management in organizations, see Garvin (2000); Selamat and Choudrie (2004); Taylor (2004); and Thompson, Levine, and Messick (1999).

[18] See, for example, Fonseca and Martin (2004) and Rowley (1994).

[19] See, for example, Karat, Brodie, and Karat (2006).

PIM stands to benefit from advances in the fields of *information retrieval* and *database management*. For example, database techniques might be applied to mine and structure personal information.[20] Other techniques might realize essential efficiencies in support of deeper levels of unification in underlying data structures.[21]

There is sometimes discussion of personal *knowledge management* (PKM).[22] Given the usual ordering of data < information < knowledge, one is tempted to think that PKM is more important, or at least "sexier," than PIM. Even though the term "knowledge" tends to get excessive and indiscriminant use when the term "information" would do just as well, some useful distinctions between the terms can be drawn. One distinction essentially says that "knowledge" is what is in a person's head or perhaps also embedded in a tool or a system. Knowledge is implicit, difficult to see, difficult to articulate.

Knowledge acquisition/elicitation has been an important area of study in its own right, receiving special prominence in the 1980s with all the (mostly unmet) expectations concerning the promise of expert systems. This area morphed into the knowledge management movement of the 1990s, with its focus on finding ways to capture, share, and better leverage the knowledge embedded within corporations and other organizations (in key people, teams, and processes).

By extension, we could say that a key challenge of PKM would be to make explicit—to elicit—the knowledge of a person. The *P* in PKM is not because the focus is on the individual person. *P* would mean, rather, that a person perceives some benefit in the elicitation of his/her hidden knowledge. Doing so could be revealing or even therapeutic.

But here's an important point: Knowledge elicited is usually written down in some form—perhaps as a list of "principles and rules that I use when I do *x*." These may be represented in plain text, if-then rules, complicated diagrams, and the like. Others may read and learn so that they acquire and internalize some reasonable facsimile of this knowledge. In this case, we can say the knowledge has been transferred. But the vehicle of transfer is information. Knowledge written down is information—to be managed like other information.

We're back to PIM.

Similarly, a discussion of *time and task management* on a personal level quickly takes us back to a discussion of PIM. Some tasks—like mowing the lawn or sweeping the kitchen floor—involve few, if any, information items (except perhaps for a to-do list or a Post-it reminder). But many other tasks we complete in a day—such as making a plane reservation or responding to an email message—make heavy use of information.

Moreover, our external representations of tasks and time are themselves informational. We may carry a finely tuned internal sense of time and also a good memory for our various daily appointments. Likewise, we may choose to keep a small number of tasks in our head. But at some point, barring extraordinary feats of mnemonics, we're forced to externalize and to

---

[20] See, for example, Dong and Halevy (2005).

[21] See, for example, Karger et al. (2005) and Karger and Quan (2004).

[22] See, for example, this web site: *http://www.global-insight.com/pkm/*.

depend on external tools. What is time without watches, calendars, timelines, Gantt charts, and other means of external representation? Similarly, what is task management without at least a to-do list? These forms of external representation are information, to be managed like other information.

3.5 Weaving PIM activities together

The previous section addresses the question of how PIM as a field of study relates to other disciplines such as HCI and cognitive science. But how do PIM activities relate to one another? Two stories help to illustrate.

At her place of work, Jill has been given a "use it or lose it" ultimatum in January concerning the eight weeks of unused vacation time that she's built up over the past few years. Neither her boyfriend nor any of her friends can join her for an eight-week-long vacation. No matter. She's excited by the prospect of traveling alone. She begins to think of all the many exotic places she can visit over the summer.

- *Finding*. Jill finds information on the Web—lots of it—relating to different vacation options.
- *Keeping*. Jill is in gather mode. As she sees vacation-related web pages, she creates bookmarks in the top level of a "vacation" folder supported by her web browser so that she can return to these pages later when she has more time to read their contents.
- *Organizing*. As bookmarks begin to number in the hundreds, Jill organizes them into subfolders by country, kind of vacation, travel options, hotels, and so on.
- *Maintaining*. Jill weeds out old bookmarks that represent activities she is no longer interested in so that her collection of bookmarks is not such a jumble.
- *Managing information flow*. Jill gets ongoing updates on travel-related information through several RSS feeds. Jill also subscribes to digital and paper versions of several travel magazines.
- *Measuring and evaluating*. Jill's web browser provides her with statistics telling her that, over the past three months of vacation planning, she has used only 3 percent of the vacation bookmarks she has created. Although Jill spends only a few seconds to create a bookmark, the total time spent so far to keep and organize several hundred vacation bookmarks is over 3 hours, vs. less than 2 hours to actually read the web pages accessed through these bookmarks.[23] Jill decides it's time to focus more. She narrows down to planning a grand tour through Europe (other continents will have to wait).
- *Making sense*. Jill has a very sophisticated trip-planning tool that makes it easy for her to plan various tours through Europe. Even with eight weeks, there is only a day, or two for each location that Jill wants to visit. The trip-planning tool makes it easy for Jill to select all the places she wants to visit in Europe. The tool also helps her to order the locations she wishes to visit, plan travel from location to location, and arrange for places to stay along the way. Jill can see several different views of her itinerary. She can even see a

---

[23] The browser measures "read time" as the time a page is in view. The clock stops if the page is switched out of view or if there is no activity (no scrolling, clicking, etc.) after a specified period of time.

speeded-up first-person video simulation of her trip as planned, including location sights and sounds, hotel check-ins, train travel, and taxi rides. After one viewing, Jill is exhausted! She decides to scale back on travel plans and a pick a few places in Europe where she can stay for longer periods of time.

Jill's efforts with the different kinds of PIM activity engaged in her vacation planning are depicted in Figure 3.4. "Manage flow" as a kind of meta-level activity helps to streamline more event-driven activities associated with finding and keeping. "Measure and evaluate" as a kind of PIM activity has application to several other kinds of PIM activity, including the management of information flow. Finally, "make sense" is a kind of PIM activity that can be applied to and build on all PIM activities and associated structures, strategies, and supporting tools. Jill used a simulation tool that was able to accept as input Jill's carefully planned, carefully organized travel itinerary—the product of many rounds of finding, keeping, organizing, maintaining, managing information flow, and measuring and evaluating. Jill was able to make sense of her itinerary as representing a vacation she was not likely to enjoy—and in time to make corrective changes.

Or consider this example involving Alice, whom we first met in Chapter 1, as she attempts to manage her email.

- *Finding.* Alice has one basic need in association with her business: she is always trying to find new clients and new work with existing clients. Toward this end, she sends out various

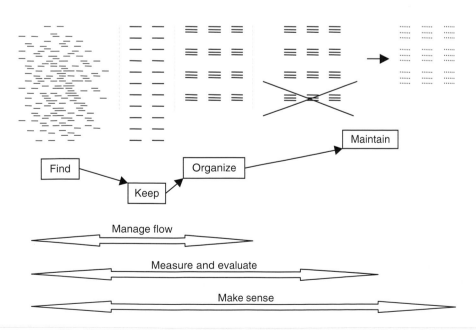

Figure 3.4 **A depiction of PIM activities as engaged to research and plan a vacation.**

email messages, ranging from relationship-building "for your information" (FYI) messages containing information of possible value, to announcements for upcoming "soirees" and workshops where clients have a chance to network and to learn more about the services she provides.

- *Keeping*. Alice receives a hundred or more email messages in a typical day. She makes quick assessments. She responds to a few messages immediately and ignores most messages altogether. Alice used to transfer messages for delayed follow-on to one of several project or to-do folders. But now she flags these messages instead and leaves them in the inbox.

- *Organizing*. Alice has in fact developed a scheme of organization applying different colored flags to email messages according to the nature of the sender and the response that will eventually follow (e.g., business partner, existing client on current project, potential client interested in learning more, etc.).

- *Maintaining*. Alice clears messages out of her inbox when she has read and responded to them or if she judges them to be "no ops" (she will never read or respond). Doing so helps Alice to focus more fully on the processing needed for remaining email messages.

- *Managing flow*. Over time, Alice has taken steps to manage the flow of email so that she sends out fewer email messages and can more quickly process incoming email. Alice has, for example, constructed several distribution lists so that a single message can be broadcast widely. She also sends out information via her web site and, especially, via a blog that also supports an RSS feed. On the input side, Alice has an aggressive spam filter that learns automatically in accordance with Alice's corrective feedback concerning what is and isn't spam. Alice also has several "smart folders" into which incoming email for selected senders is automatically sorted.

- *Measuring and evaluating*. Alice's email program takes measurements. From these measurements, Alice can tell that she is not making the best use of her time. Over the past year, about half of Alice's email time is spent responding to what Alice calls the "tire kickers"—people who express a passing interest in Alice's consulting services. For every 100 such expressions of interest, only one, on average, ever becomes a paying client. Alice decides to develop a filter for these incoming emails so that they can be paired with an automated response directing people to her web site for more information.

- *Making sense*. Even after processes are in place to manage correspondence with "tire kickers" more efficiently, Alice still notes that she spends a great deal of time in email correspondence. A typical day is often a blur of email exchanges. Although the majority of exchanges relate to current projects with paying clients, Alice often leaves her home office at the end of a long day with an empty feeling that she was mostly in reactive mode through the day, accomplished very little of substance and never managed to get to the creative, fun parts of her job. As she continues to sort and arrange a summary display of recent email threads, Alice notices how often email threads to different clients are about roughly the same thing. Through her manipulation of information items—in the form of message thread summaries—Alice comes to see a wealth of potential, but as yet unrealized, synergies between the work she is doing for different clients. Alice decides to explore the creation of several free wiki-based "collaboratives" that might draw various groupings of clients into a productive exchange of nonproprietary information. Based on Alice's hands-on manipulation of email threads, collaboratives appear to offer a way to cut down on "fyi" email traffic. Wiki-based collaboratives might also be a way for Alice to recruit new clients. Moreover, Alice's sorting of email threads yields groupings of clients and content that are a first step toward an organization of wiki collaboratives.

For both Alice and Jill, a great deal of time and effort is consumed in event-driven activities to find and keep. Many activities are prompted by various needs, such as the need to figure out connecting train schedules or a need to get the word out concerning consulting services. Or activities are prompted by information encountered, such as vacation-related information provided by friends (useful or not?) or email received from current and potential clients (standard or special response?). Significant parts of the day can be consumed reactively dealing with encountered information and immediate needs.

But leverage comes from time and effort spent on meta-level activities—activities that are seldom urgent but always important. For example, both Alice and Jill receive a great deal of useful information through friends and colleagues. Alice knows this well and makes an explicit effort to manage the flows of information, both outgoing and incoming, involving colleagues and clients.

For both Jill and Alice, "making sense" activities reflect an essential interplay between information management and information use. If the travel simulation tool represents information use, it takes as its input a travel itinerary database that Jill developed to help her manage the mounds of information she had accumulated. If the analysis of email threads is information use, the groupings that result are a basis for an organization of clients and content into wiki collaboratives.

3.6 Looking back, looking forward

PIM activities are an effort to establish, use, and maintain a mapping between information and need. This basic statement leads to a framework (see Figure 3.3) in which to place the following groupings of essential PIM activities:

☑ *Finding/re-finding activities* move from need to information. This grouping includes explicit search queries as sent/posted to a web-based search service or to a computer desktop-based search facility. The grouping also includes various activities of sorting, browsing, and "nosing around" that people use to get back to information for reaccess and reuse. And the grouping includes activities to publish (in a journal, for example), post (to a blog, wiki, or online forum, for example), or send (via email or surface mail, for example) information in an effort to meet one or more needs.

☑ *Keeping activities* move from information to need. This grouping includes decisions concerning whether to make any effort to keep information for an anticipated use and, if so, decisions and actions concerning how to keep the information. Should information items be piled (where?), filed (which folder?), tagged (with which tags?), or committed to memory? Keeping also includes the decision to attend to information in the first place. Emails received invoke a sequence of keeping decisions: What is this? Do I need to deal with this now, or can a response wait until later? If later, should I flag, tag, or file the message so that I can remember to deal with it later?

⊘ *Meta-level activities* focus on the mapping itself as a fabric weaving together information and need. Meta-level activities include efforts to organize (via schemes of piling, filing, or tagging), maintain (through backups, periodic cleanups, updates, and corrections), manage privacy and the flow of information (e.g., through subscriptions, friendships, policies of disclosure), measure and evaluate (supporting tools and strategies, current and prospective, of a PIM practice), and make sense of personal information. Since meta-level activities are rarely forced on us by the events of a day, these activities invoke a more original sense of "meta" as in "after"—after keeping and finding activities, as an afterthought, or as activities placed in a receding "tomorrow" that never arrives.

PIM relates to and provides a productive meeting ground for several disciplines, including cognitive psychology and cognitive science, human–computer interaction and human–information interaction, and the fields of database management, information management, and knowledge management. PIM distinguishes itself from these disciplines for its focus on the ways people manage information, digital and paper-based, over time in order to meet goals and fulfill various life roles. What problems do people encounter? How can supporting tools (and teachable strategies) help? In a world increasingly defined by the information we receive and send, PIM—the ability to manage this information—is one of life's essential skills.

This chapter began with Figure 3.1's depiction of a world where our life's ride is made worse, not better, by our information and informational tools. Even as demands of the physical world persist, our informational world introduces new demands on our time, attention, and energies.

Your reality or mine, informational and physical, is probably somewhere between Figure 3.1's depiction and the depiction of Figure 2.3 in Chapter 2. The phone + email device we take with us may make it possible to attend our daughter's soccer game when otherwise we might feel duty-bound to stay back in the office and work through a stack of unanswered email messages sitting in the inbox. On the other hand, as the phone rings during the soccer match or as we're distracted by the arrival of new email, our reality may begin to resemble that of Figure 3.1.

As we consider first activities and then solutions for PIM, we need to keep both depictions in mind. And with reference to Figure 2.3, we should keep the vision of an ideal of PIM that is even better than the one already described. To be sure, our information and information tools, if managed properly, can enable us to have things our own way. We work through email messages, for example, at a time and place of our choosing.

But a good practice of PIM, with good supporting tools and strategies, can do much more. Assume that you or I, as the cyclist in Figure 2.3, have a destination in mind. We have goals to achieve and roles to fulfill. A basic means–ends approach makes it clear that information, properly managed, can (should) help us to:

1. See the destination (goal state) more clearly. Is this really where we want to go? Do individual goals of our planned destination contradict or complement each other? Self-help books often encourage us to make our goals more real through detailed descriptions made explicit and external (e.g., as a written document to be pasted to the bathroom mirror or self-sent in email). There is good psychological evidence to suggest that the technique of making goals explicit works.[24]

2. Assess alternate routes to the destination. Which roads are in good repair? Should we take a chance on a shortcut?

3. Get there faster. With destination and route decided, a good practice of PIM can help us to reach the destination more quickly, with fewer stops along the way.

4. See where we are now more clearly. Maybe we're already at our destination and just don't know it.

In an ideal of PIM, we see everything more clearly—our destination, routes to reach this designation and their relative merits, and our current location. We travel the route faster and with greater comfort. Let this ideal of PIM guide us—add to it if you like—as we consider first key activities of PIM and then solutions for PIM. We begin, in Chapter 4, by considering a kind of activity we may think of most often in connection with PIM and failures of PIM: finding, re-finding, and the access and application of information to meet a need.

---

[24] For example, research suggests that people who have made a plan are more likely to recogize the relevance of plan-related information encounters by happenstance, even if they are not actively thinking about or working on the plan (Seifert & Patalano, 2001).

Finding and re-finding: From need to information

Finding is multistep. Recall something about the information. Recognize it when we see it. Repeat as needed. But also, we have to remember to find it in

the first place. Finding is not just about big acts to seek new information "out there." The many small acts to find the familiar can kill a day. *Wayfinding* treats finding as a journey—from a need and the situation prompting it, to information, and then back again.

Chapter
Four

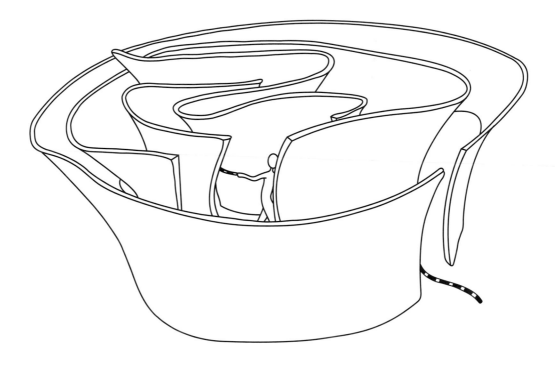

I do not seek. I find.

Spanish painter and sculptor Pablo Picasso (1881–1973)

4.1 Starting out

"Where is it? I know it's here somewhere. Where on earth did I put it?" "It" can be the car keys or a pair of shoes. "It" can be an information item such as an email message or a tax-related document. Certainly some of the more painful, memorable failures of PIM relate to failures to find information that "I know is here . . . somewhere." In my PIM seminars, people report efforts to find information—especially paper documents such as a title to an automobile they wish to sell or a birth certificate or a passport—that may extend over a period of a week or more. Finding over such a period of time may be a collaborative effort[1] involving various members of a household or an office work team. Failures to find can be a real source of discord as frustration mounts and accusations and recriminations are exchanged ("What did *you* do with it?").

If finding activities, with their focus on the location, output, and use of information, represent an endpoint in PIM, their study is also a natural place to begin taking a closer look at PIM.

---

[1] For more discussion of finding as a collaborative, group activity, see Berlin et al. (1993) and Fidel et al. (2000).

The finding stage makes apparent, sometimes painfully so, larger failings in a person's practice of PIM.

We are aware of larger acts of finding especially when these involve significant time and creative effort to complete or when these involve a conscious search as supported, for example, by a web service or a desktop facility. But large portions of a day can be consumed in many smaller acts of finding—the many look-ups required to fill out a form, for example, or the repeated references to a calendar in an effort to schedule a meeting. Though the many smaller acts of finding may each take only a little time, together they can still add up to a significant portion of a day.

In this chapter, we will see that finding is as much about interaction as about end result. There are two senses in which this is true. First, we can find the targeted information and yet still feel a sense of failure unless the process of finding the information was reasonably short, pleasurable, and trouble-free. Second, even though our focus is on the targeted information, we may gain considerable benefit from the incidental interactions with information along the way to this targeted information. To take a simple example, if a person checks her calendar to see when today's staff meeting will take place, she may happen to notice that another meeting is also scheduled for later today. More generally, the path taken to targeted information can be a source of serendipitous discovery. Finding is about the journey as well as the destination.

These topics are explored in this chapter as we move through the following sections:

☑ *Getting oriented.* Research on finding, as a PIM activity, is placed in the context of a larger field of research on *information seeking*. The challenges of finding and the opportunities for tool support vary according to whether we've experienced the items we seek before and whether these are in a store that we own and that is (nominally at least) under our control. Focus in this chapter is primarily on efforts to find (re-find) information we've experienced before and that is inside our PSI in a store that we control. This section also considers the essential movement that underlies finding activities: from a current need to the access and use of information that meets this need.

☑ *Everyday finding: Death by a thousand look-ups.* We consider the many small acts of finding that can add up to a significant proportion of a day's time—and its frustrations.

☑ *Finding is multistep.* Any act of finding involves an interplay between *recall* and *recognition*. We recall something about the item we are trying to find that might help to narrow the scope of a scan to recognize the item (e.g., in a folder or search results listing). Also, the finding process overall must often *repeat* several times so that a complete set of items is assembled. Finally, we must *remember* to find in the first place. Finding can fail because of the failure of any of these steps.

☑ *The limitations in ideal dialogs of finding.* We consider an ideal finding dialog with the computer (i.e., with a computer-based search tool) to be one that is much like the dialog we might expect to have with a well-trained human assistant. The computer can make use of anything we can recall. The computer orders and represents candidate items to aid us in our recognition of the item we seek. Support of a dialog like that between two people has many advantages but also one fundamental limitation: we may not always know or be able to express the things we need to find.

☑ *Wayfinding through the PSI.* We explore *wayfinding* as an alternate, complementary metaphor to finding as a dialog. The wayfinding metaphor gives emphasis to finding as a journey through the PSI—from a need and the situation prompting this need to information and then back again. As with any journey, a journey through the PSI can be serendipitous, yielding useful information we did not expect and would not have thought to ask for.

4.2 Getting oriented

What is information finding? We begin with Wilson's definition for information seeking (2000):

> The purposive seeking for information as a consequence of a need to satisfy some goal. In the course of seeking, the individual may interact with manual information systems (such as a newspaper or a library), or with computer-based systems (such as the World Wide Web). (p. 49)

This definition emphasizes the teleological or purposeful nature of finding: finding to satisfy a goal. Certainly goals matter. Failure to reach the goal, failure to find the sought-for information, is frustrating, costly, and memorable. For example, Sellen and Harper (2002) review studies suggesting that the average manager spends three hours a week looking for documents that have been misfiled.

But in a large number of everyday instances of finding, the end—if defined as eventually getting the information—is not in doubt. The information will be found one way or another, sooner or later. The bigger questions are how, and how long it will take. Can we find information easily and in the natural course of our efforts to get things done? Or is finding a separate, time-consuming, disruptive experience that takes us away from the other activities of a day?

As a supplement to Wilson's definition, this chapter takes the following slant on the finding activities of PIM:

> Information finding is an ongoing, minute-by-minute interaction with a large and growing PSI involving not only the needed information but also the information, organizing constructs, and tool support that are encountered and used along the way to this needed information and then back again to the situation prompting the need for this information. Needed information is found following paths through the PSI. Found information and the process of finding extend and further integrate the PSI.

Certainly the efforts of people to re-find information that they have previously saved involve interactions with the PSI. But a person's PSI is also invariably involved in efforts to find new information from a public space of information. The need behind a search on the Web for hotels in Montreal, for example, may be triggered by the glance at a personal calendar indicating that the trip to Montreal is only a month away. The search itself may be made easier, if ever so slightly, by having a favorite search service referenced on the home page—a part of the PSI. Or the web page may be quickly accessed through a web address that is specified by a keystroke or two and completed by an "auto-complete" suggestion of the browser. The information the browser uses to complete the address is also part of the PSI.

Information, once found, is often applied to an item in the PSI such as an email message or a document being created. Also, the information itself or a path to the same may be kept in the PSI so that it can stay found—easier and more likely to be re-accessed again later. The "marks" (impacts) of information found may eventually be on, or in, the person[2] in the form of new understanding or new internal knowledge structures. In the meantime, however, people can at least hope that the marks of information found are in their PSIs.

4.2.1 Finding vs. re-finding in public stores vs. private stores

Activities of information finding can be placed in one of four quadrants in Table 4.1 according to two senses of "personal" as described in Chapter 2:

- Is the information controlled ("owned") by us? Most of us control (in principle) the information on the hard drive of our personal computer. We can move or delete it (though many times we're properly reluctant to do so for fear of creating problems). Most of us control very little if any information on the Web. We can't move or delete it.
- Have we experienced (seen) the information before?

Activities of finding in each quadrant are important to a practice of PIM. Each quadrant presents its own challenges and its own opportunities for tool support.

A. Re-finding information we control (and have seen before)

Getting back to "my" information is especially important in PIM. We took the trouble to keep it and sometimes to create it in the first place. We're not done with it yet and may never be. We may have partially read an email message, for example, or a document, with the intention to read more thoroughly later. Some information—articles, contacts, or a spreadsheet with passwords—may be general reference to which we return repeatedly. Desktop search facilities can help, especially if these are integrative in their ability to search across multiple information

Table 4.1 An event of finding can vary according to where targeted information is and whether the person is trying to find this information again

The information is . . .	Controlled by us	Not controlled by us
Seen before by us	A	B
Not seen before by us	D	C

---

[2] Kidd (1994) takes an extreme position that knowledge workers rarely need to revisit an information item once they have been "informed" by its contents.

forms, and even more so as these tools are increasingly integrated into our use of other tools.[3] Generalized support for automatic completions and fill-ins can also help in the reuse of smaller pieces of information such as email addresses, phone numbers, and account numbers (see the "What next for tool development" sidebar). Also relevant are efforts to automate the tagging and grouping of information items by task and efforts to situate information items in the context of the planning of a larger project.

B. Re-finding information on the Web

We also return to information on the Web. In a study covering six weeks of web visits for 23 participants, Tauscher and Greenberg (1997a, 1997b) found that there was a 58 percent likelihood that the next page seen by a person was a page the person had already accessed at some point in the past. Jones et al. (2003) found that people use a variety of different methods and supporting tools for returning to Web information. Especially popular are "do-nothing" methods that require no keeping forethought. These methods include (1) clicking through hyperlinks from a familiar starting point such as a web portal or home page, (2) searching again, and (3) "auto-complete" facilities that suggest completions to a partially typed web address where completions are drawn from web addresses for pages previously visited.

C. Finding new information (not seen before) on the Web and other public stores

There is an extensive body of work on information seeking and information retrieval that applies especially to events in the C quadrant.[4] It is important here to note that there is a strong personal component even in efforts to find new information, never before experienced, from a public store such as the Web. For example, our efforts to find information may be directed by an outline or a to-do list that we maintain in our personal space of information. Access to new information items may be through a query that we maintain in our personal space as a bookmark or even as a list of words we keep in written form (or "in mind"). Much more can be done to use existing personal information in efforts to find new information from a public space.[5] Equally important, much more can be done to situate our searches on the Web with respect to informational situations in the PSI that prompts these searches—a topic of further exploration throughout this book.

D. Finding new information that we control

The amount of information we (ostensibly) control continues to increase along with increases in the capacities of storage devices we own. When we use a desktop search facility, we may be

---

[3] For discussions on the ongoing integration of search functionality, see Cutrell, Dumais, and Teevan (2006) and Russell and Lawrence (2007).

[4] See, for example, Marchionini (1995), Marchionini and Komlodi (1998), and Rouse and Rouse (1984).

[5] For a discussion of possible uses of personal information in support of search, see Teevan (2006).

surprised by what we find—by what we "have" already. One challenge in tool support, discussed later in this chapter, is to call a person's attention to information he or she has already and that may be relevant to the current situation—and to do this without becoming a nuisance.

Note that two other chapters in the book stand in different, complementary relationships to the current chapter. Problems experienced during finding often originate as earlier failures of keeping and organizing, as explored in Chapter 5. Searching technology, as explored in Chapter 11, can support finding in ways less dependent on careful prior keeping and organization of information.

What are the differences, really?

How much do differences in where and how we find information matter as long as we get the information we need? Certainly there's a difference between new finding and re-finding. If people have a specific item in mind, their search is more focused. They have memories from previous encounters that they can use (or ought to be able to use) in order to narrow the scope of the current search.

What about differences between finding information we control vs. finding the information "out there" on the Web and other public repositories? We may increasingly have the experience of finding new information inside our PSI in a store that we control. Such information, though newly found, is often information we ought to have experienced (that is, known was there to be found) or might want to have experienced, even if we haven't—so far. Our reaction, for example, to the discovery of an unread email message sent to us by a friend a year or two ago—even if only an "fyi" pointer to Web site of possible interest—is likely different from our reaction had we discovered a pointer to the same web site in someone's blog instead. The email message is directed to us personally.

Most important, the experience of failing to re-find an information item is different when the targeted item resides in a store we control vs. the Web or some other public store. We're less surprised when a Web page visited yesterday is not available today. An access failure could be for any number of reasons beyond our control—frustrating, to be sure, but "these things happen."

Do we generally show the same kind of equanimity when information under our control (nominally at least) can't be re-found? Leave aside documents we have authored which may represent many hours of our own work. Consider, instead, an article written by someone else which could just as easily be found on the Web as on a local hard drive. The failure to find this article inside the PSI often stands for something much larger than the loss of the information in the article itself. Failure can come to represent a larger failure in our lives . . . a loss of control. "Where on earth is it? Am I losing my mind, too?" We take it personally.

This chapter's discussion will focus primarily on finding in quadrant A—where the effort is to find (re-find) information we've already experienced from a store that is under our control.

4.2.2 From need to information (and back again)

We're almost done with this section's brief orientation. The remaining task is to consider two points in relation to this chapter's subtitle.

1. The journey from need to information is round-trip. Once information is found, it is either applied—"used"—in the situation that prompted its retrieval, or it is possibly kept for use later. Activities of finding and re-finding need to be situated in this larger context.

2. Our needs change with every step we take. Our own understanding of a current need, as reflected, for example, in our descriptions or in our seeking behavior, is constantly changing. Many changes in our understanding of a need are brought about by the actions of finding (seeking) itself and by the information retrieved.

The journey from need to information is round-trip

Information management and use are interwoven. This central theme of the book encourages us to think beyond just the location and access of information. Information revealed through browsing or "web surfing" or as referenced in a results listing returned by a search query is subject to several different keeping decisions. Is this information useful? Now, for a current need, or later for an anticipated need? If later, does anything need to be done now to ensure its availability later on? Do reminders need to be set? Should the information or a pointer to this information be kept?

But considerations of the return trip apply even if information is used immediately and then discarded. How is the information used? Is the information sent out in an email message or used in a document? Is information used as is, or are steps taken first to interpret, make sense of, and integrate the information into a larger document?

We might dream of a high-fidelity Copy & paste (or Drag & drop) in which the information found is copied into a new information item without loss of formatting. Better, the reference to this information is also copied. Portions of this reference can automatically be included, for example, in a document's bibliography. Other portions of the reference might be included in a hyperlink that makes it easy to get back to the source for more information as needed and possibly with the excerpted information highlighted in context. In some cases, we might even want to subscribe to updates in the content of web sites from which information is excerpted.

Why stop here? Why not also situate an act of finding itself with respect to an informational context. For example, we see a line item in a spreadsheet budget and send an email to our group's financial person for clarification—an act of finding. Why not record this act on an optional overlay to the budget's display? Later, when we want to review the response to our inquiry, we then have two ways to return to the email we sent and its responses: either go back to the context (e.g., the spreadsheet budget) that prompted us to send the email, or try to access email responses from the context-free jumble of the inbox. Which would you pick?

Or, as another example, we see a web site describing a new product and are moved to search for blogs giving commentary on the tool. Rather than carefully saving useful results in a separate document or through a separate bookmarking facility, why not save them as an overlay to the web site that prompted us to search?

Alas, current support for the "return trip"—from information found back to the situation that prompted its finding—still falls far short of what we might hope for. Finding tools such as search facilities and email applications still function more as worlds unto themselves rather than as an integral part of our informational context. As we use these tools to access needed information, we're still mostly on our own in our efforts to return to the informational context prompting the finding in the first place. And, as Karger (2007) notes, the transfer of information from the source back to the current situation through Copy & paste (Drag & link) is often still text-only. Or worse, we get information in paper form or as a scanned image and must then either transcribe or attempt to use character recognition software.

The larger point here is that we need to think of finding activities as part of a larger journey: from need to information and then back again, to need and the use of information to meet this need. Doing so raises practical questions that are easily overlooked if the focus is only on finding the information itself.

Needs change with every step we take

Even our effort to describe a need creates a refinement in our understanding of it and, sometimes, leads us to abandon the need altogether. "I want to see information on Paris's nicest hotels. . . . On second thought, maybe I'd rather stay at a little pension in a quiet neighborhood."

Belkin (1993) notes, "There is by now a substantial literature, from both theoretical and empirical perspectives, on the non-specifiability of information 'needs'" (p. 59). Several models of information seeking move beyond what Belkin refers to as "the standard view of IR" (information retrieval) in which a person approaches an information system with a well-specified query and "the major issues of concern" are "the representation of texts, and of queries, and techniques for the comparison of text and query representation" (p. 56). Interactions with an information system can be characterized as a process of negotiation,[6] a dialog,[7] or a process in which a person's knowledge changes through interactions with the information retrieved, leading, in turn, to a reassessment of information need.[8]

Especially evocative is M. J. Bates's *berry-picking model* of search (1989), depicted in Figure 4.1, to account for situations in which search interest and the expression of this interest evolve over time as a function of results returned by previous searches. For example, a search for "hotels in Paris" may return one result for a bed and breakfast inn in Paris. The person might then have the thought, "Hmmm, maybe I would like staying at a bed and breakfast better than at a large hotel," which is then reflected in a follow-up search for "bed and breakfast inns, Paris." The new query reflects a shift in interest—affected by previously returned results but not simply an attempt to search within these results.

---

[6] See, for example, Taylor (1968).

[7] See, for example, Oddy (1977).

[8] See, for example, Belkin, Oddy, and Brooks (1982) and Belkin, Seeger, and Wersig (1983).

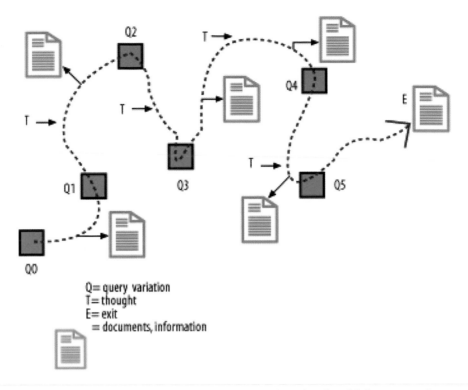

Figure 4.1 The berry-picking model describes a situation in which a person's search query (Q*n*) wanders as a function of results returned from previous queries. *Source: From http://www.flickr.com/photos/morville/84894767/in/set-1812650/.*

The concept of information need is itself subject to many interpretations. In the dialog between student and teacher, for example, who has a better understanding of the student's information needs with respect to an assigned term paper? Taking a behaviorist's position, Wilson (1981, 2005) suggests abandoning the concept of "information need" altogether in favor of only focusing on observable information-seeking behavior. Dervin (1992) refers instead to "sense-making" activities as motivated by a person's perception of a gap in his or her understanding of a situation.

However, it is difficult to assess the effectiveness of various finding activities or the tools designed to support them without making some assumptions concerning the motivation behind and desired outcomes of these activities.

Rather than abandoning the notion of need, it may be better to acknowledge that the assessment of need changes radically by person and in the same person with every step taken. The student now perceives only a need to do the bare minimum in research required to get a passing grade so that he can have more time for soccer practice. He may perceive a different need in 10 years when he is looking for a job. Even now he may be persuaded by the teacher to do more work, or maybe he will continue researching just for the fun of learning more about the term paper topic.

No matter what the need (or motivation), even if the student does the bare minimum, he will face the same basic problems of finding. Moreover, problems of finding arise in many everyday situations having little to do with canonical information-seeking situations where the search is for information in a library or on the Web. It's time to talk about everyday finding.

4.3 Everyday finding: Death by a thousand look-ups

Nancy is filling out an expense reimbursement form (Figure 4.2) for her recent trip to Montreal to attend a trade show. The form takes her more than an hour to fill out rather than the allotted half hour she'd hoped would suffice. No wonder she's been postponing its completion (even though she could use the reimbursement).

Why the extra time? The mechanics of finding just take time. Each space on the form seems to force another effort to find the required information. Nancy's internal dialog with herself, as she works to complete the form, might go something like this: "Departmental code? Note sure, better look it up. Same for budget number. I remember the destination all right but better check ticket to be sure I get the date/time of departure and return correct. And then check again for cost of ticket. Same thing for car rental. Where is that receipt anyway? I drove to and from the airport. What's the distance to the airport again? I think I wrote it down somewhere. . . . Or better to look at a previous expense report." By the time Nancy has completed the form, she is frustrated by the time it has taken, and she is even more inclined to postpone the completion of similar forms in the future.

Or consider a Web page form (Figure 4.3) that Nancy filled out much earlier in order to reserve a hotel room for the business trip. Nancy needed to decide the dates to reserve, which in turn meant that she needed to find information concerning the trade show she wanted to attend, its key events, and other events in her work life and personal life that she wanted to make room for before and after the trip. She wanted to spend enough time at the trade show, but she was thinking that she might extend the trip if she could talk her spouse, Jim, into coming with her.

*** PLEASE INCLUDE ITINERARY AND ALL RECEIPTS ***

Name:							Date:		
Departmental Code:							Budget #:		
Destination:									
Purpose:									
Date/Time Departed:							Date/Time Returned:		
Cost of Airfare or Train:							Car Rental:		
Date	Hotel Room Rate(per night)	Meals(per day)	Taxi	Parking	Miles Driven	Conference or Registration Fees	Misc.		

Figure 4.2 Finding activities account for much of the tedium in form-filling.

In that case, she would have needed to specify "2 guests per room" rather than one. But first she needed to call Jim (another act of finding) to see if he might be interested in coming along (he was but couldn't after he checked his own schedule—more finding). Nancy needed to check as

Dates

Check in: `1` `Jul 2006`

Check out: `2` `Jul 2006`

Rooms: `1`

Guests per room: `1 Adult` `No Children`

Help

Choose: ⦿ Check in | ◯ Check out

◀◀	July 2006							August 2006					▶▶
S	M	T	W	T	F	S	S	M	T	W	T	F	S
						1			1	2	3	4	5
2	3	4	5	6	7	8	6	7	8	9	10	11	12
9	10	11	12	13	14	15	13	14	15	16	17	18	19
16	17	18	19	20	21	22	20	21	22	23	24	25	26
23	24	25	26	27	28	29	27	28	29	30	31		
30	31												

▷ Need to Book Multiple Group Reservations?
If you have a Group Code, click here to book reservations.

Room Type Preferences

Your room type preferences will be submitted with your reservation and are subject to hotel availability.

Smoking: ⦿ Non-Smoking ◯ Smoking

Beds: ◯ King ◯ Two beds ⦿ No preference

Types: ☐ Accessible ☐ Suites ☐ Club/Towers/Executive

Special Accounts (Optional)

Promotion/Offer code:

Corporate account #:

Group/Convention code:

Travel agent number:

Special rates: ☐ AARP* ☐ Government/Military*

AAA number:* [   ] U.S./Canada (16-digits)

[   ] International (3-digit club code only)

Figure 4.3 Another form, more acts of finding. *Source:* Accessed through the online Hilton reservations site.

well to determine if she has a corporate account number that might apply, and she also wondered whether she should try to get the AAA discount (but she would then need to find her AAA number).

Nancy also did research on several hotel web sites before arriving at the form shown in Figure 4.3. She looked at several possible hotel alternatives, their positions on a map relative to the location of the trade show, their rates, availability of Internet access, workout facilities, and so on. It took a lot of finding. Even providing a credit card number (slot not shown) required a small act of finding to retrieve her corporate credit card from her purse and copy down its number.

Or consider the email exchange I had with someone who was hosting my trip to give a talk at the University of Eindhoven in The Netherlands. In the message depicted (Figure 4.4), reference was made (highlighted) to a hotel and a mobile phone number. The name of the hotel and the phone number were buried in a trail of previous email messages involving not only the host, but also an administrative assistant, in several different threads with different subject headings. The information was all there, somewhere, but the mechanics of getting to it consumed several minutes of time.

You may think of similar examples from your own life. Find a user ID and a password for your account on Amazon or eBay or the New York Times. Assume you have written the information down and know more or less where it is. Even so, you take time to locate this information again. Find a time when you and your friends can meet for lunch. Find an address. Find a phone number—even your own phone number if you have moved and haven't committed it yet to memory. You may have several ways to look things up. But look-up takes time and takes you away from your current task. Moreover, acts of everyday finding—especially efforts to schedule time with other people—can often cascade from one act of finding to several that involve not only the original finder, but several other people as well.

Given the scope and number of acts of everyday finding, we may be less surprised to see estimates from Feldman (2004) that knowledge workers spend 15 to 35 percent of their workday finding information. These estimates may even be low.

Hi William,

as promised some details of your stay in Eindhoven.

When you arrive to the station you can just walk to the hotel (it is at most 5 minutes walk). I attach a map to this message. The hotel is located at the North side of the central square of Eindhoven called Markt, next to the shopping center called Heuvel Gallery (red area on the map). In case you are lost don't hesitate to ask people around, they all speak English and are friendly.

I will book a dinner for us at about 19.00. Let me know if you have any preferences for the food. You can always call my mobile, otherwise let's meet about 18.45 in front of your hotel. Let me know if you also keep your mobile on.

Figure 4.4 Important information is often buried in an email exchange.

Everyday situations of finding are far removed from classic situations of information seeking and retrieval. We aren't seeking to learn something new or to fill gaps in our understanding of our world. We're just trying to get on with our daily tasks.

Two characteristics are often true of everyday finding:

- *Finding means communication and coordination.* Nancy needed to provide information concerning her stay at a hotel in Montreal. This meant not only looking at her schedule and the schedule for the trade show she was attending, but also calling her husband for his availability for the weekend after the trade show. Her husband, in turn, looked at his schedule. It is even possible that he might have made his own calls to see whether meetings scheduled might be moved.

- *The information sought is often "small."* Everyday finding often involves look-up of what might be called "property values" for an object or, more simply, statements of fact. Statements are embedded in information items such as a web page, email message, document, or the entry for a person in a contact-management database. But statements are rarely themselves information items to be retrieved on their own.

4.3.1 What can be done to help?

When finding involves communication and coordination among people, at least we now have several alternatives to phone calls or face-to-face meetings. We can email or send text messages. If Nancy needed to reach her husband today, she might even request a short instant messaging session. And her husband might participate in such even as he takes part in a meeting at his work. As part of its review of email, Chapter 10 considers the space of possibilities covered by these modes of communication and others as well. Wikis, for example, as their support matures, have the potential to complement and greatly alter email as we know it today so that problems like those illustrated in Figure 4.4 are less common.

When finding targets smaller pieces of information—statements of fact—there are simple steps we can take now to simplify or even eliminate some acts of look-up (see the "What now for you and me" sidebar for suggestions). Over the long run, we can expect continued improvements in facilities of auto-completion such as we see now to help us with the completion of web addresses, email addresses, and the passwords for some of our accounts. Increasingly sophisticated mechanisms of auto-completion might fill out or suggest easy completions for many of the fields in forms such as those in Figure 4.2 and Figure 4.3. The principle might be "write a fact once, read it/use it many times." Possibilities for a greatly improved, general auto-completion mechanism are discussed in the "What next for tool development" sidebars of both this and the next chapter (Chapter 5). A great deal may be accomplished, for example, through the consistent use, across applications, of structured and semi-structured storage and more granular searches able to flexibly locate statements of fact within such a store.

New modes of communication and coordination; better, more granular search—these and other applications of technology promise to greatly reduce the time spent and frustration felt with acts of everyday finding. But the success of these solutions depends on an understanding of finding fundamentals. As we see in the next section, any act of finding involves the same basic steps and the possibility to stumble with each step.

4.4 Finding is multistep

There are many techniques of finding and even more names for these techniques. People use browsing, directed search, logical finding, location-based finding, linking, teleporting, and orienteering. Underlying this diversity of techniques is an essential interplay between recall and recognition.

4.4.1 Recall and recognize

Figure 4.5 depicts a dialog between two people. Jerry wants to find out more about a person that he and Kate both met recently. He tells Kate a portion of what he is able to recall, and he then tries to recognize one among the list of names that Kate obligingly provides of people who seem to match Jerry's description. From Jerry's perspective, his attempt to find out more about Tony is a two-step process: first recall; then recognize. Jerry can recall Tony's gender, age, and hair color. By giving this description to Kate, he is able to get back, in return, a list of names of people who match the description, and he is able to recognize the name of the person he wants to know more about.

Lansdale (1988) describes a person's efforts to retrieve information as a similar interplay between recall and recognition. Recall may mean typing in a search string or even an exact address for the desired information. In other cases, recall is less precise and may involve spatial or temporal rather than verbal information. A person may recall in which pile a paper document lies but not its exact position within the pile. Or a person may have a rough idea when an email message was sent or an electronic document last modified. In a second step, then, information items or a representation of these, as delimited by the recall step, are scanned and, with success, the desired item is recognized and retrieved.

The steps of recall and recognition can iterate to progressively narrow the search for the desired information—as happens, for example, when people move through a folder hierarchy to retrieve a desired file or email message or when people navigate through a web site to a desired page. However, as illustrated in the depiction of the berry-picking model of

> Jerry: *"Who was that person we were talking to last week? You know... at Tom and Mary's party? A man... about 40... dark hair...?"*
> Kate: *"Sam? Dennis? Tony?..."*
> Jerry: *"Tony! That's it... What's his last name? Did he used to work at Tom's office?"*

Figure 4.5 Jerry's conversation with Kate is a give-and-take mixture of recall and recognition.

information seeking (Figure 4.1), the interplay of recall and recognition is not always a smooth progression through a general space of alternatives to a specific item or item set.

Many different finding techniques have been discussed in the literature, including browsing, directed searching, location-based searching, teleporting, and orienteering. The analysis of finding as an interplay between recall and recognition provides us with one way to compare and contrast these different techniques of finding.

For example, Bates (2002) postulates three generic techniques of finding[9]:

1. In *browsing,* the predominant action is recognition. People browse when they do not have a clear idea of what they are looking for. People also browse when they are unable to recall much (e.g., keywords, content words, properties) that might be used to narrow the scope of the search. Finally, people browse when the space is rich in relevant information so that there is little point in further narrowing the scope of the finding effort. People might browse through a journal or conference proceedings, for example, that directly targets their profession or interest area. In a PSI, the "hot" items of a desktop—items in active use—might be candidates for browsing as a primary means of access.

2. *Linking* occupies an opposite extreme in Bates's categorization. A desired item is fully specified by the information in the link. A full reference to an article is a link. A person might send this information to a librarian, for example, with the expectation of getting back the referenced article and no others. The hyperlink on a web page is also a link, with information that not only fully specifies the referenced web page (via URL), but also an associated mechanism for "jumping" to the referenced web page. People follow links to find information when the space of information is extremely large and the proportion of relevant information extremely low. People follow references to information in a library for example. People follow hyperlinks to information on the Web. People might also be expected to rely more on linking to access the "cold" (archived) information in their PSIs.

3. *Directed searching* can occupy a full range of intermediate positions between the extremes of browsing and linking. The person specifies keywords and gets back a results listing which can then be scanned for the desired item. Since search expressions can be more or less specific, directed searching can range from an activity involving mostly recall to an activity involving mostly recognition. One example is full-text searching of the kind supported on the Web.

Similar to linking or a much targeted use of direct searching, *teleporting* is described in Teevan et al. (2004) as a technique in which people try to jump directly to the information they seek. The emphasis is on recall. Recognition-based scanning is minimal. Such a jump might be accomplished, for example, through the specification of the exact address for a desired information item or through specification of a search string that only the item can match. An opposing *orienteering* technique involves an iterative, stepwise progression toward desired information in which recognition and recall each play an important role.

Orienteering is also used by O'Day and Jeffries (1993) to describe the iterative evolution of librarian-assisted searching. They describe an exploratory process in which intermediate searches are like the steps taken along a winding path through an information space.

---

[9] Bates uses the word "search" instead.

Consistent with the berry-picking model, the results of previous searches affect the next search request issued: "Like practitioners of the sport of orienteering, our searchers used data from their present situation to determine where to go next." Recall, then recognition, then recall again. O'Day and Jeffries speculate that the value for the library clients they studied was more in the accumulation of search results than in the final result set.

Related to browsing and orienteering, *location-based finding* is the term for a technique observed by Barreau and Nardi (1995) for the return to information on a personal computer. In a recall step, people take a guess as to location (e.g., the computer desktop or a particular drive or directory or folder) and then scan within that location in an attempt to recognize the desired file. The process is repeated as needed—for example, in order to move through a hierarchy of folders to a desired file.

Note that deciding on a finding technique presupposes a larger context in which other techniques, involving other mixtures of recall and recognition, have already been applied. A recognition-dominant browsing through stacks of books in a library, for example, presupposes an earlier recall-dominant step of getting to the library in the first place. The click on a hyperlink to jump to a web page presupposes an earlier step of recognition in which anchor text of the hyperlink is being used to recognize that the jump is the right one to make.

These labels for finding techniques represent useful characterizations of observed acts of finding rather than precise categories with clear boundaries. An episode of finding may admit to several different labels. More important is that underlying these various techniques is an essential interplay between recall and recognition. Problems in finding, no matter the technique, can often be traced to a problem with recall or recognition.

4.4.2 Problems of recall and recognition and some solutions

Nancy is looking for a travel reimbursement form she has filled out previously to use as a template for completion of her reimbursement request for the Montreal trip. She remembers the business trip she took to Chicago two months earlier and recalls that she created a folder called "trip to Chicago, April." Naturally enough, she looks in that folder for the file she seeks. But last month Nancy decided that it would be easier to group all travel reimbursement requests into a single folder called "travel reimbursements." Unfortunately, Nancy has forgotten her own decision during her current finding attempt. This is a failure of recall.

Nancy recovers from this failure and recalls the new "travel reimbursement" folder. However, in scanning through the files of this folder, she does not see the file for the Chicago trip. When she saved the file initially, she was in a hurry and simply saved the file under the default name provided which, perversely, was "non-wages funds disbursement request" (the name of the form on the company web site). The file is there, but Nancy doesn't see it, and she concludes, incorrectly, that she must have saved the file in a third location. Failure to see the file is a failure of recognition.

As Nancy tries to find the information she needs, what problems does she encounter, and what can be done to help her? Several points can be made.

Help can come through search, tagging support, and auto-completion

First, a desktop search facility might help Nancy (or maybe not). "Travel reimbursement" actually occurs nowhere on the form. And, since Nancy has lots of clients in Chicago, a search on "Chicago" alone will bring back several hundred matching information items.

Second, a supplemental tagging system might let Nancy organize her travel reimbursements forms both ways—as "travel reimbursements" and in association with specific trips like the "trip to Chicago, April." Or better, since Nancy does not have much time to tag, the forms she downloads might already have useful tags like "travel reimbursement." A facility able to search on these tags and on field values such as "Chicago" (as the destination) would make it easy for Nancy to find the desired form.

As part of an ideal in tool support, anything recalled about an information item sought can be used in its retrieval.[10] In some digital memory scenarios,[11] the physical location and the even measures of a person's physiological state are recorded and might be correlated with a person's recollections. A future Nancy, for example, might be able to retrieve the form based on her recollection that she worked on the form on the plane on her way back from Chicago and that she had a headache while she was doing so.

But why is Nancy trying to access an old travel reimbursement form in the first place? What need is she trying to meet? Nancy needs the old form to copy its information concerning arcane matters like "Departmental Code" and "Budget #" to the new form. If there were better ways to give Nancy this information—such as through a more general auto-complete—then maybe Nancy could sidestep the retrieval of the old form and its attendant problems with recall and recognition.

Note though, that the auto-complete mechanism can produce its own problems with recognition and recall. With reference to the form in Figure 4.2, for example, an auto-complete mechanism cannot just list one or more budget numbers as suggested completions—these numbers mostly look alike to Nancy and, even if she thinks she recognizes the right number, she wants to be sure. The auto-complete also needs to include a meaningful "display name" or description for each budget number, much like the display name of an email address or the page title listed along with a suggested web address completion.

On the recall side of auto-completion, what to do about values for fields like "Date/time departed" and "Cost of airfare or train"? Nancy certainly doesn't want a suggested completion for these fields based on past forms! Is Nancy forced to find the information for these fields?

Maybe not. The completion of the travel reimbursement form is part of a larger project. A project, as defined in Chapter 2, is composed of subprojects and basic tasks and may itself be part of a larger project. Projects have goals and constraints and often involve considerable planning. A project, in its planning, execution, and wrap-up, can last for several days to several months (or even years).

---

[10] See, for example, Lansdale (1988) and Lansdale and Edmonds (1992).

[11] See, for example, Czerwinski et al. (2006) and Gemmell, Bell, and Lueder (2006).

Nancy's trip to Montreal is a project with goals that might include "meet with key clients" and "see what the competition is up to" and "have some fun in Montreal." Components to this project might include "get travel authorization," "make travel arrangements" (a project in its own right), "arrange for meetings with key clients," and so on.

From this project perspective, the values on the travel reimbursement form for fields such as "airfare" and "departure date" are not new at all. Airfare, for example, is specified in the e-ticket that Nancy gets via email from the corporate travel agent. Dates of departure and return are specified on the travel request form (and also in email to the travel agent and also in Nancy's calendar and also in her out-of-office message). Chapter 2 discussed projects as a unit of analysis for the study of PIM. Projects in our practices of PIM can provide a basis for bringing together pieces of information that are otherwise scattered by the various tools (computers, devices, software applications, etc.) we use. We can begin now to organize our information by projects. Tool support can help us do more, more easily, in the future. Projects as a basis for information organization and reuse are discussed in greater detail in Chapter 5.

When information is in several forms, finding can be more difficult

As illustrated in Figure 4.6, Nancy, like the rest of us, may be delayed in finding information, or may experience an occasional outright failure, for the simple reason that she is looking in the wrong place. New tools and applications can make matters worse by increasing the number of possible places to look.

Figure 4.6 Relevant information may be in any or all of several places.

In one study reported by Bruce, Jones, and Dumais (2004), participants were asked to return to web pages they had visited up to six months previously by whatever method they chose. If participants remembered having saved a pointer to a target web page (e.g., as a web bookmark or in an email message or a document), they would sometimes first try to find this pointer for use in getting back to the web page. Overall people succeeded in getting back to targeted web pages in 95 percent or more of the trials (depending on conditions) and were generally quick to do so (with times averaging under a minute). But the time-out failures that did occur (after 5 minutes) often pointed to problems of information fragmentation. For example, one participant looked for a web pointer first in her Favorites list, then in selected email folders, then in folders under "My Documents," before finally locating the web pointer inside a presentation she had saved to a network drive.[12]

The information needed to complete a task is often scattered across several different computers, mobile phones, PDAs, and other devices. On a single computer, task- and project-related information may be scattered between different form-specific information organizations—one for email messages, another for e-documents and other files, and yet another for web references. Email messages may themselves be scattered between several email accounts. Documents and other files in the same folder hierarchy may be organized inconsistently by competing organizational schemes. In Nancy's case, for example, older travel reimbursement forms are still organized under folders for the trip to which they apply, whereas newer forms are organized into a single "travel reimbursements" folder.

Recognition failures are also more likely when information is fragmented. For example, a document we can easily pick out in a folder listing may be much more difficult to recognize from its appearance as an email attachment. Even subtle changes in the context of an item's appearance—its appearance in a folder listing vs. in a listing of search results, for example—may hinder us in our efforts to recognize the item.[13]

A multitude of versions and variations can make fragmentation problems worse

The difficulty in returning to information in a fragmented PSI is made worse when only one item will do. We want to respond to the latest message in an email conversation. We need the latest version of a document we are working on. Retrieving and working on an earlier version of this document can mean that the critical changes of the latest document are left behind. The challenge to get back to the right information item in the PSI increases as we keep multiple versions of a document and as still more versions of a document arrive as email attachments from other members of a project.

The specificity of the information need when re-finding items in the PSI stands in stark contrast to the much broader statements of need people often have when approaching the Web.

---

[12] Finding the pointer in her presentation was mostly luck. She had expected to find it first in the other places visited and expressed confusion and frustration when she did not. As it turned out, a pointer to the web site was in a "Favorite" she had created but in a folder different from the one she looked in.

[13] The dramatic impact that context can have on our ability to recognize is illustrated, for example, in the *encoding specificity studies* of Tulving (1983) and Tulving and Thomson (1973).

Web searches tend to define, implicitly, broad equivalence sets. Any web page in the set will do—that is, the same or similar information is available on several different web pages. Also, especially with no preconceived notions concerning what is or ought to be there, people may overestimate the quality and completeness of results returned by a web search.[14]

A person's challenges of version control increase further if, for some documents, there is no sense of the latest version. Or, rather, there are many, many variations of the document and a desired latest version of each. For example, in my conversations with the CEO of a large financial institution, he described a careful system he had developed in collaboration with his administrative assistant for the repeated use of the same set of PowerPoint presentations with different clients. Each variation was saved as a separate file and given a different name according to the naming scheme <base presentation><client name><presentation date>. Only a few slides changed between variations but these changes were critical. It would not do to have the slides targeting one client in a presentation given to another client!

The increasing challenge to manage multiple versions and variations of a document also points to another, potentially serious, limitation in search facilities. A search may return a long listing of results with each item closely matching the query. The person is then left with the difficult task of deciding which result is the right one for the current need. Finding the right search restrictions to single out the document we want—a recall step—is not at all easy to do; but neither is the recognition step of deciding which document in the results listing is the right one based on differences that are important but not at all apparent.

Fast searches give documents a chance to speak for themselves through their content. Additional terms can be associated with a document and searched as metadata. But we cannot rely on the search of document content to find the latest version of a document, nor should we necessarily trust the accuracy of a tag announcing that the document is the "latest version" (especially not when several such documents are retrieved!).

In some work situations, shared use of a formal document management system may help in version and variation control. However, such systems require extra time and effort to use and impose a level of formality that may not work in many situations of PIM. The CEO above was very knowledgeable concerning software tools and technology and certainly knew of and had used such document management systems. However, his need for management of multiple presentations grew, and became apparent only gradually, as the number of presentations and their variations also grew. By this time, he and his administrative assistant had developed their own system of management through careful use of folder and file names.

If fragmentation is bad, what's the solution?

And . . . is fragmentation necessarily bad? Over the years, several prototypes have explored variations on a theme of information unification: let all information items be of the same basic

---

[14] See, for example, Blair and Maron (1985) for research suggesting that people tend to overestimate recall rate—the percentage of relevant documents returned by a query.

form—all able to be manipulated in the same basic ways.[15] For example, Haystack represents an effort to provide a unified data environment in which it is possible to group, annotate, and reference or link information at smaller and more meaningful units than the file. In the Haystack data model, a typical document is actually an assembly of many individual information objects. Larger objects can be assembled from small objects as needed, and objects can be dynamically assembled into any number of collections. An email inbox, for example, is just another collection of special "email message" objects.

When such schemes of unification are reviewed in seminars I teach, people often feel uneasy. I liken their reactions to the uneasiness you or I might have if a "this is your life" party were being planned in our honor to be attended by everyone who has ever been a part of our lives—relatives, friends, former lovers, business associates, neighbors—everyone. Do we really want all these people in the same room? People in our lives are naturally separated from each other according to physical location, stage in our life, and our various roles and activities. Separation can be a good thing.

Likewise, with our information, separations by device, application, or email account are sometimes useful. For example, we may keep different email accounts: one for personal email and another for work-related email. Separations can help to divide a vast sea of personal information into manageable regions. Even better is when separations are under our control. We should be able, for example, to remove separations when they begin to hinder rather than help us in our efforts of PIM. And we should be able to assemble task- or project-related collections of information regardless of current separations.

But, too often, our information is partitioned not for our convenience, but for the convenience of tools narrowly focused on a particular function such as note taking or the management of "tunes." We then have trouble grouping documents, photographs, notes, music, and email together according to a larger task or project for which this information is needed. In some cases, we have little reasonable alternative but to use the interface provided by a specific tool as our means of manipulating any of the items created through this tool. This is the case, for example, in the use of Apple iTunes, Microsoft OneNote, or most email applications. Each of these applications defines special forms of information (e.g., songs, notes, email messages). The information items of a form cannot be easily manipulated other than through the application that supports this form.

Other tools, such as applications to create text documents, spreadsheets, or presentations, preserve our direct manipulation of the files (or "documents") as an information form. But even these applications can work in self-centered ways that make small acts of finding more difficult. One sign of this "app-centeredness" is apparent when we want to use the application to save a new information item, open an existing item, or compare two items, and we are thrown away from a folder representing our current task and into an application's default folder as a starting

---

[15] For a discussion of property-based approaches to unification, see Dourish et al. (1999). For discussion of time in particular, as a basis for unification, see Fertig, Freeman, and Gelernter (1996). For a discussion of a more fundamental unification based on a resource description framework (RDF) representational scheme, see Karger et al. (2005).

point. We want the notes we take and the songs we own to participate in larger activities in our lives. But sometimes we are hindered in our efforts to do so by the very tools that are supposed to help us. At other times, our information is partitioned and scattered by happenstance. Sometimes the chaos in our information reflects a larger chaos in our lives. Regardless, crossing these partitions to gather needed information can be time-consuming and error-prone.

Separations of information that work against us rather than for us and that we can't seem to or don't know how to change are a sign of *information fragmentation.* Information fragmentation is always, by definition, bad.

But decrying the evils of fragmentation does not—by itself anyway—get us any closer to a solution. Better searching, in combination with better, even automated tagging, can be an important tool in the fight against information fragmentation. But search too is limited. A single search can't yet, for example, cross all partitions in our information. And searching to distinguish among multiple versions and variations of a document can be especially problematic. Fragmentation may (or may not) diminish through convergences afforded by developments in our portable devices and on the Web, as explored in Chapters 12 and 13.

Even so, many of the agents of fragmentation are likely to remain a while longer. Whatever our reaction to visions of unification, we're not likely to see these realized anytime soon for reasons explored in greater length in Chapter 14. In the meantime, information will be fragmented in all the usual ways—by location, device, software application, and by us, too, through our own inconsistent ways of organizing our information.

But some of us already have an answer. In seminars, I often informally ask attendees how satisfied they are with their current practice of PIM on a scale from 1 (extremely dissatisfied) to 4 (so-so) to 7 (extremely satisfied). Usually about three-quarters of the people are in the middle, with ratings of 3, 4, or 5. Surprisingly, only about 10 percent of the people usually give a low rating of 1 or 2. That leaves about 15 percent of the people who give a rating of 6 or 7.

What's different about these "PIM satisfied" people? In talking with them, two points are apparent:

1. PIM-satisfied people are already actively engaged in a self-study of their PIM practice. In relation to their tools, organizational schemes, and daily habits—even their choice of friends and colleagues—PIM-satisfied people are constantly noticing what works and what doesn't. PIM-satisfied people actively explore ways of doing things better.

2. PIM-satisfied people are realists rather than purists in their practice of PIM. Not every tool is used or even paid attention to merely because it's new and cool. Not every email message gets answered. Not all information gets organized. PIM-satisfied people pick their battles, so to speak, targeting some information for special attention and letting the rest "flow by."

What is worth keeping and organizing and what isn't? We give special attention to this question in Chapter 5. But first, there's more to say about finding. We have considered recall and recognition as a kind of two-step that is done in various concentrations across all finding techniques. Each is a potential source of problem and failure in finding. Now let's consider two other steps of finding and the problems that can arise with each.

4.4.3 Remember to look

Not all problems with finding can be attributed to failures of recall and recognition. Many opportunities to re-find and reuse information are missed for the simple reason that people forget to look in the first place. In a study by Whittaker and Sidner (1996), for example, participants reported that they forgot to look in "to do" folders containing actionable email messages. Because of mistrust in their ability to remember to look, people then elected to leave actionable email messages in an already overloaded inbox. Inboxes were often further loaded with copies of outgoing email messages that might otherwise be forgotten in a sent mail folder.

Web information is also forgotten. In a study of web use, for example, participants often complained that they encountered web bookmarks, in the course of a "spring cleaning" for example, that would have been very useful for a project whose time had now passed.[16] In the study by Bruce, Jones, and Dumais (2004) mentioned earlier, participants often had bookmarks ("Favorites") pointing directly to targeted web pages to which they were asked to return. Yet these bookmarks were used less than half of the time. Marshall and Bly (2005) report a similar failure to look for paper information (newspaper clippings).

If the old adage "out of sight, out of mind" is true, then maybe the converse is true too: Keep items in view to keep them in mind. Reminding is an important function, for example, of paper piles in an office.[17] Email messages in an inbox provide a similar function, at least until the messages scroll out of view.[18] Barreau and Nardi (1995) observed that users often place a file on the computer desktop in order to be reminded of its existence and of associated tasks to be completed.

Visibility helps. But a person must still be prepared to look. Piles on a physical desktop can, over time, recede into a background that receives scant attention. Likewise, as online advertisers surely know, people can learn to ignore portions of a computer's display. Also, the ability to manage items and keep track of items in view—whether on a computer screen or on the surfaces of a physical office—degrades, sometimes precipitously, as the number of items increases.[19]

Attempts to compensate for the limitations of visible reminders can introduce other problems. People who adopt a strategy of repeatedly checking their email inboxes in order to respond to messages before these scroll out of view (and out of mind) may end up "living" in their email application with little time or attention left to accomplish work requiring sustained levels of concentration. People who immediately click through to interesting web pages, for fear of forgetting to look at these later (even if they bookmark them), may have their session of web use degenerate into an incoherent sequence of page views scattered across a wide range of topics with little to show for the experience.

---

[16] See, for example, Jones et al. (2002).

[17] Malone (1983) was perhaps the first to note this reminding function of "messy" piles.

[18] See, for example, Whittaker and Sidner (1996).

[19] See, for example, Jones and Dumais (1986).

There are many new ways in which a computer-based device might remind people of potentially useful information,[20] including, for example, the spontaneous execution of searches that factor in words and other elements of the current context (Cutrell, Dumais, & Teevan, 2006). However, these reminding devices must walk a fine line to avoid being either extremely annoying or ignored. These devices, like visible space, compete for a very precious and fixed resource: a person's attention.

4.4.4 Repeat?

In many instances, the need is not for a single information item but rather for a set of items whose members may be scattered in different forms within different organizations. Can you take a job candidate out to dinner next Wednesday? You want to say yes, but answering correctly may depend on finding several widely scattered information items (see, again, Figure 4.6).

1. What does your digital calendar say?
2. Is there anything for that evening on the paper calendar that you share with your spouse at home?
3. Is the trade show you were planning to attend next week? Better check the trade show web site.
4. You vaguely recall making another commitment for the same evening to play bridge with friends. Better check through the email messages on your personal email account.
5. What about your son's soccer match? You really don't want to miss another game. Better check the paper flyer with its schedule of games.

In finding situations such as this one, retrieval of "four out of five" is not good enough. We've all been in situations where we said yes to an engagement only to discover, belatedly, a conflict and then to be in an awkward position of having to cancel one or the other commitment. We thought we checked all possible commitments. We missed only one. Or what about the meeting we arranged or the party we hosted? We thought we invited everyone. But the person we missed is now not speaking to us. Or what about the tax return we filed? In some finding situations, "most" or "almost all" is not good enough.

When all items in a set need to be retrieved, chances of failure increase with the size of the set. Suppose the likelihood of finding any given item in a set of needed items is 95 percent. And let's assume that the likelihood of retrieving each item is independent of the others—an item has a 95 percent chance of being found no matter how many other items have already been retrieved. With these assumptions, the likelihood of successfully retrieving five items (e.g., the five items needed to answer the question above) goes down to 77 percent—that is, the chances of failure are now 23 percent, not 5 percent.[21]

But the chances of success can be worse than expected from the assumption that items are retrieved independently from one another. In situations of *output interference,* items retrieved

---

[20] See, for example, Herrmann et al. (1999).

[21] The chance of retrieving all five items is 0.95 * 0.95 * 0.95 * 0.95 * 0.95 = 0.77. The chance that at least one item will not be retrieved is 1 − 0.77, or 23 percent.

first may interfere with the retrieval of later items in a set—perhaps because the act of retrieval itself strengthens the items first recalled at the expense of unrecalled items (Rundus, 1971). Some of us may experience this effect when we try to think of everyone in a group of eight or nine friends. No matter whom we list first the last one or two people are often the hardest to remember.

The chances of successfully retrieving all members of a set can also be much better than is predicted by assuming a strict independence of individual retrievals. Every now and then we may find that the exact information needed for the current task comes to us packaged already or can be readily assembled. For this to happen, some forethought is required (by us or others). Support for larger task- or activity-based units of retrieval is discussed further in Chapter 5's discussion of keeping and organizing. But, in these instances, it makes more sense to think of the folder, pile, or collection of items sharing a tag as the unit of retrieval.

Retrieval may also be better than predicted by strict independence if the items we need to retrieve have an organization or are related to one another so that the retrieval of one item actually facilitates the retrieval of other items.[22] One everyday example of what we might call *output facilitation* seems to occur, for example, when remembering the characters of a well-told story or a good movie. The fabric of the storyline helps to connect the characters.

Does your information tell a story? How do the pieces come together? How do they interweave?

And what can our tools do to help? The computers we use have a wealth of raw information concerning our access patterns. How predictable are you in your daily patterns of information interaction? Do you usually open the same applications when you restart the computer? Do you usually go to the same collection of web sites at the beginning of the day to check news, weather, sports, and the stock market? What about the sources you check when looking up a word or a technical term? Do these include reference sources such as Wikipedia, various online dictionaries, or a trusted collection of online magazines, bulletin boards, and blogs?

Trusted tools might begin to construct *information assemblages* based on our patterns of access and use. The applications we routinely open can be preloaded on start-up. The web sites that we routinely consult might be merged into various "mash-ups" (see Chapter 13)—one for start of day, one for look-up, one for when we need an emotional lift.

A tool might even use our access patterns to help us avoid double-booking ourselves. Sources of conflict may be registered in the email messages with date information that we've received and responded to recently, and in the one or more digital calendars we use or reference (e.g., a corporate or organizational calendar) and in the web sites we routinely visit—especially those with dates prominently featured (e.g., conference or trade show web sites).

In short, there are many possibilities, still mostly unrealized, for tools to help us in the "re-collection" of the information we need.

---

[22] See, for example, Bower et al. (1969) and Jones and Anderson (1987).

4.5 The limitations in ideal dialogs of finding

Wouldn't it be nice if the computer worked like a well-trained human assistant?

In the dialog depicted in Figure 4.5, Jerry is able quickly to establish Tony as the object of conversation. Once this is done, he can ask Kate for more information about Tony, such as his last name or whether he previously worked in Tom's office. Obviously, it helps that Jerry and Kate know each other and speak the same language. It also helps that they have overlapping experiences of events like Mary and Tom's party.

Jerry is smart enough to not tell Kate everything he recalls concerning his encounter with Tony. He doesn't, for example, tell Kate that Tony reminded him, in some strange way, of his best friend in grade school. This would have meant nothing to Kate.

Kate, in turn, tries to be helpful in her responses. She does not, for example, say something like "Do you mean the person who had on a dark-blue sports jacket?" She knows that Jerry is generally oblivious when it comes to details concerning what people are wearing. Kate also doesn't do something silly like speak, in alphabetical order, the names of all men from the party who strictly match Jerry's description. She remembers which people she saw Jerry talking with, for example, and uses this as a basis for ordering her responses. She speaks her best guesses first.

As the shared context between people increases, dialogs can often become extremely efficient, even as these become nearly impossible for a third person to follow. Such dialogs can occur, for example, between two married people, people who have worked together for a long time or even people who are sharing a car on a cross-country road trip. It might even seem, at times, as if we're speaking to ourselves in altered form.

In our interactions with our computers, we're getting closer to an ideal mentioned earlier in which anything recalled about an information item or the circumstances surrounding encounters with it (e.g., time of last use or nearby "landmark" events) can be used to help find this item again. Moreover, our computer as assistant can order its responses so that the most likely object of our interest is always near the top.

We might call this the "me-speak ideal" (or, some might say, the "me-speak extreme") in which talking to the computer (possibly actual talking supported by voice recognition technology) seems like talking to ourselves—only a version of ourselves with a more exact memory for past events. The computer truly could be said to operate as an extension to our own memories (see Jones, 1986).

Here we consider more practical limitations of me-speak.

One practical problem: Not everything we need from our information can be readily articulated in a question or a search expression. The question/response of "Why didn't you tell me?!!?" . . . "Because you never asked me . . ." is a common device for sitcom laughs. But the exchange aptly expresses an underlying truth: we often have difficulty expressing what it is that we want or need.

Of course, a really smart computer—with an understanding not only of us but of the situations in which we need information—might even provide information we need but don't think to ask for. And the computer might do so with the deft, discreet diplomacy of an experienced human assistant—picking just the right times (Horvitz & Apacible, 2003) and just the right mode of delivery ("will you be going to the health club before or after your appointment with . . .?").

But, such intelligence is many years away from reality.

A small step toward me-speak might be a usage-based ordering of the items to be considered during the recognition phases of finding. Put items that are used more frequently at the top of the list; let less frequently used items fall to the bottom of the list. Certainly people do something similar when talking to each other. If Jerry asks Kate again later, "Who was that person I was talking to at Tom and Mary's party?" we would expect that Tony would now be Kate's first guess this time, not her third.

But Teevan, Capra, and Pérez-Quiñones (2007) note that dynamically rearranging a list of item referents in the human–computer interaction based on past experience does not always help and sometimes hurts. To speed up menu access, for example, Mitchell and Shneiderman (1989) tried rearranging menu items so that references to more commonly accessed items would "bubble" to the top of the list over time. However, the opposite happened. Menu access slowed. Because commonly selected items no longer appeared in the expected position in the menu, users were forced to scan the entire list. Similarly, White, Ruthven, and Jose (2002) gave people lists of relevant sentences which were dynamically reranked as the search process proceeded. Users did not enjoy the experience, nor did they perform as well as when the listing of sentences was static. Teevan (2006) completed an analysis of Yahoo query logs that focused on queries repeated by a user. Users were less likely to click through to a web page they clicked to before if its position in the results listing changed. And when they did click, they took more time.

Now what's going on here? Certainly we can think of many instances where we're perfectly happy to have the mostly likely completion listed first. Think of our email application's suggestion of an email address in response to our partial typing of a recipient's name. Or think of a web browser's suggested completion of a web address. We're happy to see the item we want listed first so that we don't have to scroll down the list. Even better if it's highlighted, so we can simply hit return to accept.

One key determinant is the influence of context on our ability to recognize a desired representation for an item based on its representation (e.g., in a list of alternatives). Sometimes context matters; sometimes it doesn't.[23] We know this from personal experience. Sometimes we know exactly what we're looking for. As long as an item's display is reasonable, we'll recognize it no matter where it is on a page or in a listing—better in these cases to list the item where we'll see it first. But at other times, context matters a great deal. In an extreme, our ability to recognize an item is totally dependent on its occurrence in a context of occurrence. We may remember, for example, that the item is "the third one down" or "in the lower left corner."

---

[23] See, for example, Murnane, Phelps, and Malmberg (1999) for an analysis of when context matters and when it does not.

More often, recognition is driven partly by the appearance of the item itself and partly by our memory for the context of its occurrence. If we repeatedly select an item from one position in a listing—the "Save as" command in a menu listing, for example—we may experience at least a moment's disorientation if this item appears in another position. It's not just "Save As" anymore but "Save As as this occurs in the fifth position." Some of us may have a comparable experience in recognizing other people. It may take us a few extra seconds, for example, before we realize the person we're talking to in the grocery store is actually someone we know from work.

In interactions with our information, space often does matter. A sense of location and context matters.[24] Visibility matters. The visible fabric of information can operate as a powerful extension to our internal, overtaxed, and limited working memories. We're reminded of things we might otherwise forget. We see relationships in our information that we might otherwise miss.

4.6 Wayfinding through the PSI

In their studies, Barreau and Nardi contrasted *location-based finding* with what they termed *logical finding*—roughly equivalent to directed searching as described in this chapter. People overwhelmingly preferred location-based finding as a method of returning to files on their personal computers. Similar to browsing as described by Bates, location-based finding places greater emphasis on recognition but as directed to information on a person's computer rather to a public store. People take a guess as to location (e.g., the computer desktop or a particular drive or directory) and then scan within that location in an attempt to recognize the desired file.

More recently, participants in the Teevan et al. (2004) study—all very technically savvy MIT computer science graduate students—expressed a strong preference for orienteering as a means of finding information, whether local to their computer or on the Web. Like location-based searching, orienteering is shifted toward a reliance on recognition rather than recall. Orienteering can include directed searches, but these are situated and represent small steps in the finding effort rather than large leaps. An orienteering style of return to a web page, for example, might follow the jump to a web site with a site-specific search for the desired web page.

Teevan notes that participants preferred orienteering even when they knew exactly what they were looking for in advance. But perhaps they preferred orienteering precisely *because* they knew what they wanted. Teevan speculates, for example, that orienteering gives people a greater sense of location and context. With a sense of location and context, people can better control the direction of their finding efforts, and they can be more confident that they've reached the right information.

4.6.1 The role of desktop search facilities

The reluctance to use directed search, even in small steps, as a primary means of returning to information in the PSI persists even as desktop search facilities show dramatic improvements

---

[24] See Teevan et al. (2004).

in speed, ease of use, and integrative scope of search results. In my own ongoing informal survey of people who have installed and use an integrative desktop search facility (e.g., one able to search quickly across files, email messages, recently visited web sites, etc.), people still express a preference for orienteering as a means of returning to information within their PSIs. In results so far,[25] more than 90 percent of the respondents indicate that they used a search facility only as a secondary means of access after primary methods of return such as scanning the inbox or the desktop had failed. Consistent with this informal evidence are results from a formal evaluation of the Stuff I've Seen (SIS) desktop search prototype involving 234 people over a 6-week period (Dumais et al., 2003). Logs of usage indicate that the majority of items accessed through SIS (54%) were last opened over a month ago.

Are you an enthusiast of desktop search facilities? How often do you use your favorite facility? During a seminar I gave in 2005, one participant said that he planned to use a search facility instead of folders as his primary means of getting back to information. When we exchanged email about a year and a half later, he was still an enthusiast and said that he used desktop search as his preferred way to get back to information—"approx. 5 times a day." Five times is a lot—especially if those instances make it possible to access information that he would otherwise not be able to access or would need to spend significant time to access. Undeniably, a desktop search facility can be a powerful addition to the tool set we use to re-find information.

But, for most of us reading this book, five uses of a search facility do not begin to account for the number of acts of re-finding (let alone the total number of acts of finding) in a typical day. Try keeping your own log and count the number of times in a typical day that you:

1. Look for a document either to open and check some fact, reuse some information, edit, or send along to someone else.
2. Look back through your inbox for email messages you have not yet processed, or search for replies to a message you sent out, or look for messages from a particular person.
3. Check and recheck your calendar—perhaps to see what's next or coming up on your schedule, or to search times you might be free for an engagement, appointment, or meeting.
4. Return to various favorite web sites to check news of the day or to look up information on a topic.
5. Look for a song to listen to or a photograph to look at or funny story to read (one more time).
6. Be sure, also, to count incidents of finding like those described above as prompted by the need to fill out a form.

Many acts of everyday finding are so routine as to escape our attention. Yet the completion of these acts of finding takes time and can take our attention away from the work we're trying to do. Email alone can be a significant distraction. As we send one email message or check for one response, how tempting it is to read other email messages as well! Similarly with the Web, in our effort to find or re-find information for our current task, we are often tempted to look at other information as well, even though it has little or nothing to do with the task at hand.

---

[25] I've asked the question to over 300 people so far in various seminars, presentations, tutorials, and courses.

Getting off track is not always bad and often we may find information that may be useful sometime later. But a problem in our use of an email application or a web browser as a separate standalone application is that we go to the application. In doing so, we leave the context of our work (even if the document prompting our excursions remains in view), and we enter the world of the web browser or email application. These problems diminish as finding activities directed toward email, the Web, and other information are increasingly integrated with one another and into the working situations from which information needs arise. But we have a long way to go.

4.6.2 Wayfinding as a round-trip

The reasons for a reliance on browsing, location-based finding, and orienteering are aptly subsumed under another term: *wayfinding*. Peter Morville, in his book *Ambient Findability* (2005), defines wayfinding as "knowing where you are . . . knowing your destination, following the best route to your destination, being able to recognize your destination and *finding your way back to your starting point*" (p. 17, emphasis added; see also the "Wayfinding" sidebar by Peter Morville in this chapter).

Another characteristic of wayfinding is the ability to reproduce the experience again later. The wayfinders who located a new uninhabited island wanted not only to return to their home island, but also to guide their fellow islanders to the new land. A person who gets to a specific web page, email message, or file on one day might like to be able to repeat the experience the next day.

The term "wayfinding" encourages a subtle shift of emphasis in finding. Certainly the destination—getting the needed information—is important. But also important is a successful return, with information "in hand," to the context where the information is needed. Also important is the experience of the journey. Is finding easily done in the context of our work, or does finding take us away from our work and down paths having little to do with the task at hand so that we leave our work at the end of the day frustrated for the lack of progress? Does finding feel like a matter of providence over which we have little control, or do we have confidence that we can reliably, repeatedly get back to information as needed?

The term "wayfinding" was coined by Kevin Lynch and used in his book *The Image of the City* (1960). Lynch developed a rich vocabulary to describe the features of a city that impact people's ability to wayfind:

- *Paths* such as streets and walkways connect the parts of a city together.
- *Districts* are major sections of the city with common identifying character—think, for example, of the SoHo and East Village sections of Manhattan.
- *Edges* such as walls, fences, and other barriers help define and separate, but also relate, different districts.
- *Nodes* such as street corners, squares, and subway stations serve as points of reference and transition.
- *Landmarks* such as large churches, skyscrapers, and museums serve as important points of reference.

PSI counterparts for these elements of a city either don't exist or they exist imperfectly:

- The paths that make it possible to move between documents or between web pages are represented implicitly in constructs such as a folder hierarchy or a hyperlink. But paths are generally not handled as objects in their own right, nor are they given meaningful, visible features. For example, a hyperlink in a web page changes color to indicate that it has recently been clicked. But people are given no indication of how frequently the hyperlink is clicked. People cannot see how the paths they take—to web pages, documents, application commands, and so on—are routinely, repeatedly combined over a period of time. Virtual paths do not deepen or widen with use.

- The concept of districts is partly represented in the folders we keep and perhaps also in various clusters of desktop icons. Folders as districts are not well integrated. For example, email folders contain only messages, and file folders generally contain only e-documents. There is little to express the size, character, or composition of a folder other than its name or possibly color.

- Folders generally have hard and fast boundaries—an item is either in a folder or not (although boundaries are softened somewhat by recent efforts to create "search" or "smart" folders). But these boundaries are not really edges that can serve to relate as well as separate. Folders are related to one another primarily by a parent–child relation. Even something as basic as ordering, as a way to relate sibling folders, is poorly supported.

- A folder in its relation to its subordinate folders can be seen to act as a node. Click on the folder to see and choose among its subfolders. Likewise, a major web site, as a hub or starting point/meeting point, acts as a kind of node. Are there others?

- What counts as a landmark in the digital regions of a person's PSI? The Start button? Desktop shortcuts? Applications with icons always in view? The home page icon and other icons always in view in a web browser?

As summarized in Table 4.2, wayfinding constructs identified by Lynch work well for the Manhattan borough of New York City but seem to stretch or break as we try to apply them to a PSI. Do gaps in the mapping of wayfinding constructs to a PSI point to basic limitations in the metaphor, or do these gaps represent opportunities to improve PIM?

Dillon and Vaughan (1997) review literature suggesting that, in navigating physical spaces, people form three distinct types of mental representations over time: landmark, route, and survey. Representations are generally seen to build on one another. For example, we might navigate first in New York City according to major landmarks like the Empire State Building or the Chrysler building in order to get to a friend's house from the 34th Street PATH station. Over time we develop a route that we follow to get to our friend's apartment. Survey representations of the kind needed to form a mental map of the environs emerge later. As we acquire a survey representation, we can begin to explore alternate routes to our friend's apartment that are shorter or that take us, for example, past a corner store where we can buy last-minute food items for dinner. Alternatively, of course, we can get a map of Manhattan.

Table 4.2 Wayfinding constructs make sense for Manhattan, but do they make sense for your PSI?

	In Manhattan . . .	In your PSI?
Paths	Park Avenue, 5th Avenue, 34th Street, 45th Street, the Brooklyn Bridge and its pedestrian walkway, Broadway	Well-trod " paths" through your favorite web pages? The series of clicks to access a network?
Districts	SoHo, Tribeca, Chelsea, the Upper East Side, the Lower East Side, Chinatown, Little Italy	Clusters of icons on a computer desktop? Folders? PICs?
Edges	Canal Street, Central Park, Avenue of the Americas	The boundaries between folders and disk drives? These are separate "districts" of information; but how are they related?
Nodes	Times Square, Washington Square Park, Grand Central Station, Pennsylvania Station	Folders? Favorite web sites? A task bar?
Landmarks	The Empire State Building, the Chrysler Building, the Brooklyn Bridge	The home page icon of a web browser? The "start" button?

However, Dillon and Vaughan question the utility of the landmark, route, survey (map), and other spatial concepts of our three-dimensional physical environment when talking about information. They note, for example, that "what constitutes landmarks in information space remains unclear" (p. 96). Perhaps the information in a PSI and its uses are too fluid, too dynamic, too multifaceted to be adequately characterized through the application of static, stationary concepts such as paths, edges, districts, nodes, landmarks, routes, and so on.

And what about the "way" in wayfinding? Sure, destination is important. And so too is a "safe" return to the situation that prompted us to get information in the first place. But how important is the way to and back?

For that matter, how important is the way to and back as we move through physical space? Most of us probably travel by plane rather than train, automobile, or ship in order to reach a remote destination. We do so for the savings in time even if the journey is often unpleasant with long lines at security checkpoints, cramped seating, and terrible food. At least the journey is short. If we could safely teleport to save even more time, we probably would. The uncertain promise of serendipitous encounters on a longer journey is not likely to outweigh the sure thing we have in the savings of time.

Wayfinding

– *Peter Morville*

"Wayfinding" as a discrete term originated within the context of what architects call the built environment. First used by the architect Kevin Lynch in 1960 to describe the role of street numbers, directional signs, and other "way-finding" devices in cities, the word was later appropriated by biologists, anthropologists, and psychologists to describe the behavior of animals and humans in natural and artificial environments.

Most recently, wayfinding has been applied to the study of user behavior within digital information environments. We talk about people getting lost in cyberspace. We create "breadcrumbs" and "landmarks" to support orientation and navigation in web sites. While these spatial metaphors are often taken too far, there is no doubting their resonance.

We do import our natural wayfinding behaviors and vocabularies into digital environments, and for that reason alone the history of wayfinding is worth our attention. But at the intersection of location awareness and ubiquitous computing, we are increasingly navigating hybrid environments that connect the physical and the digital. The history of wayfinding only grows more interesting with each step into the future.

But before we lavish attention on *Homo sapiens*, it's worth taking a look at the wayfinding skills of a few other species with which we share planet Earth. Their solutions to the challenges of orientation and navigation can illuminate our own. For example, have you ever wondered how ants find a feeding site and then return home? Lacking maps and street signs and cell phones, these tiny creatures regularly travel thousands of times their own body length to arrive at a pinpoint goal.

After decades of research, behavioral biologists have begun to figure out how. Studies show that ants use a combination of geocentric and egocentric techniques. Geocentric navigation relies on external environmental cues such as landmarks and any available map information. Egocentric navigation relies on self-awareness of distance and direction traveled and is independent of the immediate surroundings. Of course, these senses are imperfect, and errors can rapidly accumulate during the course of a trip. It's the sophisticated combination of strategies that allows for error correction and ultimate wayfinding success.

Sight. Hearing. Touch. Smell. Taste. We're often intrigued by the novel application of these five senses. Bats and whales and dolphins use echolocation to "hear" their way through low-visibility environments. Salmon rely on a powerful sense of smell to sniff out routes as they navigate back to the upstream waters where they will breed. We're also impressed by unfamiliar wayfinding senses such as the polarized vision of ants and honeybees or the biomagnetism of sea turtles, lobsters, and newts. We can't help but speculate what it would be like to possess these remarkable capabilities.

Of course, we've developed some pretty sophisticated wayfinding tools ourselves. By enhancing our natural abilities with such technologies as maps and compasses, we've turned the whole planet into what Kevin Lynch might call a legible environment. But everything is relative. Despite the ready availability of maps and street signs, we still manage to get ourselves lost. Lost in cities or inside buildings or on the way.

Fortunately we appear poised on the brink of a breakthrough. After eons of bumbling around the planet, we're about to take navigation to a whole new level. Wayfinding 2.0. And it begins with location awareness. The crown jewel of next-generation wayfinding is the Global Positioning System (GPS), a satellite-based radio-navigation system that enables land, sea, and airborne users to determine their three-dimensional position (latitude, longitude, altitude) and velocity. Equipped with a GPS receiver and map database, we can find our way like never before. Our kids will wonder how we ever survived without GPS, and not just in the car. GPS receivers and mobile devices that rely on other technologies such as Wi-Fi, Bluetooth, Ultra-wideband, and RFID grow smaller and more popular every year. Handheld units are increasingly common. No more printed maps. No more getting lost.

This is the promise of ambient findability, a world at the crossroads of ubiquitous computing and the Internet, in which we can find anyone or anything from anywhere at any time. It's not necessarily a goal, and we'll never quite reach the destination, but we're surely headed in the right direction. And wayfinding will never be the same.

For information too—notwithstanding the Teevan et al. (2004) results—wouldn't we teleport for the savings in time if we knew exactly what information we needed and we could reliably get to this information and back again? In cases of form-filling, we're happy for no journey at all. The rub of this question, of course, is in the "ifs." Needed information as a destination is rarely as certain as, say, a trip to Boston. Recognizing the needed information is often heavily influenced by the context surrounding its access. Moreover, need is itself revised and refined in the course of our efforts to find information. The way does matter.

Also, there is reason to believe that Lynch's wayfinding constructs do have application to a PSI, though perhaps in ways less direct and less literal. For example, in our work on the Keeping Found Things Found (KFTF) project, we see considerable longevity in the top-level organizations people impose on their information. Top-level folders, for example, often reflect projects, areas of interest, roles, and responsibilities that endure for years (Jones, 2004). Do these count as landmarks?

There is certainly evidence that people are creatures of habit in their access to information, taking the same sequence of steps, or the same route, each time they need to access an information item such as a web page or a file.[26] Many of us may have the experience of following the same sequence of clicks to reach a particular web page—the white pages for address and phone number look-up, for example—even though we suspect there are shortcuts. Do these count as paths? Would a web map showing our current location and likely destinations give us the courage to take a shortcut?

Maps of the physical world can have tremendous value for their ability to instill survey knowledge that might otherwise take years for us to acquire. Maps often appeal not only for their

---

[26] See, for example, Capra and Pérez-Quiñones (2005).

utility but also their aesthetics. A well-designed map can be a thing of beauty to be appreciated in its own right.

What would a map of our PSI, showing our daily activities of PIM, look like? What paths or "sea lanes" do we trace through our PSI? Where do managed personal information collections rise up as islands of relative structure and coherence? And how would we use this meta-information to improve our practice of PIM? These are fascinating questions that don't admit to easy answers.

I find that a great part of the information I have was acquired by looking up something and finding something else on the way.

U.S. journalist Franklin P. Adams (1881–1960)

4.7 Looking back, looking forward

In looking back over this chapter's exploration of finding, re-finding, and the movement from need to information, several points can be noted:

- ☑ *Re-finding is different from finding. Re-finding in a personal store is different from re-finding in a public store.* Finding activities vary according to whether we've previously experienced the information we seek and whether the information is under our control or "out there" in a public store such as the Web. Efforts to re-find information are more focused than efforts to find new information. We're looking for a specific information item and not just any information will do. In our efforts to re-find an item, we should be able to use not only our memories for the item itself, but also our memories for our encounters with this item. Failure to re-find an item in a personal store is different from failure to re-find an item in a public store. The failure can stand for a larger failure of control. If we've lost this, what else have we lost?

- ☑ *The journey from need to information is round-trip.* Information, once found, must be applied in the situation that generated a need for this information in the first place. How quickly can we return to this situation? How quickly can we reestablish context? Is the information found in the right form to be used? Also, our assessment of need is dynamic and changes with every step of finding we take.

- ☑ *Small acts of finding can kill a day.* A day is often composed of many, many small acts of finding. Find the right budget number to put in an expense form. Find the email containing a phone number. Check our calendar—once, twice, many times. Look up our account name and password for an online service. Even if small acts of finding nearly always succeed in getting the needed information, and even if each takes only a few minutes to complete, these can add up to much of a day's time and its frustrations.

- ☑ *Finding is a multistep process with a possibility of stumbling at each step.* What we *recall* about the information we need could be wrong, so that we look in the wrong place or search on the wrong words. Or we may fail to *recognize* an item even though it's "right there." We may fail to *repeat* the finding process enough times to assemble the complete set of items needed for a decision. And we may fail at the outset because we do not *remember* to look.

☑ *Wayfinding and finding as a dialog* with a trained assistant (or the computer as a "me-speak" extension to ourselves) each provide unique, useful perspectives as we look for ways to provide better tool support for finding. Each perspective also has its limitations. The dialog falls short in the many cases where we don't know exactly what it is we're looking for or when we may not even think to ask for the information in the first place. And the dialog as a model for support of finding may fall short in cases where our ability to recognize a needed information item, and perhaps to be sure we have the right version, depends on a representation not only of the information item but also of the larger context in which the item usually occurs.

The wayfinding metaphor gives emphasis to finding as a kind of journey through the PSI—from a need and the situation prompting this need to information and then back again. Wayfinding may be a means for us to increase our understanding of and control over our PSIs. And, as with any journey, a journey through the PSI can be serendipitous, yielding useful information we did not expect and would not have thought to ask for. But in cases such as form filling, where we know exactly what information we need, we're happy to dispense with the journey. Just the facts, please.

What Now for IT?

– Bob Boiko

Today's top IT talent wrestles daily with the issues of fragmentation, and they are finding no easy way out. On one hand, there are constant calls for greater integration of information sources. "Why," users ask, "can't I search across email, the Web, and my hard drive?" On the other hand, people also call for more user-friendly systems that require little or no training to use. When IT groups create monolithic systems that access all information, users complain that they are too complex, hard to use, and unreliable. When they opt for simple, single-function systems that are easy to use, users complain that information is "trapped" within the systems and not accessible without special effort.

A similar dilemma arises when IT departments attempt to make information more findable by introducing universal storage and categorization standards (such as exist in document management systems). They craft such standards in order to satisfy user demands for more findability. What they get when they attempt to implement the standards are user demands for a simpler system that does not require them to change their well-worn ways and spend time categorizing the information they are storing.

Users can't be blamed for wanting to have their cake and eat it too. IT staff can't be blamed for trying to give users what they seem to want, even if that results in a contradiction. Rather, the up-front cost to the user (in time and training) of making information findable has to be balanced against the value of making information more available. Of course, to balance this equation, IT workers must be able to calculate the value of finding information faster—something they have not yet been able to do.

Also, wayfinding constructs—such as paths, districts, edges, nodes, and landmarks, with ready application to the physical environs of a city—apply at present (or at best?) in only limited and substantially altered ways to a PSI. These problems of application may point to limitations of the metaphor, or they may point to limitations in our current ways of thinking about and designing for our PSIs.

For example, we follow what might be termed "well-trod paths" through our PSIs in our use of various applications and in our use of the Web. But our PSIs, in their supporting tools, retain little impression of our habits; nor do our current tools make much use of this information to suggest better paths or shortcuts. Maps of our PSIs, like maps of the physical world, may have tremendous value for their ability to instill survey (overview) knowledge that might otherwise take years for us to acquire. And these might be an object of beauty too. But it is not clear what such maps should look like or how they should be constructed.

This chapter has given special focus to efforts to re-find—that is, to find information already (if only briefly) experienced. The chapter has further focused on efforts to re-find information inside our PSIs in stores (such as our computer's hard drive or even the filing cabinets of a physical office) that we ostensibly control. We must remember to look in the first place. We must recall enough about the information to give reasonable scope to a follow-on effort to recognize the specific item we seek. We may need to repeat the steps of recognition and recall several times in the search for a specific item. And a larger episode of finding may require that several items are retrieved to form a complete set.

But, the journey to re-find information does not properly begin with a perception of need or a remembrance of a relevant information item. The journey begins with earlier acts to keep and organize the information in the PSI. What we do at this stage often determines whether the journey will ultimately succeed or fail. This is the topic of the next chapter.

What Next for Tool Development?

– Mike Kelly

Much of the tedium in everyday finding comes from the repeated look-up of small pieces of information. Consider:

- We may look up a budget number once and then, later the same day or the next, we may need to do so again.

- We send our cell phone number to people via email so that they can reach us later if necessary—not once but many times for different people or to the same person at different times.

- We spend many minutes sifting through email in the inbox to locate a phone number someone else has sent us. When we received it, we had the idea to make an entry for this person in the contact database we maintain, but there was no time. Now the email message is pushed far down in the inbox, and we're taking even more time to re-find it.

In situations like these, a little bit of computer smarts can go a long way. Variations on auto-complete or auto-fill already support the completion of web addresses, email addresses, and passwords. Some email applications now do limited parsing of message text to recognize dates (for suggested meetings, for example) and support the option to enter this in a digital calendar.

But current auto-complete facilities are limited in several ways. Support for auto-complete is fragmented, and so it works differently in different places. If just once we accidentally provide the wrong information—the wrong email address, web address, or password—auto-complete facilities are equally happy to propose this incorrect completion, and ways to correct this are non-obvious and inconsistent. Finally, to the extent applications do maintain auto-complete data today, it is almost always per-machine, which does nothing to solve the problem of synchronization across our different devices: work computer, laptop, home computer, and mobile phone.

It is time to consider a single, unified, and smarter auto-complete facility that can be accessed from all our machines and that works consistently across multiple applications. At the core of this would be a database with objects such as "person" and "budget" and associated properties such as "cell phone number" and "current budget amount." Email applications, word processors, web browsers, and other applications could access this either to store new information or to retrieve information.

The use of auto-complete to store (keep) information is discussed at greater length in Chapter 5. The consolidation of storage here also carries maintenance benefits (updates and corrections are much easier), which are discussed further in Chapter 6. Here let's consider how this newer, higher-functioning auto-complete could help people to find and use information:

- We type "my cell phone number is" and the application is ready to complete with the phone number. The same completion can happen whether we're typing a document (e.g., an invitation) or sending an email message.

- We type the first part of a web address and the application completes—similar to today. But it might also recognize a "well-trod path" through a sequence of web pages and so suggest a jump to the eventual destination. If we always go through pages A, B, and C to get to page D, for example, and we're currently viewing page A, auto-complete might at least suggest page D along with page B. This is tricky to get right, and we have to avoid the famous "It looks like you're writing a letter" problem.

- Budget numbers, directions, and addresses could all become pieces of information readily accessed from auto-complete and inserted into a current information item (whether document, form, or email message).

One key to success here is simple application programming interfaces that support the consistent use of this information. It is especially important that different applications storing information in the system auto-complete add to and reuse existing objects wherever possible rather than create new custom ones. Ideally, we would like all information we have about "Robert Smith" to be consolidated in a single entity—containing his cell phone, his web page address, and so on. How these higher-level objects might work, and what they might enable, is a topic for further discussion in Chapter 5.

What Now for You and Me?

Practical suggestions apply to each essential step in finding.

1. *Reminding/remembering to look.* Look around. What do you need to remember to find? Look at your *attentional spaces* (see also Chapter 5)—for instance, your desktops, physical and digital, your inbox(es), your calendar(s). What have you forgotten to look for? Many of us are in the habit of doing this at the beginning of the day. Also, look periodically through at least the top levels of your various organizations of paper documents, digital documents, email messages, bookmarks, and the like.

2. *Recall.* If you have information in several places—on different computers, different drives or shares, or in different email accounts—then make a list of these that you can easily consult. Do you need to find the correct version or variation of an item? Then hopefully you already have in place at least an informal process of version and variation management. Think broadly about the places you might look. Use your friends and colleagues as information sources too (and reciprocate). For example, rather than sifting through old email messages for a pointer or a phone number, consider simply asking the sender again.

3. *Recognition.* Look once. Look again. It seems such an obvious and unlikely mistake not to recognize the information that is in view. But this happens to us all the time. In the longer range, of course, a failure to recognize may best be fixed in the manner of an item's keeping—for example, with better names for documents or a name of your choice for a web bookmark. The subject line of an email message, as the counterpart to the name of a document or file, is worth a few seconds of crafting before you send it out so that you are more likely to recognize and attend to replies that arrive in the inbox later. In a group collaboration, some minutes spent agreeing on subject-line conventions can be an investment that pays for itself many times over.

4. *Repeat?* What else? Where else? Be clear on whether a complete set is really needed. There is no "complete set" of information anytime the Web is involved. We may spend too much time chasing an illusory complete set of information needed

to write an article or purchase a product or plan a vacation, even as we overlook completion with respect to more mundane matters such as scheduling a meeting.

Some other suggestions:

- *Get a desktop search facility* if you don't have one already. Use it. They are free and generally "well behaved" in their uses of your computer's resources. But recognize its limitations. The search facility you acquire has its place as one of several tools supporting several methods of finding.

- *Note the bits and pieces of information* you find and repeatedly re-find. Write down for easy reference the budget numbers, phone numbers, departmental codes, names, and the like that you repeatedly need. If you are organized enough to have a database of contacts, then use it (for example, make a budget or a department into a "contact"). But for information we repeatedly access but never seem to commit to memory, it may be more effective simply to write the information down on paper in a notebook close at hand or in a "scraps" file that can be read by a software application we nearly always have open such as a word processor or a spreadsheet application.

- *"Begin with the end in mind."* This maxim from Covey (1989) applies with special force to activities of finding. Where will you need the information you're trying to find? In what form? Stepping back further, what need are you trying to meet? Not all needs are equally important, and some apparent needs take care of themselves in good time without your intervention.

- *Become a student of your finding activities.* When finding fails, ask yourself, How could I have done things differently? The answer may lie in better execution of one of the finding steps listed above. But many of the problems of finding information originate and are best dealt with during the keeping and organizing of the information. The "What now for you and me" sidebar for the next chapter deals with that.

Keeping and organizing: From information to need

Keeping is like throwing a ball into the future to be caught at a time and place of anticipated need. Where and how to keep? On which device? In what form? Should information be filed away or left in a pile? Eventual failures of finding may actually be initial failures of keeping. Suppose we keep everything? Suppose we organize nothing? Both approaches have problems. But information can sometimes get organized as a by-product of its use. And we can "PIC" our battles to keep and organize.

Chapter
Five

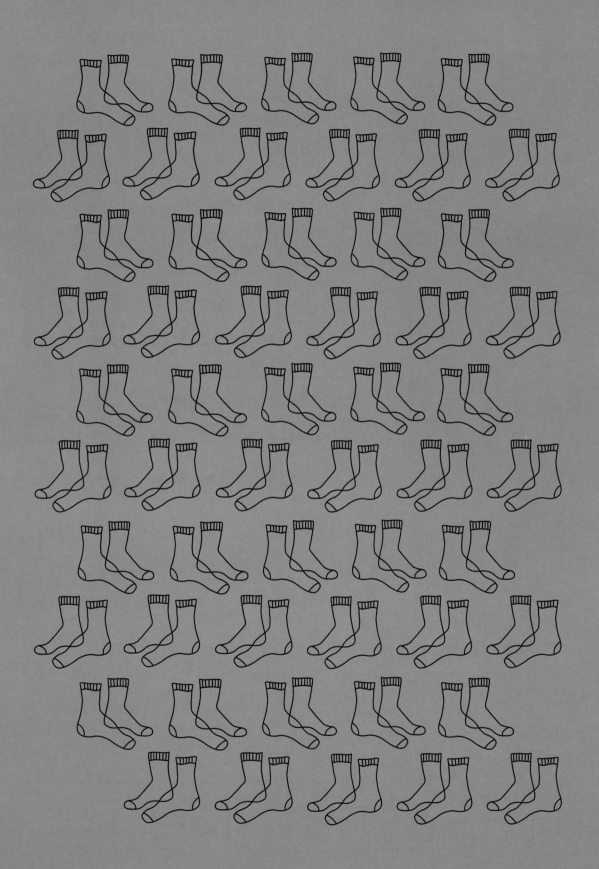

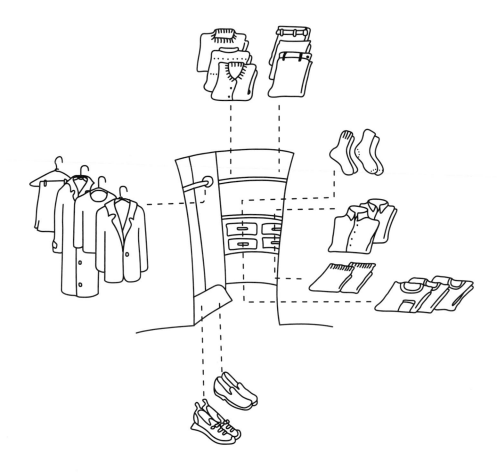

Be regular and orderly in your life . . . so that you may be violent and original in your work.

Gustave Flaubert (1821–1880)

5.1 Starting out

Finding and keeping. Finders, keepers? Keeping found things found. In general use, finding and keeping stand in a natural, complementary relationship to each other. And so it is in PIM. We find information but don't need it right away and don't have time to process it. We keep information—whether found by our actions or encountered by happenstance—to make its finding again later easier or simply possible.

We keep information to meet anticipated needs of a future which may be a minute from now or years from now. Sometimes items are kept with a specific need in mind as when, for example, we keep an agenda and relevant documents in preparation for a scheduled meeting. Sometimes the circumstances of a need are open-ended. For example, we may take and keep many photographs and barely look at them again until some point 20 or 30 years later when they can help us to tell a story that we'd almost forgotten. Also, like some physical items such as stamps or coins, information items are sometimes kept just for the sake of keeping: the book (or photograph, article, or joke) may simply help to complete a collection.

As these examples illustrate, our information needs are multifaceted and so are the keeping decisions we make and the keeping actions we take. Where and when will we need this information later? On what computer—home or work? Can we trust that the web page will still have the information we need later on, or should we make a local copy? Will we even have access to a computer and from this computer to the Web when an opportunity to use this information later arises, or should we make a paper copy? Will we remember to look for this information later, and will we know where to look?

In Figure 5.1, the act of keeping personal information is likened to throwing a ball into the future to be caught by our future selves at a time and place of anticipated need. Finding and keeping are reciprocal activities. Items poorly kept can still be found again later, though possibly at a greater expense of time and energy. We can make a good catch of a badly thrown ball. Moreover, keeping now and finding later go together better for drawing on a shared understanding of where things ought to be—a scheme of organization. With the play established, the ball's receiver can focus on running his route knowing that the ball will (should) be there, an arm stretch away, when he arrives at the end point.

Figure 5.1 **Keeping information for future use can be likened to throwing a ball to your future self and having it fall into your hands again later at just the right time and place.**

Of course, passes are not always caught and information is not always found again when (and where) a need for it arises. When failures occur, these are often traceable to failures in the initial act of keeping or to failures in an organization's utility as a route between information and need. How do we keep and organize our information? What considerations apply? What problems arise? How can we do better, and how can tools help?

These topics are explored in this chapter as we move through the following sections:

- ☑ *Getting oriented.* Keeping is given broad definition to apply to a range of activities, specific actions, and decisions associated with the attempt to connect current information—information "at hand"—to anticipated need. Keeping and organizing are often used inter-changeably and, indeed, one can prompt the other. But important distinctions are made between these two kinds of activities. Organizing, with its overall focus on a collection of information, is the first of the meta-level activities we consider in connection with PIM.

- ☑ *Everyday keeping and organizing: To each his own.* People show large variation in their habits of keeping and organizing. Variations partly reflect informational circumstance and need. Patterns of keeping and organizing vary according to available tools and technologies at work and home and according to the roles we mean to fulfill, work-related and otherwise. But people also vary with education, past experience, and personality. Some of us like to organize; some of us avoid organizing like the plague.

- ☑ *Keeping is multifaceted.* Keeping, like finding, is multistep, and failure can happen at any step. But keeping activities are also aptly characterized as having many facets to their completion. Facets reflect uncertainty concerning the information itself and uncertainty concerning the need(s) to which the information will be applied. Is information needed now or later or not at all? Here or there? On what device? In what form? Should it be filed away or left in a pile? Items can also be organized in several ways, depending on information and anticipated need. As with finding, challenges of keeping and organization multiply with increases in the number of information forms to be managed.

- ☑ *The limitations of future perfect visions.* What challenges of keeping and organizing go away, or at least get a lot easier, with advances in technology? What challenges remain? Given the pace of advances in the technologies of storage and search, we can imagine a "keep everything" vision of the future. Why not keep a record of all the information we experience? Storage is cheap and plentiful. Search can help us pinpoint the information we need, no matter how big the "haystack" in which we're looking. Or, what about a "keep nothing" vision of the future, in which nearly all the information we need is located on the Web or in organizational intranets. Why bother keeping anything at all?

- ☑ *PICing our battles.* Notwithstanding visions of the future, most of us will still need—want—to organize selected collections of our personal information. We consider two important kinds of personal information collections: *reference collections*, in which items are selected for repeated use but with no specific use in mind, and *project collections*, in which all items relate to a specific project.

5.2 Getting oriented

Keeping and organizing go together but are different. Placing a document in a folder is keeping. Deciding on a scheme for how folders should be created, named, and related to one another is organizing. Organizing, with its overall focus on a collection of information, is the first of the meta-level activities we consider in connection with PIM.[1]

> *Information keeping* (or just *keeping*). Decisions made and actions taken to relate current information (information at hand or under consideration) to anticipated needs. Decisions can include (1) "ignore, this has no relevance to me," (2) "ignore, I can get back to this later" (by asking a friend, searching the Web, or some other act of finding), and (3) "keep this in a special place or way so that I can be sure to use this information later."

> *Information organizing* (or just *organizing*). Decisions made and actions taken in the selection and implementation of a scheme to relate the information items in a collection to anticipated needs. Decisions can include (1) How should items in this collection be named? (2) What set of properties make sense for and help to distinguish the items in this collection from one another? (3) How should items within this collection be grouped? Into what piles or folders?

Keeping, more broadly considered, applies not only to information but also to channels of information. Subscribing to a magazine or storing the car radio setting to a particular station is a keeping decision. Even the cultivation of friends and colleagues can be seen partly as acts of keeping. The friends and colleagues you keep can be an important source of information.

Keeping activities are also triggered when people are interrupted in the midst of a current task and look for ways of preserving the current state so that work can be quickly resumed later.[2] People keep appointments by entering reminders into a calendar. People keep good ideas or "things to pick up at the grocery store" by writing down a few cryptic lines on a loose piece of paper.

Keeping activities are often prompted by finding activities and, in turn, prompt more finding activities. For example, Nancy's search on the Web for "fun things to do in Montreal," as described in Chapter 4, will produce a lot more information than she has time to "consume." Moreover, many of the web pages she finds have information concerning addresses, phone numbers, and times of operation that she will want to refer to later.

Nancy decides, therefore, to create web bookmarks for some of these sites. She wants to place the bookmarks in a special bookmark folder she has already set up for her trip to Montreal. But, since Nancy can't recall what she named the folder, she scans through the top-level listing of bookmark folders—a finding activity—until she finds the right folder ("Montreal trip"). She then places the bookmarks in this folder to complete the keeping activity.

---

[1] What about creating a folder? Is this keeping or organizing? It's likely a mixture of both. Creating a folder is more purely an act of keeping if the folder is created just to have a place to put some item and without regard to an overall scheme for organizing information. Creating a folder is more purely an act of organizing if the folder—possibly an empty, placeholder folder—is created mostly to implement a scheme of organization.

[2] See, for example, Czerwinski, Horvitz, and Wilhite (2004).

Efforts to organize or reorganize a collection of personal information, such as the email messages in an email account or the paper piles in an office, occur much less frequently. Organizing is a meta-level activity. Focus is on (about or above) a *personal information collection* (PIC), rather than on an individual information item. In a typical day, if organizing happens at all, it is after more immediate, more urgent activities of keeping and finding are completed. And this often means not at all. There are few, if any, external events in a typical day to prompt people to organize or reorganize their information.

Organizing and maintaining also go together but are different:

> *Information maintaining* (or just *maintaining*). Decisions made and actions taken relating to the preservation and upkeep of personal information. Decisions include how information is stored (where? in what formats? in what kind of storage? backed up how?), how information is updated or corrected, and what happens to older information (e.g., is it deleted or archived?).

The object of maintaining, like organizing, is to develop a collection of information. Maintaining personal information, especially for the long run, is discussed in Chapter 6 and is not a topic of further discussion in this chapter.

5.3 Everyday keeping and organizing: To each his own

Consider the following situation: Six people in a work situation, different from one another by nearly every measure of life (e.g., age, gender, ethnicity, education, personality) have two things in common: (1) they work at the same company, and (2) they are members of a committee that was formed to plan a big retirement dinner and a good-natured "roast" for Vera Cruz, long-time administrator of the business unit in which they all work. The actions and reactions of each person in relation to the retirement dinner planning reveal very different approaches to keeping and organizing information:

Tess, a mid-level manager in her mid-forties, is taking the lead in organizing the retirement dinner for Vera. She has given special attention to the this-is-your-life, all-in-good-fun roast of Vera. Tess still uses paper as her primary means for saving information and for sending information to other people. When she meets with Ron, Sally, and Udo to plan the retirement dinner, for example, she distributes her script for the roast via paper printouts.

Ron, a business unit sales manager in his late thirties, is well organized with respect to most of his work-related information but less so for information that "doesn't fit" in his current scheme of organization. When Ron receives paper printouts from Tess containing plans for Vera's party and a script for her roast, he's not sure what to do with the information. He lets it build up in his briefcase where it gets intermingled with other paper documents.

Sally, an entry-level programmer and self-proclaimed cyberpunk enthusiast in her early twenties, lets things pile up in both physical and virtual space and doesn't much care if she can't get back to a particular item of information. Instead she makes heavy use of both her excellent memory and the friends and colleagues around her. When unsure about details of the party, she simply asks Ron, Tess, or Udo.

Udo, a senior programmer in his mid-thirties, has made a deliberate attempt to put nearly everything onto his tablet PC. He wishes Tess would distribute party planning information via email rather than by paper printouts. However, his approach is to take digital notes immediately and then discard the paper printout.

Vera, the administrator who is the object of everyone's attention these days, is nearly 65. She is looking forward to retirement and, especially, to the opportunity to spend more time with her two new great-grandchildren. If the past is any indication, Vera will likely want to save one or two of the paper party napkins from the party along with the paper invitation. Vera saves things, including information items, with no clear purpose in mind other than to be reminded of a pleasant time she had with friends and family. (She thinks of many of her workplace colleagues as both.)

Walter[3] is the senior vice-president of the business unit in which Ron, Sally, Tess, Udo, and Vera work. Walter is not directly involved in the planning of Vera's goodbye party, but let's consider his approach to keeping and organizing information anyway. Walter is nearing retirement and embraces what he describes as "the old school" with respect to the way he keeps and organizes information. He lets incoming paper information sit in the inbox for one week. At the end of a week, he moves all of this information to a "pending" pile. At the beginning of each month, all pending information over a month old is thrown in the trash. Walter does something similar for incoming email messages. He rarely replies to incoming surface mail or email. Instead, he counts on those who work for him—especially his administrative assistant—to draw his attention, in face-to-face meetings or over the phone, to matters requiring a response from him.

These stories about Ron, Sally, Tess, Udo, Vera, and Walter illustrate several key points concerning the keeping and organizing of personal information:

- *People vary greatly in their approaches to keeping and organizing information.* Even people in the same work situation show tremendous variation.[4]

- *Keeping and organizing are related but distinct activities.* For example, as Ron continues to keep party-related paper printouts in his briefcase, he may reach a "time to get organized" saturation point that prompts him to devise a better way of organizing this information. Or maybe not.

- *Challenges of keeping and organizing are greater when several devices and applications are involved.* Udo, for example, must manage information on both his cell phone and in the several organizations of his tablet PC. He is nevertheless happy that he now has one less device to deal with (his PDA).

- *People don't always keep information with a specific purpose in mind.* As the example with Vera illustrates, people may keep information for decoration or to evoke memories.[5] People may also keep and share information such as photos or lists of favorite songs or favorite web sites to represent something about themselves[6] or "just because."

---

[3] The story of Walter is based on an actual fieldwork interview.

[4] See Gwizdka and Chignell (2007) for an exploration of individual differences and PIM.

[5] See, for example, Marshall and Bly (2005).

[6] See, for example, Kaye et al. (2006).

The notion that information items are sometimes kept not for the information they contain but for what they say about ourselves is not new. Some of us may have, or know of someone who has, an office in which books (e.g., reference books, college textbooks, and even newly published books) are carefully arranged in bookshelves for all to see. Many of these books haven't been read in years; some have never been read. But the books say something about us (or the person we want to be). Differences between people are especially apparent in their approaches to the organization of their information. Malone (1983) distinguished between "neat" and "messy" organizations of paper documents. "Messy" people had more piles in their offices and appeared to invest less effort than "neat" people in filing information. Comparable differences have been observed in the ways people approach email,[7] e-documents,[8] and web bookmarks.[9]

The examples of Ron, Sally, Tess, Udo, Vera, and Walter illustrate one other important point about keeping and organizing:

> *Keeping and organizing are about strategy as well as actions and structures.* We can observe our daily actions of keeping. We can see some representation for the structures and categories of an organization through visible folders or tags. Less visible is the strategy behind activities of keeping and organizing. We can't understand a practice of keeping and organizing, not even our own, without some assessment of the strategy behind observable actions and visible structures.

For example, Walter's minimalist approach works for him because he is a senior vice-president. He has an advantage of power over most of the people with whom he interacts. They come to him. And he can rely on his administrative assistant to flag the instances where he needs to take more initiative. Sally also depends on the people around her in lieu of her own efforts to keep and organize. Whether this strategy will continue to work for Sally may depend on whether the affection her colleagues have for her continues to outweigh their annoyance at her requests for information.

The examples of Ron, Sally, Tess, Udo, Vera, and Walter illustrate a diversity of approaches to keeping and organizing information. Whom do you most resemble in your approach to keeping and organizing information?

Given how much people are observed to vary in their approaches to keeping and organizing, there is a good chance you'll say "none of the above." Variations are especially apparent as we move from broad descriptions to a consideration of specific keeping methods and organizational schemes. For example, one KFTF study[10] observed how people keep web pages for later access. Participants created bookmarks, of course. But participants were also seen to keep web pages in many other ways including (1) sending them in a self-addressed email

---

[7] See, for example, Bälter (1997), Gwizdka (2002), Mackay (1988), and Whittaker and Sidner (1996).

[8] See, for example, Boardman and Sasse (2004) and Bruce, Jones, and Dumais (2004).

[9] See, for example, Abrams, Baecker, and Chignell (1998) and Boardman and Sasse (2004).

[10] See Jones, Dumais, and Bruce (2002).

Keeping Things Where They Need to Be Found

A doctor told me about her approach to keeping things. "My kids think I'm whacky, but I put things where I think I'll need them again later, even it doesn't make much sense." As an example of her system, she told me that she keeps extra vacuum cleaner bags behind the couch in the living room. Behind the couch in the living room? Does that make any sense? Don't they belong in a proper place like a storage closet? Well, actually, her system makes a lot of sense. It turns out that when the vacuum cleaner is used, it is usually used for the carpet in the living room. Other rooms in her house don't have carpeting and are not vacuumed as much or are cleaned using a broom instead. When a vacuum cleaner bag gets full and a new one is needed, it's usually in the living room. And that's just where the vacuum cleaner bags are.

We could do no better than to follow such a "whacky" approach to keeping our information. Put it where we think we'll need it again later.

message along with a short note; (2) printing out the web page; (3) saving the web page as a file; (4) pasting the web address into a document; (5) doing nothing and counting on getting back by search again later (or by hyperlinks from another web site or by use of auto-completion); and (6) even writing down web addresses in a notebook or on a sticky note that was placed on their display monitor. In a functional analysis, each keeping method scored high on some functions and low on others. No method scored high across the board.

5.4 Keeping is multifaceted

Finding in Chapter 4 was described as multistep. Keeping can also be described this way: Is information relevant or not? If yes, can the information "keep" until later (or does it need to be analyzed immediately)? If yes, do actions need to be taken to ensure that the information is there later when it's needed? If yes, what actions? Set reminders? Tag? Place in a folder?

But keeping can also be described as multifaceted, reflecting the multifaceted and uncertain nature of the needs for which keeping decisions are made and keeping actions taken. Is information relevant? Relevant for what? We have many different interests. We have many different goals and may be actively working on several different projects. The information we encounter may be relevant to any or several of the interests we hold, roles we play, or goals we pursue.

Can the information wait? Suppose we wait and we're wrong? What's the cost? An angry boss? A missed opportunity? Suppose we deal with information immediately and we're wrong? What's the cost? Wasted time? Or, worse, a response made too soon and before other relevant information could be analyzed?

What do we need to do to ensure that information is available later when a need for it arises? Where and when will we need the information? In what form? Do we need to set reminders?

Consider Ron, the sales manager. In the course of a typical day, he gets lots of email, encounters lots of web pages of potential value, and sees lots of documents, both as attachments in email and in paper form. Ron also gets handed many business cards. In a typical day at work, Ron will encounter several hundred different information items, in various forms, and must make roughly the same decisions for each. The business card someone has just handed Ron at the end of a meeting will illustrate.

Is the information potentially useful? Ron gets business cards from people he has no intention of contacting later. He has acquired a habit he first observed in Japan of respectfully studying the card for a moment before placing it in his right front pocket. Cards in this pocket are later discarded.

Do special steps need to be taken to keep it for later use? Assuming that the item represents useful information, does anything need to be done to be sure the item can be accessed later? Again, Ron may decide the answer is no in the case of the business card, for any of several reasons. Perhaps he knows the person already and has his/her contact information, or perhaps he is confident that he can easily locate this information from the Web or from a colleague.

How should the item be kept? Where? On what device? In what form? To be accessed again when? If Ron decides to keep the business card, he has many choices. Ron generally places cards representing near-term to-dos in a special place in his briefcase. He has another spot in his briefcase for "rainy day" cards that he'll sort through and possibly use as he has free time (e.g., while waiting in airports). Ron also tries to write a note on a business card he keeps in order to remind himself of things to discuss with the person who gave him the card. This too is an act of keeping.

For some cards, Ron will want to transcribe contact information to a contact management database so that people can be added to mailing lists, holiday card distribution lists, and the like. In these instances, information is transformed to appear in a new information item: the record of the contact management database. Ron will also sometimes enter the phone number from the card and an abbreviated name into his cell phone—another transformation.

However, neither transformation, to database or to cell phone, necessarily eliminates the need for the original business card that, for example, acts as a visible reminder of actions to be taken. Ron experiences both the contact database and his cell phone as "black holes" into which information disappears, to be forgotten. Out of sight; out of mind. But if Ron needs to be sure to contact someone, he may keep the business card information in still other ways—by sending himself an email message with card information, for example, or by entering a name and phone number from the card into his electronic calendar. Here we see that even a routine event—the receipt of a business card—can prompt a sequence of keeping decisions.

5.4.1 Damned if you do, damned if you don't

Keeping decisions often enter a gray area where the determination of costs, reciprocal benefits, and outcome likelihoods is not straightforward. In the logic of signal detection, this middle area presents us with a "damned if you do, damned if you don't" choice: no matter which way we decide, we will be wrong some percentage of the time. The bias toward keeping or not keeping is partly governed by the costs of a *false positive*—keeping information that turns out to be useless, for example—vs. a *miss*—not keeping information that turns out to be useful and needed.

For example, if Ron keeps a card, he may never use it, but he still pays a small cost in time to put it in one of his piles, and he pays a small extra cost to sort through the cards with each new card added. If Ron doesn't keep the card, he may find that he really needs its information later. Ron may pay double for finer-grained failures of keeping. If he places a document in the wrong folder, for example, he may not find it later when he needs it. Worse, the document in the wrong folder may hinder later access to other documents in the folder.

5.4.2 A proliferation of information forms increases challenges of keeping and organizing

The information world described by Malone (1983) was largely paper-based. Today, paper documents and books are still an important part of the information space for most people.[11] In addition, people must contend with the organization of e-documents, email messages, web pages (or references to these) and possibly also a number of additional forms of digital information (each with its own special-purpose tool support), including phone messages, digitized photographs, music, and videos. The number of keeping and organizing considerations further increases if a person has multiple email accounts, uses separate computers for home and work, or uses a PDA, smart phone, or any of several special-purpose PIM tools.

As the example for Ron illustrates, people freely convert from one form of information to another. People sometimes keep information in several different ways to be sure of having it later.[12] But doing so can increase the later challenges of updating and synchronization (e.g., when the phone number changes). And still not all needs are met. Neither the calendar nor contact entry will help, for example, if Ron needs to contact the client on his cell phone while stuck in traffic.

The fragmentation of information by forms poses special challenges for organizing information. Folders with similar names and purposes may be created in different information organizations. Maintaining consistency is difficult, and organizations can easily get out of synch. For example, people may have a "trips" email folder and a "travel" e-document folder.

The fragmentation of information across forms also poses problems in the study of PIM. There is a natural tendency to focus on one form of information in order to manage the scope of

---

[11] For research illustrating the persistence of paper, see Sellen and Harper (2002) and Whittaker and Hirschberg (2001).

[12] See Jones et al. (2002).

inquiry—to study only email, for example, or the use of web bookmarks or the organization of paper documents. But a focus by information form can have the effect of endorsing current tool-centric partitions of information and the information fragmentation that results from these partitions—certainly one of the most vexing problems of PIM today.

From the small number of studies that have now looked at how the same person manages across different forms of information,[13] the following composite emerges:

- People do not generally take time out of a busy day to assess their organizations or their PIM practice in general.

- People complain about the need to maintain many separate organizations of information and about the fragmentation of information that results.

- Even within the same folder organization, competing organizational schemes may suffer an uneasy coexistence with one another. People may apply one scheme on one day and another scheme the day after.

- People sometimes make extraordinary efforts to consolidate organizations. One participant in the Jones, Dumais, and Bruce (2002) study, for example, reported saving web references and email messages into a file folder organization. Another participant sent e-documents and web references in email messages.

5.4.3 File or pile? Each approach to keeping has its limitations

One essential decision people face, across forms of information, is between "filing" and "piling" the information at hand. The decision is most apparent for paper documents, which can either be placed in physical piles or filed away in a filing cabinet. For any form of information, piling is the path of least resistance. Piles[14] of paper documents can be created with minimal effort. Filing takes manual and mental effort (which folder in which filing cabinet?). Analogously for email, it is easier to leave incoming email in the inbox untagged than it is to tag email messages or place them in a folder.

Both options—filing and piling—have their advantages and disadvantages. There is no practical limit on the number of items that can be filed. But filing information items—whether paper documents, e-documents, or email messages—correctly into the right folders or in association with the right tags is a cognitively difficult and error-prone activity.[15] Difficulty arises in part because the definition or purpose of a folder or a tag is often unclear and then may change in significant ways over time.[16] Worse, people may not even recall the folders they have created and so create new folders to meet the same or similar purposes.[17] Also, items filed—especially if filed into folders—are "out of sight, out of mind" and so are likely to be forgotten.

---

[13] For greater detail on these studies, see Boardman and Sasse (2004); Jones et al. (2005); and Ravasio, Schär and Krueger (2004).

[14] For some desktops, even "pile" may connote more organization than is really present. Documents are not arranged in piles. Instead, documents are scattered or "mounded" for maximum entropy.

[15] See, for example, Bälter (2000), Kidd (1994), Lansdale (1988, 1991), Malone (1983), and Whittaker and Sidner (1996).

[16] See, for example, Kidd (1994), Whittaker and Hirschberg (2001), and Whittaker and Sidner (1996).

[17] See, for example, results by Whittaker and Sidner (1996).

What Now for IT?

– Bob Boiko

IT departments the world over are trying desperately to get ahead of the flood of information. As even a cursory glance at your own hard drive will tell you, useless and barely useful information outweighs truly useful by orders of magnitude. Network servers (web, email, and file) are even worse. The process is completely natural and completely pernicious. People act reasonably when they keep back versions of files or files that are marginally useful. They don't know if they will need to get back to them. By the time they move on to other projects or jobs, they have forgotten what is in all those files. Even if they have the inclination to go through old files, they certainly do not have the time. No one else knows where the old files came from either, so there is no one in a position to say they are not necessary.

The common rule of thumb in the information management industry (and confirmed by most server logs) is that less than 10 percent of the information stored on a web or file server is ever accessed after it is put there. While the cost of storage (measured in dollars per gigabyte) continues to drop, the cost of access (in minutes or, sadly, hours to find the item you want) continues to rise as the information you want is diluted ever further by the information you don't want.

Relatively simple tools built into our standard file management system would go a long way to help. Rudimentary version control and file comparison, for example, built right into Microsoft File Manager, for example, could help you see quickly how many copies of "the same" file are stored on your hard drive. You could then continually weed out old and useless versions of your information.

But is it just laziness and inattention that causes the buildup of information that is never used? Even diligent people end up keeping redundant and extraneous information. What most of us are lacking is not intention, but understanding. We lack the basic information literacy (and often the basic tools) to track versions and archive or delete obsolete information. But even more fundamentally, we lack the advanced information literacy to be able to effectively anticipate what information we are likely to need in the future. Without this wisdom, we are too frightened to get rid of anything!

Items placed or left in a small number of piles have visibility and high accessibility. But our ability to manage information by piling alone is limited. In Malone's study (1983), participants indicated that they had increasing difficulty keeping track of the contents of different piles as their number increased. Experiments by Jones and Dumais (1986) suggest that the ability to track information by location alone is quite limited.

Also, support for piling digital information varies greatly, and the impact of different kinds of support on our ability to manage information is poorly understood.[18] For example, computer desktops may serve as a place to pile items for fast access or high visibility. But if the desktop

---

[18] For explorations of the pile metaphor, see Mander, Salomon, and Wong (1992).

is often obscured by various open windows, the accessibility and visibility of its items is much reduced. The email inbox provides pile-like functions of accessibility and visibility, but these functions are clearly reduced as the number of items in the inbox increases and especially for older messages that scroll out of view.

5.5 The limitations of future perfect visions

Just as we explored the appeal and limitations of a "me-speak" perfect dialog between person and computer to support finding in Chapter 4, we consider here some future perfect visions for keeping:

* *Keep everything.* Keep a record, for example, of every document, email message, web page, photograph, song, and video that we ever created, encountered, received, down-loaded, or sent.

* *Keep nothing.* Depend instead on access to the Web and to corporate intranets.

* *Keep automatically.* Depend on our future computer to recognize and keep the information we need (e.g., based on our past interactions with information and our future plans).

Looking beyond the technical and economic limitations of each vision, which might possibly be ameliorated, we see more basic limitations that reflect inadequacies in our own ability to attend and remember and also a basic need for some level of hands-on interaction with our information.

5.5.1 Keep everything?

Why bother to decide whether or not to keep information? Keep everything—just in case.

But what is "everything"? Definitions vary. Vannevar Bush (1945) described a memex device "in which an individual stores all his books, records, and communications" and that functioned as "an enlarged intimate supplement to . . . memory" (p. 6). Ongoing dramatic improvements in the economics, reliability, and capacities of digital storage encourage us to dream even bigger. What about "digital memories" that automatically record first-person views of our daily experi-ences, through digital photographs taken at regular intervals[19] or even through sound and full-motion video.[20]

We're reminded of Chapter 1's quote by Herbert Simon. Even as the storage capacities of our devices continue to increase dramatically, there is no evidence to suggest that the basic human capacity to attend is increasing at all, let alone at comparable rates of exponential growth.

The digital capture of information is straightforward compared with the challenges of organizing captured information in useful ways. For example, the old adage "out of sight; out of mind" still applies. Older e-mail messages in the inbox are pushed out of view by newer messages and

---

[19] See, for example, Gemmell et al. (2004).
[20] See, for example, Czerwinski et al. (2006).

frequently forgotten. Documents in a folder or associated with a particular tag compete with one another for our attention. As their number increases, so too does the likelihood that we will overlook an information item when its time of need arrives. What about search as a way to stay focused on the most relevant information even as the total amount of information increases? The problem here is that as more information is kept, we can expect the results listing for the same search query to lengthen as well. Extra matches to a search query can be an especially serious problem when multiple versions of a document are saved—as was noted in Chapter 4.

5.5.2 Keep nothing?

Recent developments invite speculation about a second extreme in keeping. When so much of the information we need is on the Web or in an organizational intranet, and is readily accessible by powerful search facilities, why bother keeping anything at all?

The success of "keep nothing" methods for reaccessing web information has already been noted. People may often decide that web information can be easily accessed again, when needed, via the auto-complete facility of a browser, a search service, or another web site. And people may decide that the costs of doing so are smaller than the costs of creating a reference to this information (e.g., a bookmark) locally.

Improvements in finding support may also favor the storage of work-related documents on a corporate intranet. For example, a friend of mine who works for a software company recently told me that he now keeps very few work-related documents on his computer's hard drive. He has more or less constant access to the corporate intranet and prefers to leave work documents on the intranet. Fast, reliable access to these intranet documents is supported by full-text search support and a logical (to employees at least) project/subproject folder organization.

This vision of a keep-nothing future is limited in at least three ways.

1. We can't expect that information "out there" will be labeled according to the activities we need to complete in our lives. It may make sense to rely on the shared organization of a corporate intranet for access to certain kinds of work-related information. But this organization reflects a considerable amount of work to achieve a shared vocabulary and a shared viewpoint among its users.

2. More fundamentally, we can't find what we forget to look for. Even if the organization of information "out there" perfectly aligns with our needs, we may still need to keep something locally in order to remember to use this information.

3. Information "out there" is not under our control and could change or disappear entirely without prior notice.

5.5.3 The egg in the mix

In the actual future, we're likely to see trends toward both extremes in keeping. We may have the option and the motivation to have increasing amounts of information kept automatically—especially information describing our interactions with our world. And our reliance on public stores for information may also increase. Neither trend, however, will altogether eliminate the need to organize personal information or to keep (e.g., by filing or tagging) according to the organizations we create.

There is the story, famous in advertising circles, of the initially failed attempt by Betty Crocker Foods to introduce a "just add water" cake mix back in the 1950s. Members of the targeted audience of that time—American housewives—were not buying. The problem? Housewives did not feel good about presenting a cake as "theirs" to which they had added so little. The solution? Change the mix so that an egg needed to be added.

Freudian theory in vogue at the time pointed to the egg-fortified cake as an act of birthing. But other explanations are more straightforward.[21] Perhaps the egg really did improve the quality of the mix. Also, by adding the egg (maybe it could have been another ingredient, like baking powder, instead), the person using the mix had a stronger connection to the cake as the end result.

Now consider minimal levels of keeping and organizing as a kind of metaphorical addition of an egg to the mix of our management and use of information. Keeping and organizing strengthen our connection to our information and the potential uses of this information to meet needs in our lives. More than this, our activities of keeping and organizing can deepen our understanding of the information we have so that we make better uses of this information.

An organizational scheme (e.g., of tags or folders) should meaningfully reflect our needs for information as used in the various projects we are trying to complete, the decisions we need to make, and the roles and obligations we need to fulfill. Keeping according to such a scheme

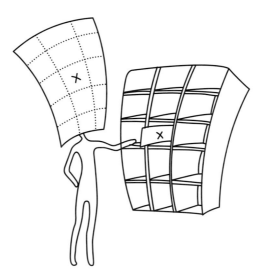

---

[21] See ChangingMinds.org (*http://changingminds.org/analysis/betty_crockers_egg.htm*) for more on the Betty Crocker story.

What Next for Tool Development?

– *Mike Kelly*

How would a system-provided framework for capturing information schemas (like that described for a systemwide auto-complete in the "What next for tool development" sidebar in Chapter 4) help with the various keeping and organizing tasks described in this chapter? Part of the power of capturing information in software databases rather than paper systems is the ease with which information can be connected—for instance, I can easily find all the files modified on a particular date, which is obviously much harder using traditional paper systems unless I've thought in advance to organize in that way.

Today's file systems already provide schemas for organizing common information such as size, modified date, and the like. We sometimes call this "metadata" because it is data about the data—the file, in this case. Imagine if every time a file was saved by an application, the application had to provide the underlying file system with this metadata—the date, the size, and the creating application of the document. In addition to being an added burden on each application, a single bug in one application would make all the information stored about files suspect. The fact that the system automatically tracks this also allows the system to provide common user interfaces to find files: view > details > sort by modified date is one of my favorite ways to find that document I was working on last week. Because these are system-provided interfaces, it is no additional work for any application that manipulates files to provide that capability for me.

The problem is that the set of common "metadata" captured by the system is far too limited and is captured today only at the file level. But if we imagine that more complex and customized information schemas with common elements become first-class citizens of the operating-system-maintained database, the situation changes quite a bit.

One of the frustrating experiences of information overload is feeling like a glorified file clerk, forced to sort bits of information like contacts, email messages, and voicemail into various categories. Who hasn't asked oneself at some time, Why can't the computer do this for me?

With common schemas such as "Contact," "Bill," or "Project," we not only allow for auto-complete as described in Chapter 4; we also start to make it possible to *connect* disparate information in natural ways:

- Show me all pictures of this Contact.

- Find Bills I paid to this Contact.

- Show me all messages, meetings, and documents related to this Project.

These common schemas also automate what are now some manual keeping tasks and make possible natural ways of finding information which leverage the partial information we often have: "I don't remember anything about his name, but I paid a bill from him sometime last week." By breaking the data out of silos of vertical applications, we help make it even more powerful and reduce the amount of manual keeping tasks we need to do. The computer really *can* do some of that for you.

Some of the work being done on Language-Integrated Query (LINQ) is relevant here. LINQ allows query primitives to be integrated into the syntax and flow of programs, regardless of the source of the data—so a LINQ query can be applied across an in-memory array, a relational database, or perhaps, in this case, a file system, or XML representation of common data types like "Contact." (For more information on LINQ, see *http://msdn.microsoft.com/data/ref/linq.*)

affects our memories and even our understanding of the items we keep.[22] Participants in a KFTF investigation of folder use said as much, with comments such as "Folders help me to see my information better" and "Putting things into folders helps me to understand and remember the information better."

Chapter 4 reviewed research telling us that organizations of personal information have value for the "ways" they give us to get back to our information. But organizations do more than this. The visible structure we impose on information (even if only a basic folder hierarchy) can serve to highlight key relationships among the information items in a collection. Organizational structure can help us to make sense of our information and its applications. This is a topic to explore further in the next section.

Keep what is worth keeping. And with the breath of kindness blow the rest away.

English novelist Dinah Mulock Craik (1826–1887)

5.6 PICing our battles

If some hands-on organizing of personal information is useful, there is neither time for nor value in organizing everything. Where to focus our efforts?

Chapter 2 described personal information collections, or PICs, as islands of relative structure and coherence in the vast sea of a PSI. PICs are the regions of a PSI where we try to "make a stand."

A PIC contains information items or references to these (such as shortcuts or aliases). A PIC can be created using grouping mechanisms such as folders, piles, binders, and albums. Each of these ways to group has physical and digital variations. For example, we may stack papers on our (physical) desktop that all relate to a particular project, or we can have an analogous

---

[22] See Jones and Ross (2006) for a review of relevant research in cognitive psychology connecting the memorability of information to the methods of its keeping and organizing.

grouping of icons on our computer desktop for project-related documents. PICs of digital information can also be created automatically through applications of a persistent query in connection with a *virtual folder.*[23]

For any PIC that we create and maintain, we have some notion of what should and should not be in it; that is, items of a PIC cohere even if this is through a pattern of "family resemblances"[24] rather than through enforcement of a formal definition. For some PICs, such as those created using virtual folders, the notion of what belongs is made explicit (imperfectly so). For other PICs, the notion of what belongs is implicit in our choice of items to go into the folder (pile, album, binder, etc.).

5.6.1 Reference vs. project collections

Let's consider two important kinds of PIC:

Reference collections. Items in a reference collection are selected for repeated use but usually with no specific use in mind. Examples include (1) the books of a personal library, (2) digital articles kept in an "articles" folder, (3) dinner recipes downloaded from the Web, (4) conventional, paper-backed pictures kept in a photo album, (5) digital songs managed by an application such as Apple iTunes, (6) various Microsoft PowerPoint presentations organized for use on different occasions by different audiences.

Project collections. Items in a project collection are selected to relate to a particular project that we are trying to complete. Examples include (1) Ron's "search folder" collection of all email correspondence addressed to the special "Vera's-going-away-party" distribution list; (2) the hanging folders in one of Tess's file drawers containing paper documents relating to Vera's party, including paper printouts of menu options and pricing from different restaurants, printouts of funny stories about Vera that people have sent in email, and a schedule of events for Vera's goodbye party; (3) the web bookmarks you or I might gather relating to a summer vacation we're planning.

A comparison of two collections—one a reference collection and the other a project collection—points to some interesting differences. Figure 5.2 provides a view of some of the nearly 700 articles I have assembled that relate to the work and various publications of the Keeping Found Things Found (KFTF) project. Articles cover a diverse set of topics and range in size from short conference papers of four pages to book chapters to downloaded books.

Notwithstanding these variations, articles share in common a set of questions—properties—about which we can expect sensible answers, as property values. Property/value pairs help to distinguish articles from one another. For example, each article has an author(s), a year of publication, and a title. On the other hand, properties such as "camera model" or "date picture taken" do not make sense for articles (though these do make sense for a collection of pictures).

---

[23] See the Wikipedia article on "virtual folders" (*http://en.wikipedia.org/wiki/Virtual_folders*).

[24] For a classic discussion on the disjointed nature of our categories for everyday things, see Wittgenstein (1953).

Kuny, 1998, Digital dark ages
kwasnik, 1999, the role of classification in knowledge representation & discorvery
Kwasnik, 1989, How a personal document's intended purpose
Kwasnik, 1999, role of classification in knowledge
Lamming et al, 2000, Satchel
lamming newman 1992, activity-based IR
Landauer & Nachbar, 1985, selection from menus
Landay & Myers, 2001, Sketching interfaces
Lansdale & Edmonds, 1992, Using memory for events
Lansdale et al, 1996, Developing practice with theory in HCI
Lansdale, 1988, Psychology of personal information management
Larkin & Simon, 1987, Why a diagram is (sometimes) worth

Figure 5.2 **A personal reference collection of articles.**

Notice that several properties are embedded in article file names through the following naming convention: file names begin with an author field, followed by the year of publication, followed by an abbreviated form of the title. Why such funny names? Current versions of both the Macintosh and Microsoft Windows operating systems make visible a property dialog for a selected item in which it is possible to modify many useful properties. However, support in both operating systems is limited in several ways,[25] and even with great improvements in the ease with which properties can be modified, I might still use this funny naming convention. Naming files in this way is reasonably fast and easy. Filling in values for properties is not.

Someday we might hope these property values for an item would come along as metadata of the item. In fact, some of the articles I've downloaded do have associated values for "Author" (or "Authors") and "Title" fields, but most do not. And for articles that do, values are inconsistently assigned or assigned in ways that aren't useful. For example, the author value of some articles is simply "author." On many others, the field begins with the first name of the first author, making it impossible to sort by last name.

Two final points to make concerning this reference collection before moving on to a consideration of a project collection example:

- *Organization is relatively flat* with respect to use of folders and subfolders. The organization is, rather, in properties and their values—here given expression in structured file names.

- *One property is key.* In this example, the last name of the first author is key. I make an effort to remember an article by this property. The file manager, as my computer counterpart, essentially promises to sort-by-name on this key property. The key property may vary depending on the kind of items in a collection. For photographs, the date that a picture is taken or the date it is downloaded may be the key property.[26] For songs, the artist may be key.

---

[25] See *http://arstechnica.com/reviews/os/macosx-10.4.ars/* for a longer discussion on the advances and persistent limitations in support for properties (aka "metadata").

[26] For research into how people organize digital photographs, see Rodden and Wood (2003).

What about search? If I could search on article content or, more narrowly, on article titles, would I really need to make it a point to remember the last name of the first author of an article? I've tried this. Perhaps you have too. The trouble with such keyword searches is that they often return more than I'm looking for and, in worst cases, searches may miss the article I'm looking for. Seemingly trivial differences in spelling (e.g., "organize" vs. "organise") or a natural substitution of words (e.g., "figure" or "picture" for "diagram") can mean failure. I'd rather pay the price of learning an article by its first author (which, in any case, is also a useful way to refer to articles in conversation).

Now let's consider an example of a project collection. Figure 5.3 displays a listing of files and folders collected by someone near the beginning of 6-month period in which she was making arrangements for her own wedding.[27]

Figure 5.3   **A personal project collection near the beginning of efforts to plan a wedding.**

---

[27] Depictions of project information in Figures 5.3 and 5.4 are based on participant data first presented in Jones et al. (2005). Both are taken from screenshots that have been reformatted to remove any personal identifying information.

One difference between this wedding project collection and the article reference collection of Figure 5.2 is immediately apparent. The items (files) of this collection are much more diverse with respect to file format and, more important, with respect to the nature of information content. Items include JPEG pictures of the ballroom where the wedding reception will be held, other JPEG pictures of choices in wedding dress, a Microsoft Word document describing a complete wedding package, a Microsoft Excel spreadsheet containing the guest list, and another spreadsheet containing an overall plan for the wedding. What set of properties might usefully describe and distinguish such a diverse set of items?

Note that Figure 5.3 also includes folders. Six months after the screenshot of Figure 5.3 with the wedding only a few weeks away, the folder organization has grown to be very elaborate indeed, as depicted by the folder view of Figure 5.4.

The participant's comments made it clear that the folder structure of Figure 5.4 functioned as more than simply a way of getting back to files. The folder hierarchy represented important

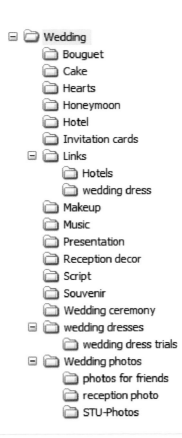

Figure 5.4 **A view of folders and subfolders for the same wedding, six months later (and three weeks away from the wedding).**

information in its own right. In one view, the participant could see a record, albeit intermingled, of tasks completed, decisions made, and a reminder of tasks and decisions still to be addressed.

The folder hierarchy, then, was an external representation, albeit partial and far from perfect, of the participant's efforts to plan her wedding. Planning of the wedding and its results are also distributed across people and processes in the participant's environment. For example, the bride's parents, the groom, and the groom's parents are involved in planning. And planning is "wired" into the participant's environment in ways that make it unlikely that she would forget important aspects of the wedding even without the folder hierarchy. The seamstress will call, for example, with questions concerning the wedding dress, even in the unlikely event that the bride has forgotten all about the wedding dress.

Notwithstanding this overlapping and redundant support for wedding planning, the folder representation appeared to realize some of the benefits observed elsewhere for external representations (ERs) of a problem or project.[28] For example, subfolders of the wedding folder represented not only the information kept within, but also the information that was still needed or might be relevant. To be sure, the folder hierarchy as ER is a guide for the bride rather than anything approaching an algorithm to be followed lockstep.[29] But participant comments made it clear that the hierarchy was an important part of her planning efforts, and that losing it, even if the information it organized remained, would be a serious loss.

If a folder organization helps in project planning, it may support a person not only to "keep faster," by providing a ready location for incoming information, but also to "keep smarter," to see more readily the relevance of encountered information to a given project, even if the project is not the current focus of attention.[30] These examples of a reference and a project collection were selected to bring out points of general contrast between project and reference collections, which are summarized in Table 5.1. There are many variations in reference and project collections that begin to paint a gray area between the examples of Figure 5.2, Figure 5.3, and Figure 5.4. Some reference collections have an internal structure of folders. Digital photographs, for example, may be grouped into folders by year and month or, alternatively, according to vacation or special event (e.g., "Vera's going-away party"). Articles are sometimes grouped by a folder structure of topics, subtopics, and even sub-subtopics.[31]

---

[28] For more discussion on the use of the environment and external representations in support of decision making and problem solving, see Hutchins (1994), Larkin and Simon (1987), and Russell et al. (1993).

[29] See Suchman, 1987.

[30] See, for example, the work of Seifert and Patalano (2001).

[31] Before the flat, author-ordered listing illustrated in Figure 5.2, I had an organization of articles by topic and subtopic, but several problems became apparent. Articles often belonged under several different topic folders. Later, I never knew where to look. Searches on author returned results quickly, but I was not nearly so fast at accessing the search facility and specifying the search. I began to make copies of articles—one per topic folder or subfolder in which it belonged. But then I faced a problem of version control—I might highlight key passages in one copy of an article but then be frustrated later when accessing another copy only to see that these highlights were missing. I still maintain a one-level hierarchy of topic areas, but folders within contain shortcuts pointing to articles in a single "articles" folder.

Table 5.1 Differences between reference and project collections

Are items in a . . .	reference collection	project collection
Kept with a specific use in mind?	No, multiple uses perhaps but no specific use	Yes, the associated project
All described and distinguished from one another by a single set of properties?	Yes	No. Items are not all of the same content type (e.g., articles, photos, songs, etc.)
Often organized into a hierarchy of subfolders?	Sometimes, by subject area or date interval (e.g., Summer 2007)	Yes, in accordance with subprojects and tasks

On the other hand, some project information is naturally organized by properties, even if items in the overall collection of project-related information share few meaningful properties in common besides "last modified" date. The wedding dress pictures (JPEG files) referenced in Figure 5.3, for example, might have been described by properties such as "style," "price," "time to sew," and "general comments." Or consider another example, where a student is working with other students on a team term paper as part of a larger project to complete a course. If the term paper is passed back and forth in email, versions as separate files may have file names coded, in an ad hoc manner, to represent properties such as base name, date, and person who last reviewed.

In a person's choice of PICs, reference collections and project collections may compete for the same information items. This was illustrated in the example from Chapter 4 where Nancy had organized some travel reimbursement requests by project (e.g., different business trips) and had grouped other requests into a folder called "travel reimbursements."

Or consider Figure 5.5's depiction of a college professor's organization of information for the various courses he teaches. Some images are stored in "Images" subfolders under project collections for "course 424" and "course 541." Other images and some copies of these project collection images are also stored in a reference collection represented by a top-level "Images" folder under "My Documents." Trouble arises later when this professor wants to locate an image for use in a third course. A more serious problem arises because the professor sometimes copies images to put into both the project collections and the "Images" reference collection, and he sometimes makes changes to one or more of these copies. Finding the "right" copy later is not easy. Notice that a similar competition occurs in Figure 5.5 among articles: are these stored in the "Articles" reference collection or in the "Readings" subfolders under course folders representing project collections?

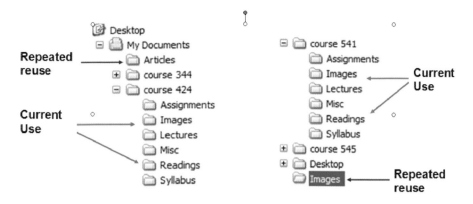

Figure 5.5 "Images" are organized both for current use (as subfolders under course project folders) and for repeated reuse (in a single larger folder).

Let's summarize some of the points covered so far in this limited look at reference and project collections.

- Regarding support for metadata (properties, tags) as an alternative to or enhancement of hierarchical folder organization, the devil is in the details.[32] Is support exposed in a general way through applications such as the Macintosh Finder or the Windows Explorer? Or is support specific to special-purpose applications (e.g., to manage photographs or music)? How easy is it to specify property values? Is there support for the consistent use of property values (e.g., in the form of property-specific drop-down menus)? How easily can new properties be added? How easily can property values be exposed for use to sort and search on items? It might be best for items to come prepackaged with useful metadata. But what incentive do content providers have to provide data that is accurate? And can there be consistency in the conventions followed by different content providers?[33] These are not new issues, to be sure.[34] And they don't go away easily.

- "Flat," factorial combinations of property values as a means of organization are sometimes placed in an unnecessary either/or opposition to hierarchical organizations.[35] But there is ample reason to believe that both kinds of organization are needed and that support for their integrative use is far from straightforward. A related challenge is to support people in their use of both reference and project collections.

- Folder hierarchies are more than a means to one end—the organization of information for reaccess. Folders can also provide information in their own right, as a summary of the information content within. Folder hierarchies can provide visible, external representation

---

[32] For a discussion of some issues of metadata, especially as these apply to the Macintosh, see the metadata section of John Siracusa's Ars Technica review (*http://arstechnica.com/reviews/os/macosx-10.4.ars/6*).

[33] See, for example, the web site for the Dublin Core Metadata Initiative (*http://dublincore.org/*) or W3C discussions concerning namespaces in XML (*http://www.w3.org/TR/REC-xml-names/*).

[34] See, for example, Bliss (1933).

[35] See Dourish et al. (1999).

to a mapping from information to need. As applied to a project we're trying to complete, a folder hierarchy can give rough, external representation to a plan for completing the project. This observation points to an interesting possibility: Don't focus on the organization of information. Focus, instead, on planning the project and let the information follow.

This last point is explored further in the next section.

5.6.2 Plan the project and let the information follow

Figure 5.4 suggests that folder structure can serve as a kind of a project plan. Suppose we switch things around so that focus at the outset is not on the organization of project information per se, but on the planning of a project? Can a useful organization of a project collection emerge as a by-product of project planning?

This is a possibility being explored through a Project Planner prototype being developed in the KFTF project.[36] The Planner essentially provides a rich-text, document-like overlay to the file system. Using the Planner, people can begin their work on a project top-down, by building a project outline with high-level components representing subprojects and lower-level components representing tasks.

Or users can start bottom-up, by typing in notes and gathering bits and pieces of information from web pages, email messages, and e-documents through a Drag & link operation. With Drag & link, information is hyperlinked back to the source so users can drag only a small, key part of a larger document (email message, web page) with the assurance that more information is only a click away.

Over time, an entire project plan emerges such as that depicted in Figure 5.6. An important point is that the plan is essentially another view of a person's file folder hierarchy, where headings are folders, subheadings are subfolders, and links are shortcuts.[37] In addition to linking text and typing formatted notes, users can order headings and subheadings in ways that help them to make sense of a plan or to see things in order of importance—just as they might like to do in a word processor.

One especially important feature of the Planner is its support for *In-Context Create*. Using In-Context Create, people can send new email messages and create new documents *in the context of a project plan*. Documents so created reside in the nearest containing heading/folder. For email messages, links are placed in the nearest containing heading/folder, and the email messages themselves are still managed by the email application (Microsoft Outlook).

---

[36] See Jones et al. (2006).

[37] Behind the scenes, the Planner is able to support its more document-like outline view by distributing XML fragments as hidden files, one per file folder, that contain information concerning notes, links, and folder ordering. The Planner assembles fragments on demand to present a coherent project plan view, including notes, excerpts, links, and subfolder ordering. The distribution of XML fragments in association with file folders has more general application as a way to support a variety of views into a hierarchically structured collection of personal information. Other potentially useful views include workflow, decision tree, and tabular.

Consider the benefits of In-Context Create with respect to an email message. After an email message is sent, a common question later arises: Did I get a reply? If so, what? When many email messages arrive in a day, it is easy to lose track of responses to a particular email message. One way to check is to locate the sent email message, either in the Sent Mail folder or possibly in the inbox if the message was copied to the sender. A query can then be issued for all responses to the email message. But locating the original email message can take time, especially if this is done several times per day.

A project plan such as that in Figure 5.6 provides an alternate way to locate a sent email message and, through this message, responses. One task in the home remodel plan, for example, is to "find out what the budget allows" for countertops. Underneath is a link to an

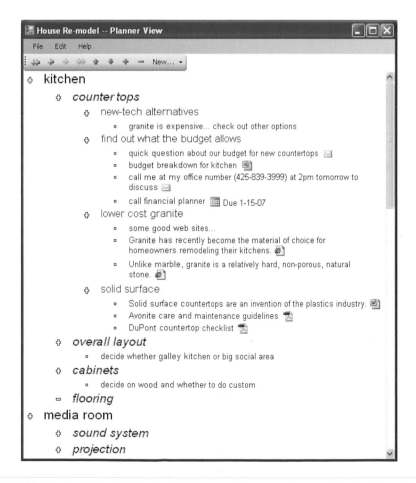

Figure 5.6 **A plan built in the Project Planner also organizes project-relevant information.**

email message from the homeowner to the contractor, with the subject line "quick question about our budget for countertops." If the homeowner later wants to locate the contractor's response to this message, she can do so with reference to the project plan and its representation of the need that prompted the email message in the first place. In this manner, information is more closely connected to need.

The Planner takes simple steps toward two important integrations:

- *Integration of different forms of information.* Through the actions of Drag & link and In-Context Create, a plan can bring together, in a single view, references to the documents, email messages, and web pages that relate to a task or subproject of the plan.

- *Integration of information and time/task management.* Folders, representing tasks, can be associated with appointments that appear in the Microsoft Outlook Calendar. An appointment includes a hyperlink that can be clicked to quickly retrieve information relating to a task.

Initial evaluations of the Planner have been very positive. One participant said, for example: "That's all I do all day long—go back and forth, back and forth between programs. How much time could I save by having all project-related documents together in an integrated whole? One click and I am right there, rather than opening 4 to 5 folders and repeating the same things. The planner will save me a lot of time."

Organizing is what you do before you do something, so that when you do it, it is not all mixed up.

English humorist and creator of Winnie-the-Pooh, A. A. Milne (1882–1956)

What Now for You and Me?

We can't wait for new tools to help us keep and organize better. What can we do now? First, let's return to the steps of finding. Each is a source of potential failure that can often be avoided by some keeping forethought:

- *Reminding/remembering to look.* It's not enough to keep information. We keep lots of information and then forget to use it later. We need to think about how we'll remember to look for the information again later when it is needed. Realize that, with information in hand, you're apt to be overconfident of your ability to remember this information later. "Of course I'll remember this. How could I forget?" Set reminders, send email messages, make appointments in your calendar—do what it takes to remember. Also, try to think specifically about the circumstances of need later on. Where? When? How (in what form) will you need the information later? Finally, assess and make use of your *attentional surfaces* according to your observation of your own habits. Where does your attention go in a typical day? Where do you look? What do you notice? For most of us, the visible portion of the inbox is an attentional surface. What about a computer desktop? If you routinely look on your desktop, it may be a good place to put items that need your attention later. But if you rarely look at the desktop or it is already cluttered with other information, it may not be a good place to put information. Consider simply dragging a copy of a reference to information you'll need later into a special appointment in your calendar (scheduled for roughly the time when you'll need the information).

- *Recall.* Pick a scheme of organization and stick with it. If you later decide to change to another scheme, then change completely. Don't let two inconsistent schemes coexist, using one on one day and the other on the next day. Don't let overlapping folders or tags like "trips" and "travel" coexist. Be clear with yourself concerning the definition of a folder or tag and how it should be used. Consider consolidating organizations for different forms of information so that you have one primary organization. For many of us, our primary organization is file folders. If so, consider dragging important email messages and web addresses into this organization as well. For some of us, our email folders (or the labels of a system like gmail) are a primary organization. If so, consider sending important documents and web references in self-addressed email messages so that these can also be kept in this email organization.

- *Recognition.* Don't be afraid to use long descriptive names for files. Rename web references too if their default name is not descriptive. In your email exchanges with others relating to a particular project, consider establishing conventions for the first part of the message subject line (e.g., all messages relating to "project A" should begin with "project A").

- *Repeat?* Group together (by tag or folder) items you are certain to need together again later. Or group together references (e.g., aliases, shortcuts) to these.

Other suggestions:

- When making keeping decisions, always consider two different costs: the cost of a "false positive" and the cost of a "miss." Ask yourself: What bad things can happen if I keep (respond to, deal with) this item of information and it turns out I didn't have to? Time lost? Task disruption? Conversely, ask yourself, What bad things can happen if I don't keep (respond to, deal with) this item of information and it turns out I should have? Lost opportunities? Angry colleagues and bosses? Since we can't be perfect in our predictions of the future, we can't be perfect in our keeping decisions. But we can at least make some assessments for the costs of an error. If the costs of errors are higher on the side of misses, then we should be more inclined to keep (respond, deal with now) an item of information even if we suspect we may not need to. Likewise, if the costs of errors are higher on the side of false positives, we should be more inclined not to keep (to ignore or postpone dealing with) an information item.

- Make reference collections; make project collections. Make collections for the items you use repeatedly. Make these flat if you can. Organize instead by properties—even if properties can only be realized through funny names. Make a folder for each of your major projects. Make subfolders stand for subprojects and tasks. Do this top-down if you know the structure of the project (e.g., if it is like other projects you have done before). Otherwise, simply "pile" information into the folder at first and build a structure of subfolders over time as the subprojects and tasks become apparent.

- Pick your battles. Don't organize everything.

5.7 Looking back, looking forward

What have we covered in this chapter?

☑ *Keeping and organizing are distinct kinds of PIM activity.* The terms "keeping" and "organizing" are often used interchangeably. But each is a distinct kind of PIM activity. Placing a document in a folder or tagging it is keeping. Deciding on a scheme for how folders or tags should be created, named, and related to one another is organizing. Organizing, with its overall focus on a collection of information, is the first kind of meta-level activity we have considered in this book.

☑ *Large, visible variations in habits of keeping and organizing need to be understood with reference to underlying strategies.* Some of us are neat; some of us are messy. Some of us are organized in one place, for one form of information, and not so organized in others. We can't understand a practice of keeping and organizing, not even our own, without some assessment of the strategy behind observable actions and visible structures.

☑ *Keeping is multifaceted.* Keeping, like finding, is a multistep process, and failure can happen at any step. But keeping activities are also aptly characterized as having many facets to their completion. Facets reflect uncertainty concerning the information itself and uncertainty concerning the need(s) to which the information will be applied. For a keeping decision we might take or a keeping action we might make, there are two kinds of possible error and a cost with each.

☑ *"Keep everything" and "keep nothing."* Both have drawbacks as extremes in keeping strategies. In the actual future, we're likely to see trends toward both extremes. We may have the option and the motivation to keep increasing amounts of information—especially event information describing our interactions with our world. And our reliance on public stores for information may also increase. Neither trend, however, will altogether eliminate the need to organize personal information or to keep it (e.g., by filing or tagging) according to the organizations we create.

☑ *Not everything is worth our time and trouble to keep and organize.* When deciding where to focus our efforts, we should give special attention to the creation of reference collections—collections of items we may use repeatedly—and project collections—collections of items relating to a specific project we want to complete.

Studies of how people manage their information over time can provide valuable information for understanding better the rules of the game for PIM. One exciting possibility is that, as a by-product of tools devised to better support us in our efforts to plan, we may also get effective organizations of the information needed to fulfill these plans. Organization as a kind of PIM activity that many of us prefer to avoid ("like the plague") is then interwoven with an activity that many of us like to do and need to do: plan for the future.

If this is true, our PIM future looks bright. But a very dark cloud looms on the horizon as well. All of a person's efforts to keep and organize personal information could disappear in an instant for want of proper maintenance of the information. This is the topic of the next chapter.

Maintaining for now and for later

Suppose we move into an enormous mansion bequeathed to us in the will of a long-lost uncle. When one room reaches an unbearable state of clutter, we simply shut its door and move to a new room with comparable functions and furnishings. We dispatch a servant to retrieve items left behind in the old rooms. We never, ever, have to houseclean again. An analogous situation now holds for much of our personal information. But what if, one day, the doors won't open? Or the mansion burns down?

Chapter
Six

Everybody gets so much information all day long that they lose their common sense.

U.S. author Gertrude Stein (1874–1946)

6.1 Starting out

"The house is a mess." If we give guests a tour of our house, we may find ourselves making a statement like this. We may even tidy up as we go along—straightening the pillows on living room sofas, for example, or removing a pile of dirty laundry from the bedroom floor. We want guests to judge us not by the current state of the house, but rather by the higher standards of tidiness to which we mean to adhere.

In studies of PIM, participants sometimes provide interviewers with analogous tours through their organizations of books and paper documents, e-documents, email messages, and web bookmarks. Participants, in their words and actions, often act like hosts entertaining guests within their PSIs. Boardman and Sasse (2004) reported that 12 of 31 participants in their study performed "ad hoc tidying" during the interview itself. In the Jones et al. (2005) study, all 14 participants made comments during the interview such as "I really should clean this up." Four participants actually insisted on interrupting the interview while they moved or deleted files and whole folders as "old stuff that really shouldn't be there anymore."

Moving old stuff—whether old clothes or old information—to make way for the new is an act of maintaining. Maintaining, like organizing, is meta-level—important over the long run but rarely urgent in the current moment (unless guests are present!). The prospect of maintaining and organizing, in an actual house and in a personal space of information, often elicits, in equal parts, feelings of avoidance and guilt for doing so.

Maintaining is not just for now or the near term, but for the long term as well. Issues of maintenance vary considerably with the duration of time for which personal information needs to be maintained. Accordingly, the chapter is divided into the following sections:

☑ *Getting oriented.* Just as keeping and organizing go together but are different, maintaining and organizing go together but are different. Key distinctions between maintaining and organizing are made in this first section of the chapter. Modern challenges of maintaining personal information can be likened to the challenges of maintaining one, or possibly several, mansions containing a large number of rooms—many of which we haven't yet visited.

☑ *Maintaining for now.* Maintaining our personal information for the present means dealing with issues such as how best to back up computer hard drives and other storage devices, how to handle these backups, and how to move old information out of the way periodically so that focus can be on the working information (currently in use). We also must address how best to correct or update information—in all its copies and versions—and to do this not only for information we control, but also for information (especially financial and medical information) about us that others control.

☑ *Maintaining for later.* Maintaining information for the next 10, 20, or 30 years requires that we think about longer-term issues such as which formats we can trust to be around and supported decades from now. For example, will we still be able to see digital photos and videos in 30 years at the same level of fidelity? What about the storage medium itself? For how long is it reliable? If information is on an old computer, will we still be able to boot it? If information is password protected, where do the passwords go? These are questions of maintenance to face if information is to be kept for decades rather than years.

☑ *Maintaining for our lives and beyond.* Questions change again as we maintain our information for its impact on us and on the people who come into our "space" through visits to our offices, our web sites and blogs, through the music and photos we share, and possibly even by over-the-shoulder peeks at our computer desktop. How does our information reflect, remind, and reinforce our values, goals, hopes, and fears? Our information as legacy is not only for us, but also for those who survive us.

A point concerning the book's scope bears repeating, in particular for this chapter: Our focus is on "what about?" rather than "how to." The aim is to define a space of larger considerations and then to place the person—you or me—in the center of these considerations rather than shunt us to the side as an afterthought in the design of a larger system.

One simple example will illustrate: In a description of data backup procedures, we may think we see ourselves represented somewhere in the diagram as the "user." But do procedures handle the backup of our personal computer at home? What about the backup of contact information on our mobile phones that we use with at least half of all the calls we make? What about the backup or transfer of the pictures on our digital camera? As we begin to answer these questions, we begin to explore our personal space of information.

6.2 Getting oriented

Chapter 5 noted that, though the words "keeping" and "organizing" are often used interchangeably, a useful distinction can be made with respect to focus and triggering events. In keeping, the focus is on the item; in organizing, the focus is on a collection of items. Keeping may prompt organizing ("there's no more space; time to reorganize"). And organizing may prompt keeping ("where does this item go under the new organization?"). But the two types of activity are distinct. In a typical day, we continuously encounter items—from business cards proffered during a meeting to incoming email to pages on the Web—for which some keeping activity is required. By contrast, people generally do little, if anything, in a typical day to organize, other than perhaps to guiltily express the need to "get organized" (one of these days . . .).

The words "organizing" and "maintaining" are also frequently used together, if not interchangeably. This chapter is about maintaining personal information. The definition for *information maintaining* or simply *maintaining,* as introduced in the last chapter, is repeated here:

> *Information maintaining* (or just *maintaining*) includes all decisions and actions relating to the composition and preservation of personal information collections. Decisions include what kind of new items go into a collection, how information in the collection is stored (where? in what formats? in what kind of storage? backed up how?), and when older items leave the collection (e.g., are deleted or archived).

By contrast, *information organizing*, or simply *organizing*, is focused on how items in a collection are interrelated to and distinguished from one another through the assignment of names and other properties and through their placement in folders. The analogy to a house is instructive. If we're fortunate enough to be able to pay someone to clean our house, what is the activity we often do right before the housekeeper arrives? We straighten up. We organize or reorganize. Cleaning the house is something we entrust to someone else. But if we leave it to the housekeeper to put our things away, we may spend many hours finding them again later. Organizing preserves an essential connection between us and our things—whether these are clothing, toiletries, and the other physical items of a house, or the email messages, e-documents, paper documents, and other information items of our PSI.[1]

Maintenance of a house means not only housecleaning but also handling other matters like cleaning the gutters, repairing the roof, and checking the fire alarms. Maintenance of information collections in the PSI includes matters relating to the storage of information, its

---

[1] People do sometimes entrust other people with their information's organization. I interviewed an ex-governor of Washington state, for example, who, until he retired recently, left the organization of nearly all of his information—articles, upcoming meetings dates, invitations, and so on—to his assistant. In this case, the personal assistant was very smart and had considerable experience with the governor's preferred way to categorize and organize his information.

backup, and the preservation of information items in "good working order" (so that items can later be opened up, viewed, and manipulated). Maintenance also includes efforts to purge the collection of information that no longer belongs there.

The debate continues over whether hands-on organizing of information is essential to PIM or whether, as computers get smart enough, we might be able to delegate organizing to the computer, the way we might to a highly trained personal assistant.[2] There is less debate concerning many maintenance activities such as periodic backups, updates of software (especially system software and virus definitions), and the migration from one storage format to another (to keep pace with changes in standards and application support). Most of us would happily entrust these activities to a paid professional, if only we could.

Maintaining, like organizing, is a meta-level activity. Maintaining requires that people take a broader look at what a personal information collection is or should be *about*. And since maintenance activities are rarely forced by the events of a typical day, these activities often occur *after* other work is done—which is to say rarely or not at all. In a study of office workers in the midst of a move, Whittaker and Hirschberg (2001) found that 74 percent of the 50 people interviewed had not cleaned their archives of paper documents in over a year. When cleanups did occur, 84 percent were in response to external events such as job changes or office moves. Whittaker and Hirschberg concluded that people "seldom rationalize their archives." As one participant noted (p. 155), "More stuff just keeps coming in, and the pace of things is such that you can't say 'I'm going to take a week out, and I'm going to go through my files to clean them.' "

Many of us are fortunate to have trained professionals to help us, through the services of the information technology (IT) department where we work. And we can also take advantage of IT-established facilities for backup. However, any such work-related maintenance coverage frequently defines another fault line in our PSI. The computer we use at work (and perhaps even take home with us if it's a laptop computer) is covered. But not the computer or the other devices we use at home for our digital music, videos, and photographs.

6.2.1 A fantasy mansion

Large amounts of cheap storage mean that some maintenance chores—disk cleanup, for example—no longer need to be done as frequently, if at all. Again, the house analogy is instructive. Suppose we move into an enormous mansion bequeathed to us in the will of a long-lost uncle. The mansion has more rooms than we can possibly ever use. When one room reaches an unbearable state of clutter, we simply shut its door and move to a new room with comparable functions and furnishings. As the need arises, we dispatch a servant to search for and retrieve items left behind in the old rooms. We never, ever have to straighten up or houseclean again.

A great mansion with an inexhaustible supply of rooms is the stuff of fantasy and fairy tales. But an analogous situation now holds with respect to much of our personal information.

---

[2] For an argument in support of search to obviate organizing, see Cutrell, Dumais, and Teevan (2006). For counter-arguments, see Jones et al. (2005) and Marshall and Jones (2006).

Certainly, paper filing cabinets still fill up, thus forcing basic decisions concerning what to keep and what to toss (or archive in less accessible storage). The keep-or-toss decision often prompts meta-level considerations concerning whole collections of personal information. For how many years do tax records need to be kept? Will these old magazines really ever get read? And so on.

People once made similar decisions of maintenance and organization for digital PICs as prompted, for example, by a disk-full event or the notice from a system administrator or an Internet service provider (ISP) that allocated space has been reached or exceeded. Though these cleanup events can still occur, they are more likely to be the manufactured product of a corporate (or personal) "clean desk" policy than the result of actual limitations in available storage.

For those of us with many media files—sound and especially video—our needs may continue to outstrip the capacity of our storage devices. But some of us may also remember a time in the early 1980s when personal computers either had no hard drive or hard-drive capacity was very limited.[3] Digital storage could be extended only through the cumbersome use of "floppies" for active data or tape drives for archives. Hard drives with only text and software still filled up quickly. Disk cleanups prompted by "Disk full" events were a frequent, sometimes daily occurrence. Careful thinking went into decisions impacting the use of hard-drive storage. Those days are gone.

For personal digital information, then, many people already have their fantasy mansion with more space than they are likely to use and no one or no situation to ever force them to straighten up. The realization of this fantasy, like many others, is a mixed blessing.

On the positive side, people are freed from the need to make time-consuming and difficult (sometimes emotionally wrenching) decisions concerning what to keep and what to delete or archive. Bergman, Beyth-Marom, and Nachmias (2003) refer to the *deletion paradox* to describe a situation where people may spend precious time on information items that are, on average, of least value to them (e.g., old, never-used information items that are candidates for deletion). And decisions may not be that good. According to the so-called *old magazine effect*,[4] an old item is difficult to discard because its potential uses are momentarily, at the point of the decision, much more salient—literally more visible—than are the ongoing costs of keeping the item. If we look through the table of contents for an old magazine, for example, we may see several potentially interesting, useful articles. As we decide to keep or toss, we may weight the potential benefits of reading these articles more heavily than we weight the more subtle, ongoing, ever accumulating costs associated with keeping the magazine (e.g., the cost of the space the magazine takes up and the clutter it adds and the time it takes to move it every time we are looking for something in the same space).

---

[3] The IBM Personal Computer XT, first released in 1983, was one of the first personal computers to come equiped with a hard drive. Its capacity was 10 MB (see Wikipedia, *http://en.wikipedia.org/wiki/PC_XT*).

[4] See Jones (2004).

6.2.2 A gothic horror story?

Nevertheless, people often express an unease with their current maintenance of information in such apologetic comments as "this is a mess" or in references to themselves as "a pack rat."[5] Or, as one participant in Boardman and Sasse's study (2004, p. 585) said, "Stuff goes in but doesn't come back out—it just builds up." Kaye et al. (2006) report that the participants in their study were "almost always disappointed in their archiving system" (p. 277). Study interviews can themselves provide a therapeutic or cleansing experience, as exemplified by one participant in the Boardman and Sasse study who remarked, "it's like a confessional getting all my computer problems off my chest" (p. 585).

For many of us, our digital information storage might better be compared to a situation where our rich uncle has left us with several different mansions—one in the city, one in the country, one on the shore, and each with a vast number of rooms—but with only a skeletal staff to help. We now have large amounts of storage on the hard drives of our personal computers, more storage available for free through our web-based email accounts, and still more available through email accounts and share points at our workplace. Our cell phones, digital cameras, and MP3 players each come with ever-increasing amounts of storage as well.

A proliferation of digital tools, each with abundant storage, can create special problems relevant to maintenance:

Information fragmentation. Personal information is scattered across several devices, each with its own storage. The time involved in maintenance tasks, including data backups, transfers, and cleanup and synchronization between devices, is multiplied by the number tools (devices, gadgets) we use. Information is further fragmented as new computers and new devices replace older versions. Some information is transferred; other information remains behind. Hafner (2004) writes, "Desk drawers and den closets are filled with obsolete computers, stacks of Zip disks and 3 1/2-inch diskettes, even the larger 5 1/4-inch floppy disks from the 1980s."

Decisions delayed mean circumstances forgotten. An abundance of storage allows us to delay certain tasks, but this is not always good. Sometimes, much of the context we need in order to complete a task is inside our heads—in memories that fade with time. Given the large amount of memory on a digital camera, for example, we may be able to wait for weeks or even months before we must upload pictures to another device such as our personal computer. Waiting that long (or even longer if we have several different Flash memory cards) may mean that we forget many important details surrounding an event represented in the photograph.

Where's the help? We often don't have good help as we struggle with maintenance decisions concerning how to back up our data and which formats to use. Hafner (2004) notes, "Professional archivists and librarians have the resources to duplicate materials in other formats and the expertise to retrieve materials trapped in obsolete computers. But consumers are seldom so well equipped. So they are forced to devise their own stop-gap measures, most of them unwieldy, inconvenient and decidedly low-tech." C.C. Marshall (2007) notes that "many individuals keep their computing environments running by enlisting ad hoc IT support—relatives, friends, or colleagues" (p. 64).

---

[5] See, for example, Marshall and Bly (2005).

Finally, the volatility of our digital information invokes another house metaphor—that of a fire waiting to happen. Gigabytes of personal information stored on the hard drive of a personal computer, for example, can go up "in flames" with the crash of the hard drive or the corruption of its data by an intruding virus. Protecting our information from such catastrophic loss is certainly the most immediate, if not the most important, challenge of our maintaining activities and is explored further in the next section.

6.3 Maintaining for now

Our first concern is to maintain information for its immediate use. An exploration into issues of maintaining-for-the-present begins with two simple questions: What do we collect and why? Across different forms of information—paper and digital—we collect different kinds of information for different reasons:

Precious, irreplaceable information. Included in this category are pictures and videos we have of our family and friends, as well as letters from family and friends. Also included in this category, for some of us, may be working notes recording some occasional flash of insight. As one participant in a Whittaker and Hirschberg study (2001) observed, "sometimes when I look at them I wonder, 'How did I think of that?'" (p. 156).

Extremely difficult-to-replace information. Included in this category are legal documents such as automobile registrations and deeds of sale. Also included in this category, for some people, may be the information to establish priority on patent claims or the information relating to completed projects. For example, a participant in the Whittaker and Hirschberg study (2001) described collecting information that was "partly personal, partly social. I continue to work on projects, and sometimes documentation like that is of use to the group, just to sort of see what we've done before." Information items in this category may be maintained even though they are seldom accessed, because when items are needed, the cost of locating the information elsewhere requires extra effort and time.

Reference collections. The value of a personal information collection is often in its composition and organization rather than in the individual items themselves. People assemble reference collections of photographs (whether of them or by them), illustrations, music, articles, recipes, and even jokes. Reference collections may be used repeatedly for various reasons (to cook a meal, get in a better mood, cheer up a friend). Individual items in a collection are often easily replaced (sometimes with a simple visit to the Web). But the memory of what went into a collection is not so easily replaced. What is the collection meant to include? To exclude?

Working information. Included in this category is the information in collections for projects we are currently working on. The category also includes reference information, such as the phone numbers of a rolodex, that we need to have at hand to get our work done. We may make copies of this information so that it can be where we are. People sometimes copy information to a USB or "thumb drive," for example, so that it can be accessed from home as well as work. Visibility as well as accessibility is an important factor for working information. Working information in one view vs. another may help us see key relationships (e.g., task B depends critically on the outcome of task A) and remind us of associated tasks to be done. Preservation of the current state of working information is important too—even though support for this is limited. Some of us, for example, may be reluctant to reboot our computer (even in the face of messages telling us to do so in order for system updates to take effect) because that would mean losing the current state of open windows (and their position, the position of the insertion points within, etc.).

6.3.1 Challenges and considerations

Maintaining these kinds of information for their purposes now and in the near term means addressing the following challenges and considerations.

Data protection and backup

Hard-drive crashes happen and can be catastrophic if data is not backed up. Even the loss of a few days' worth of data—the days not covered on the recent backup, for example—can be terribly disruptive. But backing up the hard drive of a personal computer or computers is only part of the answer. What about the backup or synchronization of the contact information we have carefully entered into a mobile phone? What about a plan for transferring pictures from our digital cameras before these are accidentally deleted or overwritten with new photographs? Certain paper documents are also very difficult to replace in the event of a fire—a birth certificate or the title to a house or an automobile, for example. Such documents might be placed in a safe deposit box at a bank or, if left at home, at least placed in a fire-resistant box.

Cleanup—if not for storage, then for attention

Regions of a PSI need to be cleaned up periodically and information either deleted or transferred to another region. If we're no longer limited by physical storage, we are, as human beings, still limited by our capacity to attend. We can view this in another way, with respect to the capacity of our "attentional surfaces." An *attentional surface* contains some display of information which, given our daily habits, is in our field of vision for—pick a period of time—at least 15 minutes every day. What qualifies? The surfaces of our physical desktop, the computer desktop, the inbox, perhaps a personal web site or a web site we visit regularly, or even the notes and paper fragments held up by magnets on our refrigerator door. The top-level views of folders and files in a region like "My Documents" and perhaps also the top-level view of files and subfolders in the folder for an active project also count as attentional surfaces. For these surfaces to retain their attention-getting power, they need to be cleared of the detritus of old "stuff" that builds up.[6]

Synchronize, update, and correct

Another maintenance activity—perhaps the most thankless of them all—is to synchronize, update, and correct information. Synchronization is particularly an issue for people who work on several different computers.

---

[6] Of course, some attentional surfaces are renewed without our intervention. The viewable portion of the inbox, for example, is renewed as new incoming messages displace older messages which then scroll out of view. A home web page renews periodically on its own or through the actions of its webmaster.

but small changes and updates must be made even if most work is done on a single computer. Phone numbers and email addresses change. Personal last names change with marriage or divorce. Company names change with mergers or spin-offs. Projects and initiatives also come and go or their terms change with time.

Consider the challenge of updating a person's email address. Locating all listings of an outdated email address and updating may mean looking in several different places across different email accounts, different distribution lists, different email applications, and in the same email application but as cached in different modules, sometimes on multiple computers. In spite of these efforts, many of us have still had the experience of using an outdated email address that may have lingered as a suggested completion or possibly in the text of a document inviting us to copy and paste into the "To:" field.

The information we use is rarely normalized in the manner of well-designed databases. We generally copy rather than reference information. Doing so is often easier and more robust in the short run, especially as we work across different applications on different devices. And why not? Storage is cheap. Of course, the "gotcha!" is that updates and corrections later can be extremely difficult to do—even with the aid of a desktop search facility that is able to search across documents, email messages, and web pages.

With respect to updates and corrections, we are concerned not only with the information directly under our control (the first sense of "personal information" as listed in Table 2.2 of Chapter 2). We also need to be able to correct information kept about us by other people and organizations. In particular, we need to be able to correct and update financial information and, even more important, medical information that is kept about us.

Ross and Lin (2003), in a review of several medical studies, note that patients found inaccuracies in their medical records in several of the studies. Many errors were minor, but some were quite serious. In one instance, for example, a pregnant woman corrected her medical record to indicate that she was Rh-negative.[7] In another incident, a patient identified an error that, if left uncorrected, might have permitted a potentially serious drug interaction.

6.3.2 Support and solutions

What can be done to improve the ease and effectiveness with which our information is maintained? Here are a few approaches.

Get someone else to maintain

Not all the information we use needs to be maintained by us. Often, we can use libraries or the Web instead. Sometimes we can also depend on friends, family, and colleagues. Some division of labor often happens among people sharing a household so that, for example, one

---

[7] Complications can develop during pregnancy if the mother is Rh-negative and the fetus is Rh-positive; they are preventable, however, if this combinatoin of blood types is detected in time (see, for example, *http://www.drspock.com/article/0,1510,4429,00.html*).

parent keeps track of all the medical information for their children while the other keeps track of all the photographs and videos for their family. A similar mutualism, or sometimes parasitism, occurs in workgroups as well. Whittaker and Hirschberg (2001) noted the emergence of "informal librarians" in a work setting, with one participant admitting, "I'm selfish. I say that if colleagues have all this, why should I store it? Why should I store duplicates?" (p. 158).

Portable hard drive on call?

Many people who once worked on one desktop computer at home and another at work now carry a notebook computer back and forth with them to be used both at home and at work. The dramatic increases in processing power, memory, and disk capacity on a notebook computer are such that many of us no longer miss the extra power (and expansions slots) of a desktop machine. With a consolidation to one computer we take with us also comes a consolidation of maintenance tasks: one hard drive to back up and clean up instead of two, and no more need to synchronize between two different machines.

I have a colleague who no longer carries the notebook computer either. Instead, he carries a USB or "thumb drive" with him between work and home. At home he has a desktop computer; at work he has a notebook computer. But, from his standpoint, what he has is the thumb drive. This is where he keeps his working information. The capacity of thumb drives is still limited and not everyone would want to adopt the discipline of deciding what information goes on this "life boat" between home and work.

However, there is one device that many of us now carry by habit wherever we go: the cell or mobile phone. As flash memory continues to decrease in cost, and hard drives continue to decrease in physical size even as they increase in storage capacity, we can imagine a time when a working set of information travels with us as a part of the cell phone we are already in the habit of carrying with us. The cell phone would readily "plug" into a computer that happens to be available—whether desktop or notebook. But the phone would also provide a standalone interface for basic interactions with personal information.

Backup services, web-based

Backups of work-related information can happen as supported by the IT department of the place where we work. But we may be reluctant to entrust our personal information (tax records, personal photographs, etc.) even if this were allowed by our workplace (and frequently it is not).

We can back up our information onto CDs, DVDs, or tapes that we keep, but this takes time. And then we need to store the backups. Moreover, backups produced and stored for our personal use—in our homes, most likely—provide only one level of insurance. We're protected against hard-drive failures. But what about a fire that destroys both the original devices (computers, phones) and the backups for information on these devices?

One emerging alternative to "local" backups (on CD, DVDs, or tapes) is web-based backup. Web-based backup would seem to have several advantages. For example, as the sophistication of backup software improves, backups can potentially happen nearly automatically and regularly with very little effort on the part of the user—perhaps as an ongoing background task or as a scheduled event that happens the same time every day. The Web, as a medium of backup, does not have the longevity issues of other storage media since data can be continually copied to newer, "fresher" storage devices. Even so, there are longevity issues. How long will the company providing backups be around? What happens if the company goes bankrupt?

As a variation on web-based backups, Marshall, Bly, and Brun-Cottan (2006) note that people are increasingly using web-based email services as a way to archive information (e.g., by including documents as attachments in self-addressed email messages). However, there is again no assurance that information stored in this way can still be accessed should the company disappear.

Visualize to understand

What information do we have? Where? In what form? How much space is it taking up? How often do we access it? These are important questions to answer first when making important maintaining decisions concerning what information to archive or to move out of the way. Yet many of us may have, at best, only vague answers to these questions. Tools of visualization can help. Several tools derive, for example, from a *treemap* algorithm[8] which provides summary information for a folder hierarchy displayed in a two-dimensional view.

Auto, in-place archiving

Better support of cleanup may come in the form of automated, in-place archiving of old information. People may work for weeks or months in a cluttered space before making any effort to reduce its clutter—and then perhaps only as prompted by an external event such as the visit of an earnest researcher or an especially troubling failure to find information that "is right there in front of me." After all, who has time to delete or move old information? Also, moving information within the hierarchical structures that still predominate in today's information organizations means leaving behind some of the organizing context—the connection to containing folders in the hierarchy.

As already noted, old information doesn't just take up storage space on a computer; it can also take up attentional space. Suppose that the visibility of an item is itself a property that changes over time according to use. Old items could fade gradually from view, perhaps stepping through shades of gray from a state of normal visibility to a state of "invisibility." Invisible items remain searchable and can easily be returned to a state of visibility. Other properties of an item, including its position in an organizing hierarchy, need not change at all. More generally, as Malone (1983) noted so long ago, visible, attention-directing properties might ideally change dynamically as due dates near, projects are completed, or simply with use and disuse. A person can't be expected to manually tinker with attention-directing property values for items. Why can't the system help?

---

[8] See Shneiderman (1992). For more information on the technique of treemapping and links to available tools, see the "Treemapping" Wikipedia article at *http://en.wikipedia.org/wiki/Treemapping*. For more information on DirGraph, a related but alternate approach, see *http://www.spillett.net/~dirgraph/#what*.

What Now for IT?

– Bob Boiko

What should IT organize and maintain? For better or worse, most of your information life takes place at your workplace. Most of the information you consume and output is work-related, and the majority of what you keep, organize, and maintain has to do with your avocation.

What that means is that there is an inevitable overlap between personal and organizational[9] information management and an all too blurry distinction between the two. IT departments have been slow to recognize the implications of this overlap. Two kinds of policy have usually been considered sufficient to cover the breadth of this complex issue:

- *Personal information at work.* Generally, some policy exists that states the restrictions on using the organization's hardware, software, and storage for "personal" information. In the most lax cases, only people who use a noticeably large amount of the organization's storage or bandwidth are sanctioned. In the most strict cases, even a single email message from a friend or family member delivered to your work address can be cause for disciplinary action.

- *Intellectual property.* Generally some policy exists that stipulates what information is owned by the individual and what is owned by the organization. In extremely strict cases, any tangible artifacts created while under the employ of the organization belong to the organization. In more lax cases, the policy prescribes a limited set of work products for which it retains sole or dual ownership.

While undoubtedly useful, these policies provide little direction on these and other wider issues of personal and organizational information management:

- *Personal vs. organizational search and retrieval.* What types and instances of information created by individuals should and must be locatable by which other kinds of employees? Solutions can range from no communal indexing of any personally created information to indexing every hard drive in the network for completely open search and retrieval.

- *Future-proofing.* Very few organizations have any sort of policy on what information types and items must be continually converted to the most recent formats and how to view items that are in old and unsupported formats.

- *Legacy.* When someone leaves an organization, there are few guidelines for what to do with that employee's information. It is usually either deleted or archived. No provision is made for deciding what part of the collection to maintain, who to reassign ownership to, or even what items the former employee can legally take with him or her.

---

[9] In this discussion, we need to use another sense of organization—an organization of people in a workplace (e.g., a private company, a nonprofit, a corporation, or a governmental agency).

- *Archiving and retention.* Most organizations have some sort of archiving policy, but it is most often designed to meet government regulations and address liability issues. No attempt is made to understand the long-term value, or eventual access and reuse, of important information.

IT departments and the policies they create are primarily focused on the hazards of information. Leaked secrets, liability, company property, and viruses are well covered. Less well covered are the opportunities that information can offer. This gap reflects the fact that the value of information is poorly understood by most organizations. If you can't distinguish valuable information from junk, you have to either save all information on the chance that some of it is valuable or get rid of it all to ensure it can do no harm to you. What is needed is greater clarity concerning the relative value (and threat) of the information that an organization, through its people, produces. From such an understanding might come a balanced policy for keeping, organizing, and maintaining the information of an organization as produced by its people.

6.4 Maintaining for later

Maintaining for later (over the next 10 to 30 years) does not mean maintaining later on; it means doing what must be done now with an eye toward longer-term preservation of personal information. Maintaining personal information not only for now but for the future makes each of us a curator, of sorts, of our personal information.

Considerations and concerns that apply to the longer-term maintenance of personal information are again prefaced by questions of what and why: What kinds of information would we want to access again in 10, 20, or 30 years, and why? A partial answer includes some of the same categories listed for "now," but the composition of these categories and the reasons for maintaining this information change somewhat with a longer view in mind:

Precious, irreplaceable. The photographs and videos of friends and family, letters from same, the scrapbooks (paper or digital) with mementos of our lives' events—these items gain value with age—especially as we find we have more time to look at them and as we rely on these information items to resurrect our own fading memories of the people and events from long ago.

Extremely difficult to replace. This category retains all members listed in the previous section, though the reasons to maintain may shift. For example, people may want to maintain information associated with projects completed decades ago as a "for the record" protection in case of legal disputes. They may want to keep the plans from the construction project they did on their house a decade ago, to be available as a reference for the next remodel. Also in this category, when maintaining for the longer run, is information that, though currently available from the Web or other external sources, is not likely to be around indefinitely. As one participant in the Whittaker and Hirschberg (2001) study commented, "I'm not sure that I believe that 10 years from now, stuff that is available on the Web now will still be available. I have no reason to believe that. Zero."

6.4.1 Challenges and considerations

Maintaining personal information for the future, as well as for the present, raises several additional issues.

Version control, context, and shifting from wayfinding to search retrieval

A document or presentation that we are actively working on is likely to exist in multiple versions, each in its own file. This is especially true for documents done in collaboration with or under review by others. Occasionally we may need to decide which of several versions is the correct or current version. Even with computer support for document comparison, deciding between or merging two versions can be a time-consuming, tedious, and error-prone activity.

For the most part, though, we probably avoid version confusion in the near term. We know which folder to look in for the correct version; and perhaps we know it has "current" in its name or "latest." And, of course, we can sort by date.

But the information we use to reach the correct version is only partly "out there." Much of it is "in here," in memories that will fade over time. Moreover, some of the contextual information surrounding a document's access may not be preserved in the process of archiving the document. For example, some information concerning the document's original position in a folder hierarchy may be lost.

For these and other reasons, our preferred method for locating documents, say, 10 years later, is likely to shift from wayfinding to direct search. And a direct search will faithfully return several versions, each of which, like pretenders to a throne, appear to be the "one true one." To avoid major headaches later, attention needs to be given now, at the point of archiving, to methods for indicating which version of a document is the correct, "blessed" version or, alternatively, to methods for eliminating all other versions prior to archiving.

Storage degrades, formats change, passwords are forgotten

Many things change with the passage of time. As already noted, CDs, DVDs, and magnetic tapes degrade with time, and their contents may become unreadable. If we mean to use these media for long-term storage, therefore, we need to follow a companion procedure that includes the periodic transfer or "refresh" of archived information.

Formats change too. New formats emerge; old formats are no longer supported; a format may continue but change considerably over a period of time. Issues of format migration and obsolescence are especially important to address for digital pictures and videos. Even small changes in the nature of a format or its support can seriously alter the appearance of pictures and videos. A larger point is that, in the archiving of digital information, unlike the archiving of paper-based information, we must think about not only the information itself, but also the means for its retrieval, display, and manipulation.

Setting and following a policy for what not to keep

Companies are advised to establish and then enforce policies for what is *not* kept over the long run. Documents and email messages beyond a certain age—their own or that for a larger project or approval process to which they relate—should probably be purged. A document management policy that includes such a document disposal policy—and proof of diligence in its enforcement—can be very important should the company ever be involved in a lawsuit. People are sued too. A verifiable policy concerning what is not kept or what is disposed of with time may be an important element in a person's practice of PIM.

Planning for job departure

We take our work home with us, and occasionally we also deal with personal matters at work. The result is that work-related and non-work-related information becomes intermingled on our computer, in our email accounts, and perhaps also on other devices such as a cell phone or a PDA. C.C. Marshall (2007) notes: "Curation usually starts to be an issue when the individual leaves a job." But perhaps it is better to plan for this eventual separation much earlier and not as we're about to walk out the door. Most of us will change jobs several times during our lives. Even as we begin a new job, therefore, prudence argues for making some plans for an eventual departure from this job. Plans might include some agreement with the company concerning what information is "mine" and what information belongs to the company. Plans might also include ongoing processes to separate one kind of information from the other.

6.4.2 Support and solutions

Many of the concerns and considerations listed above point to the need for more comprehensive document management support for the long-term maintenance of personal information. We now often keep multiple versions and variations (targeting different audiences) of documents and presentations, suggesting a need for version control support. Some of us may need to set and follow policies, which can be documented and verified, concerning what information we keep and for how long. We need help in the preservation and consolidation of password information so that archived information is secure from intruders but still accessible by us. In short, we need some kind of document management system. A challenge is to provide such support without imposing an overly formal, restrictive system of document management that further complicates our individual burdens of information maintenance.

Format assurance

Maintaining support for legacy formats has become a topic of discussion not only among researchers but also in the popular press.[10] Efforts currently under way in support of the archiving and preservation of public information may find eventual application to the

---

[10] See, for example, Hafner (2004).

archiving and preservation of personal information. Various methods proposed or currently under development include:

- Development of a special archival format such as PDF/A[11]
- The emulative support of legacy formats[12]
- Format registries[13]
- Format migration services[14]

We might hope that somewhere—perhaps at the Library of Congress—legacy applications will be preserved that are capable of rendering and supporting the manipulation of information kept in legacy formats, although support for legacy applications, in turn, may require preservation of legacy operating systems and even legacy computers to run all of the above. Better for most of us might be a web-based service to which we could submit information items in legacy formats—especially photographs and videos—and have them returned in a current format of our choice—in a manner reminiscent of the way we once sent exposed film to a film development lab for processing into prints or slides.

Or perhaps the backup service to which we subscribe can also provide a format conversion service so that our digital information is periodically converted from older formats to current formats. However, given the current pace of format migration, such conversions might need to happen every few years.[15] Kuny (1998) questions whether such conversions can ever be perfect. Errors, however small for a given conversion, may be magnified with repeated conversions, in much the same way that a message is distorted as it is passed between kids in the "whisper chain" game that many of us may have played as children.

Information assurance, information insurance?

Maintaining information for the long run brings us back to a discussion of backups. Even all-in-one services like Microsoft's OneCare[16] use backups (onto CDs or DVDs) that are local to—that is, in the same physical space as—the user. Several problems are apparent with this approach: (1) keeping track of various disks becomes a maintenance headache in its own right. (2) Disks last reliably for only 5 to 10 years, or less if not stored properly. (A single scratch can render the disk unreadable.) (3) Backups provide only one level of safeguard—against hard-drive crash or corruption. Backups that are co-located with the computer being backed up may suffer a common fate with the computer for other kinds of disasters—ranging from theft to fire to natural disasters such as flooding, tornadoes, or hurricanes.

---

[11] See LeFurgy (2003).

[12] For a discussion of this approach, see Lorie (2002) and Rothenberg (1998).

[13] For more on format registries, see Arms (2000).

[14] For more discussion on format migration services, see Hunter and Choudhury (2003).

[15] Format changes happen especially often for information items high in multimedia content—pictures, sound, video, and, someday, three-dimensional pictures and holographic projections as well.

[16] See *www.windowsonecare.com*.

Web-based backups, by contrast, can happen with no need to manage local backup disks. The encrypted data that is transferred is, in principle, highly resistant to decoding by a "sniffer." But we are left with a nagging question concerning the companies that provide this backup service—no matter how big and enduring they now appear. Will these companies still be here in 30 years?

We, as consumers, need the assurance that our information will still be there even if the company providing web-based backups disappears. A rough analogy can be drawn to the Federal Deposit Insurance Corporation (FDIC) and the insurance it provides consumers against bank failure. For banks so insured, checking and savings accounts of bank customers are currently each insured up to $100,000. The analogy is imperfect, of course, since money is money and we don't expect to get back exactly the same bills and coins we deposited in the bank—FDIC or no FDIC. But we certainly do expect to get back the same information we "deposited" and would not be at all satisfied if we were to get back an equivalent quantity (i.e., measured in gigabytes) of someone else's information!

Consumers can get another kind of information insurance, however, if—either as mandated by law or on a voluntary basis—companies that provide a backup service also back up their back-ups, so to speak, through arrangement with an accredited, independent company (perhaps itself another backup service). This chapter is certainly not the place to begin a consideration of all the issues that arise and all the details to be worked out. But the discussion reflects a change in attitude concerning our information and its long-term preservation. Information is not just a thing of short-term value. Our information, as a reflection of us, has enduring value in its own right. This is a theme to be explored further in the next section.

What Next in Tool Development?

– Mike Kelly

One serious maintenance problem we all face now are the ghosts of incorrect or outdated information which seem to haunt our efforts to reuse the information in our PSI (Personal Space of Information). We're especially haunted by smaller bits and pieces of outdated information. Months or even years after these change, we may still find ourselves using outdated, incorrect information—the budget number that has been superseded or the email address for a person who has since changed email providers.

Outdated, incorrect information lingers mainly because we don't have a single source of the "truth" and because current facilities of auto-complete, like those described in Chapters 4 and 5 are limited. Our email application, for example, may continue to pro-pose an outdated email address in the "To:" field even though the contact information has been updated. Outdated, incorrect information also lingers because, in our efforts to save on look-up (a finding activity), we are often tempted to copy. We copy from a previous form or document or whatever is close at hand because we would rather not undertake the more time-consuming task of verifying that the information is still correct We also copy to multiple devices which have limited or nonexistent ways to synchronize updates and maintain "one version of the truth" in multiple, loosely connected places (our home computer, our work computer, our mobile phone, etc.)

In Chapters 4 and 5, we considered the benefits of a system-supported auto-complete facility to support finding and keeping, and suggested a common structured storage for personal information. The consistent use of structured storage for the myriad details of our PSI also yields a major maintenance benefit: updating and correcting are also much easier once we access essential facts—the email address or phone number of a person, the budget number for a project—from a central repository maintained by the auto-complete facility rather than simply by grabbing some occurrence of these facts that happens to be close at hand. Moving forward, a fact needs to be updated or corrected in only one place, not in several. If a project's budget number changes, this change is registered in one place for future use and then is automatically propagated out to other places it is needed.

Of course, the facts used by an auto-complete facility need not reside in a single store. The system might use one local store with facts specific to you, and many other stores for facts not specific to you. Facts relating to a company project might be maintained on a corporate intranet site, for example. Contact information for the people we work and socialize with might be maintained on the Web. Sites such as Plaxo (*http://www.plaxo.com*) provide this capability now for e-mail addresses. The emergence of Identity 2.0 standards like "Open ID" (*http://openid.net*) promise to extend knowledge about people to the Web in a decentralized way.

Be careful that what you write does not offend anybody or cause problems within the company. The safest approach is to remove all useful information.

U.S. cartoonist and author Scott Adams (1957–)

6.5 Maintaining for our lives and beyond

Try closing your eyes to take a "mind's eye" tour through familiar regions in your PSI. Do you have an office or workspace? What does it look like? Do you have books? What kinds of books? How are these arranged? Are these books you have read or books you hope to read? Or both? Do you keep textbooks you haven't opened since you were a college student? Books for a vacation in the Alps you hope to take next year? Books on personal information management? And maybe books you borrowed from a friend and have not yet returned?

Do you have a desk? A table? Open shelving? Are there piles of paper on the surfaces of these? On the floor too? What do the piles represent? Tax documents that need to be filed? Articles you hope to read some day? Projects you are working on? Unfinished projects you are no longer working on but hope to get back to some day?

Now continue your tour by looking at your primary computer. Do you frequently use and visit its desktop? How does this virtual desktop appear to you? Does it also have its piles or clusters of icons? What do these represent to you? Are these also projects in various stages of completion (or abandonment)? Do some represent enduring areas of interest? Or web sites to look at on a "rainy day" when you have the time?

Continue your tour by looking at the folders you have taken the trouble to create to hold the different forms of information you work with. Let your, mind's eye scan the folders you have created under "My Documents," a "Home" folder, or something similar. Look at the folders you have created through your email application or your web browser. What are these folders for? Do they represent projects, areas of interest, or "stuff"? Are these folders still active, or have you forgotten what some of them contain?

Now one last thing: Imagine how regions in your space of information appear to other people as they have occasion to see them. If you have your own web site or your own blog, this is an obvious place to start. What are you sharing about yourself? What impressions do you hope to convey? Do you have pictures, lists of activities, projects, organizations, areas of interest? Do these tell a story of you as you are now, as you once were, or as you would like to be? Or a little of each? What about your physical office or workspace? How does this appear to other people when they visit? Consider the books, the pictures, the awards on display, the piles of paper—the overall neatness or messiness of your space. What impression are people likely to form of these informational places, and of you?

This mind's eye exercise brings home the point that the maintenance of our information space is done for reasons that go beyond retrieval and use of personal information for either now or later. Our PSI is a reflection of us—an imperfect, watery reflection, to be sure, with some gaps and distortions, but a reflection even so. Our PSI tells us and those we come into contact with a story about us and our lives—our successes, our aspirations, and our failures too.

In a study involving tours of office spaces maintained by university professors and graduate students, Kaye et al. (2006) observed that the primary purpose of some archives appeared to be to "allow visitors to make a visual sweep of the room in order to take in important aspects of the subject's personality and life's work." Kaye et al. referred to these as "legacy archives" (2006, p. 277). Similarly, in a study by Voida et al. (2005) on the sharing of iTunes libraries, participants were observed to carefully construct a publicly visible portion of their music collection as a means of building a public identity for themselves. Kaye et al. (2006) noted that the "focus of this construction is not just outward, but is also part of the archiver's reinforcement of their perception of their own identity" (p. 279).

6.5.1 Considerations and only a few solutions

How do our personal spaces of information work as a mirror of us and our lives? As seen by others as well as by us? Even after we are dead and gone? How does our information reflect and reinforce our goals, aspirations, and core values in life? These questions bring out a whole new set of maintenance questions—many considerations but only a few tentative solutions.

How can our information reflect and reinforce our goals and values?

We can use our information not just as a means to complete our daily tasks, but also as a means to bring better balance to our lives and to reinforce core goals and values. There are many ways in which people do this already. For example:

- People paste inspirational sayings or goals on the bathroom mirror.
- People place pictures and paintings in view on walls in their office or home—representing loved ones or places they have been or would like to go, or invoking feelings they wish to have.
- People tack up information they want to learn in places where they are likely to spend idle time.
- People have computer screensavers that cycle through a comparable set of pictures.

These methods of bringing information into our lives come for free in the sense that they make idle-time use of our attention. Our attention might otherwise drift to the events of the day or to what we want to have for dinner. Instead, for a time, our attention can be drawn to the people, aspirations, and values of enduring importance to us in our lives.

What else can we do? Pictures on walls and desktops are currently static, and these may fade into a background that we mostly ignore with the passage of time. But now digital picture frames can cycle through a series of pictures. Is this a good thing, or will the constant change (even if change happens only every half hour or so) prove distracting?

Should we (allow ourselves to) forget?

Sometimes management of information is about removing and forgetting rather than saving and remembering. The attentional advantages of moving information out of the way when it is no longer needed on a regular basis were discussed earlier in the "Maintaining for now" section. Old information left lying around can distract and get in the way as we try to attend to current information for current tasks.

When maintaining personal information for life, cleanup takes on a deeper meaning. We need to scrub our spaces, where *scrub* has two meanings of relevance: (1) to clean or scour, and (2) to cancel or eliminate.[17] Sometimes we need to scrub our spaces of old, abandoned projects so that we can get on with our lives. Scrubbing can mean tossing or deleting the

---

[17] As defined in Merriam-Webster Online (*www.m-w.com/cgi-bin/dictionary*).

information associated with scrubbed projects. Trashing paper information is often especially satisfying. Alternatively, some people may prefer to archive information for scrubbed projects as a kind of "final interment." Perhaps in this spirit, Kaye et al. (2006) note that sometimes "archives were meant for storage, but not necessarily for retrieval: putting things away and into the right place was much more important in this type of archive than ever retrieving items again" (p. 277).

A last will and testament

Our information is not only for us. Our information can also be for those who survive us. Just as surely as our physical effects are bequeathed to our loved ones and friends through a last will and testament, we can think of bequeathing our information to those who survive us.

Our paper-based information (books, working notebooks, and other papers) can follow along with our other physical effects. For our digital information, we may need to take extra care to ensure that passwords and access permissions are also provided. C. C. Marshall (2007) notes, for example, that modern password protection "has proven to be a very real obstacle in military situations in which soldiers' email cannot be accessed by relatives after the soldiers' deaths" (p. 68).

Will we ever replace paper?

We use paper in the here and now as a very flexible, portable, disposable form in which to represent information. Paper printouts, for example, can be bent, folded, stuffed in a briefcase, taken with us to be read on the bus or while we wait for a meeting to start. Paper doesn't need a computer or a power supply. And when we're done, we can simply throw the printout away, secure in the knowledge that the same information can be printed out again later if needed.

However, when backing up data either as an immediate precaution or for access a few decades later, the focus is mostly on digital backup. Printing out a paper copy of even a small subset of our information can prove time-consuming and cumbersome. Paper also takes an enormous amount of space, and paper-based information is not in a form that can be used by our scores of digitally based tools and gadgets.

But when we think about keeping information for generations, consideration must return again to the benefits of paper. I have a *McGuffey's Reader* used by my grandfather when he was a school child at the turn of the last century. The pages have browned with age but are still perfectly legible. Under favorable circumstances and when the paper is of good quality, information as recorded on paper or its precursors, such as parchment and papyrus, can last for centuries or even millennia (as the Dead Sea Scrolls attest). To be sure, paper-based information can literally go up in the smoke of a fire, or be washed away in a flood, but barring such disasters, its degradation is gradual.

Compare paper to digital information. Digital information can disappear in a microsecond through device failure, a mistake in copying, or the actions of a computer virus. The lifetime of CDs, DVDs, tapes, and other magnetic storage is measured at best in decades, not in centuries and certainly not in millennia. The Web, in theory, can be forever, as digital information is continually copied to newer, fresher storage media. But will there be a Web in 2,000 years? Given the turmoil of the past 2,000 years, what can we say with confidence? A future civilization may learn about our own civilization, including our fantastic Web, from the few surviving paper documents it is able to uncover.

What Now for You and Me?

Here are some steps we can take now, without waiting for better tools or better IT support, in order to improve the maintenance of our personal information:

- *Offload, delegate, collaborate.* Not all the information we need has to be maintained by us. The maintenance of some work-related collections can be delegated to subordinates or coordinated with colleagues. Similarly, in a household, different household members can agree to maintain different information collections of shared use and relevance (e.g., one parent may maintain medical information for the children, while another maintains all tax-relevant information).

- *Consolidate.* Placing all working information onto a thumb drive or some other portable drive may be too radical a solution for many of us. But if we find ourselves moving between several different computers and other gadgets in a typical day, we might ask ourselves if all are really necessary. Can we simplify? Simplification reduces information fragmentation, with savings across several activities of PIM.

- *Back it up!* Consider sending important information between backups in self-addressed email messages. A backup plan should cover not only the hard drive of your primary computer(s), but also email accounts (even if you decide to entrust this to others, you should still inquire into their backup plans) and other gadgets, including cell phones and PDAs. Backup plans should be realistic. If you find yourself putting off a backup because of the time and trouble, consider an alternate plan. Consider web-based backup services. Consider even backing up on your spouse's computer if the alternative is not to back up at all.

- *Clean up!* But move, don't delete, digital information. Avoid the "deletion paradox" and the "old magazine effect" as described previously in this chapter. Simply move digital information out of the way with the assurance that you can always move it back or search for it later if necessary. Not sure where to put it? How about a folder called "Stuff I moved on <date>"?

- *Scrub.* Toss or give a decent burial to old projects you will never do. Get on with life.

- *Anoint the "correct, current" version of a document or presentation.* Adopt a naming convention and then stick with this convention. Not sure what convention to use? How about <name of document> followed by "current"? And then make it so! Make sure there is only one "current" file for this document on your primary computer, and make sure this version is in fact the latest, greatest version.

- *Avoid archival use of exotic, application-specific formats.* Fortunately, many applications are now supporting standard formats such as XML, MPEG, and JPEG. But exercise care even in the use of these formats. These too will change over time, and the ability to render your information at a later time may depend on elements of each (e.g., a specific document type definition) that are no longer supported. For information that is especially precious, consider non-digital archiving—perhaps on high-quality paper or even microfiche.

This list is only a beginning. You will think of other maintenance dos and don'ts. Add to it.

6.6 Looking back, looking forward

This chapter has considered maintenance as a kind of PIM activity related to and often occurring with organizing but with its own set of challenges and potential solutions. Maintaining is for now, for later, and for our lives and beyond:

- *Maintaining for now.* We need to back up not only our computer hard drives, but also the storage on other devices such as our cell phones and our digital cameras. Backups need to happen regularly and, as nearly as possible, automatically. What takes our time and attention is apt to be postponed. Web-based backups show special promise, but what happens to our information should a company providing such a service go out of business? Tools also need to help us in the updating and correction of our information—not only the information we own, but also information about us (especially medical and financial information) that is kept by others

- *Maintaining for later.* Will we still be able to see our digital photographs and videos 30 years from now and at the same level of fidelity? What about the storage medium itself? For how long is it reliable? If information stays on an old computer, will we still be able to boot it later? If information is password protected, where do the passwords go? These are questions of maintenance to be faced if information is to be kept for decades rather than years. Web-based backup again shows promise as a way to address problems in degradation of the storage medium. Problems of format obsolescence are less easily addressed. Approaches to difficult solutions range from the development of special archival formats (where possibly some ability to manipulate information is lost but essential content is preserved) to format registries and format emulation to services supporting format conversion.

- *Maintaining for our lives and beyond.* How does our information reflect, remind, and reinforce our values, goals, hopes, and fears? These are questions we'll look at again in the final chapter as we consider what it means to have an informational home (rather than simply a house). Also we need to think of our information as a legacy. Who owns or has access to our information when we are gone?

Many issues of maintenance discussed in this chapter were first met in other disciplines, including information and library science, information retrieval, database management, document management, and even software development. There are concerns that our society may be entering a "digital dark age" for want of a sustainable, coherent policy to guide (and restrain) us in our head-long pursuit of digital conversion of information.[18] These societal concerns have their counterpart in the management of our personal information.

This chapter's discussion of maintenance has often turned to the treatment of information as an object to be saved and preserved much as the curators might work to preserve artifacts in a museum. But certainly our information is not at all inert. If flows in and out of our lives, often pulling us along as it moves. The next chapter is about managing the flow of personal information.

---

[18] See Kuny (1998) for a provocative discussion of potential failures associated with exclusive reliance on digital information.

Managing privacy and the flow of information

Information flows from us and to us. We manage flow to protect our time, our attention, our money, . . . ourselves. Who sees what information when? What information, from whom, gets our time and attention? We're easily pushed and pulled by individual informational events. If the television is on, we'll watch. If the phone rings, we'll answer. Managing flow means focusing on channels of information and not individual events. We manage information not just to protect, but to project. We manage not just for privacy, but for power.

Chapter
Seven

The closing of a door can bring blessed privacy and comfort—the opening, terror. Conversely, the closing of a door can be a sad and final thing—the opening a wonderfully joyous moment.

U.S. commentator, producer, and author Andy Rooney (1919–)

7.1 Starting out

Bob was late to his appointment last week to see a specialist about an apparent heart palpitation. Bob was also a week late in paying the monthly bill on one of his credit cards. And late the month before, too. Bob and his wife Carol sold their old house for $349,000 in April and purchased the house they currently live in that same month for $449,000. They are currently remodeling the kitchen. Their three children Christopher, age 10, Molly, age 8, and Sidney, age 6, all attend the elementary school a half mile from their house.

What do these private facts about Bob, Carol, and their children have in common? They are all, to different degrees, a matter of public record. Bob's visit to the specialist, the outcome of the visit, and even the fact that Bob was late (and seemed "slightly agitated") are part of a report that the specialist sent back to Bob's primary care physician and that is now a part of Bob's medical record. Information about Bob's tardiness in paying his credit card bill is kept by the credit card company. Bob's pattern of being late in payments is a part of his credit history and possibly available to banks and lending institutions for inspection should Bob ever apply for a loan. Information about the sale of Bob and Carol's old house and their purchase of their current house is maintained by the government of the county in which they reside and is available online via the Web.

Bob's story is not unique. Technologies of storage and search enable others—government agencies, private companies, authorized parties, and unauthorized parties—to keep large amounts of data about each of us in readily searchable, accessible, combinable forms. As noted in Chapter 6, technologies in support of keeping and finding have outpaced technologies and procedures for properly maintaining the data stored and ensuring its integrity. As a result, even a simple update—of a person's email address, phone number, or marital status—becomes extremely problematic. Bob is still receiving email, for example, on an old email account that he had hoped to decommission two years ago.

This chapter is about privacy and, more generally, about the flow of information. How can we control the flow of our personal information—and also personally relevant information—to our best advantage? For personal information as kept and maintained by others, we seek control over who sees what and when (and under which circumstances). We don't want our tax records "flowing" to telemarketers, for example. But often the best way to control information about us "out there" is to keep it from getting there in the first place.

This chapter is also about the constant flow of information directed toward us. People stop by our office at work. Telemarketers call us during the dinner hour. The dryer beeps loudly to tell us the cycle has ended. Alerts on our computers tell us of new email, new updates, the restoration of a lost connection, and other information that distracts us from and is not relevant to our current task. This too is a flow of information—directed toward us. The inflow of information, in many forms, must also be controlled if we're to keep our concentration, our productivity, our precious time with our family, our solitude, and our sanity.

Consider some more examples of flow involving Bob.

Bob receives a message sent by a colleague at work to a large distribution list. The message describes an upcoming reorganization. Bob replies to the colleague expressing concerns and asking that his comments not be shared with others. Unfortunately for Bob, the entire distribution list has been included on his response. Bob's "private and confidential" message is now resting in the inboxes of 300 fellow employees.

At home, Bob downloads the update to a free software application, clicking "OK" and "I accept" along the way without taking the time to really understand what he is agreeing to. Bob clicks "OK" on one page before realizing he left checked a box requesting that he receive regular email updates concerning "news and announcements" from the software maker. How else will Bob's email address be used or circulated? What else has Bob agreed to?

Bob's day has been a blur of interruptions and interruptions of interruptions. He has moved from meeting to meeting, handling phone calls, email messages, and instant messages in between meetings and also within meetings. Most meetings, phone calls, email messages, and instant messages relate to an upcoming reorganization within his company. Bob is working hard to be sure that he and his group are minimally affected. By the day's end, Bob feels exhausted, but he can't really point to anything that has been accomplished. As Bob tries to relax with his family over dinner, they receive several unsolicited phone calls.

Bob remembers the blissful feeling he had a few weeks ago of "running on all cylinders" as he moved through the work of his day. Everything just seemed to fall into place. The information he needed to write his group's marketing plan was readily at hand. Bob was very happy with the report's organization and direction. At the end of that day, Bob felt energized and even decided to stop by the hardware store on the way home to complete a task he'd been putting off (the return of a drill that wasn't working).

Each scenario involves flow. Information flows from us. Information flows toward us. And sometimes we're in a "flow" with concentrated time to complete a task and all the needed information at hand.

The management of privacy and information flow is explored in this chapter through discussion that moves through the following sections:

- ☑ *Getting oriented.* Issues of privacy and information flow arise for each sense of personal information described in Chapter 2 (see Table 7.1).

- ☑ *Managing the outflow.* This section deals with issues commonly associated with privacy. Focus is primarily on the second sense of personal information—information about us. The best place to exercise control is at points where information about us (e.g., our credit card number or email address) is about to flow outward from regions of the PSI we control to regions under the control of others (such as companies we do business with on the Web).

- ☑ *Managing the inflow.* This section deals primarily with the third sense of personal information—information directed toward us. We want to protect not only the privacy of our information, but also the privacy of our time and our solitude. Even good information can become too much, resulting in information overload. In managing this kind of information, the challenge is less to protect the information itself than to protect ourselves and our precious time and attention from incursions.

- ☑ *Staying in the flow.* A lawyer once told me that he felt that he got 90 percent of his "real work" done in 10 percent of his time. Most of us occasionally have periods when everything seems to come together, our energy levels are high, and a great deal is accomplished. Not only is more work accomplished during such periods, but the quality of this work is often better. There is no sure formula for getting into such periods of flow, but this section will review some of the requisites for creating opportunities for such periods of flow to occur.

7.2 Getting oriented

The previous two chapters have talked about the meta-level activities of organization and maintenance as an extension to the keeping of information. This chapter is about the management of privacy and the flow of information. This too is a meta-level activity in both the "about/above" and "after" senses of "meta."

- *About/above.* Questions about privacy and the flow of information are better addressed from a broader perspective. For example, how do costs and benefits for different policies accrue over time?

• *After.* Dealing with issues of privacy and information flow is not a primary goal for most people. People are busy trying to get things done. Also, people are unclear how best to address these issues. The result is that the management of privacy and information flow becomes an afterthought to be dealt with in a "later" that never comes.

Table 7.1 Issues of privacy and flow arise for each kind of personal information

	Relation to "me"	Privacy issues	Flow direction and means of control
1	Controlled by, owned by me	Security against break-ins or theft	In/out: virus protection, firewalls
2	About me	Who sees what when (under which circumstances)? Does it ever go away?	Out: security controls in web browser (e.g., disabling certain uses of "cookies"); legal protections; support for P3P; detection of "phishing"
3	Directed toward me	What information gets our attention (energy, time) from whom (or what source) and when? What's the right balance between blocking everything and blocking nothing?	In: junk email filters, pop-up blockers, do-not-call lists
4	Sent (posted, provided) by me	Who sees what when? Did the message get through?	Out: distribution lists, "Do not distribute" requests
5	Experienced by me	Do we want a web site to know that we've been there? Can people see what books we've checked out of a library?	Out: security controls in web browser (#5 is a special case of #2—information about "me")
6	Relevant (useful) to me; about to be experienced by me	How to filter out or otherwise avoid information we don't wish to see. (How to do likewise for our children.)	In: filters, content blockers

Concerns of privacy bring us back to the several senses of "personal" described in Chapter 2 and summarized here (see Table 7.1).

1. Information controlled by, owned by me

Included in this category is the information we keep on our computers, in email accounts, on network shares, and the like. We need security protections not unlike those we seek for protection of our physical belongings—our houses, cars, and the valuables within. We need protection against break-ins, vandalism (e.g., in the form of computer viruses that may corrupt our data), theft, snooping, and outright takeover (e.g., the use of our computer to store and distribute pornography). Issues of computer and data security are beyond the scope of this book.[1]

2. Information about me (outflow)

Information about us often starts out under our control but then flows into the hands of others and out of our control. The best place to exercise control, then, is often at the point where information passes from our immediate control to an outside person or organization. In practice, such control is often difficult or impossible to exercise. When reading through a document filled with legalese—whether online or on paper—our inclination is often simply to mark "I accept" to get on with the task we're trying to complete. And we're generally not given alternatives short of "take it or leave it." Information concerning our finances and our health is especially sensitive. Yet forms relating to both kinds of information often give us little choice other than to sign to release (if we want advice or treatment).

3. Information directed toward me (inflow)

The whole world, it sometimes seems, is trying to get our attention (and our time and money). Phones ring, TVs blare (especially during commercials), billboards loom. Web pages include advertisements that move to grab our attention. Even trusted applications and the operating system of our personal computer may distract. The Microsoft Office Assistant, dubbed "Clippy" (actually officially "Clippit"), distracted people even though it was designed to help. If Clippy is gone, other distractions still abound, ranging from the balloon notifications that pop up (and disappear) without warning to the red squiggly lines under words in a document that invite us to break our train of thought to fix a spelling error.

4. Information sent (or posted) by me (outflow)

Many of us have had the experience of pressing "Send" only to realize that a response intended for only one or two people is going out to an entire distribution list. Even as we send information outward, we desire to keep some control over who sees this information. We might at least like to slow the spread of information through requests we include in the message (e.g., "This information about the company reorganization should not be shared with your direct reports for the time being").

---

[1] See the computer security article in Wikipedia for an excellent introductory discussion of the issues (*en.wikipedia. org/wiki/Computer_security*).

5. Information experienced by me (outflow)

Our access to information is personal even if the information itself is not about us or owned by us. We may prefer to keep private the books we check out of a library or purchase at a bookstore ("brick-and-mortar" or online). Similarly, we may prefer to disable Web "cookies" that might provide the web sites we visit with personal information concerning who we are and how we can be reached.

6. Information I will (will want to, will not want to) experience (inflow)

We try to create a private space for ourselves and our children in which our values are preserved—a space that is free of offensive or gratuitously disturbing encounters. In our physical world, we may accomplish this by avoiding the proverbial "red light" district and maybe also by avoiding certain people. It is harder to do this online as we read our email or surf the Web. We seek filters that can screen out material that is offensive or "junk."

Note that sense #6—information we will (will want to, will not want to) experience—is in opposition to #5—information we have already experienced.[2] After we've experienced the information, it reverts to sense #5 of "personal." If the information is useful, we might later want to return to the information. Search support for filtering new information both out and in and for re-finding information already experienced is explored in more detail in Chapter 11.

Issues of privacy that relate to #5 have to do with the record of what we've experienced. This record, separate from the information itself, is a kind of private information, and we may want to control who has access to this information. One important aspect of #4—information sent (or posted) by us—is the email we send, and this is discussed in greater detail in Chapter 10.

The remaining sections in this chapter focus primarily on control over two other senses of personal information—information about us (sense #2) and information directed toward us (sense #3). Discussion is cast in terms of managing flow—managing outflow and managing inflow. Again, aside from legislation, we can't stop other people from directing information our way. Our main control is over what gets in to grab our time and attention. Similarly, leaving aside legislation, the best way to control the information that others have about us is to keep them from getting this information in the first place.

I've never looked through a keyhole without finding someone was looking back.

U.S. actress and singer Judy Garland (1922–1969)

---

[2] Sense #6 can also be contrasted with #3—information directed toward us. Both are about the inflow of information. Sense #3 is information as "pushed" to us from other people (and organizations); #6 is information that we "pull" toward us. Even when the initiative is ours, even when we're doing the pulling, we can still make mistakes. We can stumble onto offensive information we would rather not experience. Even more likely, our children are at risk of doing this as they browse the Web.

7.3 Managing the outflow

With each email we send, with each item we buy, with each web page we view, possibly with every step we take, we potentially provide information about ourselves that can be used by others. Living—even living as a reclusive shut-in—provides information to others. This fact is not new, as anyone in a small town can attest. What is new is the extent to which information about us—about the impression we make on the world around us—is recorded in digital forms that can be stored, transmitted, and then later retrieved by nearly anyone, anywhere, at any time. Our digital information age has brought several profound changes that impact our privacy:

1. *Digital storage continues to increase in capacity and decrease in cost.* Michael Shamos (2007) notes that, by the year 2010, according to current projections, "$1000 will be able to buy 50 terabytes of disk, enough to store 200K bytes of information on every person in the United States." Keeping information about people is cheap. Ever-increasing amounts of information are maintained, including our credit history, medical information, tax records, purchase decisions, academic records, employment histories, and so on.

2. *Devices to record information digitally are becoming ubiquitous.* Certainly, our computer-mediated interactions with people and information sources are easily recorded, including our exchanges via email and instant messaging, our web site visits, and our web-based purchases. Digital records are also made of purchases done offline—at the grocery store or a gas station, for example. Moreover, cameras may record us as we stand in line to make the purchase.

3. As supported by computer-based tools of search and data mining, *large quantities of digital information can be rapidly searched and combined* in ways that would have been far too costly and time-consuming to complete for paper-based information. Items of information combined can tell a story concerning who we are, where we live, the names of our children, and the assessed value of our house, even though each item by itself might seem to say very little.[3]

4. In our digital age, *the advantage of anonymity is not with us, who wish to protect our privacy, but with the people who wish to violate this privacy.* A peeping Tom in physical space risks discovery. Not so his cyber analog, who may be able to sift through large amounts of information about you or me in complete anonymity and from the privacy of his (not our) home office or a coffee shop. There is now a verb reflecting the enormous popularity of the Google search service: We talk about "googling" someone. "Googling" limited to the publicly available information on the Web seems harmless enough. But maybe not. How much of our life is available somewhere online for someone to piece together if they take the trouble?

5. As a corollary to observations #1 and #2, *information kept in digital form can readily stay in digital form—forever.* The pictures and viewpoints a person posts to the Web in an act of youthful indiscretion can lie dormant in a web archive only to come back decades later when the person is trying to build a life.

---

[3] See Malin and Sweeney (2004) and Sweeney (2002) for discussions on how to protect privacy when a person can be identified through a "process of elimination" assembly of information pieces, none of which are identifying in their own right.

One comment I sometimes hear in discussions of PIM and privacy is that young people seem not to care much about privacy. The conclusion is sometimes reached that a generational shift has taken us to a point where issues of privacy matter less than they used to. Perhaps the young are merely the first to accept Scott McNealy's dictate that "you have zero privacy anyway. . . . Get over it."[4] But there are reasons to believe that youthful nonchalance concerning matters of privacy will fade when age brings careers, families, and reputations that might suffer or even be lost through the revelations of youthful acts. Even if we understand our acts to be those of a distant self we barely recognize, others may still attribute these actions to us.

Michael Shamos, an attorney specializing in matters of personal privacy, provides an example from his own life that illustrates the points above and the ways in which large quantities of information kept in digital form profoundly alter the privacy landscape. A Web-accessible database is kept by the government of the county in which he resides[5] that contains information about houses and other buildings in the county:

> You'll learn my wife's name, how much we paid for the house, its assessed value, how many bathrooms it has, that we have central heating and air conditioning, how much we pay in real estate taxes, whether we were ever delinquent in paying, how much we were assessed in penalties, and a lot more data you didn't imagine the county even knew. You will also be treated to a photo of my house and its floor plan. (Shamos, 2007, p. 261)

The county provides the information as a public service, with many legitimate uses. In particular, people can view the database to judge the fairness of their property assessment. But this public disclosure of personal information can be used in harmful ways too. Thieves planning a break-in would find it very useful to know the layout of the house and of neighboring houses as well. Knowing that a particular house doesn't yet have central air conditioning could certainly provide a useful cover should a concerned neighbor discover the would-be thieves and ask what their intentions are ("We're here to install central air conditioning . . .").

The database has obvious commercial value as well. Companies selling the installation of central air conditioning, for example, would certainly find it useful to have a listing, nicely sorted by homeowner's last name, of addresses and phone numbers for houses that do not yet have central air conditioning.

Shamos notes a problem with an asymmetry in our digital information age: a great deal of information about a person is a matter of public record, but the access to and use of this information is not. Personal information kept in a web-based database can be accessed quickly, easily, and *anonymously* by anyone, anywhere, anytime. The person being studied is none the wiser. In olden times (that is, just a few years ago), retrieval of like information would have required a trip to the county courthouse and the issuance of a formal, traceable request for the information. Farther back, with no public record to inspect, would-be thieves would have had to go to the neighborhood to case the house—thus creating the possibility that they could be reciprocally observed by the homeowner.

[4] See Springer (1999).

[5] Allegheny County, Pennsylvania (*www2.county.allegheny.pa.us/RealEstate/Search.asp*).

Grudin (2001) notes that when vast amounts of information can be kept cheaply, and indefinitely, in web-accessible form for global access, "we never truly know the full context in which we act—where, when, or by whom our actions may be interpreted. Casual e-mail can turn up in a court case years later, for example" (p. 280).

7.3.1 Don't let it out in the first place?

Once personal information is out, it's out—"the genie is out of the bottle." There is very little we can do to control or even correct the information that others have about us. To the extent that we have any control at all, it is usually in deciding what information gets out in the first place.

One policy is to let out as little information as possible. But this is not a practical solution for most of us. Some distribution of personal information can be very useful. Alan Westin (1967) noted that "each individual is continually engaged in a personal adjustment process in which he balances the desire for privacy with the desire for disclosure and communication of himself to others" (p. 7).

Grudin notes, for example, that "[d]espite well-circulated accounts of the extensive collection, aggregation, and interpretation of credit and debit card transactions to identify purchasing patterns, people would rather use them than make the effort to carry cash" (p. 279).

In general, people accept some risk in disclosure for compensating benefits. It is now common for people in an organizational setting to provide at least a busy/free level of access to their calendar information. There are risks of even this rough level of disclosure—a workplace enemy might use this information to plan an office "coup." But people consider these risks to be more than offset by the advantages of disclosure, including much greater ease in scheduling meetings.[6]

A Harris Poll conducted in 2003[7] divided the 1010 adults who responded into three categories based on their privacy concerns: (1) "Privacy fundamentalists" (24%) were strongly resistant to any further erosion in their privacy. (2) "Privacy unconcerned" people (10%) had no strong concerns about privacy. (3) The large middle ground (64%) was occupied by "privacy pragmatists." Privacy pragmatists feel strongly about the protection of their privacy against abuses or unauthorized uses of their personal information. But they are also willing to share their information with others when the apparent benefits outweigh the risks.

Most of us, then, are busy pragmatists. We don't mind taking some chances in order to get things done. We'll take a calculated risk by clicking "Yes" or checking "I accept," especially if there is little alternative other than to abandon the transaction or the inquiry altogether.

But would we like to establish a middle ground between no disclosure at one extreme and full disclosure at the other? Studies show that the willingness to share personal information can vary considerably, depending on the type of information, who wants to see it, and for what

---

[6] See, for example, Palen (1999) for a discussion of costs and benefits relating to sharing calendar information.

[7] See Taylor (2003).

reasons.[8] Our concerns and our desire to restrict public access to private information are also likely to vary with gender and, perhaps more generally, according to our perceptions of our own vulnerability and the likelihood of being harmed.[9]

We may have vague, difficult to articulate notions concerning different classes of personal information and different classes of people with access to this information, under different circumstances. For example, under normal circumstances, we may want only our doctor and close friends and family to know about a diabetic condition. But in cases of an emergency, it becomes essential that the people treating us have this information.

Phishing

Phishing refers to a kind of deception practiced through the Internet. The perpetrator poses as a legitimate company—often a bank or credit card company—and attempts to trick people into providing personal information—an account number, password, or credit card number, for example. The email message in Figure 7.1, for example, is pretending to be from PayPal, a legitimate service (*www.paypal.com*).

People who follow the email's instructions are directed to a fake PayPal web site where they are asked to enter their PayPal password. The ruse is easily detected in this case (we might hope the sender of a genuine PayPal message could spell better). But a more skilled attempt might not be so easy to detect. Moreover, the information (e.g., account number/name and password) is precisely the information you would be asked to provide at the legitimate site.

Phishing or its analog is not just practiced on the Internet, of course. Is the parking lot attendant who is asking for your car keys legitimate or an imposter who will steal your car? Not a bad idea to check. What about the phone message you receive, purportedly from your credit card company, informing you that "there may have been an unauthorized use" of your credit card and directing you to call a number where, naturally, you are asked first to give your credit card number? Again, this is the same information that you might be asked to provide when calling a legitimate credit card company. How do you know whether the caller is legitimate or not? Check the back of your credit card and call the number listed there, no matter what number you're given.

> Paypal Inc Departament   2:12 AM
> Online Update !
> Activate with PayPal Mobile - You Could Be a Winner.
> Activate your phone now for PayPal Mobile, and you could win one of 45,000 mystery cash prizes of up to $1,000.

Figure 7.1   A clumsy "phishing" attempt.

---

[8] For research relating to the conditional nature of our willingness to share personal information, see Ackerman (2000); Ackerman, Cranor, and Reagle (1999); Bellotti and Sellen (1993); and Consolvo et al. (2005).

[9] See, for example, Friedman et al. (2006).

7.3.2 Walking the talk

Regardless of what we mean to do in order to protect our privacy and security, we're often drawn into situations where we must (quickly) make decisions impacting our privacy and security without clearly understanding the implications of the decisions being made.

How many of us click "No" to the questions posed in either dialog of Figure 7.2? And yet how many of us really understand the implications of clicking "Yes"? Or, similarly, how many of us carefully read the terms of an online agreement (for a download, for example) before checking "I Accept" and clicking "Continue"? The problem now is that we often have little choice between "Yes" and "No" and lack the time to decide even *between* these two alternatives.

Certainly we need to avoid *phishers* (see sidebar) who try to con us into providing sensitive information such as a credit card number or account number and password under the guise of being a provider with a legitimate need for such information. But, all too easily, we can be drawn into dialogs with legitimate providers where we wind up providing information we would prefer to keep private. Do we faithfully enter our home, work, and mobile phone numbers into a form when none of these is logically needed for completion of the transaction? Or, where forms insist on some non-null entry, do we think to satisfy the form by filling in a single number—such as a main reception number for our office—for all three questions?

Figure 7.2 How many of us click "No" to dialogs such as these?

Spiekermann, Grossklags, and Berendt (2001) describe a study in which people interact with a simulated online service (a "shopping bot") as they shop for either a compact camera or a winter jacket. Study participants—even those who rated themselves as privacy conscious—answered most questions posed by the service. Participants generally answered personal questions that had little to do with the purchase (such as "How photogenic do you consider yourself to be?").

Other studies reinforce an impression that people may be overly trusting of online services. Jensen, Potts, and Jensen (2005) found that people are inclined to read too much into indicators such as the TRUSTe mark or a privacy policy. The actual content (sometimes pages of "legalese") may differ widely from consumer expectations, and the means of enforcing these policies may diverge still further. Jensen and Potts (2004) found that while most surveys of user concerns about privacy show high rates of such behaviors as reading the privacy policy or taking concrete actions to protect their privacy, informal analysis of log-file data suggests that the actual rates of these user behaviors are much lower.

Business can frequently make matters worse. Karat et al. (2006) note that business privacy policies are often vaguely expressed (e.g., "Customer service reps will only use your personal information for the efficient conduct of our business") and subject to considerable variation in interpretation when translated into rules that can actually be enforced (and upheld in a court of law). Based on a meta-analysis of 30 consumer studies, Teltzrow and Kobsa (2004) concluded that the great majority of businesses still provide inadequate controls for the storage and access to personal information. Worse, businesses do not provide adequate means for the verification and correction of data stored.

Enhanced legal restrictions with strict penalties for failures of implementation and adherence could be a useful step toward better privacy protection. For example, privacy laws in European Union (EU) countries mandate the registration of data gatherers, who are highly constrained in the data they are allowed to collect from people. Moreover, the subjects of the data being collected must give permission before this information can be shared with others, and information can only be shared with other approved data gatherers. Data gatherers who fail to follow these rules essentially lose their accreditation—a very serious penalty indeed for companies whose business depends on the ready availability of consumer information. However, these rules create serious problems for non-EU companies who want to do business in Europe and for European companies who want to partner with companies based elsewhere in order to provide basic services to their customers.[10] Moreover, as Shamos notes, EU-style privacy laws are not likely to be adopted in the United States and, in fact, conflict with a variety of state-level freedom of information and "sunshine" laws.

For some time to come, then, protections of privacy and personal information—its collection, use, and dissemination—are likely to be a "lumpy" patchwork that varies by country, by local governments within countries, and according to standards voluntarily adopted by companies—especially companies doing business on the Web.

---

[10] For a discussion of business challenges presented by EU privacy laws, see Swire and Litan (1998) and Wearden (2002).

Given this great diversity in privacy standards, the burden seems to remain with each of us to determine whether the privacy practices of a company or organization (web-based or not) provide us with acceptable protection or, at least, acceptable risk when balanced against the services provided. Consumers beware.

7.3.3 Privacy controls people can understand

We may need to decide, case by case, what information to provide to whom and when. But that doesn't mean we should have to decide alone or without assistance. We can benefit from help to:

1. Articulate a privacy policy we can use consistently and that we can use to "center ourselves" against our inclinations to be too chatty, too trusting, or too hurried in actual interactions.

2. Match our privacy policy against the stated policy of the organization with which we mean to interact.

3. Verify that the organization is actually following the privacy policy it espouses.

Item #2, matching our privacy preferences against the privacy policy espoused by an organization, lies at the heart of what P3P is about (see sidebar). Unfortunately, there appears to be little yet in support of item #3, verifying that organizations actually follow their privacy policy as advertised. Sites can earn a TRUSTe seal, for example, based on a privacy policy that they don't actually follow (though this seal can later be withdrawn if valid complaints are registered with TRUSTe). Perhaps TRUSTe or a similar agency will evolve in the sophistication of their testing so that sites that don't adhere to their published policy can be detected more quickly.

Articulating a privacy policy that accurately reflects our preferences and that can be flexibly applied to the many situations we face is a challenge in its own right. Giving people "security controls they can understand and privacy they can control for the dynamic, pervasive computing environments of the future" has been identified as a major research challenge by the Computing Research Association (CRA) Conference on Grand Research Challenges in Information Security and Assurance (*Computer Research Association*, 2003). Whitten and Tygar (1999) point out that "security mechanisms are only effective when used correctly."

Several efforts are under way to support people in their efforts to articulate privacy preferences that they can live with. As part of their development of a Server Privacy Architecture and Capability Enablement (SPARCLE) workbench, Karat and her associates[11] have explored variations in a user interface that allows people to enter privacy preferences as natural language statements. Olson, Grudin, and Horvitz (2005) describe an effort to determine meaningful groupings of information types and information recipients based on a small set of qualifying questions. Clustering is used to generate a hierarchy of classes for both information type and information recipients. Using categories within these hierarchies, users can choose to exercise a coarse-grained or fine-grained control over who has access to what information.

---

[11] See C. M. Karat, Brodie, and J. Karat (2005, 2006); C. M. Karat (2006); and J. Karat et al. (2005).

As efforts such as these develop, we can imagine a day when each of us has a coherent, enforceable policy of personal information sharing. Such a policy would be applied, for example, to a personal web site, not only to control access but to determine who is notified concerning what updates in web site content. The policy would also apply to the information that others—credit card companies, medical providers, tax agencies, and the like—keep about us. And we might even hope that the policy could travel with the information as it is transferred between organizations.[12]

P3P: Platform for Privacy Preferences Project

P3P (Platform for Privacy Preferences Project) is a World Wide Web Consortium (W3C)-sponsored initiative aimed at support of a common language for representation of privacy preferences and policy. P3P provides for the expression of personal privacy preferences and web site privacy policies in a comparable XML format, as well as mechanisms for locating and transporting these expressions.

Statements of preference and policy can be compared automatically through a browser add-in such as Privacy Bird®[13] and discrepancies are noted and displayed to the user. If, for example, a person's privacy preferences specify that contact information (such as email address or phone number) should not be shared with third parties but the web site's privacy policy allows for such distribution, this discrepancy can at least be called to the person's attention. The person can then decide to abandon the transaction or proceed—forewarned in any case.

P3P includes provisions for expressing policy and preference as these apply to the kinds of personal information a web site may collect, how this information is used, how long this information is kept, and whether or not the person can access and correct it later on.

To better understand the motivations for P3P, consider Figure 7.3 with its representation of a portion of the web page that appears when I begin the process of downloading an update for the iTunes software on my computer. Notice, first of all, that boxes are checked by default to add me to a regular distribution list for the iTunes newsletter and to keep me generally up to date on Apple news, products, and services. Leaving these boxes checked will certainly increase the inflow of information into my personal space—the topic of the next section in this chapter.

If I uncheck the boxes, what then? What happens to my email address? A click through to the Apple Customer Privacy Policy presents me with a lengthy 2000-word document that includes the following: "There are also times when it may be advantageous for

[12] For a discussion of ways that privacy restrictions might travel with the information as it is transferred, see Cranor (2002).

[13] See *www.privacybird.org*; see also Cranor (2005).

Figure 7.3 A portion of the web page for downloading an iTunes update.

Apple to make certain personal information about you available to companies that Apple has a strategic relationship with or that perform work for Apple to provide products and services to you on our behalf."[14] Which companies? Only for products and services I order through Apple? Or will independent companies then be able to bother me with offers and come-ons? The answer appears to be no, but this is only apparent after a careful reading of the privacy policy.

Questions of privacy practice become even more involved when we try to order things online for physical delivery to ourselves or other people—flowers for our mother on Mother's day, for example. Obviously, there is a need to provide our mother's street address for the flowers to be delivered, and maybe also her phone number so that arrangements can be made for her to be home to take delivery. But what happens to this information? Is it used later for follow-on marketing, or only to complete the current transaction (the delivery of the flowers)? Is the information shared with other companies? How long is the information kept? These are important questions that can't be easily answered even if we do take time to carefully read a site's lengthy statement of privacy policy.

Tools based on P3P can help us to "get to the point" concerning a web site's policies and whether or not they match our preferences. However, P3P is also limited in several ways. For example, there are gray areas concerning the sharing of our personal information. A web site that takes our credit card number to complete a transaction may need, for example, to share this number with another company to whom they have outsourced their order processing. More important, P3P may work in relation to web sites for reputable companies like Apple who have a great deal to lose (in reputation and possibly lawsuits) and little to gain through lack of adherence to the policy they advertise. But in general, support for P3P by itself does not protect us against cheats—web sites that advertise one privacy policy and then act in ways that go against that policy.

As discussion on the Web will attest, P3P is far from perfect or complete. Ultimately P3P or it successor needs to be put in its proper place—as a way to give more precise computer-readable expression to policies and preferences of privacy so that mismatches are quickly identified. We can also hope that tools will be developed to test sites for adherence to the policies they advertise (e.g., by signing up fake people and then tracking what happens to their personal information). And we can hope for strong legislation to punish companies that falsely advertise their privacy policy through their web sites.

---

[14] See *www.apple.com/legal/privacy.*

What Now for IT?

– Bob Boiko

Can corporate IT be a "Big Brother?" Does your corporate IT group have the ability to look at your information? Absolutely. Does your IT group have the right to look at your information? Probably. Does your IT group have the staff and time to look at your information? Probably not. It's very likely that all of the information you store on a company computer is immediately and entirely accessible. Your hard drive is networked, and a simple operation is all it takes to open it up completely to others in your organization. The network locations where your email, shared files, and backups are stored are already open to system administrators. In addition, it is likely that you have entered some sort of agreement with your organization that stipulates that the work product you create (and information is a work product) is the property of your organization to which you ultimately have no special right. Many of us have also agreed to stipulations that we will not store personal information or even receive personal emails on our organization's systems. So, you have little or no private information that your IT department cannot find and deliver to whomever it sees fit.

On the other hand, will your IT department look into your personal files? What would it cost them to look at your personal files? Do they have anywhere near the staff they would need to determine whether your information is "safe?" I think not. Even with today's most sophisticated data mining and analysis tools, the job is too large. As the US government recently learned when it attempted to data-mine the mobile phone records of US citizens to find potential terrorists, even the best tools are not good. The sheer volume of information you need to retrieve and process continues to outstrip our ability to automate the analysis of that information. Unless your IT department has a particular reason to pay attention to your information, it remains unlikely that they can pay much attention to it.

Considering the current nature of our employee–employer relationships, we should not be too surprised that IT has the ability and the right to access our information. However, given the difficulty of making use of the information they can so easily collect, it should also be no surprise that there is an enormous amount of "private" information that remains out of sight and out of mind to corporate IT.

7.4 Managing the inflow

Once upon a time, a group of students working on their PhDs at Carnegie-Mellon University would gather together every Saturday morning for breakfast at a little hole-in-the-wall diner in Pittsburgh called Ernie's. I was one of them. Breakfast at Ernie's was active entertainment. Everyone played. Each of us, in our turn, said something funny or silly or thought provoking. Then one day a television appeared, mounted high up near the ceiling on the wall. It was always on. Our breakfast at Ernie's changed forevermore. We gaped helplessly at the television even as we observed ourselves doing so. The harder we tried not to look, the more we looked. Conversation happened only in fits and starts, engaging only some of us while others attended, openly or surreptitiously, to the television. We stopped going to Ernie's.

More than 20 years ago, Ries and Trout, in their 1986 book *Positioning: The Battle for Your Mind*, described an "assault on the mind" brought about by a revolution in modern communication that "has so jammed our channels that only a fraction of all messages get through. And not the most important ones either" (p. 11). The battle for our attention has only increased in intensity since these observations were made. There is now an active area of discussion called the "attention economy" and "attention economics."[15]

As human beings, we are wired to attend to the ring of a phone, the appearance of a new email alert, or the blare of a television set. We can't easily change our nature. What we can do is adjust the flows of information in our environment in order to create spaces and times in which we are relatively protected from these informational intrusions. Control over the inflow as well as the outflow of information is essential if we're to protect our privacy. This section explores additional reasons why the management of inflow is important.

7.4.1 Attention capture

We often get distracted by sights and sounds that have nothing to do with the task at hand. Psychologists call this *attention capture*.[16] We're especially wired to attend to movement and "looming" on the periphery of our vision. Certainly sensitivity to change had survival value for our ancestors, who were threatened by the warriors of a hostile tribe or by predatory animals (for whom our ancestors were targeted as actual meat, not just the "money, energy, attention, time" of an information assault). Sensitivity to movement and looming has value even today as a way to alert us to the danger of an oncoming car or a mugger.

People working in the media, in general, and advertisers, in particular, have been very adept at developing devices for exploiting these sensitivities in order to grab our attention and keep it. Consider television. Southwell and Lee (2004) note that there has been a marked increase in camera cuts, where a *camera cut* is defined to be "transition to a different camera perspective that results in the depiction of a new visual environment or entirely new visual information" (p. 655). In an analysis of Dutch episodes of *Seasame Street* between 1977 and 2003, for example, Koolstra and colleagues (2004) found that the mean number of camera cuts per minute doubled between 1977 and 2003, from four to eight.

MacLachlan and Logan (1993) found the number of camera cuts per minute to be especially high on programs and channels targeting teen and twenty-something markets, such as on MTV. Their analysis of camera shot lengths—the time between camera cuts—showed a steady decline in shot length between 1978 and 1991. For example, the shot length on a 30-second commercial declined from 3.8 seconds in 1978 to 2.3 seconds in 1991. On average, shot

---

[15] See, for example, *http://en.wikipedia.org/wiki/Attention_economy*.

[16] For a review of research on attention capture, see Folk and Gibson (2001).

lengths for commercials were at least 50 percent shorter than the shot lengths of the programs in which these commercials occurred.

The high number of camera cuts and the corresponding shortness of camera shots have the effect of keeping us glued to the television set. We may find it difficult not to attend even when the volume is muted. Some studies suggest that we're more likely to attend to an old object that moves than a new object that doesn't move.[17] This raises the possibility that the attention we pay may not always align with our expectations concerning information value. We may, for example, be more likely to attend to the blinking advertisement of a web page—even the same advertisement that was there the last time we visited the web site—than a new hyperlink possibly pointing to useful information.

Data also suggest that we may be nearing a breakdown in our ability to apprehend the message in a video segment that is laced with camera cuts. MacLachlan and Logan (1983) present data suggesting that as the length of a camera shot goes below a certain duration (2.5 seconds in their study), the memorability and impact of the commercial also declines. Lang and colleagues (2000) also found less memorability for short shot length (and more camera cuts). In a worst of both worlds, then, we may sit in rapt—stupefied—attention and then recall nothing later.

7.4.2 The availability heuristic

Research in human cognition provides a second effect, called the *availability heuristic*, which is also of direct relevance to a discussion of inflows and the management of personal information. The term was coined by Tversky and Kahneman (1973, 1974) to describe a human tendency to estimate "frequency or probability by the ease with which instances or associations could be brought to mind" (1973, p. 208).

To illustrate the effect, let's imagine a person named Tom who is running for office in a small local election—a position, say, on the city council. Tom wants to know the likely percentage of people that will vote for him, but he lacks the money to commission a poll. He decides, instead, to trust his own gut estimate that he is doing really well—so well, in fact, that he decides to take a vacation rather than campaign during the final week before the election.

Tom loses by a landslide. What happened? He was so sure he would win! Tom's problem is that he based his estimates on the people he met personally who said "we're going to vote for you" or some similar expressions of support. Tom is much more likely to meet supporters than not. The people who didn't plan to vote for him weren't at his campaign rallies.

We are frequently in situations like Tom's. We must estimate likelihoods. If I go this way to work, what are the chances I'll be late because of a traffic jam? What are the chances that so-and-so will finish the project on time? Do I need to take my umbrella? (What are the chances for rain?) For some decisions, like the chances of rain, we can consult the newspaper or the Web. For many other decisions, we base estimates of likelihood on a sampling of information readily at

---

[17] For a review of research on the relative attraction of novelty vs. movement, see Franconeri, Hollingworth, and Simons (2005).

hand—information we can recall from memory, or information we can readily apprehend from the hot regions of our PSI—the headlines of today's newspaper, the papers on our desktop, or the email messages still listed in view on our screen.

What else, after all, are we to do? Decisions requiring some estimates of likelihood come up many times in a typical day. We certainly can't hire a pollster or statistician each time we need to decide something! But what we can do is to be aware of the ways in which our use of the availability heuristic biases our estimates (even our perceptions) of reality and of the decisions based on these estimates.

The media tendency to focus on sensational events has been linked to a tendency for people to overestimate the likelihood of these events.[18] Sensational events such as terrorist attacks, incidents of road rage, or molestations by pedophile priests actually get a double boost in availability: (1) We are more likely to hear of them through media coverage (compared with, for example, the many more frequent deaths that result from disease). (2) The lurid nature of the events covered means we are more likely to remember these events later on.

Efforts to counter the biases of the availability heuristic need to be multi-pronged. First among these is the simple awareness that we are subject to this bias. When important decisions must be made, getting more objective data is often worth the trouble. In buying a car, for example, objective data on maintenance records should trump our memories for how many times friends with a model we're considering have been in the shop. Second is the awareness that other people are subject to this bias as well. If we want to convince our manager to consider an alternate course of action, a direct assault alone—as in "alternative B really is better"—may not be effective. Exposing the manager to examples (the more noteworthy the better) where alternative B has worked may be more effective.

Third, we might want to change the "information diet"[19] for ourselves and our families. For example, many of us are exposed via television and newly released films to a steady stream of "action" narratives in which the "bad guy" is truly evil and disagreements are resolved only through physical violence. How can such narratives not affect the perceptions we have of the intentions of people in real life with whom we come into conflict? How can they not have an effect on our thinking concerning the means of resolving these conflicts? And, if not for us, then what about for our children?

7.4.3 Information overload

Some of us have seen the classic *I Love Lucy* episode called "Job Switching" (often simply referred to as the "Candy Factory episode"). Lucy is trying to manage in her new job as a

---

[18] See, for example, Combs and Slovic (1979) for a discussion on the impact that media coverage has on our estimates of the likelihood of various events.

[19] There are a number of interesting mappings between information and food. People can "forage" for information as they do for food (Pirolli & Card, 1999). In Chapter 2, information technologies, by analogy to technologies for the storage and distribution of food, permit us to have things our way. The concept of an information diet raises additional questions. What does a balanced diet of information look like? The information served up by commercial television can be seen as poor in fiber and high in the information equivalent of fat and sugar. Can we become "infobese" from overconsumption?

Figure 7.4 **Lucy with unwrapped candy in the "Candy Factory" episode of** *I Love Lucy.*

worker on a candy factory assembly line. The candy comes down the line. Lucy carefully wraps each individual piece. So far so good. But then the flow increases. More pieces of candy go down the line. At first Lucy tries to go faster too. The individual pieces are not wrapped as carefully, but they're still wrapped. But when the flow of candies goes still faster, the situation turns chaotic. Lucy has to stuff candies in her mouth and in her blouse when she cannot keep up so that unwrapped candies do not flow by and out the other end (Figure 7.4).

If we move beyond the slapstick hilarity of the episode, we can easily relate Lucy's situation to many we face in our own efforts at personal information management. Information comes in. And then more information . . . and then still more information. The email messages that arrive on the first day of our job may be answered with care. As more email messages arrive, our responses become briefer. And as the flow of email increases still further, we may begin to ignore or overlook email messages altogether.

Email for many of us certainly seems to be a prime example of *information overload*. The term is itself overloaded with meaning. Information overload is sometimes equated with the exponential growth in the amount of available information. But an explosion in the world's supply of information needn't cause us personal stress unless we're a "Renaissance" scholar hoping to keep pace with it all. Scholars dropped any pretense of doing this well before the onset of the Renaissance.

Kirsh (2000) suggests another sense of overload related to the notion that, while the amount of available information is rising exponentially, the supply of "quality" information is growing only linearly. This Malthusian relationship is leading to a steady decline in the density of quality information. But again, this needn't be cause of personal distress either, because we're blissfully ignorant of the information we're missing or because we've found effective ways of locating the needle in the haystack (e.g., through use of search tools).

Information overload becomes personally distressing when our personal systems for managing information begin to break down. As discussed in Chapter 5, signs of breakdown are evident in ever-increasing mounds of paper documents waiting to be filed. Signs of breakdown are evident in a sense of having lost control over the files of a computer desktop or the email messages in the inbox.

People also experience information overload when they begin to fall behind in their plans for handling incoming information relating to a project or a decision to be made. Perhaps the information is in the form of paper job applications awaiting review for a position to be filled. Or perhaps the information relates to alternatives in the purchase of a new computer or digital camera. Up to a point, people continue to master the material though perhaps by taking short-cuts as flow increases—skimming rather than reading in depth, for example. But as a certain point is reached, the whole process begins to break down, and the degradation in a person's ability to keep up is far from graceful.

Email messages scroll off the screen unanswered. The job applicant or the computer or the camera is no longer selected based on even a cursory consideration of the evidence. Instead, people may say something like "Oh, the heck with it. They're all the same" and go with some gut instinct having little to do with the available information. Or people may establish a growing list of "fatal flaws" that immediately disqualify an alternative from further consideration.

There are no easy, certain solutions to this personal breakdown in the processing of decision- or project-related information. But here are some approaches to consider:

- *Satisfice rather than optimize.* The term "satisfice" was coined by Herbert Simon (1957) in reference to a strategy of searching only until an alternative meeting some minimal level or set of criteria is found. Satisficing is in contrast to optimizing, which requires that all alterna- tives be considered in order to locate the very best one.

- *Triage (sort) candidates into "no," "yes," and "maybe" categories.* Triage is especially useful when attempting to find a set of acceptable candidates—the players who will make a team, for example, or the papers to be accepted at a conference. More concentrated focus can then be given to the "maybe" pile.

- *Sample and then optimize within this sample.* Set a limit on the amount of information that is collected or the number of alternatives or candidates that are accepted for consider- ation. A job review process, for example, may specify that only the first n job applications will be considered. The sampling approach is especially useful in cases where (1) criteria for selection are not well understood ahead of time (and only become apparent through a comparison of candidates); and (2) there is reason to believe that the sample is unbiased and representative of the population as a whole.

7.4.4 Manage the information channel, not the information itself

A theme throughout this section's discussion of inflow is that management works best when focused on channels of information—and strategies associated with their selection and the processing of their information—rather than on the information itself. We can't help but attend and be distracted by the television if it's on. Willpower alone won't change things (and exercising willpower is itself a drain on our energy). Turn the television off instead of leaving it on in the background. Disable the television as a channel of information.

Likewise, we can't avoid using the availability heuristic. In many situations we have few other alternatives. However, we can try to select our channels of incoming information so that the information "available" gives a more balanced representation of the likelihoods we need to estimate.

Finally, with information overload—discussed here as a breakdown in our ability to keep pace with incoming information—focus needs to shift to the channel of incoming information and to overall strategies for its processing. Do we satisfice, triage, or sample? This is a choice of strategy involving a consideration for the channel of information (or set of alternatives) as a whole.

What Next for Tool Development?

– Mike Kelly

The cell phone rings while we're in a meeting or listening to a concert. What a distraction! How embarrassing! We meant to mute it and forgot. Our cell phones may never be smart enough to mute themselves based solely on an assessment of the current situation and external conditions, the way we expect our children to do after about age 6. But we can hope that phones will make much better use of other information we take the trouble to enter elsewhere. After all, wasn't it this same cell phone that just 20 minutes ago buzzed with a reminder for this very meeting?

Taking advantage of information about meetings scheduled using a digital calendar is a no-brainer and in fact already exists. Today, my Cingular 2125 phone has an "Automatic" profile that cycles between the "Normal" profile (where the phone rings) and the "Meeting" profile (where the phone only vibrates) based on the calendar information synchronized to the phone from my central email and calendar server. Other phones have similar features. Imagine taking this to the next level:

- When we call someone now, we may get the message that he/she "is on the phone." In the future, we may get the message that "… is in a meeting that is scheduled to last until 11:30."

- Our tools could notice when we're working on documents related to an important project (based on task due dates and email traffic) and so automatically start holding new email that might distract us, responding with an auto reply to the effect that "… seems to be very busy now, with average response time of up to two days." This would help set expectations for people awaiting a response, and possibly offer an option for circumventing the screen ("If you need immediate attention, resend your email with Urgent priority.")

- Using information about travel plans, or information we enter in appointments, tools could notice when we're not in our usual office. For instance, suppose next week I'm going to be in our Paris office. Simply blocking out the time as "Out of Office" on the calendar complicates scheduling meetings with my Parisian colleagues; yet not indicating that I won't be in my usual office allows others to schedule meetings I won't be able to attend. The system could filter meeting requests based on the location, or provide feedback when scheduling meetings about where I will be that day.

All this sounds good until we start to think about the nuances. What about the time blocked out on my schedule to drive from one meeting to another? I blocked it out so that no one would schedule a meeting during that time, but do I really want the phone not to ring because I'm "busy"? And if I receive many calls, do I really want my phone constantly vibrating during meetings, disturbing me? Maybe I want calls only from certain key contacts—perhaps my wife and my direct manager—to be able to interrupt my meeting, while others just go right to voice mail. Similarly, we might like for all phone calls—whether to cell phone or land-line phone—to be directed to voice mail during the dinner hour. But what about the call from my sister with news of my father's surgery? Once again, we learn that seemingly no-brainer, rules-based systems are too simple-minded to accommodate the complexity of our real lives. Eventually tools may learn from our behavior what is important to us and when we should be interrupted.[20] There is also considerable room for a better integration of tools to manage the flow of information as mediated, for example, by emerging standards such as iCalendar.[21]

When I am . . . traveling in a carriage, or walking after a good meal, or during the night when I cannot sleep; it is on such occasions that ideas flow best and most abundantly.

Austrian composer Wolfgang Amadeus Mozart (1756–1791)

7.5 Staying in the flow

We have all, it is to be hoped, had occasional moments of supreme concentration and productivity when we feel as if we're working at a higher level—as a super version of the person we normally are. Not only do we get a great deal done, but the quality of our work may be better too. Even better, moments like these—often referred to as being "in the flow" or "in the zone"—are also restful and fun—even blissful.

Mihaly Csikszentmihalyi (1991) writes: "It does not seem to be true that work necessarily needs to be unpleasant. It may always have to be hard, or at least harder than doing

---

[20] For one effort to give computers the smarts to decide when to interupt, see Horvitz, Apacible, and Koch (2004).

[21] For a brief description of iCalendar and references to more information, see Wikipedia (*http://en.wikipedia.org/wiki/ICalendar*).

nothing at all. But there is ample evidence that work can be enjoyable, and that indeed, it is often the most enjoyable part of life." Csikszentmihalyi identifies several characteristics of being in the flow:

- A challenging activity that requires skills.
- A merging of action and awareness.
- Clear goals and feedback.
- Concentration on the task at hand.
- A feeling of being completely in charge.
- A loss of self-consciousness.
- A transformation of time, in both extremes: small actions go on for a long time, but the day goes by in no time at all.

Each of these characteristics makes good intuitive sense. However, there is little beyond intuition or personal experience to suggest that any one characteristic is necessary to the experience of flow. Nor is there reason to believe that some combined realization of these characteristics is sufficient to reach a state of flow. Some characteristics, such as challenging activity, concentration or clear goals, and feedback, seem to be ours to achieve through the actions we take. Others, like feeling completely in charge or losing self-consciousness, do not seem so easy to control, other than possibly through a program of meditation.

There may be no reliable set of steps we can follow to get into a state of flow. But there are certainly events and conditions that can take us out of a flow once we're there. Ringing phones, people at our doorstep demanding our attention, screaming babies, even the alerts that persistently pop up on our computer monitor—these events, always distracting, can also shake us out of any flow we've managed to achieve.

Studies suggest, for example, that task interruption is built into the fabric of a typical workday and that people spend an average of only three minutes on a task before switching to another task.[22] Sometimes the task is completed. Many times people "self-interrupt" as they reach a stopping point—for example, a point where more information such as an email confirmation from a co-worker is needed before the task can be continued. But people are also frequently interrupted by external events—an average of four times an hour according to one study by O'Conaill and Frohlich (1995).

To reduce self-interruptions, try to assemble all of the task-requisite information (including confirmations from co-workers) ahead of time. To reduce interruptions by others, clear the calendar, close the door, forward or mute the phone, and turn off email. Reductions in inter-ruptions surely increase the chances of entering a state of flow and, in any case, reduce the chances that, once "in the flow," we'll be untimely wrenched out of this state.

Interruptions can come not only from outside agents, but also from our very own computer. Shneiderman and Bederson (2005) describe the importance of minimizing the disruptive

---

[22] For a review of research relating to task interruption and task switching, see Czerwinski, Horvitz, and Wilhite (2004); Gonzalez and Mark (2004); and Mark, Gonzalez, and Harris (2005).

effects of computer alerts as one way of helping people to stay in the flow. With this in mind, they explored a redesign of the balloon alerts in Windows XP. Many notifications that now appear as balloons are not urgent but, rather, just of the nature of "for your information." Yet users feel compelled to self-interrupt their task to look at the alerts since they don't know how long the balloon will last or where to find the notification after the balloon has disappeared. Simple changes can give users some control over how long a balloon remains in view and also ways to retrieve the information again later.

Finally, consider that for a period of being in the flow, there may inevitably be periods of preparation during which, for example, requisite information is assembled and assimilated.

The quality of the imagination is to flow and not to freeze.

U.S. philosopher, poet, and essayist Ralph Waldo Emerson (1803–1882)

7.5.1 Personal liquidity

Flow suggests a liquid state. Water flows—but not always. When the temperature of water goes below 0 degrees Celsius (32 degrees Fahrenheit), a profound transformation occurs. Water freezes into ice. Flowing water, before freezing, becomes dense and flows more sluggishly.

An analogous thing happens in other situations of flow when we replace temperature with measures of utilization as a percentage of capacity. Traffic flows at off-hours when there are only a few vehicles on the roadway and the percentage of utilization is low. As the number of vehicles reaches and then exceeds capacity, traffic "freezes" and we have traffic jams. Traffic stops flowing. It is a solid. The flow of people leaving a building or stadium can also freeze when capacity is exceeded—sometimes with terrifying and disastrous consequences.

People may experience a sense of freezing with respect to the things in their houses. The house that once seemed to have so much space is now in a frozen state in which daily activities no longer flow as they used to. In a cluttered house, movement becomes blocked, and rearrangements (of furniture, the kitchen utensils in a drawer, the food in the refrigerator) become especially difficult. Moving one item provokes a chain reaction of other movements. Worse, the frozen world of too much stuff becomes opaque. We can't find the one spice jar because so many other spice jars are in the way. We can't easily find one item in the refrigerator because so many other items are blocking its view. Freezing can also happen for the items in a duffle bag or toilet kit or medicine cabinet.

Freezing can happen, too, with respect to our schedule of workday meetings or our calendar of social events. If the schedule or calendar is filled beyond a certain level, any change—short of canceling a meeting or event outright—becomes extremely difficult to make. Moving one meeting can't be done without moving another meeting, and so on. Freezing can happen with respect to the paper piles on a desktop or with respect to the icons of a computer desktop. Again, beyond a certain point, there is not enough free space left: any movement forces a chain of follow-on movements.

A concept from economics, referred to as *capacity utilization*, seems to have direct relevance.[23] A company, or a country, has some maximum capacity with respect to the goods it is able to produce. But well before this maximum is reached—as utilization rises above 80 percent or so—signs of stress—inflation for a country, increases in per-unit cost for a company—will begin to appear. At what levels of utilization—of our desktop, our schedule, our hard drive, our ability to juggle different tasks or assignments—do we begin experience an analogous stress in our ability to manage our lives and our information?

What Now for You and Me?

We don't have to wait for the future. There are many choices we can make now to better protect our privacy and to better control the flow of personal information—in each of the six senses of "personal." A sampling of some of these choices is listed in Table 7.2. Most steps are obvious and straightforward but easily overlooked even so.

Table 7.2   Steps we can take now to manage privacy and flow

Sense of PI[24]	Object bearing or controlling flow	Choices we can make	Comments
#1	Personal computer	Virus protection current? System updates installed?	So important, yet so easy to put off. Virus protection updates can be automated. So can installation of system updates.
#2	Web forms	Entries for phone number and email address—fill? If so with what?	Leave blank or leave a number or address that works for you, not for them.
#2	Credit card slip	Scratch out all but the last four digits of credit card number (if this hasn't been done already)	Restaurants can still connect a slip to a transaction if you want to leave a tip. Scratching out the number decreases the chances that someone will copy it after you leave the restaurant.
#2	Bank statements, health records, etc.	Shred before tossing	

Continued

---

[23] For a discussion of capacity utilization, see Berndt and Morrison (1981).

[24] Personal information.

Sense of PI	Object bearing or controlling flow	Choices we can make	Comments
#3	Office door	Wide open, shut, mostly shut	Wide open if you're happy to have company. Shut if you want to be alone. Mostly shut to say "I'm here but don't bother me unless it's important."
#3	Email application	Out of office notice	Manage people's expectations.
#3	Word processor	"Check spelling as you type" on or off?	The red squiggly line can be a distraction, especially when you're still trying to get your thoughts down.
#3	Word processor	Draft (outline) or final (print) view?	Final (print) is good for the final stage of a paper, but often bad for early stages. The temptation is high to "fuss" with formatting when you need to get your thoughts down first.
#3	Television	On or off; TV channels, programs selected	Don't expect meaningful conversation to happen while the television is blaring in the background. Likewise, don't expect to do cognitively demanding activities (like answering most email) while also watching a television program. Establish television-free times of the day or, better, limit the amount of time the television is on.
#3	Web forms	Boxes (e.g.,"Add me to monthly newsletter")—checked or unchecked?	These boxes are often checked by default. If you receive too much email already, consider unchecking them.
#3	Telephones	Answer when ringing? Mute or lower ring volume?	Ringing phones are hard to ignore. Establish a policy of not answering when in meetings or at the dinner table. Or, if it must be answered, take the phone somewhere else or ask the caller if you can call back later.

Sense of PI	Object bearing or controlling flow	Choices we can make	Comments
#4	Email messages you send	Send good things; speak bad things	Email is forever. Old messages can come back months or years later.
#5	Web browser	Level of "cookie" security?	Leave at "medium" level (usually the default) to block out transmission of personally identifiable information (that might be used to record your web visits).
#6	Web browser	Enable the content advisor (off by default)	Enable the content advisor for help in screening out material according to web site self-ratings for language, nudity, sex, and violence (see the InternetContentRating Association site, *http://www.icra.org/*).

Dwell as near as possible to the channel in which your life flows.

U.S. essayist, poet, and naturalist Henry David Thoreau (1817–1862)

7.6 Looking back, looking forward

Issues of information flow arise for each of the senses in which information can be personal. This chapter has given special attention to the management of the outflow of information about us and the management of inflow of information directed toward us.

☑ *Managing the outflow.* The best place to exercise control is at points where information about us (e.g., our credit card number or email address) is about to flow outward from regions of the PSI we control to regions under the control of others (such as companies we do business with on the Web). We need several kinds of help: (1) to articulate privacy preferences that establish who can see what information about us under which circumstances; (2) to interpret corresponding company policies concerning the handling of personal data as these are posted to the Web and elsewhere, and to detect mismatches between company policies and our privacy preferences; (3) to determine which companies and which web sites are following their own policies as posted.

☑ *Managing the inflow.* Large amounts of time, money, and creativity are being invested in ways to capture our attention. We are wired to respond to peripheral motion, noises, pop-ups, and sudden changes in scene. Our best means of controlling inflow is not at the level of individual event, but rather at the level of the channel through which information presses in upon our resources. Turn off the TV, unplug the phone, disable notifications of incoming email. Also, manage the balance of incoming information, since this information impacts our impressions of the world around us as surely as our direct sensory experiences of the world do.

☑ *Staying in the flow.* There may be no reliable set of steps we can follow to get into a state of flow. But there are steps we can take to reduce the chances of being pulled out of our "zone" once we're there. Create times of the day when flows of incoming information are blocked or diverted (e.g., to an answering machine or an "out of office" message). Make sure that the requisite information is at hand. Also, recognize that some amount of information assembly and assimilation may be a necessary precondition.

A dominant theme of the chapter is that our focus needs to be on the channels of information as these impact the inflow and outflow of information. Absent control of the channels and associated strategies for dealing with the information on these channels, we're easily pushed and pulled by individual information items and events. If the television is on, we'll watch. If the phone rings, our first inclination is to answer.

P3P has been discussed as an effort to establish a common language for the expression of personal privacy preferences and the expression of provider (e.g., web site) privacy policies. Tools are under development to support the expression of preferences and policies, and their comparison for conflicts or disparities, and also to monitor provider compliance in meeting the conditions of the privacy policy they espouse.

We can also hope for tools that learn from us to elaborate on our policy for what gets in and what goes out as new cases are encountered. The management of information flow, inflow and outflow, is one kind of meta-level activity that, given the right tool support, can improve if given a more incidental, incremental, integrative treatment (as outlined in Chapter 3). Rules for deciding what information to let out do not spring from our minds fully formed. These are more easily, more accurately abstracted from a consideration of many cases that arise naturally or are possibly manufactured.

However, there is no need to wait for these tools; nor is there a need to be totally dependent on P3P or other proposed standards. Each of us can articulate our own privacy plan so that we begin to gain a measure of independence from the push and pull of daily events. If we're getting too much email already, for example, then perhaps we should make it a habit to routinely decline (uncheck) offers to keep us informed of "exciting new offers."

Moreover, effective management of information flow—incoming, outgoing, and as this relates to the flow of work—means thinking about more than just privacy and protection. Flow is not just about what we stand to lose if our privacy and security are compromised. Flow is also about the many ways we benefit from the effective dissemination of information. The management of flow is about privacy and protection, but it is also about power and projection. The use of our information is a means of affecting desired changes in our world.

But how do we know whether our plan for the management of information flow is working? For that matter, how do we know which parts of our personal information space need our attention most urgently? Earlier in the chapter we talked about achieving a "balanced diet" of incoming information. But how do we go about measuring our information intake? These are topics for the next chapter.

Measuring and evaluating

"Should I change?" With the wisdom of hindsight, we may regret a change we've made. Or, we may wish we'd made it much sooner. We measure and evaluate in our practice of PIM so that we can act with more foresight and spend less time regretting. A yardstick for measuring and evaluating a change considers its impact on not just one but several activities of PIM. A tool that makes it easier to keep items has little value if items go into a "black hole" and cannot be found again later.

Chapter
Eight

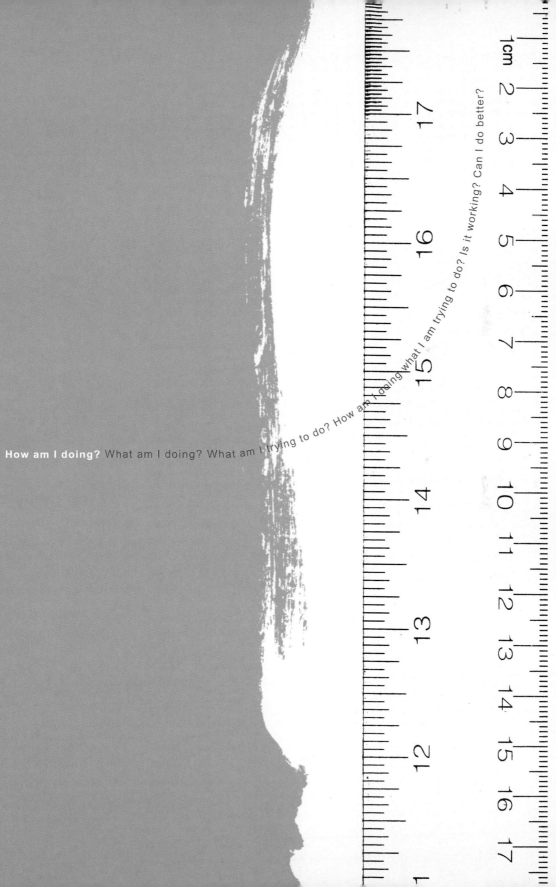

How am I doing? What am I doing? What am I trying to do? How am I doing? What am I trying to do? Is it working? Can I do better?

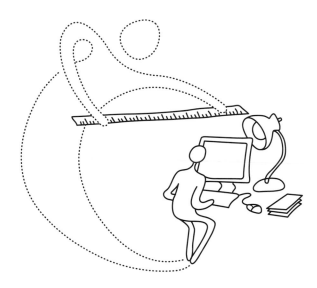

The only person who behaves sensibly is my tailor. He takes my measure anew every time he sees me. All the rest go on with their old measurements.

English dramatist and critic George Bernard Shaw (1856–1950)

8.1 Starting out

"How am I doing?" The former New York City mayor Ed Koch often asked his constituents this question—especially when campaigning for their vote. How often do we ask this question of ourselves? Are we ready for the answers we might get back? This question has relevance to a practice of PIM. Are the strategies we use effective and sustainable? Are our schemes for organizing maintainable? Are we making good use of the information we have? Do we know how to use the available tools? Should we consider acquiring new tools, or will these prove to be more trouble than they are worth?

These questions reach out to a still larger context for their answers. PIM is a means to an end. We manage our information in an effort to fulfill goals and roles, large and small, in our lives. How are we doing in our lives? Are we fulfilling the roles we've taken on with respect to family, friends, education, career, community involvement, and so on? Are we making effective use of our precious resources, most especially our time, in pursuit of our life goals?

How am I doing? also begs answers to related questions: *What* am I doing? What am I *trying* to do? *How* am I doing what I'm trying to do? *Is it working? Can I do better?*

The principal question behind many of these questions is, Should I change? This chapter applies this question to the elements of a PIM practice. Should we change? If so, what and how? Should we change our strategies? . . . our schemes of organization? . . .

our supporting tools? Or should we make better, more consistent, smarter use of what we have in place now?

The answer to variations on the "Should I change?" question depends on information that's frequently missing and on assessments of risk and reward that can vary greatly—even depending, for example, on our mood from one day to the next. Changing to use a new software tool can mean significant improvements in the speed and quality of our work. But a new tool can also be terribly disruptive. Existing software may no longer work properly, for example, or the new tool may place excessive demands on the resources (processing speed, memory, battery) of our computer.

With the wisdom of hindsight, we may regret a change we've made. Conversely, we may wish we'd made it much sooner. Can our activities of PIM make us smarter so that we act with more foresight and spend less time regretting? The previous chapters have considered organizing, maintaining, and managing information flow as kinds of meta-level activity. The questions above bring us, in this chapter, to another kind of meta-level activity: *measuring and evaluating*. Activities to measure and evaluate, like other meta-level activities, require that we take a broader perspective. Questions are about strategies, schemes of organization, supporting tools, even a practice of PIM overall. Broader still, some measures can tell us something about our lives, what is and isn't working and whether we're "walking the talk" in our use of our precious resources.

Sections of this chapter take us on a walk through the following topics relating to measuring and evaluating:

- ☑ *Getting oriented.* A distinction is made between measuring and, more generally, data collection on the one hand and evaluating on the other. Measuring is about raw information: How many apples? How many oranges? Evaluating is about making comparisons and assigning value: Do I like apples or oranges more?

- ☑ *A yardstick for measuring PIM practice elements* looks at questions we should ask when considering any PIM element, current or candidate. To properly evaluate a PIM strategy, scheme of organization, or a supporting tool, its impact on not just one but several activities of PIM must be measured. A tool that makes it easier to keep items, for example, has little value if items cannot be found again later.

- ☑ *What can research tell us about methods of measuring and evaluating in our practices of PIM?* We pick up again the theme that study and practice are interwoven and at two different levels. PIM is a new area of study, and relatively little is known about how people go about deciding whether and how to change their PIM practice and its elements over time. However, points of relevance from the study of human decision making will be selectively explored. At another level, methods for the study of PIM have obvious relevance to an individual's practice of PIM. We are all researchers with respect to our own practices of PIM.

- ☑ *Measuring and evaluating in real life* looks at ways to take and make measurements more relevant to our lives' goals and the various roles we seek to fulfill. Time spent in a web browser or an email application is easily measured. But these measures are a reflection of light cast by existing applications and their own partitioning of our information. We might like to know how much time we spend on a task, project, or activity. These units are real to us but much less so to our tools. Evaluation is made more real through integration which clearly shows the implications that measurements have for our ability to complete our projects, fulfill our roles, and live our lives.

☑ *Can self-study PIM practices contribute to the larger study of PIM?* The study of PIM defines an enormous space with dimensions for time, variety of information forms, tool configuration, tasks, situational requirements, individual differences, and many others. Researchers, using methodologies developed for the study of human–information behavior (HIB), human–computer interaction (HCI), and human cognition have resources to explore only small regions of this space. Can ordinary people, as researchers of their own practices of PIM, help out?

8.2 Getting oriented

Similar to keeping and organizing or organizing and maintaining, measuring and evaluating frequently go together and are sometimes used interchangeably.[1] But distinctions can be drawn that are useful to this chapter's discussion. If our choice is between two grocery bags of apples and oranges—one marked "status quo" and another marked "change"—we can measure to determine that one bag has 7 apples and 15 oranges while the other bag has 11 of each. But then we need to place a value on each bag. Which do we like more, apples or oranges? Or perhaps we seek a balance with equal numbers of each.

Measuring is often equated with the assignment of a number. But a more general definition of "to estimate or appraise"[2] is needed to make room for the informal, qualitative measurements we often need to make. We measure the likelihood of a new tool causing problems as "low," for example, or that the amount of time it will save us is "a lot." These qualitative measures are often the best we can do, and we'd be hard pressed to provide numbers such as "4 percent" or "5 hours over the next 2 months."

Not everything that can be counted counts, and not everything that counts can be counted.

Albert Einstein (1879–1955)

More generally, measuring is part of a stage of inquiry and data collection that can also include more subjective, qualitative observations. If we're considering adoption of a new tool, we ask: What is this? What will it do for me? How would I use (apply) it? What's it going to cost me

---

[1] For example, the *Oxford English Dictionary* (online version) defines measurement in one sense as "The action or an act of measuring or calculating a length, quantity, value, etc." The definition for evaluation includes "The action of evaluating or determining the value of."

[2] See the Merriam-Webster Online Dictionary (*www.m-w.com*).

(in money, time to learn, time to use, and potential hassle to install)? Analogous questions apply to the consideration of a new strategy or scheme. Similarly, if we're assessing elements of our current practice, we might ask: What's working? What's not? What problems seem to happen again and again? Where did my time go today? What did I really accomplish?

Measuring/data collecting and evaluating/deciding are two steps we take when deciding whether to change and what change to make. In order to decide what notebook computer to buy, for example, we can gather measurements, ready-made, concerning price, brand name, operating system supported, processing speed, hard-drive capacity, and reliability. We can try the computer ourselves. We can ask friends what their experience has been with the same or similar model. After data has been gathered, we must still evaluate. If hard-drive reliability goes down as capacity goes up, for example, what value do we place on each? Is there a sweet spot that gives us an acceptable combination of both?

In a strictly logical world, we might hope to derive an expected value for each alternative that factors in all measurements and a weighting for each, reflecting their relative value to us. But choices can rarely be reduced to expected values—one per choice—so that all we have to do is pick the highest value.

In the real world, information is often missing for many important measures. The information we have may be inaccurate or highly variable. Information expressed as probabilities is especially problematic. For example, the likelihood of a hard-drive failure on a notebook computer in the first year of its operation may be given as once every 300 times. But we must reckon with the variability of this estimate itself and with a distinct possibility that the measures provided were made under conditions more ideal than those we will subject our own notebook computer to in daily use.

Finally, our assignment of value to different measures can vary greatly depending on the context. Initially, as we think about all the music, pictures, and videos we'd like to store on our new laptop, we place a premium on disk capacity—the higher the better. Later, however, as we hear about a friend's lost week struggling to recover from a hard-drive failure, we rethink our values and place a higher weighting on drive reliability.

What to change about a practice of PIM? At the core of a PIM practice is the creation, maintenance, and use of a mapping between information and need. In this chapter, we consider three things—referred to as the elements of a PIM practice or, simply, *elements*—that affect the nature a PIM mapping:

- *Schemes of PIM organization* guide the naming of information items and their organization into folders or by various tags and property/value combinations. For example, Chapter 5 considered two example schemes of organization, one for the organization of items in a reference collection and the other for organization of items in a project collection.

- *Tools of PIM is a broad category* that includes the computers, telephones, PDAs, "thumb drives" and other devices we use. Also included are the operating systems for these devices, the larger, feature-aggregating software applications that run on these devices (e.g., word processors, email applications, web browsers), and more specific facilities and features (e.g., search facilities, bookmarking facilities, sorting features, history, and recently used features). Tools needn't be digital. For paper-based information, the paper clip, stapler, three-ring notebook, and traditional filing cabinet are all tools of PIM.

- *Strategies of PIM* tie together one or several schemes of organization, available tools, and various aspects of a person's daily environment, including predictable flows of information (e.g., through web sites, the radio, television, routes to and from work and other people). A modified version of the game theoretic definition of strategy offered in the *Oxford English Dictionary*[3] applies to a PIM strategy: a plan for successful action based on the rationality and interdependence of the moves of other people (of whom some are adversaries, some are allies, and most are indifferent). For example, Sally and Walter, as described in Chapter 5, both pursue strategies of PIM that rely heavily on the people around them. Strategies may be partially, but are rarely fully, articulated by their practitioners.

8.3 A yardstick for measuring PIM practice elements

When Henry Kissinger asked Chinese Premier Chou Enlai about the importance of the French Revolution, Chou reportedly answered, "It's too soon to tell."[4] The same can often be said concerning the evaluation of a PIM practice and its strategies, schemes, and tools. It's too soon to tell.

There are basic reasons why this is so. Recall the depiction of a personal act of keeping in Figure 5.1 of Chapter 5 as a toss of an information item to a time and place of anticipated use in the future. An item may be kept for an anticipated use weeks, months, or, as is certainly the case for digital photographs and videos, years after the initial act of keeping. We can't truly assess the effectiveness of an act of keeping, nor can we evaluate the utility of strategies, schemes, and tools involved in keeping without knowing whether the item was eventually "caught." A tool that makes keeping easier has little value if items go into a black hole and cannot be found again later.

Personal information has a life cycle involving various activities of PIM. Information is found, kept, re-found, and reused (sometimes repeatedly) and possibly re-kept (e.g., under a new folder, with new tags, or in a new form on a different device). Collections of information are organized, reorganized, and maintained (both for the near term and the long term).

We don't want to wait (and usually can't afford to wait) months or years before changing an element of our PIM practice. But we can at least ask better questions up front to anticipate the impact that a change is likely to have over the long run. As we do so, we're trying to reduce the number of times that we later say things like, "Why didn't I think of that?" Any element, current or proposed, for a PIM practice needs to be considered for its impact on and support for each

---

[3] The *Oxford English Dictionary* provides the following among its defintions for strategy: "In (theoretical) circumstances of competition or conflict, as in the theory of games, decision theory, business administration, etc., a plan for successful action based on the rationality and interdependence of the moves of the opposing participants" (*http://dictionary.oed.com*).

[4] See Knickerbocker (2002).

activity of PIM—whether or not the element (tool, scheme, strategy) was explicitly designed to support a given PIM activity. Two examples illustrate.

8.3.1 Setting reminders: From information to time of anticipated use

The Bookmarks and Favorites facilities, available respectively in FireFox and Microsoft Internet Explorer, make it easy to bookmark web pages for later use. Simply click on "Bookmark This Page..." in one case and "Add to Favorites..." in the other.

So far so good. Keeping seems easy. But what about finding again later? Once created, neither facility provides much support for remembering to use bookmarks later. Forgetting to look is a common failure of finding. Specifically, people report creating bookmarks and then forgetting all about them—only to discover them again much later and long after the opportunity to use the associated web information has passed.[5]

One simple remedy might be an ability to set reminders for bookmarks as a kind of alarm clock that "rings" to remind us sometime later to use the bookmark. There is just such a feature for email messages in Microsoft Outlook. But the reminder facility has its own problems: (1) Reminders set can "go off" (come due) at inopportune times. (2) Dismissing reminders can become a maintenance headache in its own right, especially if additional reminders are also created automatically for other items (such as appointments in a person's calendar).

A more basic problem in the reminding example is that setting reminders, whether at the level of individual email messages or bookmarks, is often the wrong level in the first place. We don't want to set, see, and dismiss several different reminders—one per email message (or web bookmark)—each pertaining to the same task. Better would be to set a single reminder for a task-relevant grouping of email messages, web bookmarks, and other information items.

Suppose, for example, we have a task to "make hotel reservations in Boston by May 3." Information items that relate to this task might include pointers to web pages providing information on various hotel alternatives, email correspondences with colleagues concerning recommended hotels in downtown Boston, and perhaps even a spreadsheet we've created to compare alternatives (e.g., for price, location, exercise facilities, etc.). We would usually rather see a single reminder for such a task rather than multiple reminders—one each for task-related items.

How does such a grouping come about? Task-related items might all be grouped together based on a distinguishing task tag or label they share in common. Better tool support may eventually help us to tag according to task. Later in this chapter we consider approaches, still at the prototype stage as of this book's writing, that support the tagging of items by task either

---

[5] See, for example, Jones, Dumais, and Bruce (2002) for a description of the "forgetting to look" problem.

automatically, incidentally (as part of project planning), or by extension to existing support for threaded email conversations.[6]

8.3.2 The ongoing costs of organization and maintenance

Sometimes a tool is enthusiastically embraced for its obvious benefits, only to be abandoned later as unforeseen, daily costs of its use accumulate. In one KFTF survey, two respondents reported attempting to put all their information into Info Select,[7] a special-purpose PIM tool, as a way to obviate the separate maintenance of organizations for email, files, and web bookmarks. One respondent used InfoSelect for over a year.

But both respondents eventually abandoned the tool. As it turned out, InfoSelect was used in addition to, rather than instead of, the file system as a means of organizing information. Respondents were apparently unwilling to abandon the filing system and commit to InfoSelect entirely as an alternate means of organizing information. But then, InfoSelect represented an extra cost of PIM that was not sufficiently offset (in respondents' estimation) by its benefits.

Two respondents reported a similar pattern in their use of Microsoft OneNote. The application was initially embraced as a means of taking digital notes. But both participants eventually abandoned its use because OneNote required the use of a special tabbed system for the organization of notes which did not integrate with existing organizations for files, email, or web references.

Consider Jonathan's experience with a scheme for organizing paper bills and monthly account statements. Jonathan placed each bill or statement in a folder labeled by bill sender or account name and then sorted within a folder according to date. He spent on average 30 to 40 minutes each month filing new bills and account statements in their proper folders. But then he eventually made an observation: He rarely went back to old bills or account statements. Given this realization, he decided he was better off lumping bills and statements into a single large folder by year—last in, most forward. Filing time each month is greatly reduced, and finding time is only a few minutes longer on those rare cases when he needs to retrieve a bill or statement.

8.3.3 Measurements and considerations

Elements of a PIM practice need to be usable. Key concepts of usability as defined by the International Organization for Standards are effectiveness, efficiency, and satisfaction (ISO document 9241).

- *Effectiveness*. Does the tool (scheme, strategy) help people to do what they want and need to do? Error rates and accuracy are relevant to a discussion of effectiveness. If we frequently fail, our effectiveness obviously goes down.

---

[6] *Virtual folders* (see the Wikipedia article on same at *http://en.wikipedia.org/wiki/Virtual_folder*) as realized through "smart folders" on current versions of the Macintosh computer or through "search folders" in the Microsoft Vista operating system provide a means for grouping together items that all match the restrictions of a search expression. However, items so grouped must already share something in common through their content or property values and tags that are assigned.

[7] "Info Select 7.0 adds more information capture capabilities, numerous new features," see *http://www.informationweek. com/news/showArticle.jhtml?articleID=193401525.*

- *Efficiency*. How much time and effort is needed? Efficiency and effectiveness are different. An organizational scheme, for example, can be effective at organizing information for later use but still be inefficient for the demands it places on a person's time to keep and organize.

- *Satisfaction*. How happy are people in the use of an element? Clearly, satisfaction is an inherently more subjective measure than either effectiveness or efficiency. Doesn't effectiveness plus efficiency equal satisfaction? Not necessarily. Suppose that Ron, as he was described in Chapter 5, is eventually promoted to Walter's position? Should he assume Walter's strategy for pushing PIM responsibilities onto his assistant and the people that report to him? The strategy has proven effectiveness and efficiency for Walter but may still be deeply unsatisfying to Ron.

Kelly and Teevan (2007) offer additional measures to consider, such as *usefulness* and *ease of use*. Most clearly distinct from the measures above is *ease of learning*:

- *Ease of learning*. How easy is an element to learn? How much must be learned before an element can be used with effectiveness, efficiency, and satisfaction? For example, an elaborate scheme of organization that takes many hours to learn before we can begin to use it can fail for the simple reason that we never find the time to learn it.

A set of more PIM-specific considerations follows directly from a consideration of the seven kinds of PIM activity described in this book (including activities for measuring and evaluating activities themselves and also for *making sense activities* as described in Chapter 9). Table 8.1 lists questions we might ask (and measurements we might make) for each kind of PIM activity.

Table 8.1   A checklist of questions when considering an element (current or proposed) in your PIM practice

Activity	Does the (current / new) (strategy / scheme / tool) …	Feature examples
Keeping	Help the initial decision to assess usefulness?	Summarization, highlighting, search terms in context in a search-results listing
	Support the tagging or filing of an item to reflect the time, place, and form of anticipated use later on?	Automated tagging, suggested folders[8]
Finding	Help me to remember to look for the item later?	Reminders, preferably set at the level of a task-related grouping of items
	Make use of what I'm able to recall to help me narrow the scope of my search?	Full-text search support
	Support my recognition of an item?	Results list displayed with search terms highlighted

Continued

---

[8] See, for example, Segal and Kephart (1999).

Activity	Does the (current / new) (strategy / scheme / tool) …	Feature examples
Organizing	Consolidate or leverage existing organizations?	
	Support the reuse of organizational structures?	
	Support the use of organizing templates?	
Maintaining	Make it easy to move or archive items no longer in active use?	
	Make backups easy and automatic?	Scheduled, web-based backup
	Preserve the ability to use (view, edit) an item over time even as formats migrate?	
Managing flow	Provide controls for incoming information?	Junk email filters; caller ID
	Provide controls for outgoing information?	Privacy initiatives such as P3P (see Chapter 6).
Measuring and evaluating	Collect useful measures concerning my use of information or elements (tools, schemes of organization, strategies) of my PIM practice?	
Making sense	Help me to arrange my information in new ways that make useful, new patterns and relationships more apparent?	

Not every tool (strategy, organizational scheme) is designed to positively impact every PIM activity. No matter. You may see uses of a tool not foreseen by its designers. But be sure, at least, that you aren't overlooking ways in which a change in PIM practice could make things worse as well as better.

Note also that another kind of checklist can be devised with respect to each of the six senses of "personal information" as described in Chapter 2. The number of "don't know/doesn't apply" answers is likely to be high. On the other hand, you may be surprised at some of the answers that occur to you. Consider, for example, Sally's strategy of asking others for information when she needs it. One side effect of this strategy that might not have immediately occurred to Sally is that she is providing a great deal of information about herself—her interests, the projects she is working on, her progress—through the questions she asks others. Sally might not care. Would you? Or, to consider another example, the "What Next for Tool Development?" sidebar describes a potential revolution in software release and usage monitoring that may result from web-based applications. We certainly stand to benefit. But also important is the protection of information about us (the second sense of personal information described in Chapter 2).

What Now for IT?

– Bob Boiko

Every day, new and improved personal information applications become available. How can an IT group even keep up with the flux? Moreover, how can you evaluate this endless stream of products and measure their impact on your organization? How can you form an opinion about which of these new applications to permit, encourage, or even promote as standards?

A good method of getting ahead of new product offerings is to approach the market with a framework of what you expect to see. In the area of personal information management, you might naturally expect to see these sorts of communication applications:

- *Point-to-point communication*. Email, instant messaging, and mobile phone applications are of this variety. They allow conversations between individuals and small groups.

- *Broadcast communication*. Blogs, podcasts, and image-sharing applications are of this variety. They permit an individual to get a message out to a wide audience.

- *Collaboration applications*. Wikis, social bookmarking, and groupware applications are of this sort. They allow a small group to work together toward some end.

While not exhaustive, you can see how this simple framework covers a very wide range of applications. Having a framework like this allows you to make sense of an exploding market. We have always had these needs. The new products are simply new ways to meet the same old needs.

But what about evaluation? How can you measure the benefit of a potential new application? Using a framework, you can turn this question around and instead ask which areas need the most help. For example, there are a lot of new, interesting broadcast applications available, but do you need to do a better job of broadcasting? If not, then you can safely ignore a large range of applications. On the other hand, you may be able to identify significant and pressing issues with collaboration (low productivity, poor quality, and so on). If so, you can focus on this segment and create a more detailed framework to further narrow down your field of view until you find an application that seems to solve a real problem in your organization.

But how will you know for sure whether your investment in a particular tool will return value? Begin by establishing a benchmark. For example, if you believe that collaboration on team reports is inefficient, begin by documenting how long the average report takes to create. Then establish a target. If the average report takes two weeks, can you cut it down to one week? Of course, you also have to convince yourself that a time reduction of one week per report is worth the cost of tool acquisition, development, deployment, training, and maintenance of, say, a collaboration web site.

Having done the work to establish benchmarks and targets, you also have to commit to measuring outcomes. You have to measure how long the average report takes to create after your tool is in place.

Efficiency is not the only useful and measurable benefit. You can target productivity. Does giving employees instant messaging increase the volume of customer questions that they can effectively answer? You can target missed opportunities. Does giving sales staff a collaboration web site increase the number of product inquiries they can respond to?

Clearly, only very small tools deal with only one benefit. But even in larger tools (say an entire document management system) the logic is the same. Know that the market is not going to identify new problems, just new solutions to the same old problems. Approach the market with a clear idea of what problems you have. Identify benchmarks for how well you are doing against your problems now and targets for how well you have to do to justify the expense of new applications. Then be willing and able to continually measure the impact your tools have on your problems. In this way, you can make year-over-year progress against your biggest needs, even in the face of a seemingly endless stream of new and improved applications.

8.4 What can research tell us about methods of measuring and evaluating in our practices of PIM?

We run across new elements we might want to include in our practice of PIM all the time. Open any trade magazine, walk down the self-help or computing aisle of any bookstore, or simply browse the Web. We can see advertisements for schemes to get organized, strategies of time and task management, and tools to do nearly everything.

Generally missing, though, are objective measurements that might relate to the considerations listed in Section 8.3.3. Trade magazine tool reviews, naturally enough, focus on the tool and its features, leaving readers with the difficult leap to real situations of use in their own lives.

Even were we to find a study that might apply to our PIM situation, we need to season its results with a few grains of salt, as the saying goes. Who were the participants? What kinds of tasks did they do? Over what period of time? In what situations: in a laboratory or a participant's natural working environment? What kinds of measurements were taken and by whom? Certainly a healthy skepticism should be directed toward studies done by the tool provider.

Studies of any kind that directly apply to the decision we need to make are rare. Good studies with believable results are still more rare.

A larger problem is that PIM-relevant measurement and evaluation are very hard to do. The challenges we face in measuring and evaluating our own practices of PIM are mirrored by those that researchers face in their efforts to better understand how people do PIM and to better assess the likely utility of various potential PIM solutions. For example, the answer to the question, "Is it working?" is often "That depends" or "It's too soon to tell."

Measurements need to be made over a period of weeks or months, and the new element (e.g., a tool) must be exercised in many different situations of PIM. The appeal and benefits of a tool may be immediately apparent, while its costs are only evident later. Also, people's subjective assessment of a tool may not align with objective measures of their use of it.[9] Doing this kind of study is very time-consuming and expensive, even when participants can be recruited. And recruiting people to participate over an extended period (and not to drop out along the way) is very difficult indeed.

We shouldn't expect, therefore, that the supply of PIM-relevant, user-relevant studies will increase dramatically any time soon. Of course, we don't wait. We do our own research. We try out new strategies, new schemes of organization, new tools, and new features of existing tools, just as we discard older versions of the same.

As we do our own research, we make mistakes. Perhaps we embrace a "Get organized!" New Year's resolution and then devise an elaborate scheme of filing. We follow it zealously the first week but ever less so afterward. The "to be filed" pile—whether paper or digital items—gets ever larger, and soon we are faced with another failed attempt to organize. Or perhaps, as noted above, we enthusiastically embrace a new tool, but as time goes on, we use it less and less and then not at all. The converse can also happen. We continue with the same old tools and strategies and suffer the same frustrations over and over again. We think about changing but never seem to find the time to do so.

In one survey,[10] people were asked to list strategies they tried that had worked well for them and also to list strategies that had not worked. Across respondents, the same strategies were listed in both the "works for me" and "doesn't work for me" columns, including "file everything immediately," "file nothing," "keep the folder hierarchy broad but only one or two levels deep," and "develop a deeply nested hierarchy with only a limited number of subfolders at each step."

We can't expect that researchers will have answers that directly apply to the decisions we need to make in our practices of PIM. But we can learn from the methods used in PIM-related research. We can become better researchers of our own practices of PIM. The next subsection considers two research methods that might work for you in your efforts to observe and better understand your practice of PIM. The second subsection provides some suggestions to consider when making decisions concerning the elements of your PIM practice.

---

[9] For example, Cockburn and McKenzie (2000) note that people can express a preference for one tool even though their performance may be as high or higher with alternate tools.

[10] See Bruce, Jones, and Dumais (2004).

8.4.1 Methods for studying your practice of PIM

A very large number of methods of inquiry (and methodologies specifying a "logic" to the application of methods) have potential relevance to the study of your own practice of PIM.[11] Methods vary along several dimensions, including:

1. Participants: What kinds of people are being studied (e.g., by age, gender, ethnicity, profession)?

2. Place: A controlled laboratory setting or a setting in the participant's life?

3. Individual or group?

4. Active or passive participation?

5. What tasks are being done? What's the situation?

6. Time period: A single session? For how long? Multiple sessions? How many? Over what period of time?

7. Measurements taken: Objective measurements of time to complete a task and success are often taken in studies where the task is well specified. Subjective measurements can also be useful. Participants are sometimes asked to think aloud as they work to complete a task.

For example, the focus-group method generally takes place in a controlled setting, involves a group of participants, and encourages their active participation. The traditional usability study generally involves a single session taking place in a controlled setting, using a single individual as a participant, with tasks selected by the person conducting the study. As a general rule, participants initiate discussion or otherwise actively participate only at the beginning (to ask questions about the task) or at the conclusion of the session and possibly only in response to a "Do you have any questions or comments?" query during the debriefing.

In studies of human–computer interaction, and especially in studies about how people do PIM, increasing emphasis is given to methods of inquiry that are situated (i.e., take place where a participant does PIM), minimally disruptive, and occur over extended periods of time.[12] As noted earlier, recruiting people to participate in these studies is not easy.

But you have a ready participant: yourself! We make assessments of ourselves and our situation all the time as we ask questions like, "How did that go?" or "What could I have done differently?" Unfortunately, many of these assessments are done away from the situation or event we're assessing—as we walk away from a meeting, for example, or as we drive home from work. And these assessments depend on memories that may not always be accurate. Here we consider methods of self-study inspired by two more formal methods of inquiry.

---

[11] For a partial overview, see Naumer and Fisher (2007); also see *http://www.usabilitynet.org/tools/methods.htm.*

[12] See, for example, Holtzblatt and Jones (1993) and Naumer and Fisher (2007) for discussions of less intrusive methods of inquiry.

Critical incident technique

Critical incident technique (CIT) emerged from the study of aviation psychology and has been usefully applied in aviation, health care, and other domains where "human error" can cost not just time and money, but lives. A critical incident is defined "in a situation where the purpose or intent of the act seems fairly clear to the observer and where its consequences are sufficiently definite to leave little doubt concerning its effects."[13]

Failures and near-failures in our practices of PIM are, we can hope, generally not life threatening. But several incidents deserve more than a shoulder shrug, as in, "Oh well, better luck next time." Consider, for example, failed efforts to re-find an information item that you know is "here some-where." You may fail outright or fail in your initial attempts so that accessing the item takes much longer than you anticipated. Ask yourself the following questions: What were you trying to find? How and where did you look? How long did you spend looking? Over what period of time? If you eventually found the item, how did you find it? What finally worked? Most important: What will you do differently to avoid a similar incident in the future?

As an exercise in PIM tutorials and courses I teach, participants interview each other with respect to a specified recent failure to re-find. The discussion that ensues is usually lively and interesting. Other PIM incidents worthy of attention include (1) incidents in which your privacy has been seriously compromised (e.g., you were tricked by a phishing attempt, as described in Chapter 7); (2) incidents where you lost or nearly lost data (e.g., the computer crashed before you could save changes in a document or, much worse, your hard drive fails); (3) incidents of email exchange where misunderstanding led to hurt feelings or serious disruptions in a project collaboration.

The best time to analyze an incident is immediately after it occurs and before memories begin to fade. Unfortunately, timing does not always allow for this. (Indeed, one of the reasons an incident may be considered "critical" is because of the overall time pressures of the situation.)

Experience sampling method

With experience sampling method (ESM), participants are interrupted at intervals (random or regular) throughout their day and asked a series of questions.[14] My advisor, Professor John R. Anderson,[15] used a variation of this method in a self-study of his own productivity. He charted his productivity at half-hour intervals throughout his working day as marked by a recurring buzzer on his watch:

> It did occupy at least a 5-year period of my life.[16] I think the measure I was trying to get was the number of hours of actual productivity. I do remember I never liked the overhead and interruption but I often found myself not being particularly productive

---

[13] See Flanagan (1954, 327); see also Wikipedia for an excellent article and good pointers to information on the critical incident technique (*http://en.wikipedia.org/wiki/Critical_Incident_Technique*).

[14] For more on the experience sampling method, see Barrett and Barrett (2001) and Consolvo and Walker (2003).

[15] See *http://act-r.psy.cmu.edu/people/ja/*; see also the Wikipedia article on John R. Anderson at *http://en.wikipedia.org/wiki/John_Robert_Anderson_%28psychologist%29*.

[16] The period described was roughly from 1977 to 1982.

when the buzzer rang. One of the reasons I quit was that the behavior I was trying to produce had finally become automated and when the buzzer rang I always found myself at a pretty high level of productivity. I would like to think I have maintained my good ways but maybe I am kidding myself.[17]

If you try this method, consider the following questions: What were you doing (at the time the "buzzer" went off)? What PIM activities, if any, had you done recently? What forms of information were you working with? Email? Files? Web pages? What other interruptions had you had recently? A significant advantage of *ESM* is that you have access to memories that have not yet faded. Even regular intervals (e.g., half-hour or hourly intervals) through a day are likely to sample broadly across the activities that take up your day. A disadvantage, as Professor Anderson notes above, is that the interruption can be very annoying.

Research in PIM provides one more suggestion for the self-study of your PIM practice: using a PSI confidant.

Find a PSI confidant

In PIM studies, when participants are asked to give tours through regions of their PSIs, the study session often turns into something more. Participants are initially embarrassed at "this mess." Participants see things through the fresh eyes of the observer which they routinely overlook when on their own. Participants are able to assume a different, more objective perspective on their PSI and the ways in which it works and does not work for them. And participants are motivated to change. Participants may make big changes in their organizations for files, email messages, paper documents, and the like, as revealed in a follow-up study session several days later. Boardman and Sasse (2004) quote one participant as saying, "It's like a confessional getting all my computer problems off my chest." It is no exaggeration, then, to note that for some people, a review of their PSIs and their practices of PIM may be a kind of informational therapy.

8.4.2 Suggestions for evaluation

Considerations change as we move from measurements, observations, and the gathering of data to evaluation. To use the earlier example, you are no longer asking, How many apples? How many oranges? Now you must decide, Which bag of apples and oranges? How you approach and frame this question can make all the difference.

Consider these two points:

- *Situate your evaluation.* Make the alternatives, including the status quo, as real as possible. Don't consider the purchase of a new tool while at a store or while looking at the web site. Consider the purchase while in your workspace. Try out the alternatives—if not in actuality, then at least in your mind.

---

[17] Email communication with Professor Anderson, April 10, 2007. Over the past 25 years (as of this communication), Professor Anderson has published 9 books (several in multiple editions) and is first or supporting author of more than 250 articles.

- *Evaluate at several points in time.* The same question ("new tool, or not?") may yield different answers at different points in time. You may recall things about the way you do things at one point in time that you did not, could not, recall previously. You may value things differently. ESM can work as a way to evaluate as well as measure over time. Alternatively or in addition, you may consciously select different points to reflect different situations in a workday or a work week (e.g., meeting preparation or status report writing).

Here are some additional points that should be considered as you evaluate.

Frame decisions as a choice between specific alternatives

Research on user evaluations of prototypes demonstrates that whether alternatives are specified makes a big difference in evaluation ratings.[18] If people are shown a prototype and asked to evaluate it in isolation, ratings are significantly higher than if the prototype is evaluated in the context of alternatives (e.g., Which do you like better? Prototype A, B, or C?). This research suggests that the format of the basic "Should I change?" question is problematic. Should I change the organization of my files? Should I change to a new web browser? These questions are difficult to answer reliably since answers depend on assumptions made, but not specified, concerning the status quo and alternatives. Making a question more specific is not enough. Should I stick with the Internet Explorer? As opposed to what? A better question: Should I stick with the Internet Explorer or switch to using FireFox as my primary web browser? This is a question that makes the alternative(s) clear.

No change can be risky too

Consider the decision about whether to buy a new software tool or a new PDA that is loaded with cool features. Not deciding, or waiting to decide later, can be costly in its own right. Possible payoffs are summarized in Table 8.2. Think of the points listed as a relative gain in our information management situation or, possibly, on our competition.

The change to a new tool (or scheme or strategy) could turn out to be a bad change. A software tool may not work as advertised, so that we abandon its use and have then lost the time (and possibly the money) involved in its acquisition.[19] This is represented by a false

Table 8.2 Advantage points for different outcomes in a decision to change or not to change some PIM practice element

	Change	Don't change
Good change	A **hit** = 10 points	A **miss** = –2 points
Bad change	A **false alarm** = –5 points	A **correct rejection** = 0 points

---

[18] See, for example, Tohidi et al. (2006).

[19] Costs for a bad change can be much worse. The tool can interfere with other tools we have already or, in extreme cases, might even "infect" our computer with some malicious computer virus.

alarm in Table 8.2 and the loss of five advantage points. But a decision not to make a good change can be costly too. This is represented by the costs of a miss in Table 8.2. Our situation never stays the same. If we stick with our status quo as others around us successfully upgrade to new, faster machines, improved operating systems, or more PIM-specific tools, we fall behind.

The foregoing analysis is an application of the theory of signal detectability (TSD). TSD first appeared back in 1954[20] and is grounded in statistical decision theory. TSD has been applied elsewhere to a basic question of information retrieval—what does and does not get returned in response to a user's query?[21]—and also to keeping decisions.[22]

In practice, we'll rarely have the requisite data needed to fully apply TSD to a change decision involving our practice of PIM. To do so, for example, we must assess the conditional likelihood and associated value ("advantage points") of different outcomes, given available information concerning the change under consideration. Even so, it is often useful to devise payoff matrices such as the one in Table 8.2. Even qualitative descriptions of different outcomes (e.g., hits, misses, correct rejections, and false alarms) can be useful. And we should always recognize that "playing it safe" by sticking with the status quo or deciding not to decide can carry its own costs, as measured by missed opportunities or preventable failures.

Be careful how you frame the choice

Tversky and Kahneman (1981) describe experiments in which the relative preference for the options changed dramatically depending on the "framing" of these choices. In one situation, an "Asian disease" is expected to kill 600 people if no action is taken. Different groups of participants were given choices for different programs of action, as summarized in Table 8.3.

Table 8.3 Preferences can change depending on whether choices are expressed as gains or losses

With no action	"600 are expected to die" (if no action is taken)
Option A	"200 people will be saved."
Option B	"There is a one-third probability that all 600 people will be saved and a two-thirds probability that nobody will be saved."
Option C	"400 people will die."
Option D	"There is a one-third probability that nobody will die, and a two-thirds probability that 600 people will die."

---

[20] For original discussions of the theory of signal detectability, see Peterson, Birdsall, and Fox (1954) and Van Meter and Middleton (1954).

[21] See, for example, Swets (1963, 1969) for a discussion of the application of TSD to information retrieval.

[22] See Jones (2004) for an application of TSD to the keeping decision.

One group of participants was given a choice between Option A, in which "200 people will be saved," and Option B, in which "There is a one-third probability that all 600 people will be saved and a two-thirds probability that nobody will be saved." Of the two choices, 72 percent of the participants preferred Option A. A second group of participants was given a choice between Option C, in which "400 people will die," and Option D, in which "There is a one-third probability that nobody will die and a two-thirds probability that 600 people will die." Between these two, 78 percent of the participants preferred Option D.

But note that Options A and C are essentially identical, as are Options B and D. Observed effects of framing are summarized in Table 8.4.

Why the dramatic change in preference? Tversky and Kahneman (1979) explain the results with respect to *prospect theory*. Prospect theory predicts, as verified empirically, that when choices are framed in terms of relative loss, we're more likely to take a riskier option (an option with greater variability in outcome) rather than accept certain loss. But when choices are framed in terms of relative gain, we're more likely to take the certain gain over a riskier option that could leave us with nothing. The preference for A over B might be paraphrased with reference to the colloquial expression "Quit while I'm ahead," while the preference for D over C might be paraphrased with reference to the expression "in for a penny, in for a pound."

Now consider a variation in Table 8.5. You currently have an Internet service provider that you're not particularly happy with. Your service is down 6 hours in 1000, which didn't seem like much at first but the 6 hours always seem to happen in work-critical periods. Worse, your provider is raising prices. You're definitely changing. Which option would you pick, A or B? What about your choice between C or D?

This discussion can't begin to do justice to the many subtleties of prospect theory or to the richness of supporting empirical data. However, one practical implication for us as we consider alternatives (even alternatives in which one option is the status quo) is to approach choices both from the standpoint of their relative costs and the variability of these costs, and then again from the standpoint of relative benefit and the variability of benefit. Does your preference change? If so, you may need to consider more carefully the costs and benefits of each choice and their relative importance to you.

Table 8.4 People prefer a certain gain (A) but avoid a certain loss (C)

	Preference	
A (certain gain)	>	**B** (risky gain)
‖		‖
C (certain loss)	<	**D** (risky loss)

Table 8.5   Which ISP would you choose: A or B? C or D?

Current provider	Six hours downtime per 1000
Option A	Two hours extra uptime
Option B	One-third chance of zero hours downtime, two-thirds chance of no improvement
Option C	Four hours downtime
Option D	One-third chance of zero hours downtime, two-thirds chance of six hours downtime

8.5 Measuring and evaluating in real life

We now consider how to measure and evaluate with respect to our lives and what we want to do, rather than with respect to our applications and what they are designed to do.

8.5.1 Measuring according to what we want to do

Some measures are easy to take; others are not. The "What Next in Tool Development?" sidebar discusses some measurements that our software applications can make. Measurements can have obvious value for software developers seeking to improve their products. Some of these measurements can have value to those of us who use these products as well.

A software application is like a lamppost casting a light that makes it easy to measure things like "time spent in this application today."[23] Figure 8.1, for example, shows the display of measures available to the Eudora user.

We can expect an increasingly standard inclusion in software tools of some ability to collect measurements from us, as users, on the way these tools are used. We hope we'll have a choice concerning whether these measurements are collected and whether measurement data is shared (in ways that preserve our anonymity) with the tool developers.

Measurements can shed light on various questions of usage. Which tool features are used? How often? In what sequence? Which menu items are selected? Which options? How long do people spend in an application, and in which parts of the application? Some of these measures would surely be of interest to us as users, especially if presented in the right way. Measures

---

[23] Time spent in an application would likely be based on the times a window owned by the application is the active window. As such, some distortion is possible, since we may answer the phone or leave to go to lunch while the clock is ticking, so to speak, on an active window. However, this is a problem easily finessed by a rule that, for example, stops the clock if there is more than a minute pause between keystrokes.

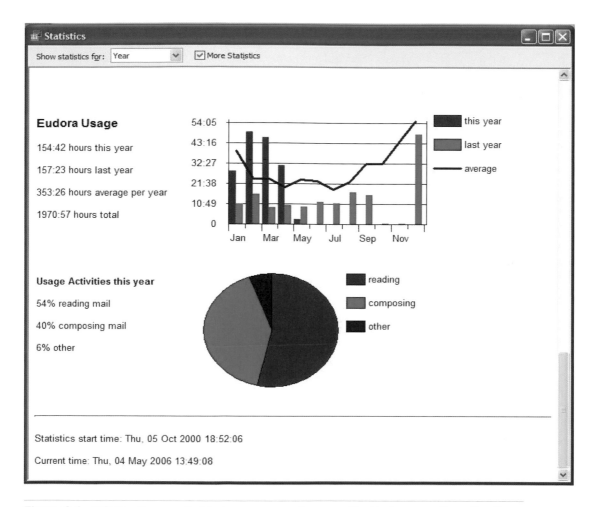

Figure 8.1 Information available to a person who uses the Eudora email application.

that showed us, for example, that we could save three hours in a month by making better use of an application might have real impact.

But the light of an application lamppost goes only so far. Consider the following examples involving measures that are not easily collected by current software applications or other tools.

Alice calls her husband to say she'll be late coming home from work. How late? She has no idea and so guesses "an hour." An hour later she calls to say she's still not done. She needs another "half-hour." And so on. Wouldn't it be nice if Alice could accurately estimate the time she will need?

Martin is asked if he would be willing to volunteer to put out this year's school phone book for his son's elementary school. He'll take over from another volunteer, Larry, who completed the phone book last year. Larry estimates that it took him "20 to 40 hours" to complete last year's phone book. Is this an accurate estimate? How can Martin be sure?

John is asked to take on an additional group as part of his managerial responsibilities at work. He'll get no more pay but expects that the added responsibilities will put him closer to the promotion he has been pushing for. On the other hand, he's promised his family he won't take on new responsibilities at work and will, instead, spend more time at home. What to do? One thing he would like are some good estimates of the extra time and extra distraction (demands on his attention, his energy, his ability to multitask) managing this extra group will require. His manager can only give him a very vague assurance that extra demands are "minimal."

Alice and John want to move to a better neighborhood. They also want to plan for their children's college education and for their own retirement. The have a long list of chores to complete around their house, including a yard sale to get rid of some the clutter that has built up everywhere around their house. They have many other hopes and dreams as well—a family vacation to Disney World, for example, and, later, a vacation for just the two of them to Hawaii. But month after month goes by and it sometimes feels that all their money, energy, attention, and time are spent just getting by. They have no clear sense about the synergies that might exist between goals and the additional sacrifices they may need to make now to achieve their goals.

The measures that would help in these examples are not easy to collect. For example, the measures needed to accurately estimate the demands of a new project or role are very difficult for people to make when they are working as fast as they can just to complete the work involved. People are constantly switching or being switched between tasks in a typical day.[24] Unless they have the time-tracking discipline of a lawyer or a consultant (and the associated tools), they are not likely to track the time involved in a role or a project.

It would be nice if tools could help, but they can't keep track for the basic reason that they have little or no awareness of the "roles and goals" in our lives. Even sophisticated tools that attempt to detect shifts automatically work only with lower-level, specific tasks done in support of a project or a role.[25] Moreover, automated tagging is still limited by severe tradeoffs between error rate and coverage. These tradeoffs give us a choice between either mislabeling the work we do or not labeling it at all. Finally, automated tagging may not be able to keep pace as new tasks emerge or old tasks are redefined.

What to do? An approach being pursued in the KFTF project is to support people in the external representation of tasks, projects, and roles. This approach has led to prototyping work on a *Personal Project Planner* as described in Chapter 5. Prototyping research is motivated by a basic observation: people plan. And people often give expression to their plans in external representations (ERs) that range from to-do lists, to planning documents, to sometimes intricate

---

[24] For examples and data on task switching, see Czerwinski, Horvitz, and Wilhite (2004) and Gonzalez and Mark (2004).

[25] For descriptions of one such approach, see Bao, Herlocker, and Dietterich (2006) and Shen et al. (2006).

nestings of folders and subfolders. ERs reflect, complement, and facilitate the further expression of companion internal representations. Even a simple to-do list—whether expressed on a scrap of paper or in an electronic document (e-document)—serves as a powerful complement to a person's often fallible internal memory of a situation.

A basic premise of the Planner is that people will, if given sufficient support, create ERs for various projects and roles in their lives and will then make repeated use of these ERs over time as a basis for planning and managing. Given the right tool support, people will then willingly communicate the project they are working on. This communication does not happen as a separate task, but rather as a natural by-product of their efforts to manipulate, map, and make sense of goals and roles.

Another approach is to leverage the email thread since it frequently corresponds to a task people are working together to complete. Bellotti et al.'s TaskMaster (2003), described in more detail and illustrated as part of Chapter 10's coverage of email, builds on email *threads* to define "thrasks." Thrasks provide a way to group together both email messages and documents that relate to a task. The TaskMaster also supports the specification of additional task-relevant properties such as due date.

We need tools able to understand and measure tasks and projects as we would define them and not as defined under the "lampposts" of our software applications. What resources—our time, our money—are we spending on which projects? Which recurring activities? What problems do we encounter? Where can we improve? And, especially important, are we making real progress? Visible, meaningful measures of progress on goals we care about has been shown to have a strong motivating effect.[26] If we can see that we're making progress, we're encouraged to continue.

8.5.2 Benjamin Franklin's efforts at self-observation

Measuring and evaluating needn't be limited just to activities and elements of our PIM practices. Measuring and evaluating can look more broadly. Are we living up to our hopes, dreams, and principles? And we needn't be solely dependent on computing tools for the answers to these questions. Both points are illustrated in Benjamin Franklin's description of his efforts at improvement with respect to "the thirteen virtues" (Figure 8.2):

> I made a little book, in which I allotted a page for each of the virtues. I rul'd each page with red ink, so as to have seven columns, one for each day of the week, marking each column with a letter for the day. I cross'd these columns with thirteen red lines, marking the beginning of each line with the first letter of one of the virtues, on which line, and in its proper column, I might mark, by a little black spot, every fault I found on examination to have been committed respecting that virtue on that day.

> I determined to give a week's strict attention to each of the virtues successively. Thus, in the first week, my great guard was to avoid every least offense against *Temperance*,

---

[26] See, for example, Freitas and Higgins (2002).

leaving the other virtues to their ordinary chance, only marking every evening the faults of the day. Thus, if in the first week I could keep my first line, marked T, clear of spots, I suppos'd the habit of that virtue so much strengthen'd, and its opposite weaken'd, that I might venture extending my attention to include the next, and for the following week keep both lines clear of spots. Proceeding thus to the last, . . . I should have, I hoped, the encouraging pleasure of seeing on my pages the progress I made in virtue, . . .

I enter'd upon the execution of this plan for self-examination, and continu'd it with occasional intermissions for some time. I was surpris'd to find myself so much fuller of faults than I had imagined; but I had the satisfaction of seeing them diminish.

Virtues such as "order" actually do relate to a practice of PIM. Ben Franklin remarks that "Order . . . with regard to places for things, papers, etc., I found extreamly difficult to acquire." But note also that Ben Franklin's table tracking virtues by day of the week is information to be

TEMPERANCE.						
EAT TO DULLNESS DRINK NOT TO ELEVATION						
	S.	M.	T.	W.	T.	F.	S.
T.							
S.	*	*		*		*	
O.	* *		*			*	
R.			*			*	
F.		*			*		
I.			*				
S.							
J.							
M.							
C.							
T.							
C.							
H.							
J.							

Figure 8.2 A depiction of the table Benjamin Franklin used to track the times in a week that he failed with respect to each of the thirteen virtues.

managed like other information. The basic table in all its many variations is a very effective way to make sense of certain kinds of information. This is a point we'll explore further in Chapter 9.

Everything that we see is a shadow cast by that which we do not see.

U.S. civil rights leader and clergyman Martin Luther King Jr. (1929–1968)

What Next in Tool Development?

– Daniel M. Russell, Google

The web-based applications world is full of surprises and opportunities *because* of the very nature of the Web. Because web-apps run remotely over a common interface portal (the web browser), the end user experience is often heavily based on common UI idioms and styles. Web-apps also offer the chance to work with a lighter memory footprint than traditional apps, and because the data is held remotely on the server, the work being done is not as subject to local machine failures. Things really are different.

But there's another, even deeper magic at work: In a world of web-apps, users come to expect that everything is instrumented. That is, every app streams use and measurement data back to the mothership with information about what features get used, what's not used, and under what circumstances. As you can imagine, this is a huge and radical change for the application developers. Suddenly, the development cycle has shifted from years to weeks as the development cycle can quickly discover bugs and misfeatures. What used to be tested in usability labs with small numbers of users has become a continuous information flow back to the developers. Not only do the developers gain an insight into what works, but in a tacit exchange, the users expect things to get better over time.

What's more, customer support now has *real data* to work with, and not just the pale, lightly sampled shadow of what they believe users are doing. At the same time, the behavior measurement data needs to be privacy-protecting, providing an anonymized and unrevealing stream of *use* data for analysis by the provider to improve services, and not *user* data that would be potentially compromising. Web application providers have to provide mechanisms at many levels to ensure the privacy and security of the information that is processed and the behaviors recorded.

What's equally important is that the web-apps can also be continually updated to reflect improvements and bug fixes. This simple change has led to a dramatic shift in the way users expect applications to work: Because features large and small can be constantly upgraded and improved (even without the user being aware of the changes), the basic philosophy behind the software development cycle has changed as well. Rather than shipping a major revision of software in yearly (or biannual) installments, major applications can now be revised and pushed out for use almost immediately as users dynamically load their AJAX applications.

At Google, major applications such as GMail and Google Finance are changed frequently as new interface ideas are invented and new back-end service capabilities come online. These applications are loaded at page-viewing time, essentially giving the user a new update of the application whenever they reconnect to the service-providing web page. When a new GMail instance is pushed out to the Google servers, users who are connecting anew immediately get the update, without having to wait for months until the next software upgrade. And within a short course of time (roughly a week), nearly all users have the newest release of the app.

Of course, this means that the evolution of the application has to be somewhat subtle and careful. Ideally, a newly pushed version should be immediately usable without much (if any) incremental instruction. On the other hand, with frequent application pushes, the rate at which an application changes can be significantly higher than it was before in the old, annual cyclic pushes.

The browser-based web-application really is different—it evolves continually, both because it can and because the developers can more easily understand what's working and what's not because of the instrumentation that tells developers the reality of use in the field.

8.6   Can self-study of PIM practices contribute to the larger study of PIM?

The study of PIM—whether to understand current practices or to evaluate a proposed change, a new tool or strategy—is not easy. Let's consider again some of the challenges:

- *A person's practice of PIM is unique* and a "work in progress." It reflects the person's personality, cognitive abilities, experience, training, various roles at work and elsewhere, available tools, available spaces, and so on. Even people who have a great deal in common with respect to profession, education, and computing platform nevertheless show great variation in their practices of PIM.[27]

- *PIM happens broadly across many tools, applications, and information forms.* Moreover, people freely convert information from one form to another to suit their needs: emailing a document, for example, or printing out a web page. Studies and evaluations that focus on a specific form of information and supporting applications—email, for example—run the risk of optimizing for that form of information but at the expense of a person's ability to manage other forms of information.

- *PIM happens over time.* Personal information has a life cycle—moving, for example, from a "hot" pile to a "warm" project folder and then, sometimes, into "cold" archival storage.[28]

---

[27] See, for example, Jones, Bruce, and Dumais (2001).

[28] See, for example, Bondarenko and Janssen (2005).

Because PIM activities also combine over time, point-in-time evaluations can be very misleading. For example, a tool may make it very easy to create web bookmarks— a keeping activity—but then provide little support for remembering to use these bookmarks later—a finding activity. Support for both activities must be considered. However, for a given information item, acts of finding and keeping may be separated from each other by months or even years.

- *Getting people to participate is not easy.* Busy people who manage lots of information are of special interest in the study of PIM. But these are the very people least likely to have time to participate. College students are sometimes willing to participate for money or for college credit. Colleagues or friends may participate as a favor or out of curiosity. Every participant, even fellow researchers in an academic or corporate research lab, have something to contribute to the study of PIM.

But different groups and different individuals have very different slants on PIM. This was made clear for me as I taught a class on PIM to undergraduates—all in their early to mid twenties— at the University of Washington. I used a discussion on email management similar to one I had presented several times before to older audiences. But reactions were not the same. Instead of nods of agreement, I got blank stares. As I probed, I came to understand that these students had not yet experienced email management problems of the kind I was describing. In particular, they did not need to manage multiple conversational threads relating to multiple projects extending over a period of weeks or months. Their uses of email, intermixed with instant messaging and text messaging on their phones, was much more immediate (e.g., "What are you doing tonight?"). Conversations were short-lived, and the students had little need to manage multiple conversations over extended periods of time. On the other hand, students described their use of elaborate systems to synchronize collections of music and video between different computers and playing devices.

My research colleagues, by contrast, produce—well—research, in the form of "papers" published in proceedings and journals. They also teach courses. In their informational worlds, issues relating to the management of text and graphics are of critical importance. Such issues include version control and the appropriate reuse of components.

The challenges faced by students and researchers, in turn, are each very different from those of the proverbial soccer mom who may be shifting rapidly between several different activities in a given day as she balances between the demands of job, family, and perhaps school or community volunteer work. If our soccer mom also manages other people at her job, this adds further challenges of information management. And if some day she or a family member is diagnosed with a serious illness, she will face yet another kind of information management challenge.

Participant availability acts as a kind of lamppost. Certainly we'll look under the lamppost, and some things we see there are true for the dark spaces beyond. But … are there ways to light up the rest of the street as well? One approach is to provide new ways for a greater variety of people to contribute to the study of PIM. People are, or can be with some self-observation, experts on their own practices of PIM. How can this expertise be shared? How can our collective experiences with our practices of PIM inform the study of PIM?

8.6.1 A shared study of PIM

One approach is to engage people as active collaborators rather than merely the "subjects" of a study. Certainly, those of us who have done studies in PIM see a familiar pattern repeat: people initially reluctant to participate in a study may then, voluntarily, continue enthusiastically discussing their own practice of PIM well beyond the scheduled period of an interview or observation. Why? Obviously, self-interest may be involved. If interviews encourage study participants to reflect on their own practices of PIM, they may arrive at useful insights. Partly also, people like talking about themselves, and many participants are justly proud of their own creative, "home-grown" solutions to PIM. People do like to share their experiences for other reasons as well.

A testament to such sharing is a diversity of problem-specific bulletin boards to which people contribute. In the Keeping Found Things Found (KFTF) project at the University of Washington, we have developed a bulletin board called "Tales of PIM" *(http://talesofpim.org)* in an effort to provide people with a forum for sharing their PIM-related experiences—good and bad, successes and failures.

Are there other venues that might work as well? We might imagine highly motivated people forming collectives for the purpose of exchanging problems and insights concerning their practices of PIM. It is already a common sight to see two or more people showing each other the features of their smart phones or digital cameras and exchanging tips on how to use these gadgets. A similar exchange can happen as one person looks over the shoulder of another while a computer is being used. Tips may be exchanged concerning how to use an email application, the desktop, or a web browser. However, the context of a PIM cooperative might encourage a wider exchange of PIM-related information.

People might be motivated between meetings to keep a diary or to subscribe to a variation of experience sampling where they are periodically prompted (perhaps by their mobile phone) to relate PIM events that have happened recently. Both the diary and experience sampling are methods of data collection used in the study of PIM. These methods might also be used in the practice of PIM. And with some incentive—the recognition of a published report, for example— cooperatives might be motivated to share their results with others to further the study of PIM.

What Now for You and Me?

Methods of measurement and data collection described in this chapter—CIT, ESM, and the use of a PSI confidant—may work for some of us some of the time. In other cases, our evaluating will be guided by our memories and data already gathered or easily collected. Regardless, we should take care in the way we frame and situate our evaluations.

- Make the choice real. Be sure to consider real choices rather than "Do you like it, yes or no" questions. When considering adoption of a new tool, scheme of organization, or strategy, the status quo—the current version of same— is always an option to be included in considerations.

- Situate. Consider choices with respect to and, preferably in, real situations in your practice of PIM. For example, if you're considering the purchase of a new laptop and routinely do some of your work at a local coffee shop, then see if you can borrow a friend's laptop of the same make and model. Try it out at the coffee shop. You may be surprised by the results. That wonderful big screen is nice, but the increased size of the new laptop makes it impossible to actually use in your lap while sitting in a chair and balancing your coffee cup with one hand.

- Sample over two or more days if time permits and under different situations of information management and use.

- There is no such thing as not deciding. Recognize that any decision you make— even a decision to postpone or not decide—is itself a decision. Saying yes to a bad change means costs of a false positive. Saying no (if only for now) to a good change means the costs of a miss ("miss" as in missed opportunities, for example).

- Frame your choices in terms of cost as well as benefit. If your preferences change, then look more closely at the alternatives and at the values you are assigning to their relevant costs, benefits, and the variability of these. Consider your choices again on successive days or over some predetermined period of time.

- For any choice, consider its many impacts—direct and indirect, intended (e.g., by tool designers) and not. Consider the impact with respect to standard measures of usability as discussed in Section 8.3. More important, consider its potential impacts on your four precious resources (money, energy, attention, time), the six senses in which information can be personal to you and, especially, the seven kinds of PIM activity (as listed in Table 8.1).

8.7 Looking back, looking forward

What have we covered?

☑ A distinction can be made between *measuring* and, more generally, data collection, on the one hand, and *evaluating*, on the other. Measuring is about raw information: How many apples? How many oranges? Evaluating is about making comparisons and assigning value: Do I like apples or oranges more? When measuring and evaluating a practice of PIM, elements to consider include its *schemes* of organization, supporting *tools*, and *strategies* for the use of tools, organizations, and the surrounding environment, including colleagues and friends.

☑ A *yardstick* for measuring the elements of a PIM practice includes conventional measures of usability, but also should consider the impact of an element on not just one but several activities of PIM. A tool that makes it easier to keep items, for example, has little value if items cannot be found again later.

☑ Good quality, objective research on PIM is difficult and expensive to do. Few studies have direct relevance to the choices we weigh between the various tools, schemes, and strategies that compete for our time, attention, and money. But research methods can apply in modified form to our self-study of our PIM practices. Less formally, but inspired by the *critical incident technique (CIT)*, we can document the circumstances of our failures and near-failures in various activities of PIM. Similarly, we can use variations of the *experience sampling method (ESM)* to gain a more objective sense of what we do in a day and where the time goes. Also, we often see elements of our own practice better through the eyes of a sympathetic observer—someone we "invite" into our space. In our efforts to understand our practices of PIM, we may benefit from an interested *PSI confidant* who interviews us as we guide this person through our PSI. We can return the favor.

☑ Research also provides guidelines for evaluating our choices after relevant data has been collected. *Framing* matters, situation matters, sampling matters. Be sure that questions are expressed with respect to specific alternatives—even if one alternative is the status quo—rather than as "Yes/no" or "How much do you like this?" questions. There is no such thing as not deciding. If we make a bad change, we pay the price of a *false positive*. But if we fail to make a good change (even as others around us do), we pay the price of a *miss*. Finally, our preference can sometimes change dramatically, depending on whether we're intent on avoiding a certain cost (loss) or we're intent on preserving a certain benefit (gain).

☑ Methods of manual data collection such as CIT and ESM may work for some of us some of the time. But we also look to our tools to take meaningful measurements for us even as we retain the evaluative burden to ultimately decide whether and how to make changes in our practices of PIM. Software applications—especially web-based software applications—are increasingly becoming instrumented by default to collect measurements that provide useful feedback to their product teams and can also provide useful feedback to us as the people who use these applications.

But current applications have little concept of "real-life" tasks or projects that align with our goals and the various roles we seek to fulfill in our lives. How can we give the computer an understanding of our tasks and projects? One approach is to build tools able to automatically tag information items according to inferred task. This is difficult to get right. Another approach is to build on existing structure. For example, the messages and associated attachments of an email conversation might be expanded (through some manual effort on the part a person) to reference items involved in the completion of a task and, by tracking interactions with these items, to make useful measurements such as overall time to complete a task.

A third approach seeks to provide a rich environment of planning to which people will return again and again as they plan a project, order its component tasks, and find or create the information needed to complete the project. Working from a project plan outward to interact with project-useful information provides another basis for tagging information items, tracking project and task-relevant activities, and taking meaningful project- and task-relevant measurements.

The chapter concludes by considering the possibility that, especially given the enormity of the PIM space to be researched, each of us, as practitioners of PIM, might contribute our own observations to a shared "Tales of PIM" database.

If wishes come true and our tools begin to collect measurements of direct relevance to our goals and roles, then we may soon face a different kind of challenge—one that occupies a point somewhere between the basic collection of meaningful measurements and final steps of evaluation: What do the measurements say? What do they really mean? How do we make sense of them? More broadly, how do we make sense of our information and the needs to which it applies? This is the topic for the next chapter.

Making sense
of things

Does the information we have make sense? How? Are we making sense in the information we provide? *Making sense* involves an interplay between information and need. Making sense is about activity and outcome. Making sense engages a natural inclination to understand the world around us, to discover its patterns, to unlock its secrets, and to appreciate its beauty. Mendeleev made sense of the chemical elements. Using his methods and others, we can make sense of our information and the needs to which it applies.

Chapter
Nine

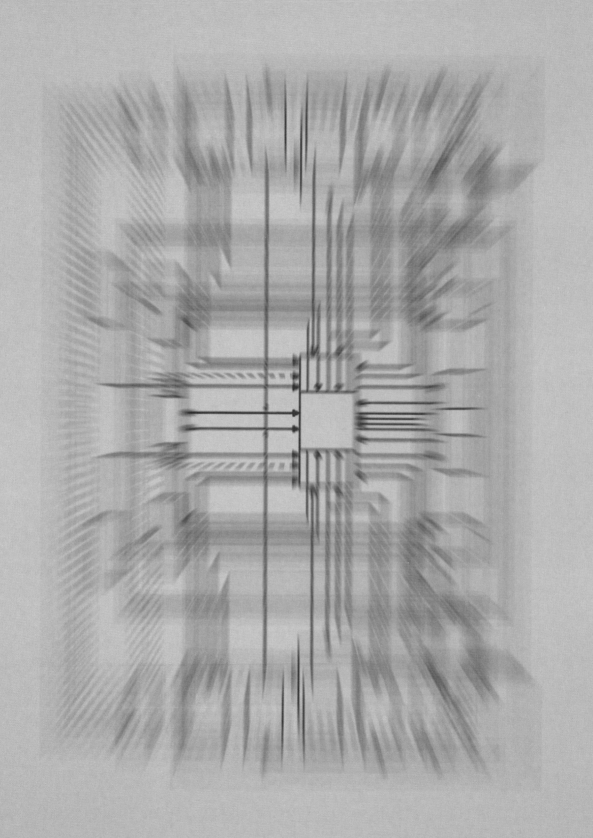

Genius is the ability to see things invisible, to manipulate things intangible, to paint things that have no features.

French essayist and moralist Joseph Joubert (1754–1824)

9.1 Starting out

What does this mean? How does it affect me? What do I need to do? These are questions we ask ourselves continuously, both as we encounter information and as we think of our needs and the things we need to be doing. Implications are often everyday and immediate. We see the weather forecast on the web site and decide to take an umbrella with us to work. We receive an email message suggesting a change in meeting time and location. Can we make the new time, or are we already booked? Is the meeting nearby, or do we need to allow extra time to travel to and from?

But implications are sometimes less obvious. We read reports of a ballooning deficit and wonder what impact this may have on our investments. We read reports of terrorism or a flu epidemic and wonder whether we should take our summer family vacation abroad as we'd planned. We may have collected a large amount of information for a project—the completion of a work-related report, for example, or the purchase of a new automobile for personal use. Collecting the information has been relatively easy. But now we ask ourselves, what does this all mean? How to structure the information so that it makes sense with respect to the goals we want to accomplish, whether it concerns writing a convincing report or making a good purchase.

Sometimes making sense is the same as understanding. But consider a statement like "I understand what you're asking me to do but it doesn't make any sense." The speaker of this sentence is drawing a distinction. He understands perfectly well the meaning of the request but may think it unreasonable or a bad idea. "Fighting rush-hour traffic to pick me up at the airport doesn't make any sense. It would be much faster for me to take a taxi."

When we try to make sense of a thing—be it a suggestion, a plan, a new tool, or the items in a personal information collection—we consider a larger, richer context of situational conditions and constraints, goals and priorities, and roles and responsibilities.

This chapter is the final in a series of chapters covering the basic activities of PIM. The chapter is about *making sense* as a PIM activity. Our attempt to make sense of making sense takes us through the following sections of this chapter:

☑ *Getting oriented*. The considerable amount of discussion about *sense-making* is a testament both to the importance of the activity and to the difficulty of providing a concise definition for what it is we mean when we talk about making sense or sense-making. "Making sense" is used in this book in preference to "sense-making" because it is a more generic term that implies less precision concerning either the outcome of the activity or the actions taken to reach this outcome.

☑ *Making sense of things as outcome vs. activity*. Making sense can be discussed both as outcome ("now things make sense") and activity. We consider an example of each.

☑ *Making sense of things as a PIM activity*. Making sense is, or should be, an integral part of all other PIM activities including activities to keep, find, organize, maintain, manage information flow, and measure and evaluate. Making sense is discussed as a PIM activity in its own right because (1) support for making sense is frequently overlooked—especially in the transition from paper-based to digital information; and (2) direct support for making sense as an activity may yield dividends across all other PIM activities as well. Making sense is a meta-level activity that is better done when the perspective is broader—it's better to make sense of a collection of information items rather than a single item; it's better to make sense of a collection of needs, *relating* to a project or a role, rather than to a single need.

☑ *Methods for making sense*. Methods to make sense of things divide into two general categories according to whether the approach is mostly data-driven/bottom-up or goal-driven/top-down. We consider an example of each approach.

9.2 Getting oriented

This chapter explores making sense both as a kind of activity and as a desired outcome (e.g., that things make sense). As we map out this exploration, we need to consider the related term, *sense-making* (sometimes referred to as "sensemaking" or even "sense making").

Sense-making has been a topic of discussion extending back to work initiated by Brenda Dervin and her associates in the 1970s. Dervin (1992) notes the following:

> The term sense-making has come to be used to refer to a theoretic net, a set of assumptions and propositions, and a set of methods which have been developed to study the making of sense that people do in their everyday experiences. Some people call sense-making a theory, others a set of methods, others a methodology, others a body of findings. In the most general sense, it is all of these. (p. 61)

Dervin goes on to say that "[i]n essence, then, the term sense-making refers to a coherent set of theoretically derived methods for studying human sense-making" (p. 62).

Russell et al. (1993) define *sensemaking* as "the process of searching for a representation and encoding data in that representation to answer task-specific questions." They describe sense-making as an iterative application of steps to:

1. Search for representations. The sensemaker creates representations to capture salient features of the data. . . .

2. Instantiate representations. The sensemaker repeatedly identifies information of interest and encodes it in a representation. . . .

3. Shift representations. Representation shifts during sensemaking are intended to reduce the cost of task operations. . . .

4. Consume encondons. . . . (p. 270)

The encondons, also referred to as instantiated schemas, are used to organize the available data and as a guide in the collection of new data, as needed, to fill in gaps.

Furnas and Russell (2005) explain, "Sensemaking can be a core professional task in itself, as it is for researchers, designers, or intelligence analysts. It arises when we change our place in the world or when the world changes around us. It arises when new problems, opportunities, or tasks present themselves, or when old ones resurface. It involves finding the important structure in a seemingly unstructured situation. It is an activity with cognitive and social dimensions, and has informational, communicational, and computational aspects" (p. 2115). Qu and Furnas (2005) note that "[s]ensemaking arises when people face new problems or unfamiliar situations; anywhere their current knowledge is insufficient."

Klein, Moon and Hoffman (2006) write that "modern researchers seem to mean something different from creativity, comprehension, curiosity, mental modeling, explanation, or situational awareness, although all these factors or phenomena can be involved in or related to sense-making." They go on to say that "sensemaking is a motivated, continuous effort to understand connections (which can be among people, places, and events) in order to anticipate their trajectories and act effectively" (p. 71).

These perspectives complement one another and are each useful in their own way. However, perspectives also underline the difficulty of arriving at—or even approaching—a satisfying, consensual definition for what sense-making (or "sensemaking") is. Devin provides a divergent view of sense-making as a set of methods, a set of findings, a set of assumptions, and a "theoretic net." Her discussion provides us with an understanding of what sense-making can be but leaves us with a desire to understand better what sense-making actually is at its core.

Russell et al. provide a description of sense-making that is specific but perhaps overly so. Is sensemaking really so mechanistic? Is sense-making done only in order to answer task-specific questions? Other descriptions tell us what sense-making is about or not (just) about and when it is triggered, but not what it is.

In our attempts to make sense of things, a picture is often worth a thousand words. And so it is that the illustration in Figure 9.1 is often presented as a depiction of sense-making. The figure aptly describes a situation that many of us face.

We're planning a trip, writing a report, making a major purchase decision. In situations such as these, we perceive gaps in the understanding we need to have (in order to complete planning, finish a report, or make the decision). We seek information to "fill" the gap so that we can continue our dash toward a desired outcome (e.g., an effective plan leading to a successful trip, a good report leading to a promotion, a good decision leading to a good purchase).

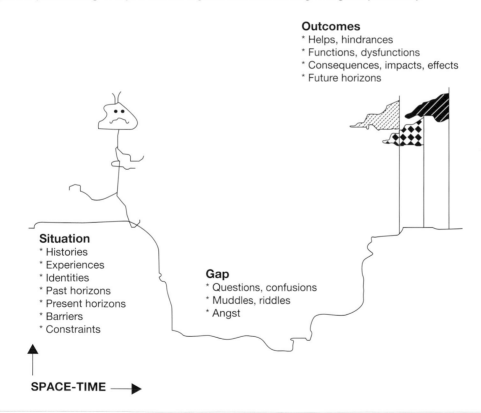

Figure 9.1 Sense-making as an attempt to bridge gaps in our understanding of a situation. *Source:* From Dervin and Frenette (2003, p. 238) Copyright © 2003 Hampton Press; used with permission.

An expanded illustration might depict the space through which the runner is dashing in two dimensions as a maze-like canyon. The runner can choose between several paths to a destination that may not always be clearly visible. In fact, the runner can choose among several destinations. Paths differ in their lengths and in the number and depth of gaps the runner must cross. Moreover, in light of our discussion of keeping as a necessary complement to finding, paths are each littered with pretty rocks. Many are "fool's gold" but others are useful "nuggets" of information that can help to fill the various gaps we encounter along the way. Gaps can be not only gaps of understanding but also gaps between a situation as we want it to be and the situation as it is or will be with no intervention.

Aspects of a classic adventure game are thus added to the runner's situation. Some rocks along the way may prove useful later on. But not every rock should be picked up. Picking up a rock costs time, energy, and attention. Momentum is lost if the runner stops even to consider picking up the rock. Picking up the rock takes time, and carrying the rock along slows the runner down and saps the runner's energy. By direct analogy, keeping information can also be costly. We are distracted, if only momentarily, from our primary task as we consider what steps, if any, need to be taken to ensure that we'll return to a web page (email message, document, picture, music clip) later on. And more items kept can mean more clutter in our attentional spaces which exerts an ongoing drag on our time and attention. Costs may be justified, provided the information is in fact used. However, unlike the standard adventure game, there is no certainty that the item we "pick up" will have any value later on.

The term "sense-making" (along with its variations, "sensemaking" and "sense making") still appears mainly in the special language of academic and technical discussions. It is an unusual term.[1] *Sense-making* is used with apparent precision by different researchers in different communities. Of concern, though, is that meanings of one researcher in one community (e.g., the community of people doing research in information science and human information behavior) are not shared, or even necessarily communicated, to researchers in other communities (e.g., people doing research in human–computer interaction or cognitive science).

May the discussions about sense-making continue. May researchers begin a dialog that crosses the boundaries separating communities of research. As such a dialog proceeds, we can hope for some convergence over time in our collective understanding of what is meant by *sense-making*, but we can also hope that the convergence is not done prematurely or in ways that squeeze out important perspectives.

In the absence of such a convergence, the more generic and more commonly used term "making sense" is used throughout this book, along with its companion transitive and intransitive verb forms. We make sense of something as an activity. A thing makes sense (to us) as an outcome.

We can borrow from the different descriptions of sense-making to arrive at a working description of *making sense* for purposes of this chapter's discussion. Borrowing from

---

[1] "Sense-making" is a gerund, for example, with no companion verb forms. We do not say "things are sense-making now" or "I am trying to sense-make things."

Klein et al.'s description of sense-making, for example, one important aspect of making sense of things is to make connections that help us to anticipate the future course of events and to determine what actions we can take to bend the course of these events to our liking.

Klein et al. speak of sense-making as a "continuous effort" (p. 71). Sense-making as a continuous effort may simply be one aspect of the information processing we're doing, as sentient beings, in each waking (and sleeping?) moment of our lives. On the other hand, Furnas and Russell describe sense-making as a process prompted by change (change in the world or our place in it) or by new opportunities, problems or tasks to be completed.

Certainly, at some level, we are always trying to make sense of things in our world. From a PIM perspective, efforts to make sense of things can be said to happen more or less continuously as we attempt to map between information and need. For example, we try to make sense of new information as a part of our keeping activities. What is this? What does it mean for us? Likewise, we try to make sense of a need—the need to attend a meeting, for example—as part of our finding activities. Where is the meeting? Do I know how to get there? What should I bring? What should I do to prepare?

But this chapter will give special attention to making sense as its own separate kind of activity—distinct from the PIM activities explored in previous chapters. Making sense is what you're doing, for example, in the following situations:

1. You have gathered lots of information relating to a report (term paper, analysis) you need to write. Now what? How do the various bits and pieces of information fit together? What are the underlying patterns? How can you structure the information so that the report makes sense? What story does the information tell? What purpose will the report serve?

2. A glance at your calendar tells you that an important visit to a client site is less than a month away. What must you do to prepare? Do you still need to make plane and hotel reservations? Has the meeting schedule been finalized? Are you seeing the right people? What do you need to accomplish during the visit?

3. As you drive home from work on a Friday afternoon, perhaps you think over the work week. Did you complete the tasks you hoped to complete? What went well? What didn't go well? How will you do what needs to be done next week?

Norman (1993) describes two modes of cognition: *experiential cognition* and *reflective cognition.* "The experiential mode leads to a state in which we perceive and react to the events around us, efficiently and effortlessly" (p. 16) whereas "(t)he reflective mode is that of comparison and contrast, of thought, of decision-making . . . the mode that leads to new ideas, novel responses" (p. 16). But reflective cognition is also "slow and laborious"—certainly not something we do continuously.

Both modes of cognition are needed. But Norman expresses a concern that many of our tools—especially those in support of music, video, and game-playing entertainment—promote a strong imbalance in favor of experiential cognition. We may spend an entire working day in a mostly reactive, experiential mode as we answer phone calls, respond to email, and go from one meeting to the next. And if the evening is filled with video games and channel surfing, is any time left for reflection?

Norman emphasizes the importance of reflective thought as a "critical component of modern civilization: It is where new ideas come from" (p. 27), and he calls for tools of reflection to support the exploration of ideas and the comparison and evaluation of alternatives. Reflective cognition is necessarily involved in each kind of meta-level activity of PIM reviewed in previous chapters. And even judgments of finding and keeping can involve reflective cognition.

We may compare, for example, alternative methods of finding the information we need. Go to the Web? Or would it be faster to ask a friend? Or we may reflect on how best to keep an item for later use. But Norman's descriptions of reflective cognition are especially apt as a characterization of our efforts to make sense of things.

The Russell et al. model for sense-making as described above can be characterized as an interplay between structure and content. Content (information) drives a bottom-up search for structuring representations which can, in turn, be used to encode and organize current content and also to guide the search for new content. Making sense as a distinct kind of PIM activity can be similarly characterized. However, the notion of task must be broadened. We make sense of our information, our PIM activities and the resources these activities consume with reference to the needs that are so served.

Making sense as a kind of PIM activity has the following characteristics:

- *Breadth of focus*. An item is assessed not just on its own but in the context of its containing collection. A need—the need to make plane reservations, for example—is assessed in a larger context of other needs. Why, for example, fly back to Seattle from the meeting in New York only to fly out the next day to a meeting in Boston? Maybe it would save time and money to take the train up to Boston instead. Focus is often on an information collection as a whole. Or focus is on a collection of needs (the needs relating to a project, for example) rather than a single need. Breadth of focus also means factoring in conditions and constraints of the current situation.

- *Depth of focus*. Making sense means understanding underlying relationships and bringing out an underlying structure that may be obscured by superficial similarities and differences. You may understand that, according to your calendar, you need to get ready for a meeting. But does going to the meeting really make sense? Does the meeting represent a necessary step toward a goal you wish to achieve? Or is the meeting a waste of your time?

- *Our senses are involved*. We quite literally try to "make sense" of things by trying to make hidden patterns, anticipated outcomes, and alternatives (e.g., choices in computer, choices in travel itinerary) as real as possible. We try to "see" things better either in our mind's eye or through a visual display. We try to see the bigger picture. We try to see (hear, smell, taste, feel) how things will be.

- *Manipulation is involved*. Making sense of things can be hands-on as when we shuffle, order, stack, and group paper note cards or the paper documents on a desktop. Our manipulation of digital information items is mediated by our tools.

When applied to an information item, how does making sense differ from keeping? When applied to a need, how does it differ from finding? When applied to a collection (of information items or needs), how does it differ from organizing? One response is that making sense implies a deeper level of analysis. We may keep an information item simply because we know we'll be asked to produce it again later. For example, we might keep a status report for an upcoming meeting but have little understanding of the item's meaning or relevance to the meeting. Or we can meet a need—say, the request from a friend for "Sam's email address"— either by simply providing the email address or by a deeper processing, leading to a reply such as "Sam is traveling for the next few days and off email, but I can give you his cell phone number if you really need to reach him."

9.3 Making sense as outcome vs. activity

Sometimes things can make sense to us without (much) activity on our part to make them make sense. But, in other cases, things only make sense after considerable, even arduous, activity to clarify what's needed. Consider the following examples.

9.3.1 City plans finally make sense

Facing Seattle on the other side of Lake Washington is the town of Kirkland, Washington. Even as Kirkland has grown dramatically in size over the past few decades, it has still retained a sense of community and a small-town feel. The heart of Kirkland is in its downtown area, with its collection of businesses along Lake Street and Central Way.

Kirkland's small-town feel derives in part from the older, lower buildings in the downtown business core. The buildings preserve a line-of-sight connection between the different parts of the downtown area and allow the sunlight to spill down onto the streets and sidewalks—quite unlike the "canyons" that might have resulted had buildings been allowed to increase significantly in height along the narrow streets.

But city plans in 2004 placed Kirkland's small-town feel in direct conflict with the forces of progress. At the very corner of Lake Street and Central Way, plans were well along to sell city property to a developer whose project for a large building significantly exceeded current building heights.

Many residents of Kirkland were uneasy about the rapid pace of city planning and what seemed to be a lack of visibility and openness in the planning process. But even so, might the building and other changes sure to follow be a good thing for Kirkland? And how much of an impact would the building really have on downtown Kirkland?

The developer provided the dimensions of the proposed building and pictures of what it would look like. But no pictures showed the proposed building in its setting. What would Kirkland look like afterward? How would it feel? Obviously a wait-and-see approach would not work. Once the building was in place, there would be no turning back.

A group of Kirkland citizens decided to create visualizations that would help residents make sense of the proposed development. The group gathered volunteers to stand along the outlines of the planned building and hold helium balloons raised to the proposed height at morning and evening rush hour. Commuters got the message. The building would have a major impact on downtown Kirkland. But how to get this messsage across at a critical city council meeting only weeks away?

Eric Horvitz, who was part of the group, remobilized the balloon team to create visualizations that would show the proposed building not as a stand-alone but rather for its impact on sight-lines in downtown. Eric describes it this way:

> While the bright red balloons were floating in the sky, marking the key points of the roofline, I drove around town and snapped photos with a digital camera. Later, I over-layed graphics on the images using simple geometric relationships to construct views of the structure from different locations. At the public hearing, the visualization led to jaw-dropping surprise from people on all sides of the discussion as the impact of the building became clear for the first time.

Things now made sense to people who attended the city council meeting; most did not like what they saw. In the face of overwhelming and determined opposition, the Kirkland City Council rejected the proposed development. One of the before and after views Eric constructed is shown in Figure 9.2.

9.3.2 Mendeleev makes sense of the chemical elements

Nearly all of us reading this book have encountered some variation of the periodic table of chemical elements (see Figure 9.3).[2] Most likely, we encountered the table early in our education, perhaps in an introductory science class. The periodic table provides, in a single view, essential information concerning all the world's known chemical elements. Moving from left to right, elements increase in atomic number and, generally but not always, in atomic weight. Elements within a grouping defined by a column in the table all have the similar properties.

The periodic table of elements has been described as "the ultimate paper tool in chemistry" (Scerri, 2001), "an icon for the order of nature" (Bensaude-Vincent, 2001, p. 133) and "maybe the most widely recognized talisman of modern science" (Gordin, 2004).

The tabular representation that was to evolve into today's periodic table was first drafted by Mendeleev in 1869 (see Figure 9.4). He was a 35-year-old professor of chemistry at St. Petersburg University in Russia. Gordin notes that "Mendeleev was not concerned in 1869 with establishing a basic law of chemistry. He wanted primarily to write a textbook for students in chemistry at St. Petersburg University" (2004, p. 43).

The world's knowledge of chemical elements was growing rapidly in Mendeleev's time. The number of known chemical elements had grown from 14 at the beginning of the seventeenth

---

[2] Portions of this section are based on a discussion from a manuscript by Claborne and Jones (2005).

Figure 9.2 A before/after visualization of downtown Kirkland, Washington, that helped its residents make sense of a proposed development.

century to a total of 63 as Mendeleev began his work. More information was being gathered all the time. How could one make sense of all this information?

Chemists in Mendeleev's time were aware that chemical elements arranged according to atomic weight had a tendency to repeat every so often in chemical behavior. This periodicity resisted a concise representation (e.g., tabular form) partly because many elements belonging in the sequence hadn't yet been discovered and partly because the elements actually needed to be ordered by atomic number (corresponding to their number of protons or electrons) rather than by atomic weight to reveal the order we see in the modern periodic table.

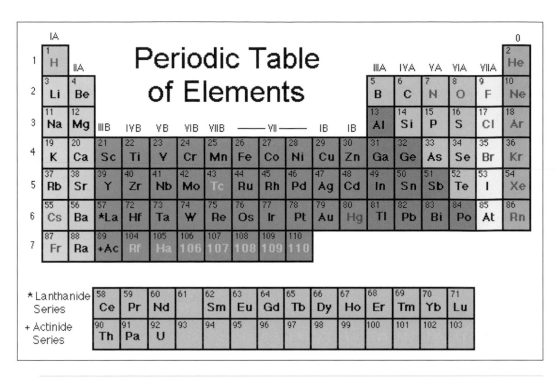

Figure 9.3 The Periodic Table of Elements, available at *http://periodic.lanl.gov/default. htm.* Viewers can click on an element's representation to learn more about it.

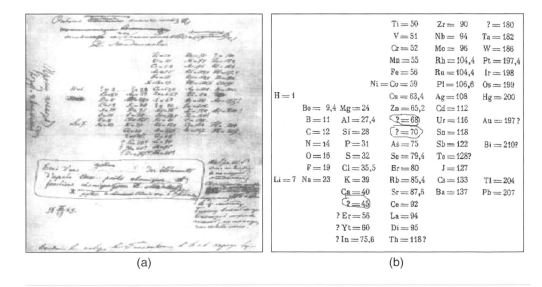

Figure 9.4 (a) This is a 1869 draft of Mendeleev's periodic system. (b) This is the first published form of Mendeleev's periodic system.

Perhaps Mendeleev's biggest contribution was to persist in ordering elements to preserve periodicity, even though this meant leaving gaps (for missing elements) and occasionally transposing elements with respect to atomic weight. Mendeleev was sufficiently confident of his table to suggest that new elements would be found to fill in the gaps in the table and, even, to predict the properties of these elements. Indeed, one such element, now referred to as gallium, was discovered in 1875 in France. The scientific world would be even more astonished at the predictive powers of Mendeleev's periodic system when later eka-boron (scandium) and eka-silicon (germanium) were discovered in 1879 in Sweden and 1886 in Germany, respectively. As theories of subatomic structure developed over the coming decades, Mendeleev's ordering was seen to correspond to an element's atomic number (i.e., the number of protons in the nucleus of element's atom). Mendeleev's periodic table can thus be said to do more than simply organize the then-available data concerning the chemical elements. The table was—is—truly ontological in making manifest an underlying reality, later verified in the discovery of additional chemical elements and given greater expression in the articulation of theories of subatomic structure.

Morris (2003) describes the process by which Mendeleev organized the elements. Mendeleev first made up cards for each of the known 63 elements, on which he wrote the atomic weight of the element and its most important chemical and physical properties. Atomic weight at that time was determined by carefully measuring the proportions, by weight, of the elements forming a compound.

Mendeleev asked several chemists all over Europe to send him the atomic weights that they had obtained. He wrote the figures on his cards as they arrived, and he did his own chemical experiments to verify the figures. He then arranged the cards in order of increasing atomic weight, beginning with hydrogen, the lightest, and ending with uranium, the heaviest at that time. "Then he pored over the cards for days, looking for patterns. Finally, he pinned the cards on the wall, putting similar elements in horizontal rows. He looked at the table that this formed, made changes, and pinned the cards on the wall again" (Morris, 2003, p. 165).

What is remarkable in this description of Mendeleev's method for makings sense is how familiar it seems. Many of us may recall using much the same method to make sense of the various pieces of a term paper we were assigned to write in school. Essentially the same process forms the basis for the affinity diagramming method described later in this chapter. Certainly the periodic table, in all its expressive elegance, did not follow inevitably from Mendeleev's card-sorting method for making sense. But could Mendeleev have discovered his table without this method? Note that this method made it easy for Mendeleev to occasionally violate an ordering by atomic weight in order to preserve periodicity. We can only hope that our tools for the manipulation of digital information can permit similar divergences, as needed, from strict orderings as defined by, for example, the property values of an information item.

What Now for IT?

– *Bob Boiko*

Language Use Groups: Whatever else an organization is doing, it is always making sense. Making sense is a messy business. It involves interminable discussions about what things are called and a constant reshuffling of meaning as different constituencies (different language use groups) vie to set the terms of discussion. In good organizations, all this sense-making periodically converges. People compromise and settle on "best-fit" terms. The so-called social tagging systems like the photo site Flickr and the web site bookmaking site del.icio.us take advantage of this process. They allow individual users to make up their own descriptive terms to tell others what their pictures or favorite web sites are about. The result is an ever-evolving but also ever-converging set of words that the user group as a whole takes on to describe information.

In really good organizations, "best-fit" terms are constantly refined as the organization strives to define its chosen field. In bad organizations, it is the same messy process, but it does not converge. Terms are never even provisionally agreed to, and the only movement of meaning is by the forceful imposition of one language use group's terms on the rest of the organization.

Given this situation, what can an IT group do to help? First, simply recognizing that making sense is an ongoing activity is a huge help. The bad IT group is constantly straining against the natural vying of opinions. They feel that "those people should just decide once and for all what they mean." This sort of IT group believes that there is some final taxonomy of terms that the organization can create once and then use forever. The good IT group understands that there is no such taxonomy. Instead there are terms that are more stable across language use groups and those that are in flux.

Second, an IT group can create processes and tools that embrace the constant change rather than resist it.

For example, a savvy IT group can harvest search logs to map language use groups within the organization. They may find, for example, that while most users consistently use the search term "news release," a small but growing number use the term "press pack." Are these terms synonymous? Why does the smaller group not use the more common term? Is the concept of a press pack up and coming in the organization, representing a shift in the way the organization perceives its relationship to the media, or just an anomaly of a group that does not know what the information type ought to be called? Armed with this data, the IT group can find out what the real issue is and either assist the transition to the new concept or help the press pack searchers come into alignment with the rest of the organization.

As another example, consider the navigation on a corporate intranet. Navigation, of course, is no more than the set of phrases users click on to find a piece of information they want. IT groups usually either decide on these navigational phrases themselves or

let each unit do its own navigation. Neither option is really satisfactory. If the IT group creates the navigation, the words they choose are not likely to be the same that users in the various groups use to find the information they want. If the navigation job is left to the individual units, it is likely to be inconsistent from section to section of the site. In addition, both solutions miss a central point, which is that the choice of words people use to look for information evolves over time. The savvy IT group should see its task as neither building nor delegating navigation, but rather constantly harvesting, organizing, and presenting (in the site navigation) the vocabulary that users need to find information.

The IT group can find the terms that are in contention and facilitate discussions around the use of these terms between the groups that disagree. Rather than looking for a static solution, this sort of IT group chooses to facilitate and guide the discussion around terms. In so doing, this sort of IT group not only embraces the inevitable, interminable process of sense-making; it also begins to drive that sense-making forward and helps the organization establish leadership in its field.

9.4 Making sense of things as a PIM activity

The PIM activities considered in preceding chapters, notwithstanding their great diversity, share a commonality noted in Chapter 3: PIM activities are an *effort to establish, use, and maintain a mapping between information and need*. Keeping moves from encountered information to anticipated need. Finding moves across the mapping in the other direction, from need to information. Keeping and finding activities happen throughout an ordinary day. Much of our day is consumed in these activities.

Meta-level activities are more squarely focused on the mapping itself. Effective performance of these activities requires a broader perspective. The proper evaluation of a PIM tool (or strategy), for example, as discussed in the preceding chapter, should consider the tool's interaction with other tools in the PSI. The tool should also be evaluated for its support of a full complement of PIM activities engaged in the life cycle of an information item. It makes little sense to keep information that can't be found again later. A tool that supports keeping and reciprocal finding may still fail if its use multiplies our headaches of organization and maintenance.

A broader perspective is also required to properly manage the flows of information. Are we getting the right information at the right time? Are we getting a "balanced diet" of information? Are we doing what we can to ensure that our private information doesn't fall into the wrong hands?

And, certainly, activities to organize and maintain information invite a broader perspective. How to arrive at schemes of information organization (through use of folders, tags, properties, etc.) that can be used consistently, economically, over time, and across various kinds of information to meet needs now and later? How to preserve information over time, even as storage media decay or are destroyed and even as formats come and go? How to retain access to this information even as our memories decay? How to keep track of the many versions of a document? How to update information consistently? How to move old information out of the way so that it doesn't continue to consume resources—most notably our own attention—that are better spent elsewhere?

Making sense, as a meta-level activity, also works better when the perspective is broader. Making sense happens piecemeal all the time, of course, in response to both information and need. We may process the immediate implication of an email message announcing a companywide meeting in two days' time and yet fail to piece it together with other email traffic to conclude that a major company reorganization is in the offing that may threaten the existence of the group we manage if we don't act quickly. Or we may meet a need to respond to email messages piecemeal by responding to individual email messages from different members of a team. However, taking a broader perspective, we might have saved time by sending out a single answer to handle variations of the same question posed by different team members.

Making sense when applied to an information collection promotes a deeper analysis that can lead to a more meaningful organization. We might organize information items based on a superficial consideration of properties such as format and associated application. Or we can organize based on a deeper analysis of similarities, differences, and interconnections among the items in a collection. Sometimes an organization is a mixture of both: the superficial and the more semantic.

Consider again the organization of wedding-related files depicted in Chapter 5. The organization emerged gradually over a six-month period of wedding planning. The screenshot showing the organization near the beginning of planning (see Figure 5.3 of Chapter 5) shows many fewer subfolders and many more files lying directly under the wedding folder (not shown). The transition from an earlier "flat" organization to the structure in Figure 9.5 reflects the person's efforts to make sense of the wedding and its planning. Subfolder names suggest, and the interview with the participant confirms, that many subfolders represent key elements of the wedding. But not all. Contents of the "Links" subfolder are defined by source and form rather than wedding task—all files within are shortcuts pointing to web pages.

When considered as a representation of the wedding and the various tasks and subprojects that need to be completed in preparation for the wedding, the organization of Figure 9.5 makes sense (mostly). So what? In Chapter 5, we considered the project management benefits of such an organization. The folder hierarchy provides an at-a-glance indicator of tasks done and remaining to be done for the wedding. Research from cognitive psychology leads us to expect additional benefits relating to the basic PIM actions of keeping and finding:

- *Serendipity (better keeping).* There are many anecdotal accounts of people who gain clarity on a goal they would like to achieve and then, providentially it seems, the means to achieve this goal appear. A person who decides one day to finish college happens upon a notice for a special back-to-school program at his or her place of work on the next day.

Figure 9.5 A person's folder hierarchy for making sense of information relating to her wedding (reformatted version of Figure 5.4).

Providence may be involved, but research in cognitive psychology also suggests that when a goal is made more "real" through planning, we are better able to recognize the relevance of encountered information.[3] We experience a variation of this effect when, after buying a car, we are surprised to see so many other cars like it on the highway.

• *Better memory (for better finding)*. Consider filing scheme A in which information items are placed in folders according to their primary associated application (e.g., Microsoft Word, Adobe Acrobat, and Mozilla FireFox). Compare this to scheme B, such as that of Figure 9.5, where items are filed according to anticipated use in the context of a project to be completed. In accordance with a levels-of-processing effect from cognitive psychology, we should expect that the act of filing according to scheme B leads to a deeper, more meaningful processing of the items filed.[4] Or, if not "deeper," the processing in any case strengthens a connection to an anticipated use represented by a folder or subfolder. By either argument, we're more likely to remember (less likely to forget) if information is organized (or tagged) according to an organization that makes sense for anticipated use.

---

[3] For example, research by Seifert and Patalano (2001) suggests that people are better able to recognize opportunities related to a desired goal when they have previously thought about the goal's preconditions and the features of the environment associated with these preconditions.

[4] For more on the levels-of-processing effect, see Craik and Lockhart (1972), Hyde and Jenkins (1973), and Craik and Watkins (1973).

Also, an organization as a representation of anticipated uses has done much of the gathering needed to assemble items for use: if subfolders represent tasks to be done, then often much of the information needed to complete the task is already organized within.

Even so, our organizations of information often don't make much sense—that is, they bear little resemblance to any understanding we may have internally for situations of anticipated use. When I show the structure in Figure 9.5 to people in tutorials and courses, some express surprise that anyone "could be this organized," especially in situations where the understanding for an information collection and its uses is rapidly changing. Others express a desire to be more organized. But they also tell me that they sometimes stick with their current organizations because they know where things are and have gotten accustomed to current ways of accessing information. The problem may be that our understanding of our information changes too quickly, and that updating these changes is too costly.

However, another possibly is that our tools are failing us. The tools make it too costly to express our thoughts in external form. Or tools don't give us enough benefit for our efforts. An ordinary whiteboard, for example, is an excellent tool for sketching out new ideas—its use is natural and the cost to express our thoughts is low. But then what? The sketch is static and can't be easily leveraged to write a report or organize information we'll need to complete a project. On the other hand, a folder hierarchy delivers some organizing benefit but can be costly to update. But why not a tool that supports us in the easy expression of our ideas and also supports the leveraged use of this external representation as a means of planning and managing a project, for example, and as a basis for organizing the information needed to achieve project goals? The consideration of making sense as a PIM activity naturally leads to a desire for such a tool. As the review of integrative solutions later in this book (Chapter 14) demonstrates, such a tool is not so far away from realization.

9.4.1 Making sense as a pleasurable activity

Let's consider another point of view on activities to make sense of things: making sense of things can be a pleasurable activity. Figuring things out can be fun. Or, to paraphrase Aristotle, all people by nature desire to know. Making sense engages a natural inclination to understand the world around us, to discover its patterns, to unlock its secrets, and to appreciate its beauty. We mostly do other activities of PIM because we have to. We find because we need information. We keep because we know we'll need the information later and may be in trouble if we don't have it. Similarly, we maintain and organize, we manage information flow, we measure and evaluate because these activities, not withstanding their immediate cost, produce later benefit—or avoid even greater cost.

Making sense of things is perhaps the one PIM activity that, once successfully completed, is inherently rewarding in a way that pays for itself—for its costs in time and other resources and independently of a later, anticipated reward. The discovery that may eventually bring a scientist a Nobel Prize in some future time is its own reward right now. In fact, the later reward of money and status is a pale reflection of the immediate bliss that scientists often report experiencing when a discovery is first made. In reference to his discovery of laws of planetary motion, for example, Johannes Kepler (1571–1630) described himself as being "carried away by unutterable rapture at the divine spectacle of heavenly harmony."[5]

We each reach our own insights and make our own discoveries. These may never be recorded in the annals of science, but insights and discoveries can have a profound impact on us personally. In school, as we finally understood a difficult topic—how to differentiate an equation or how to write a simple computer program or how to do recursion or, even, grade-school division—we may have thought, "Now I'll pass after all," but preceding this anticipated benefit was the immediate reward of learning something new.

The outcome—that things make sense—may be reward in itself. But the path to this outcome is not always easy to take. The next section describes two methods to help.

What Next in Tool Development?

– Mike Kelly

In previous sidebars, I've described how a system-provided, structured storage facility, with associated standard, simple-to-use user-interface controls, could greatly improve reuse of information now squirreled into separate application silos on our computers. But as important as the information on our private machines is, information on the Web as a whole is potentially even more valuable. Making it possible to reuse the information on our own machines lets us reuse in flexible and perhaps unexpected ways what we already know. Doing the same for information on the Web lets us use what we may not yet know.

We already can see examples of this in so-called mashups—a term of art for constructing a web site by collecting together data or capabilities from two (or more) other web sites to produce something novel. On his "Programmable Web" site (*www.programmableweb.com*), John Musser offers thumbnail descriptions of several hundred public APIs available for use in mashups, links to detailed documentation on these APIs, as well as an extensive description of existing mashups and a blog about using the Web as a development platform. Many of these *APIs* are designed to be used in AJAX-based web pages—pages that use embedded JavaScript to exchange XML-based requests asynchronously with web servers and use the responses to update the page as they arrive.

Mashups use the web-based data and APIs to construct a new web site. It isn't too far of a stretch to imagine using similar techniques to integrate new information from the Web on a local machine.

---

[5] See Brooke (1998).

The Chicago Crime mashup (*www.chicagocrime.org*) also shows another aspect of making sense of all our data: the use of graphical interfaces to understand complex data. The Chicago Police Department has long published crime data in tables and sometimes in static color-coded maps. But the mashup takes the data and overlays it with a live map, on which you can easily locate your friends, family, and the house you're thinking of buying. Rendering the data in this way makes it far more accessible and understandable because maps are a great metaphor for how we think about locations. There are many other examples of this approach: Zillow (*www.zillow.com*) is a real estate valuation site constructed as a mashup of Microsoft Visual Earth (*http://dev.live.com/virtualearth/sdk/*) and various real estate data sites; Twitter Vision (*www.twittervision.com*) is a surprisingly engrossing real-time mashup of Google Maps and Twitter which displays updates from Twitter (*www.twitter.com*) on what actual people around the world are doing right now.

One of the interesting things about mashups is that they also get better "for free"—as Google Earth adds new features, the mashups based on the public Google Earth API get these effectively for free because they are just leveraging it for the mapping. For example, many of these map sites are starting to add 3D rendering of actual buildings based on digital photographs. So, soon, on Chicago Crime you will see not only where the worst crime building is located in your neighborhood, but what it actually looks like (the better to avoid it!) Of course, providers of APIs to mashups have to be careful to maintain backward compatibility when adding features—something providers of operating system APIs learned long ago. Old programs have to work with the new APIs without requiring changes (sometimes they might have to incorporate minor changes to gain new functionality from the APIs; this is considered an acceptable tradeoff.) And sometimes even "bugs" have to be carried forward if they have come to be depended on. "Fixing" a bug in an API that 30 mashups depend on might not be seen as a step forward if the old behavior worked for those sites and the new behavior doesn't without code changes by each of those 30 dependent sites—even if the new behavior is arguably more clean or correct.

Leveraging the richness of web APIs for our PSI could help us make better sense of it. For instance, we could leverage information on the Web to find connections between two contacts that we might otherwise be unaware of (both used to work for this company, or both have this contact in common) by leveraging information on LinkedIn (*www.linkedin.com*) or some other social networking site. We might leverage mapping APIs to provide rich graphical interfaces to otherwise disparate things. For instance, as laptops and PDAs begin to incorporate GPS devices, it's not unreasonable to think of every note, document, email, appointment, and the like, being tagged with a GPS coordinate of where I was when I wrote this. Leveraging mapping APIs used in mashups, we could navigate our PSI by "where I was when I wrote this" or "where I was when I met him and created the contact" rather than anything inherent in the data of the item. APIs to allow easy geocoding and easy use of the geocoded information to display rich maps would be helpful here.

Making true sense of our PSI may require leveraging information outside it. Fortunately, the new web APIs offer a constantly growing way of tapping into the information on the Web to help.

9.5 Methods for making sense

Methods to make sense of things divide into two general categories, according to whether an approach is mostly data-driven/bottom-up or goal-driven/top-down. Here, we consider an example of each approach.

9.5.1 Affinity Diagrams

The ultimate success of Mendeleev's methods for making sense depended on the following features:

- *The basic units of manipulation were correct*. Mendeleev's units of manipulation were cards—one per chemical element. Mendeleev might, instead, have based units of manipulation on an older partitioning according to the four fundamental elements of fire, air, earth, and water. Such a partitioning was used by the ancient Greeks and was still widely used by scientists only a century prior to Mendeleev's work. Had he used this partitioning to define units, the outcome most certainly would not have been the periodic table.

- *Units could be easily manipulated*. Mendeleev could easily move, sort, juxtapose, and even pin to the wall the cards representing chemical elements.

- *The collection of units could be viewed*—in a single glance or at least in a close sequence of glances. Mendeleev did not work only inside his own head. Variations in external representation afforded to Mendeleev by the cards and their patterns of placement were essential to Mendeleev's process of discovery.

The method Mendeleev used to make sense of a buzzing confusion of chemical information was a variation on what today is called the *affinity diagramming method*.[6] The steps of this method are as follows:

1. *Make a bunch of cards*. More generally, the method calls for the creation of a large number of small, easily manipulated information items, each of which expresses a single idea. Cards can come in the form of sticky notes or can be virtual cards as supported by a software tool. Cards can represent a single issue, feature, task, deliverable, fact, person, and so on.

2. *Place all items on display* so that all can be viewed in a single (possibly sweeping) glance. The display might be a table, wall, whiteboard, or a virtual space supported by a video display and a computer application.

3. *Sort items into related groups*. If two items appear to be related to each other in some way, place them side by side and locate them in one part of the display area. Look for other items that also relate to these two and, if found, place them together with the first two. In this way, a cluster of related items is formed. Otherwise, if another pair of items relates to

---

[6] See Hackos and Redish (1998) for a more complete description of the affinity diagramming method, especially as used in support of group work.

each other but not to any other cluster of items created so far, then place them in another region of the display. Continue in this manner until all items are clustered. It is possible that one or two items will not relate to each other or to any clusters formed. These can stand alone.

4. *Create a header or summary item to stand for each cluster.* The header item may be one of the items in the cluster promoted to represent the whole cluster. Or it may be a new item with wording selected to represent the distinguishing feature or relationship held in common by members of the cluster.

An example of what results is presented in Figure 9.6. In variations of the affinity diagramming method, the display surface itself (e.g., the physical or digital whiteboard) may be used to represent aspects of a cluster or to represent the structure relating clusters to one another. If the number of summary items is large, these might themselves be clustered in a second iteration of the method.

The affinity diagramming method is often used in a group setting to facilitate the emergence of a shared understanding among members of the group, which can then form a basis for

Figure 9.6 **An example of the affinity diagramming method.** *Source:* **From Bondarenko and Janssen (April 2005). Used with permission.**

collaboration. Mendeleev used a variation as well. By placing chemical information on cards, he could then sort and resort—another way to look for patterns in the information on the cards.

The affinity diagramming method is a *bottom-up* process for making sense of things: you start with lots of items; relate these to each other; cluster; repeat—looking, all the while, for patterns and a structure that might help to make sense of the whole.

9.5.2 Mind-mapping

Mind-mapping,[7] as a method for making sense, works in the other direction—top-down vs. bottom-up. The essential aim is to do a "divide-and-conquer" decomposition of a high-level goal or concept into constituent pieces, which can then be further divided into smaller pieces, and so on (see Figure 9.7). The technique essentially creates a hierarchy not unlike those we

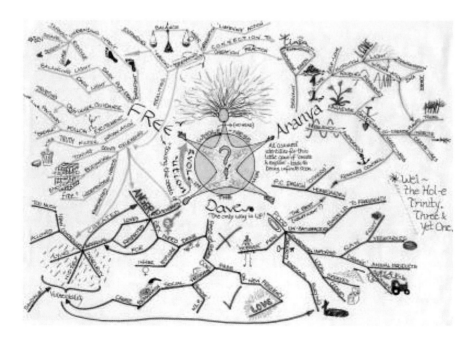

Figure 9.7 An example of a mind map. *Source:* **From the "Mind Map" Wikipedia article, available at** *http://en.wikipedia.org/wiki/Mind_map.*

---

[7] For an entertaining exposition of the mind-mapping technique, see Buzan and Buzan (2004).

learned to create in school using the outlining technique. An important difference, though, is that mind-mapping works in a two-dimensional space—for example, a whiteboard, a computer display, or simply a piece of paper. Buzan asserts that the ability to expand in a two-dimensional space engages the visual side of our brains in ways that traditional outlines cannot.

There are many other methods of making sense. Increasingly these methods are supported for digital as well as paper-based information. Given developments in tool support, we have reason to expect that our manipulation of digital information can come to feel as natural and direct as our manipulation of paper cards and paper piles of information. Moreover, computer-based tools can support methods that scale in ways that paper-based methods cannot.[8]

What Now for You and Me?

Your own efforts to make sense should not be driven by strict adherence to any method or form of representation. Methods that are primarily top-down (such as the mind-mapping method) or bottom-up or data-driven (such as affinity diagramming) both have value in different circumstances or even in combination.

A web search on "mind-mapping" or "affinity diagramming" easily produces a number of different software tools designed to help. However, many times you may be able to make do with what you already have readily available. I observe that people often have good success, for example, by using the computer desktop in support of affinity diagramming. Icons for folders and files can be readily arranged into groupings in order to make sense of the information represented. Other people make use of outlines in their word processor or folders in the filing system, as illustrated in Chapter 5.

Representations in support of sense-making activities are often variations of two basic forms: the hierarchy or the table. Each has its uses. Hierarchies often emerge as people work either bottom-up or top-down to make sense of a project. A top-down direction follows a "divide-and-conquer" approach in which bigger projects or problems are divided into successively smaller, more manageable tasks. Hierarchies can emerge in the other direction for a clustering of items and then a clustering of clusters. Tables, on the other hand, are often a simple way to compare and contrast the items in a reference collection or within the choice collection for a project (e.g., the choice of kitchen counters for a remodeled kitchen).

---

[8] In efforts to make better tools for working with digital information, there is still a great deal to be learned from the ways people work with paper. See, for example, Bonarenko and Janssen (2005) and Russell et al. (2006).

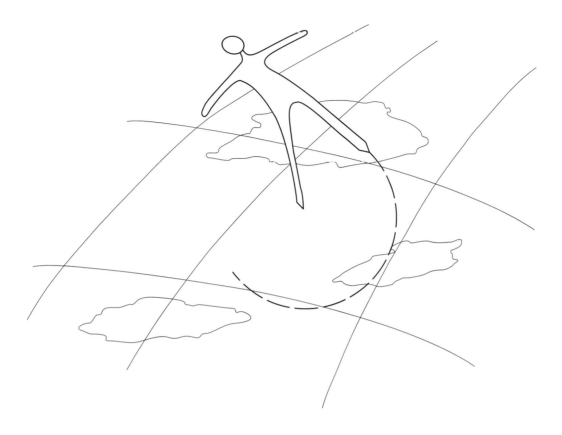

It's not the man, it's the plan. It's not the rap, it's the map.

U.S. actor, playwright, and director Ossie Davis (1917–2005)

9.6 Looking back, looking forward

The considerable amount of discussion about sense-making is a testament both to the importance of the activity and to the difficulty of providing a concise definition for what it is we mean when we talk about making sense, sense-making, or sensemaking.

☑ "Making sense" is used in this book in preference to "sense-making" or "sensemaking" because it is a more generic term that implies less precision concerning either the outcome of the activity or the actions taken to reach this outcome.

☑ Making sense can be approached as both a desired outcome (that things make sense) and as an activity. In the context of PIM, making sense is primarily considered as a kind of activity.

☑ Making sense is, or should be, an integral part of all other PIM activities, including activities to keep, find, organize, maintain, manage information flow, and evaluate.

☑ Direct support for making sense as an activity may yield dividends across all other PIM activities as well.

☑ Making sense is a meta-level activity that is better done when the perspective is broader —it's better to make sense of a collection of information items rather than a single item; it's better to make sense of a collection of needs (relating to a project or a role) rather than a single need.

☑ Methods for making sense can be primarily top-down/goal-driven or bottom-up/data-driven.

☑ Mind-mapping, for example, often begins with a general goal (e.g., remodel the house) with nodes radiating outward in all directions to represent components (e.g., "master bedroom" or "kitchen").

☑ Affinity diagramming works from basic elements (as represented on paper cards or the digital equivalent) and builds upward to construct meaningful arrangements.

But our efforts to make sense needn't follow methods with special names like "mind-mapping" or "affinity diagramming." I knew a student in graduate school who took notes in class but rarely referred to them later. What was the point? The act of taking the notes helped her to understand the lecture better and also made immediately apparent (much more so than an audio recording might have) the points during the lecture that she didn't understand—in time for her to ask questions. The act of taking the notes was often sufficient.

Those who play, as well as listen, to music often report a deeper, stronger connection to the music. In a similar spirit, Norman (1992) speculated on the deeper connection that a group of artists in China might have felt by drawing or painting the beautiful scene in front of them rather than simply "taking" a picture.

Making sense as an activity can sometimes be very pleasurable, as when we plan a vacation or figure something out that we have been puzzling over. So we hope for tools that not only will support us in our efforts to make sense, but will also help leverage the results of this activity. The structure in a good plan, for example, might also be used to organize project-relevant information needed to fulfill the plan. More important, good tools should be about facilitating a stronger, deeper connection between us and our information.

How do people need to manipulate their information so that it is truly theirs—and more like an extension of their own memories? These are long-standing questions of PIM, given new urgency with ongoing, dramatic increases in the amount and variety of information that can be stored digitally for personal use. Answers to these questions may (finally) enable us to take real steps beyond the limitations of the current desktop metaphor of personal computing. But our "digital desktops" are already being drastically altered by developments in email, search, and mobile-centric and web-centric computing. These changes are the focus of the next part of this book.

Email disappears?

Is email a very successful failure? Email messages are free and they're easy to send—good for us but good for spammers too. Email is used for tasks, documents, making contacts. It was designed for none of these activities. We may feel like we're "living" in our inbox. But are we doing the things we really want to be doing? In one vision of the future, email is extended to more fully support its currently ad hoc uses. In another vision, email as we know it today goes away altogether.

Chapter
Ten

q t c e j b u s v v

r r b a c k ; % h s

a ^ k t u b h m u p

d y s u # s h O t a

n • e p a + i v o m

e e n r x y e x k

l = t c e m p t y 7

a 4 b r C t x e n *

c i p f o r w a x d

s ” <) m $ @ h - v

h c s m p o b l 8 i

m % v o + r t i —

, p l i s t s f (t

— e w e e t a d s)

The worst thing about the miracle of modern communications is the Pavlovian pressure it places upon everyone to communicate whenever a bell rings.

U.S. journalist, author, and humorist Russell Baker (1925–)

10.1 Starting out: Is email a very successful failure?

If we talk about solutions to PIM, then we can't help but consider email. Whittaker, Bellotti, and Moody (2005) argue that "email is the most successful computer application yet invented" (p. 2). Many of us would say that email plays a critical role in the completion of everyday activities, work-related and otherwise. In a study of online users by the Annenberg School, the highest percentage of hours spent online were spent reading and writing email. (New users worked with email 16.8 percent of their time online, while experienced users spent 21.3 percent of their online time in email.)[1] Indeed, people often report "living in email" and rate it as "essential" for their everyday work.[2]

---

[1] University of Southern California, USC Annenberg School, "2007 Center for the Digital Future Report" *(http://www.digitalcenter.org/pdf/2007-Digital-Future-Report-Press-Release-112906.pdf)*.

[2] See also Whittaker, Bellotti, and Gwizdka (2007) for a discussion on email's dominance.

Email is used to communicate across the world and down the hall. As a testament to email's success, it is often used in preference to, and not just as a necessary substitute for, other, richer modes of communication, such as telephone calls or even face-to-face conversations. We may email someone when we lack time for a more interactive conversation, with its expectations of at least a minimal exchange of social pleasantries. Email also persists as a record of what was discussed. A colleague tells the story of walking down the hallway to answer a staff member's email question, only to be asked to resend the answer in email "so that we have a record of our conversation."[3]

Moreover, email is much more than simply an alternate form of communication[4]:

- Email is used for *task management*. The email message we send or receive may initiate a task (e.g., "Please review this budget and tell me what's missing"). The thread of later responses serves to document the progress of this task ("Things look good except for . . .").

- Email is used for *document management*. For example, the exchange of a collaboratively authored document provides a natural means of versioning.

- Email is used for *contact management*. Old email messages are a treasure trove of information. In particular, email messages contain information about the people with whom we communicate. We may look through old email messages to find a person's email address or office phone number ("I think it's a part of his email signature") or even the name of the person's spouse and children ("I think they were mentioned in a dinner invitation sent out back in December"). If we use distribution lists, we may also, just as readily, do a "reply all" to an old email message sent or received that happens to include the people to whom we want to send a new message.

We even send email to ourselves. For example:

- Self-directed email messages can work as a kind of diary entry to record memories before they fade.

- Self-directed email can include reminders of tasks still to be done, ranging from "pick up milk on the way home" to "Start planning trip to Hawaii." For some of us, email in the inbox may also serve as an adjunct to the calendar, reminding us of impending appointments.

- Self-directed email with attached documents provides a backup for these documents and also provides a simple way to transfer documents from one place to the next (e.g., from a computer at work to a computer at home or vice versa).

In short, email is used constantly and in ways that go well beyond its original use as "electronic mail." Email is a spectacular success.

And yet, in spite of, or perhaps because of, this success, email is also a failure. People experience information overload from the sheer volume of incoming email and its high percentage of spam. What's more, email information is fragmented in a way that makes it difficult to keep track

---

[3] Harry Bruce (2004), personal communication.

[4] Several studies look at the many ways in which email is used. See, for example, Bellotti et al. (2005); Mackay (1988); Whittaker et al. (2007); Whittaker, Jones, and Terveen (2002); and Whittaker and Sidner (1996).

of and retrieve. These two problems—information overload and information fragmentation—give email a one–two punch that can knock us right out of the ring.

What to do about email? To answer this question, we need to first explore more deeply how email relates to PIM and the special problems that email poses for PIM. Towards these goals, the chapter moves through the following sections:

✓ *PIM problems in email: The one–two punch* explores how information overload and information fragmentation can prevent us from using email efficiently.

✓ *PIM activities in email* considers email management with respect to the everyday PIM activities of finding and keeping. It also considers the meta-level activities employed to manage email flow, measure and evaluate email use, maintain and organize email, and make sense of email.

✓ *Future visions of email* consider two very different scenarios for email: (1) Email takes over as our primary means of managing tasks and the information needed to complete these. (2) Email (as we know it today) disappears.

10.2 PIM problems in email: The one–two punch

Whittaker, Bellotti, and Gwizdka (2007) note an important characteristic of email as a form of information: the expectation (at least for a subset of email) of a timely response. Timely responses are often essential for progress to be made toward completing a common task or planning a larger project. Failure to respond can hold everyone else up and cause serious delays. However, responses are often delayed or their quality is compromised because of two significant PIM problems with email: information overload and information fragmentation. The sheer volume of incoming email messages, with its abundant spam, can overwhelm us. Effectively grouping and organizing these messages is a source of additional headache.[5] Both of these problems merit closer scrutiny.

10.2.1 Punch one: Information overload

Most of us don't need convincing that email overload is a serious problem. But the problem may be even worse than we think:

- Corporate users send and receive an average of 133 messages per day, and this number is expected to reach 160 messages by 2009.[6]

- Worse, a high percentage of incoming email is "junk." One study estimates that 68.6 percent of arriving email is spam.[7] Much of this unwanted, unsolicited email remains in

---

[5] For a sampling of research relating to the special challenges of managing and organizing email, see Bälter and Sidner (2002); Boardman and Sasse (2004); Whittaker and Sidner (1996); and Whittaker, Bellotti, and Gwizdka (2007).

[6] As based on a study by the Radicati Group (2005).

[7] From the OECD Task force on Spam: *http://www.oecd-antispam.org/article.php3?id_article=244.*

the inbox even after we apply aggressive email filters. Worse still, these filters inevitably risk sorting legitimate email into the junk email folder. Even worse, some junk emails are outright attempts either to attack our computers or to trick us into giving away private information.

- Even with outright junk email filtered out (or ignored), our inboxes are often filled with enormous amounts of what might be called *semi-spam*. We receive announcements for talks, meetings, conferences, and workshops we cannot attend. We receive the happy news of weddings and births and the sad news of deaths of people we do not know. We receive FYI announcements of changes in policy and procedures that we mostly disregard.

10.2.2 Punch two: Information fragmentation

Suppose email problems of information overload could, somehow, be addressed. Spam and semi-spam are deleted or put in their place—somewhere away from the attentional surface of the inbox. The numbers of incoming email are reduced to manageable levels and are nicely sorted according to priority and expected action. We would still face a second basic problem of PIM, that of *information fragmentation*, which is especially problematic for email.

Elsewhere in this book, we've talked about the information fragmentation that results from a proliferation of information forms. But even within email—a single form of information—the information needed to complete a single task or to plan and manage a larger project is scattered widely across a time-ordered display of messages sent or received. Consider the following:

1. The messages of an email conversation—perhaps pertaining to a task we'd like to complete—are scattered over time and interleaved with many other email messages.

2. Attempts to group messages by thread or common subject line work imperfectly, since the real topic may drift considerably over the course of an email exchange and, conversely, email messages on the same topic may arrive through different threads with different subject lines.[8]

3. Moreover, even if a subject line helps to filter email messages, a great deal of time-consuming sifting must still be done, since key points are often buried within the messages that remain. The conversations represented in these messages may wander across alternatives that are discussed but no longer relevant (e.g., alternate meeting times/places) and that may also include quips, jokes, and incidental conversation ("By the way, I saw Pat yesterday and she said to say hi").

4. The fragmentary, scattered nature of email can elicit a reactive style of response even when we might be much more deliberate in face-to-face interactions. We may feel compelled to respond to an email message before it scrolls out of view (perhaps to be forgotten forevermore). How many of us, after pressing the "Send" button, have wished we'd waited until we either had more information or had a chance to cool down?

5. But because email is so difficult to organize and so easily forgotten, waiting may lead to uncompleted tasks and unmet obligations.

---

[8] See Whittaker and Sidner (1996) for more discussion on the imperfect mapping between subject lines and topics of email conversation.

The fragmentation of task-related, emailed information is an advantage of email turned on its head. An email conversation relating to a task can extend over days or weeks. Participants have the convenience of responding at a time and place of their choosing. The problem, then, is to assemble all of this information later. Time alone clearly won't help, since task-relevant email messages are scattered across a large period of time in which a great many other email messages, sent and received, are interleaved. Sorting by recipient or sender may not help much, both because a conversation may involve several different people (some of whom come and go as the conversation evolves) and because a given person may be involved in several different conversations relating to different tasks (issues, decisions).

Even a focus on subject line or email thread fails. The subject line may go unchanged long after it ceases to represent the current topic of the email exchange. People may even pick up an old email message to begin an entirely new conversation involving the same people, without bothering to change the subject line. A "reply-all" gives them a good starting list of intended recipients.

Just as task-relevant and task-irrelevant information may share a common subject line, task-relevant information may also be exchanged under different subject lines. Suppose time is short and you need to send an important follow-on email to your team members concerning an additional constraint on a task that must be done soon. The best thing might be to find the recent email you've received relating to this task and then "reply-all" to properly situate your new email. But . . . where is that email? You may not have time to sort through the email you've sent and received to find out—certainly not if you are in a hurry or working on a handheld device such as a Blackberry or a Smartphone. So you send your email with a new subject line that, in the worst case, has no words that even overlap with the words in the subject lines of other task-related email messages. The result? More email fragmentation.

One more part—perhaps the hardest part—of the email fragmentation problem remains even after all and only those emails related to a task are assembled in a single list. Now we must extract, organize, and make sense of the information within. The information still lies buried, often in several different versions, scattered across the email messages that have been collected.

The problem of information fragmentation is illustrated by the email conversation I had several years ago as I arranged my visit to give a talk at the Technical University of Eindhoven in The Netherlands. Consider a figure from Chapter 4 repeated here in Figure 10.1.

An email conversation, like any conversation, naturally makes reference to (but doesn't repeat) agreements previously reached and information previously communicated. The highlighted word "mobile" in Figure 10.1 refers to a telephone number in an email message sent several days and many messages before. The reference to "hotel" (also highlighted) was more problematic. The email message includes an attached map for downtown Eindhoven, but this map does not identify the hotel's name, address, location, or phone number. This information was communicated instead in another email sent two days earlier and completely disconnected from the current email thread. The message was sent by a different person (the administrative secretary) and under a different subject line.

From: ███████████████████
Sent: Thursday, May 12, 2005 4:26 AM
To: William Jones
Subject: RE: Presentation J.F. Schouten School 17 May 2005

Hi William,

As promised some details of your stay in Eindhoven.

When you arrive to the station you can just walk to the hotel (it is at most 5 minutes walk) . I attach a map to this message. The hotel is located at the North side of the central square of Eindhoven called Markt, next to the shopping center called Heuvel Gallery (red area on the map). In case you are lost don't hesitate to ask people around, they all speak English and are friendly.

I will book a dinner for us at about 19.00. Let me know if you have any preferences for the food. You can always call my mobile, otherwise let's meet about 18.45 in front of your hotel. Let me know if you also keep your mobile on.

Figure 10.1 Information referred to is buried in the email exchange.

The message in the figure was one of the later messages in a conversation that began with an email sent some two weeks prior and was to conclude a few days after the actual talk with a mutual exchange of "thank you's" and reimbursement information—a period lasting just over three weeks altogether.

The email discussion during this period moved through several phases:

1. What is the nature of the collaboration? An agreement is reached that I should visit and give a talk.
2. What is the topic of the talk? Several topics are discussed, and one is agreed on to best match the interests of the people planning to attend.
3. When can the visit take place? Several possible dates are considered before agreement is reached concerning a date that works for me, my hosts, and key members of the audience and that doesn't overlap with school or bank holidays.
4. What is the travel itinerary? The schedule must leave me enough time to make a plane-to-train connection in Amsterdam and another train connection during the trip.
5. What is the schedule on the day of the visit? Time must be set aside to meet with key people. An afternoon time for the talk seems to work best for those interested in attending, but there needs to be enough time for me to catch a train back to Amsterdam after the talk.
6. A wrap-up includes an exchange of reimbursement information and a discussion of possible next steps.

At various points, plans were made and changed. The proposed date of the visit changed a number of times. Once the date was determined, several different plane and train schedules were considered. Different schedules for the day's events were also considered.

Table 10.1   Statistics for email exchanges to plan a visit to Eindhoven

Number of email messages that I sent	26
Number of email messages that I received	28
Number of different subject lines	3
People involved at various points in the exchange (including me)	4

In the course of this exchange, smaller pieces of unasked-for information were provided and proved important to my planning:

> To get from our campus to the train station in Eindhoven should take maximum a 10- to 15-minute walk.

Or in response to my questions:

> Schiphol is the name of our airport near Amsterdam, and it takes maybe a 5- to 10-minute walk to get to the check-in desk at the departure hall, which is again in the same building as the train station.

Some relevant numbers for the email exchange are summarized in Table 10.1.

These statistics do not include my interactions with the airline, which were required to book the round-trip flight between Stockholm and Amsterdam. This interaction began as I filled out information on the web site. I received not one but three subsequent email confirmations from the airline. One included itinerary, another was meant to count as a receipt, and the third appeared to have both kinds of information. Which to keep?

As the travel date itself approached, I needed to refresh my memory concerning key aspects of the visit. What topic did we agree on for the talk? When does the plane leave from Stockholm? How, again, do I get to the train station from the airport in Amsterdam? I decided to paste relevant email information addressing these and other important questions into a single e-document and then to print it out for easy reference during my journey.

But what to do when the information I needed for assembly of my travel-plan printout was scattered across, potentially, 54 different email messages? Fortunately, most (but maybe not all?) travel-relevant information was in email messages that shared a common subject line. The number of emails to peruse went down to 38. I could focus further on only those email messages sent to me. There were 18 such messages.

Extraction of the right information, even from this reduced collection of email messages, was tedious and time-consuming. The information was "there," but I certainly did not want to open each individual email message. I opened email selectively. As I did this, I needed to take care that I had the latest version of the relevant information.

Odds are, you've had similar examples of email conversations from your own life. Maybe the email conversation plans an important work-related meeting. Who should come? What dates work? How do we need to prepare? Or maybe planning is for a non-work-related event like a potluck dinner party in your neighborhood. Who will bring what?

Email is a great way to communicate between people across distances and over time. Email is much less effective in its support for an external representation that preserves the results of this communication. The nature of the email conversation means that key pieces of information relating to a project we wish to plan are widely scattered across different email messages by time, sender and, often, subject line as well.

We may think to ourselves that at least the information is "in there somewhere." But this is sometimes a false reassurance. What if we don't have time to sift through our collected email? What if, in a hurry, we select information from an email message that has been superseded? Getting the current version of information is even harder when information is updated in a "by the way" inclusion to an email message with a different subject line. Moreover, we may often underestimate the extent to which the interpretation of email information depends on supplemental information in our own heads—memories that were strong at the time of the email conversation but fade with time.

The more elaborate our means of communication, the less we communicate.
English chemist, political theorist, and clergyman Joseph Priestley (1733–1804)

10.3 PIM activities in email

Email, as one form of information, engages keeping, finding, and each of the meta-level PIM activities as discussed in Chapters 4 through 9. Before considering the future of email and possible solutions to the one–two punch of information overload and information fragmentation, this section considers the special challenges that email poses for each kind of PIM activity.

10.3.1 Keeping: From email message to need

We encounter email messages repeatedly in a typical day. New email messages arrive in the inbox. And as we look at this new email, we may take a second look at less recent email messages that are slipping ever farther toward off-display oblivion.

As with other forms of information, the most basic keeping decision is how much time and attention to give an email message in an initial screening. We routinely look past the various announcements, FYI messages, and spam that often still clutter the inbox despite our use of an aggressive filter. Or we try to. Inevitably we end up attending to email messages that turn out to have no importance in our lives, even as we ignore or overlook messages that turn out to be important after all.

Many of the decisions David Allen prescribes in his popular book *Getting Things Done* (2001) are keeping decisions: What is it? Is it actionable? Can the action be completed in less than two minutes? Can the action be deferred or delegated? If it is not actionable, should it be organized for later retrieval? How?

Similarly, Whittaker, Bellotti, and Gwizdka (2007) analyze email processing into four basic steps: (1) allocating attention—look at the email now, later or never? (2) deciding actions—quick response, delayed response, or no response? (3) managing tasks—for which task(s) is an email relevant? How to relate and to remember the email later on? (4) organizing messages and message folders.

Effectively organizing email messages is a challenging, error-prone activity in its own right. People may create a folder, for example, that they never use, even as they place "to-do" messages in other folders and then forget all about them. Moreover, the email message is often only an intermediate step toward some other form of information. An attachment may need to be dragged to the file system or printed out. An agreement concerning the time and place of a meeting may need to be included in a calendar appointment.[9]

Like all keeping decisions, decisions pertaining to email are subject to the "damned if you do, damned if you don't" logic of signal detection.[10] We could be wrong. Worse, we could be wrong in two different ways. If we're biased toward taking action, we'll certainly end up answering email messages that aren't really "actionable" or, at least, not worth the time of our action. Does it make sense to respond to a friend's "How is it going?" email inquiry when we know we'll be seeing this friend later in the week (and can respond then in person)? Such repeated *false positives* can add up to hours spent in email with very little accomplished to show for the time. On the other hand, if the threshold for taking action is set too high, we're certain to overlook messages for which immediate response is important. The cost of such *misses* can also be high as measured, for example, in the hurt feelings of friends, the anger of bosses, and the frustration of teammates.

We can look for ways to reduce the costs of false positives and misses. Better search support, for example, can help us retrieve important email messages that slipped past our initial scan. We can also expect that the sensitivity or "smartness" of automated filtering will continue to improve and will help not only by detecting and sorting out junk email, but also by sorting and prioritizing the email that remains.[11]

10.3.2 Finding: From need to email messages

Although keeping is sometimes subordinated to finding in the realm of PIM, this situation is reversed with regard to email management. Our overloaded inboxes naturally raise issues of

---

[9] We are now seeing efforts to integrate email and the calendar better, as, for example, in Gmail's feature that scans each email as it's opened for potential scheduling information (and hyperlinks by the side of the screen that allow users to add these as appointments to their calendars).

[10] See Jones (2004) for a description of the theory of signal detectability as applied to keeping activities.

[11] Research prototypes designed to filter and prioritize email are described, for example, by Bälter and Sidner (2002) and Segal and Kephart (1999). Comparable support is increasingly provided in commercially available products such as ClearContext (*http://www.clearcontext.com/*).

keeping, ranging from whether an email message needs our attention to questions of how best to handle email for later access (flag it? set reminder? leave in inbox and mark as unread? move to folder?).

But not all email activity is about *keeping*, even as broadly defined to include all decisions made and actions taken in response to an email message. Sometimes, instead, we begin with a need and look for (or create) an email message that can meet that need. Consider some expressions of need that can drive us to re-find email: "Was I clear? Was I too harsh? Better check the Sent Mail folder and take a look at the email again." "Did he ever get back to me? Better look for a recent email from him (from both email accounts he uses)." "What did we finally agree to anyway? Better check the email thread." Or a person may ask, "Did you get my email?" prompting us to look. Did we overlook it? Or was it filtered into a junk email folder by mistake?

Just as it is convenient to refer to activity triggered by the information under consideration as keeping activity, it is convenient to refer to activity triggered by a perceived need as finding activity. Most of these activities fit our conventional notions of what finding is. But others do not. For example, in response to a need to make plane reservations for a trip, we may send an email message to our travel agent with destinations and a preferred schedule.

Finding (and re-finding) email messages, like other acts of finding, is multistep, with a risk of failure at each step. To avoid failure, we must:

- *Remember to retrieve*. Important email messages often go unanswered until it is too late, for the simple reason that we forget. We flag, tag, set reminders, file, or even "mark as unread" email messages (all keeping activities) in the hope that we'll remember to process messages in time. Even so, we forget. Reminders or flags become so numerous that we stop attending to them or using them as a basis for remembering. Or we forget to look in the special place we put a message so that we "would be sure to remember." Whittaker and Sidner (1996) describe failed efforts by people to sort email messages into a "to-do" folder. Efforts failed because this keeping activity was not matched by a reciprocal finding activity later on. People were simply not in the habit of looking in the to-do folder and so went back to a reliance on scanning through the crowded inbox. The habit of looking through the inbox was at least well established. The habit of looking in a to-do folder was not.

- *Recall*. Sending or receiving an email message is an event that has an associated date, people (sender and recipients), and subject. This information can be used to direct a search or sort that can narrow the range of email to be considered. For incoming email, we can often recall the sender, the date received, the email subject, or the email content. But not always. A friend of mine described a situation where arrangements for him to visit a company and give a talk had been worked out months in advance of the visit itself. His host at the company had thoughtfully sent him an email summarizing all particulars of the visit. However, my friend could recall neither the name of the host, the subject of the email, nor even an approximate date range for his receipt of the message. In the end, he was able to locate the email message by first remembering that he had been initially introduced to his host via another email sent by a mutual friend.

- *Recognize*. The message(s) we seek can be "right there" in a listing and we may still fail to recognize it. Recognition failure often happens, for example, because the email subject in a listing has little to do with the actual topic of the email.

- *Repeat*. Are we done? One additional finding step that can be especially troublesome in email is to decide whether more email messages must also be retrieved in order to complete a task. Task-related email messages can be scattered widely in the inbox, sent mail, and other folders. Re-collecting the complete set is not easy.

Finding specific email messages presents one set of challenges. As we move to a more general consideration of email's uses as motivated by a current need, an additional challenge is apparent: to use email, we must frequently leave the context in which a need is recognized and enter a very different context provided us by our email application. For example, as we look at a web site's information describing an upcoming concert, we may think to send an email message to friends of ours asking if they might be interested in going too—an act of finding.

But to send an email message means going to an email application, with its inbox in view by default. As we do so, we pay double for the resulting disruption in context. We must leave the context that prompted us to send the email. Worse, we are drawn into a new context defined by the email application, not by us. Who can see email messages newly arrived and not be tempted to look and perhaps send a quick response? A hour or more may pass before we manage to return to our original context.

10.3.3 Meta-level activities

Email engages each of the following meta-level PIM activities as well.

Maintenance and organization

People vary in their approach to the organization and maintenance of email in ways that parallel their handling of paper documents, electronic documents, and web references. Some people are highly organized, some don't bother to organize email at all, and others periodically "spring clean."[12] Some people choose to invest their primary organizational efforts in email, even to the point of routing e-documents and web references through email messages so that these items can be filed according to the email organization.[13] But for most people, studies suggest that email is generally less well organized than e-documents and files.[14]

Several developments support an inclination not to organize email messages into folders and to instead leave messages "flat" in the inbox. Storage available to the inbox is usually

---

[12] For a description of various styles of email management, see Whittaker and Sidner (1996).

[13] For example, some participants were observed to "organize all" by email folders in a study by Jones, Dumais, and Bruce (2002).

[14] See, for example, Boardman and Sasse (2004) and Jones et al. (2006).

plentiful (unless rationed by corporate policy). Sort and search facilities are getting better and faster. Some email applications such as Gmail encourage a "leave it and label it" approach to organization, in which messages are left in the inbox and tagged, creating an alternate kind of organization. Also, inboxes can generally be seen from multiple computers, at least via a basic web interface. But mail moved to a separate folder is then sometimes local to one machine and not accessible elsewhere.

Managing the flow

Issues of information flow are especially apparent for email. Certainly a junk email filter provides one control for email inflow. Many email applications also support the use of rules to direct incoming email to specific folders and tagging the email that remains in the inbox. We subscribe or unsubscribe to distribution lists as a means of controlling email flow. On the out-flow side, we exercise control through the selection of email recipients. We may also include "confidential" notices that ask recipients not to distribute the message more widely.

Some email applications also support a measure of outflow control through support of an option that delays the sending of an email message. I've spoken to people who use this feature in order to have time to reconsider the wording of an angry email message or so they can insert additional requests that occur to them after the message's initial composition. The "out-of-office" feature is also useful in our efforts to manage inflow, outflow, and the expecta-tions of people who send us email. One person's out-of-office message cheerfully told the world, "Email I receive while on vacation will be deleted, so please resend after I return if you want a reply."

Measuring and evaluating

One question that comes up especially often with email is, Where did my time go? Perhaps an email message we thought would take only a few minutes to answer ends up taking nearly an hour to answer instead. Or perhaps we expected to take an hour to catch up with email upon arriving at work, only to realize that it's lunchtime and we're still not done. Some email applications provide basic data concerning our email usage.[15] What else can be done to give us a better sense of how we use email and how we might use it more effectively?

Making sense

Making sense of an email conversation or a series of task-related email conversations can be especially challenging. The individual messages of an email conversation are exchanged over a period of days or weeks. Related messages don't always share a common subject line, and they do not always carry along a sequence of preceding messages to provide context. Under these circumstances, it can be difficult to make sense of or construct a bigger picture for a conversation's progress and its conclusions.

---

[15] See the example of Eudora in Chapter 8.

Table 10.2 Email features, current and potential, can be grouped according to the kind of PIM activity most directly supported

Keeping	Filtering, prioritizing, summarizing, and highlighting of key passages in email or agreements reached ("Okay, I think we've decided to..."); automated tagging by task. Semi-automated entry of message information into structured databases (e.g., date information into a calendar, telephone numbers into a contact database).
Finding	Searching, sorting, grouping by task, "incidental querying."
Maintaining	Automatic archival; semi-automated updates of calendar and contact information based on new email information. ("I can't make tomorrow lunch after all. How about Wednesday, noon, instead?")
Managing the flow	"Out of office messages" that can be set from the calendar. Variations based on "inbox load" ("John is especially busy this week and is answering email messages an average of 2 days after their receipt"); filtering rules that learn from labels given to incoming messages ("Junk" and other labels).
Measuring	Where does the time go? How much time do I spend on email messages that never seem to go anywhere (e.g., no follow-up conversation with the person).
Making sense	Form groupings of people based on email traffic ("If you emailed John and Susan, you might also want to email Ben").

Some possible ways to improve email in support of PIM activities are summarized in Table 10.2. The table is far from complete. The table is meant, instead, to illustrate the value of approaching a tool such as an email application with respect to its support of PIM activities.

10.4 Future visions of email

What is the future of email? One response might be that the question is not especially interesting or relevant. The consensus among undergraduates in a class I recently taught is that email is old-fashioned and "not cool." Students mostly bypass it in favor of other forms of digital communication—instant messaging (IM) or cell phone text messaging. So perhaps email stays much like it is today but is increasingly irrelevant; it goes the way of the telegraph.

---

[16] The list is obviously incomplete. For example, teenagers may post to their MySpace account with the full expectation that their friends will read what they post; they, in turn, will look to their friends' postings. Is this yet another (web-enabled) mode of communication?

Not likely. Table 10.3[16] provides a rough comparison of features for several modes of communication. Each mode has some advantages relative to other modes, with the exception of the telegraph, now defunct, which is at an overall disadvantage to email. The students who now use IM or Short Message Service (SMS)[17] will someday have jobs. And on those jobs, they will certainly sometimes need to communicate with others over distances and extended periods of time. IM or SMS or a quick phone call may work in many cases. But, in other cases, email will remain the best alternative. For asynchronous communication across great distances, there is no substitute.

Table 10.3 Each of the different modes of communication have relative advantages and disadvantages

	Number of people	Time and place	Interactivity	Immediate response?	Permanent record?
Face-to-face	One-to-one; some-to-some; one-to-many	Same time; same place	High	Yes	No (unless special efforts made to record)
Video conferencing	Some-to-some	Same time; most places	Medium to high	Yes	Maybe
Telegraph	One-to-one	Any time; any place	Low	No	Yes
Telephone	One-to-one; (some-to-some with special setup)	Same time; different places	High	Yes	Hopefully not
Email	Some-to-some	Any time; any place	Medium	No	Yes
SMS	One-to-one	Near time; different places	Medium	No	?
IM	One-to-one (mostly); some-to-some	Same time; different places	High	Yes	Yes
Wiki	Many-to-many	Any time; any place	Medium	No	Yes
Blog	One-to-many	Any time; any place	Low to medium	No	Yes

[17] SMS is a way to send short text messages to and from mobile phones; for more information, see *http://en.wikipedia.org/wiki/SMS#Premium-rated_short_messages.*

It is useful to distinguish between email as interaction and email as technology. Email as technology enables a very useful mode of communication. This section will focus, instead, on changes in the email interaction as manifest in today's standard email application. Here we consider two very different possibilities:

1. Email "takes over" in an email application that expands to work as a primary PIM tool—the central clearinghouse, as it were, for access to all our information and all other PIM-related tools.

2. Email "disappears" or, rather, today's standard email application with its inbox, outbox, and sent mail folders disappears.

Let's explore each possibility in its turn.

10.4.1 Future vision #1: Email takes over

Future vision #1 goes like this: Face it, email has won. We use email to communicate—with ourselves as well as others. We also use email for task, document, and contact management, even though email applications were not explicitly designed to handle these functions and even though email applications such as Outlook come packaged with modules "nearby" that are explicitly designed to support these functions (e.g., through "tasks" and "contacts").

We use the inbox because we're already there. Why look up the email address for someone in a contact database when it's easily found in a previously sent email message and may even be suggested as a completion if we type in the first few letters of the person's name? Moreover, previous emails contain information about the person that we don't have time to enter into a contacts database or for which there may be no "slots" or fields.

Task management, too, happens in the inbox because we're already there. Incoming emails frequently refer to or implicitly represent tasks to be done. We may respond with requested information or a promise to do something later. Similarly, we often initiate tasks or track our own requests through email we send out. We may even blind-copy ourselves on an email we send so that it also arrives in our inbox as a reminder to follow up with the person/people from whom we need something. Again, the email serves as a record of the task and its current status and also provides a basis for follow-up. Who has time to create and enter tasks separately in a dedicated task module, even if it is nearby as another module in the email application?

Rather than forcing people to go outside the email inbox, why not build the functions people need into the inbox itself? As one illustration of this approach, consider a view of the Taskmaster[18] prototype in Figure 10.2.

---

[18] For more on Taskmaster, see Bellotti et al. (2003).

Thrask used as Google bookmark

Clusters of actions associated with a thrask

Selected thrask

Actions; red for me, blue for other

Reminder has been set

Semantically neutral flags to mark up items

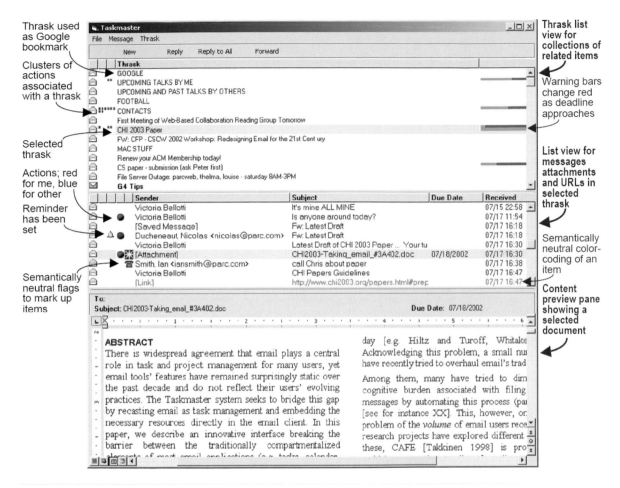

Thrask list view for collections of related items

Warning bars change red as deadline approaches

List view for messages attachments and URLs in selected thrask

Semantically neutral color-coding of an item

Content preview pane showing a selected document

Figure 10.2 The Taskmaster prototype groups email threads and documents by thrasks.

Taskmaster begins with the principle that the task and not the message is the main element of interest. Email message threads and associated documents are placed in task-related groupings called "thrasks"[19] (listed in the top panel of Figure 10.2). A selected thrask expands into component email messages and documents (middle pane of Figure 10.2). Naturally, thrasks can be assigned task-relevant property values (e.g., deadlines and percentage complete) which can then be displayed to remind and provide status.

One potential problem with a task-based approach such as TaskMaster is that so much of what demands our attention in the inbox cannot be easily associated with a well-defined

---

[19] *Thrasks* are "semiautomatic task-centric collections of mail and related content" (Bellotti et al. 2005, p. 121)

task. Other prototypes explore more contact-centric interfaces in which email messages are grouped by and accessed by email recipient.[20]

The "everything through email" approach has two potential drawbacks:

1. Existing email applications are already overloaded. Adding more features, no matter how carefully designed, may only make matters worse.

2. There are times when people may actually feel the need to turn off email (or at least ignore it) in order to make real progress on a task or a project—even tasks and projects that are highly collaborative.

Some of us may have the wish that email would "just go away"—if only for a little while.

10.4.2   Future vision #2: Email disappears

Today's email applications show relatively little variation in their user interface which, in turn, has evolved little since the inception of email nearly 40 years ago. To be sure, some email applications such as Google's Gmail, support labels rather than folders as the primary basis for organization. And many email applications are now primarily web-based.

But current email applications share in common their support for an inbox and for list views of this inbox through which messages can be sorted and grouped. Email applications support the inclusion of a document or file as an attachment to an email message. Looking forward, Whittaker, Bellotti, and Gwizdka (2007) see little variation in these common email features in the next few years. Certainly these features are well entrenched—not only through their common appearance in current email applications, but also through their repeated use in our daily routines of email interaction.

How could email applications and our use of email change so that, in a few years' time, we might look back and say that email as we once used it is gone? Here's roughly how this could happen:

1. *Start with shared external representations* as a basis for communication among people. This shift is happening already in the increased use of web-based forms, blogs, and wikis in preference to or in support of email.

2. *Don't email; communicate!* Provide integrated access to different modes of communication. People choose among several modes of communication, including the telephone, SMS, IM, blogging, a conventional web site, or old-fashioned face-to-face communication. Which mode to use depends on various factors, including the number of people involved in the communication, their availability, and the level of interactivity that's needed. Many smart phones already provide their owners with a full range of communication options, though options are often scattered into separate applications accessible through separate user interfaces—one to call, another to send a text message, another for email, and still another

---

[20] See, for example, Whittaker (2005) and Whittaker, Jones, and Terveen (2002).

for instant messaging. Suppose there were a general "Ask/Tell" command providing a consolidated listing of alternatives?[21]

3. *Situate the conversation.* The need to communicate often arises in the context of the work we are doing. We want to ask about a budget line item displayed in a spreadsheet we are viewing. Or we might want to tell others a funny joke or an interesting fact we came across on a web page. Make the "Ask/Tell" command available "everywhere" in a space of digital information (e.g., as a context menu choice). There is then no need to jump out of the current context and go to a separate email application.

4. *An Attention Central provides an at-a-glance listing of all matters in need of our attention.* This *digital dashboard* replaces the inbox for viewing all things we must attend to.

A shared external representation

Let's pick up the Eindhoven example to explore how this might work. Once planning was complete, I carefully combed through the reduced set of 18 email messages mentioned previously. Even after sorting and filtering, several messages had to be looked at one by one in order to extract the summary of key information shown in Figure 10.3, which I then printed out for reference throughout the trip. The summary was roughly divided into sections reflecting components of the visit.

Suppose this summary were available online possibly as a wiki or some other form that I, my host, and her assistant at Eindhoven could all have modified over time as needed? Support for wikis today is still basic but will improve over time. In a few years' time, the dialog to arrange the Eindhoven trip might have gone something like this:

My host might still have sent an email message to open our conversation. But soon after, once we agreed on the visit, she might have sent a follow-up message pointing me to a wiki representing the visit. Sections representing aspects of the trip would be filled out over time. I would provide some information; my host and her assistant would provide other information.

We might still need a more interactive form of communication to resolve aspects of the visit (e.g., what kind of talk and when). But in such cases, the communication could take any of several modes, depending on the availability of participants and the level of interaction needed. Sometimes a quick phone call or an IM conversation is more effective than an extended email conversation. Moreover, conversations, when they do occur, are situated by the shared representation of the wiki.

What a difference this makes! We now have a shared representation through which to situate and enrich our conversation. Moreover, for agreements reached and recorded in the wiki, there is a connection back to the conversation providing background—another kind of context—for the agreement reached.

---

[21] Use of communication mode will likely vary by culture according to convention. For example, according to Sandra Hirsh (personal communication), people in Japan prefer using email from their phone to calling a person directly, which is considered rude unless agreed to by prior arrangement or as part of an established relationship (e.g., friendship or collaboration).

Visit to Einhoven, May 17, 2005

1. talk

"Don't take my folders away!..."

2. travel

plane trip to amsterdam & back to stockholm

11:05 am Depart Stockholm (ARN)
Arrive Amsterdam (AMS) 1:00 pm Mon 16-May
Duration: 1hr 55mn   SAS 1551
Nonstop flight

9:25 pm Depart Amsterdam (AMS)
Arrive Stockholm (ARN) 11:25 pm Tue 17-May
Duration: 2hr 0mn   SAS 558
Nonstop flight

train to Eindhoven, May 16

| Dep. | 13.51 h. | Schiphol |
| Arr. | 14.04 h. | Duivendrecht |

| Dep. | 14.11 h. | Duivendrecht |
| Arr. | 15.24 h. | Eindhoven |

Hotel

Crown Inn (former Tulip Inn hotel)
Markt 35
5611 EC EINDHOVEN
Tel.: +31 (0)40 2454545
Fax +31 (0)40 2435645

Train back to Amsterdam, May 17
Dep. 16.00 h.???

3. schedule for visit

12:30 lunch

When	What	Who?	Comments
??			
12:30	Lunch	Xxx, xxx	
14:00			

Figure 10.3   A portion of the summary I made for the visit to Eindhoven.

Consider the advantages of such a wiki-based interaction:

1. Aspects of the plan still in question can be selected explicitly for focus during the conversation. If I think the time entered for the talk doesn't leave me enough time to catch the train, I can select both times (for talk and train) and send a short email expressing my concern. The email message is situated not only with respect to the wiki overall, but, more specifically, with respect to items selected within.

2. The wiki provides, at a glance, a record of what's been done or agreed to already and what remains to be done. Each of us can get a much clearer picture of where things stand with

respect to the wiki than with respect to a long email thread in which important information is buried. In many cases, the wiki itself serves as the mode of communication, with no need for a separate channel.[22]

3. At the end of this process of wiki-based negotiation, we each have the wiki as a current record of the agreement reached. I can print it out and take it with me, just as I did for the document shown in Figure 10.3. Given integration with a mobile phone or PDA (see Chapter 12), I might be notified of last-minute changes in the schedule even as I travel from Stockholm to Eindhoven.

The shared representation of the wiki, then, has some similarities with the shared representation people have when they are in the same physical space.[23] Teenagers working on an old car or a couple working together to cook a dinner for guests can take advantage of a shared physical space in which much of the project's status is visible and self-evident. Are the spark plugs back in place or not? No need to ask; just look. Is the table set? Again, a quick look either obviates or accelerates verbal communication.

Many questions remain, of course. It's easy to imagine shared representations for scripted situations such as the trip to Eindhoven. Services, such as Evite,[24] can already greatly reduce the email traffic relating to planned events. But what about the many other, less structured occasions where we use email to coordinate and negotiate agreement? Even in situations where there is a mutual attempt to work from a shared representation, it's easy to "fall off" the representation in favor of a quick email exchange. A quick email exchange in the Eindhoven example updating the time of the talk could have begun a process of undermining the wiki as the final, complete record of the arrangements.

At the same time, the potential advantages of a shared representation are significant and more than sufficient incentive to continue explorations into the uses of wikis and other forms of web-enabled support for shared representations in support of communication and collaboration.

Don't email; communicate!

Email is one of several modes of communication. Which to choose depends on factors discussed previously, some of which are summarized in Table 10.3. If both (all) people are online at the same time, and if a short, highly interactive "burst" of conversation is needed to resolve an issue ("Does a late afternoon time for the talk give me enough time to catch my train back to Amsterdam, or is there a later train I can take instead, or should I consider staying an extra day, or . . .?"), then IM might be the best way to communicate. If the channel of communication needs to be richer still (for example, to pick up on nuances of voice tone favoring one vs. another option) or if one necessary party of the conversation is not online, then a phone call

---

[22] As an option, all participants in the wiki might elect to receive a periodic (daily) notice summarizing changes made to the wiki.

[23] See Carstensen and Nielsen (2001) for a discussion of different modes of coordination.

[24] See *http://www.evite.com/*; see also, for example, *http://upcoming.org/*.

Figure 10.4 **"Ask/Tell" can be accessed from any information item to communicate in any of several ways.**

may be the best way to resolve things. In other cases, one party of the conversation may be in a meeting and can only provide a quick SMS message to confirm or to promise to get in touch later when the meeting is over.

Email still has its place as well, of course. When people are separated by time zones, synchronous forms of communication like IM and phone calls are more difficult to arrange. There are also times when we don't want an interactive conversation—even when other participants in the conversation are just a few feet away. Or we may want a record of our conversation, as previously noted. For these and other reasons, email remains a very useful, essential mode of communication. But email is one of many alternatives.

In Figure 10.4, a simple "Ask/Tell" command groups options in communication together. We choose the one that makes the most sense under the circumstances. The "Ask/Tell" user interface of Figure 10.4 is basic and intended only to illustrate. Better, for example, might be a communication dialog that begins by specifying the people with whom we wish to communicate. The choice of communication mode can then be made based on the online availability of these people.

Situate the conversation

A step further away from the traditional email application interface is to be able to access the Ask/Tell command wherever we are in our digital space of information and not just when we're working on a shared wiki-based plan. The need to communicate—whether via email or some other mode of communication—is frequently prompted by elements of the current context. Many of these elements are now digital.

A problem with email now is that we must generally leave our current context and go to our email application in order to send an email message. As we do so, we leave the current context behind. What little connection there is between the current context and the email message we send is either in our heads or, weakly, in the subject line we craft for the email message.

Let's consider an example where things work very differently. Sally is working to complete a marketing report for a big semi-annual meeting coming up in two weeks. She's working mostly on her own. This is her chance to really shine. The report is long—more than 25 pages—and based in Microsoft Word. As she works on the report, questions keep coming up. "What do we know about the new product from . . . ?" "Where are the current statistics on product demand growth in Europe?" and so on. Different questions arise for different sections of the report.

Sally prefers communicating via IM if the people she needs to reach are online; otherwise, she uses email. In either case, she does so by selecting the Ask/Tell command from the context menu (Figure 10.4). She has a question now that requires an answer from Mel, one of the company's accountants, who is away for the afternoon. Sally sends Mel an email message.

The next day, Sally is back working on the document. She wonders, did Mel respond? She could check her inbox, but instead she returns to the section of the report that prompted the email message in the first place. There she can see an indicator of her original email message but no indication that Mel has responded. Just as well. She had an additional question to ask Mel. Sally clicks open the email message to add her new question.

In this scenario, the email application works for Sally as it does for most of us. Incoming email still arrives in the inbox; a copy of outgoing email is still kept in the sent mail folder. New is the option to access a conversation (email or otherwise) from the information item that triggered a need to converse in the first place. Sally could have accessed the email from the sent mail folder, but she sends out at least 50 emails in a typical day. Finding the right email message would not have been easy—especially after several days had elapsed. Sally finds it much easier to locate the message she sent along with all responses by going back to the context— the section of the report—that prompted the email exchange.

The key features of this example are (1) the ability to access Ask/Tell and options in communication mode from any information item; (2) the conversation initiated can later be accessed by returning to the information item (document, spreadsheet, web page, email message) and the point in the item (as defined by insertion point) where the exchange was initiated.

The second feature obviously requires that something persists anchored to an information item and pointing to the conversation (whether based in email or IM). But changing the document itself seems like a bad idea. Also, in other cases Sally may not have permission to change an item prompting an exchange—when she is looking at an intranet web page, for example.

The answer is likely to be some form of support for an overlay to the information item.[25] A challenge with any overlay is to reposition elements of the overlay as content is added, moved, or deleted from the underlying information item. Overlays promise to do more than simply situate a conversation prompted by the information item. The overlay can also include highlighting or comments on the item. Overlays can also support the associational trails so eloquently described by Vannevar Bush back in 1945.

---

[25] For approaches to the support of annotations and overlays, see Brush et al. (2001), Churchill et al. (2000), and Murthy et al. (2004).

Attention Central

So far we have wiki-based conversations in which email is used much less frequently, especially for routine matters like planning visits. Much of the communication is done implicitly via changes in the wiki. When problems or questions do arise, these may be resolved via a short IM discussion rather than a more protracted email discussion. An Ask/Tell command gives us a choice between several different modes of communication. This Ask/Tell command can be accessed from any open information item. Later, a return to the information item can provide access to the message sent and the responses. Frequently, people may prefer this method over searching though the inbox and the sent mail folder.

But the email application and its inbox are still with us. A final step away from email as we know it today will come when the inbox is replaced by an *Attention Central* that provides consolidated access to all matters demanding our attention.

When I think of Attention Central, I think of the day-at-a-glance report that many managers receive from an administrative support person. For example, Cleo Davidson, administrative assistant to Dan Evans, two-term State of Washington governor, routinely provided Governor Evans with a day-at-a-glance list that included meetings to attend, tasks to complete, important communication to address, and looming projects to prepare for (whether or not due on the current day).[26] In the spirit of Attention Central are various efforts to provide "digital dashboards."

Will email really go away? Certainly not as a mode of communication. Also, you may notice that Attention Central bears some resemblance to Future vision #1 but with two important variations: (1) Attention Central is part of a larger effort to support shared representations that summarize and eliminate the need for at least some email traffic; (2) Attention Central provides integrative control of several modes of communication.

Until Then . . . Some Practical Guidelines for Email Management
– Olle Bälter

A great deal of good practical advice is available for management of email. Guy Kawasaki of Macintosh fame provides a list of 12 suggestions.[27] He suggests, for example, that we should take care in the wording of subject lines for email we send out. Bad subject lines ensure that an email is filtered into junk email or, if it gets past the filter, is ignored or postponed indefinitely (same thing). Emails with good subject lines communicate clearly the relevance of the email to recipients. In some cases, the email subject line can even communicate the point of the message so that reading the message itself is optional.

---

[26] Personal communication from Cleo Devidson, March 11, 2006.

[27] See "The Effective Emailer" at *http://blog.guykawasaki.com/2006/02/the_effective_e.html*.

Kawasaki also advises that we keep email messages short and to a single point (send more messages to make additional points). Also, quote back to previous email messages to establish context or reply to these messages, and use plain text. Minimize the use of URLs (which force a wider consideration of information), attachments (which require an extra step and some waiting to view), and unanswerable questions with no clear alternatives in response. Also, "chill out" (take some deep breaths before responding to contentious email) and avoid the use of all caps which SEEMS LIKE SHOUTING.

I have been doing email-related research and consulting for over 13 years. Over the course of this work, the following additional suggestions continue to recur:

For incoming email

- Turn off the beep. Each and every time you are interrupted—by your email, your phone, or anybody passing by your room—you have to make a context switch from the focus you had, to the interruption, and then back to your previous focus. Now, where was I? This takes between 30 seconds and 3 minutes, depending on you and your task. With 60 incoming email messages a day, can you really afford to lose one hour a day? Read email in breaks between other tasks.
- Read the most recent message first. Many problems solve themselves if you just stay out of it long enough. The last message contains the latest information on the issue, so work from there.
- Get a proper spam filter. If you still have problem with spam, your IT department has not done its job properly.

For outgoing email

- Use the phone for sensitive exchanges. As soon you realize you have been misunderstood in an email, use the phone. Resolving misunderstandings without the clues you get from tone and intonation is far more difficult and time-consuming.
- Write messages for your enemies. Never leave a digital or paper trail that can be used against you, because it will. When you need to send sensitive information, ask someone to read the message before you press Send, or use the phone.
- Use (only) the subject line. The probability that you will get an answer is inversely proportional to the time it will take to answer it. With a short, clear message, you will get an answer. If you manage to place a yes/no question in the subject line, you will get an answer right away.
- One message—one subject, for the same reason as above. If you send too many unrelated questions in the same message, you increase the risk of not getting answers to all. Most people read email carelessly, and the longer the message, the more they will miss.
- Wait. Many problems will solve themselves if you just stay out of it long enough. If you do not have a solution to the problem immediately, just wait until you, or someone else, figures out the smart solution.

I waited and waited, and, when no message came, I knew it must be from you.

English-U.S. writer, cartoonist, and columnist Ashleigh Brilliant (1933–)

10.5 Looking back, looking forward

Email may be the most successful computer application ever made. But its very success is a source of failure. Each strength of email seems to come accompanied with a weakness:

- ☑ Email costs no money to use and can be used in an unrestricted way to send as many messages as we like to as many people as we want to reach. On the other hand, email spammers can load our inbox with messages ranging from annoyingly irrelevant to offensive or outright dangerous.

- ☑ Email is flexibly used in ways that go far beyond its basic support for sending messages between people who may be separated from one another by location and temporal availability. Email is used for task management, document management, and contact management. On the other hand, email was not specifically designed to do any of these activities and may not do any of them especially well.

- ☑ Email is extremely popular. Email produces *information overload*.

- ☑ Email enables us to carry on a conversation across distances and over an extended period of time. But the result can be *information fragmentation* in which important points of the email conversation (decisions made, agreements reached, information shared) are widely scattered across messages in the inbox and the sent mail folder.

Two other points were made in this chapter:

- ☑ *Email can be a microcosm* not only for our practices of PIM, but also for our lives in general. Email engages all PIM activities, including keeping, finding, and meta-level activities such as managing the flow of information. Moreover, a great deal of who we are and what we do may be represented in the email we send and receive. A casual observer with access to your inbox and your sent mail folder might be able to infer a great deal concerning the friends you keep and the tasks that fill up a typical day in your life.

- ☑ *Now where are we?* As we experience "living in email," we face the unpleasant irony that email provides a poor sense of position or connection to the larger world outside that prompts its use. Unless we are in our email application already, we must leave our current activity and go to the email application in order to send a message or check for a response. Even though other items—a document we are working to complete, a form we are trying to fill out, a web page we run across—may prompt the use of email, there is little connection between our work with these items and our use of email. Also, there is little integration currently between email and alternate modes of interpersonal communication such as face-to-face meetings, telephone calls, instant messaging, or the use of blogs and wikis.

We have considered two future extremes for email. In the first, email is extended to more fully support its currently ad hoc use in task, document, and contact management. In the second, email as we know it today goes away through integrations that enable us to initiate and return to an email conversation, as one of several options in communication, from the context of any item we're working on. One such option in communication, as listed in Figure 10.4, is search.

Search as communication? The next chapter will explore several other ways of viewing search to make a general point that search has a wide range of applications, most of them unrealized.

Search gets personal

Search can get personal both as an interaction and as an underlying technology. Search as an interaction supports finding and re-finding and possibly other PIM activities too, like keeping and maintaining. Search-as-technology produces a text database with many uses. Search can help track information about us or posted by us as this information travels around the Web. But search, like email, needs to be better connected to the situations that prompt its use.

Chapter
Eleven

I have always wanted to be somebody, but I see now I should have been more specific.

U.S. actress and comedienne Lily Tomlin (1939–)

11.1 Starting out

In a chapter about search, the first thing to do is to define what we mean. "Search" is a usefully ambiguous term that can refer to different activities in different situations. Searching on "search" in Wikipedia, for example, results in a disambiguation page, listing 20 possible topics of exploration.[1] Search can be about finding and rescuing people; police search a home or a person (as in "strip search"); visual search tasks are used by cognitive psychologists to understand how people think; and so on.

---

[1] See *http://en.wikipedia.org/wiki/Search*.

But for most of us, "search" is usually associated with our use of a computer—especially in accessing the Web. We type in a few words; we get back a listing of results. Information from somewhere—anywhere, possibly authored by someone on the opposite side of the world—is now displayed in front of us in a matter of seconds. When things work and we get back useful information, the process can seem like magic. Our search genie is prepared to meet our every informational wish any time of the day or night.

The ability to search is essential to our effective use of the Web: just as the telegraph helped to "tame" the American West, search is helping to tame the Web. Chapter 10 introduced the notion of search as another mode of communication like the telegraph, instant messaging, or email. Placing information on the Web in the hope that a nonspecified "other" will find it can seem a little like casting a bottle with this information into the great blue ocean. But certainly web search services greatly increase the chances that the information will find an audience.

Advertisers know well the communication value of search on the Web. Web search can support the conditional presentation of advertisements based on keywords used in the search, so that advertisements are more targeted to audiences. For a person searching on "London," for example, advertisements displayed might offer vacation packages to London.

Because advertisements placed by search technology can be very targeted, search technologies enable what is sometimes called "micromarketing"[2] as an alternative to conventional mass marketing: customized ads are selectively displayed to reach a very targeted group of customers, enabling a kind of communication between potential customers and companies with products for sale. The words we type into the search box, as an expression of need, can be used to provide a targeted return of advertisements for services that might meet this need. In Figure 11.1, for example, a Google search on "micromarketing" produced an advertisement for eBay as a sponsored link.

Targeted advertisements sometimes realize a happy win/win situation. Advertisers get high "click-through" and are able to track the effectiveness of each advertisement. More generally, advertisers realize a much more targeted communication with customers. Searchers, in turn, may actually see more value than nuisance in the advertisements that are returned. The party that benefits most from this search-enabled communication channel, though, is the search provider: MSN Search, Yahoo! and, most of all, Google have made billions in revenues through the sale of targeted ad placements on search results pages.

Now, the storyline might go, the search technology that tamed the Web is on our desktops ready to tame our overgrown gardens of personal information. Moreover, desktop searches allow us to access personal information in ways that eliminate PIM as we know it today.[3] A nice story, but as with other stories, the reality is more complicated.

---

[2] See, for example, Bianco (2004).

[3] See Cutrell, Dumais, and Teevan (2006).

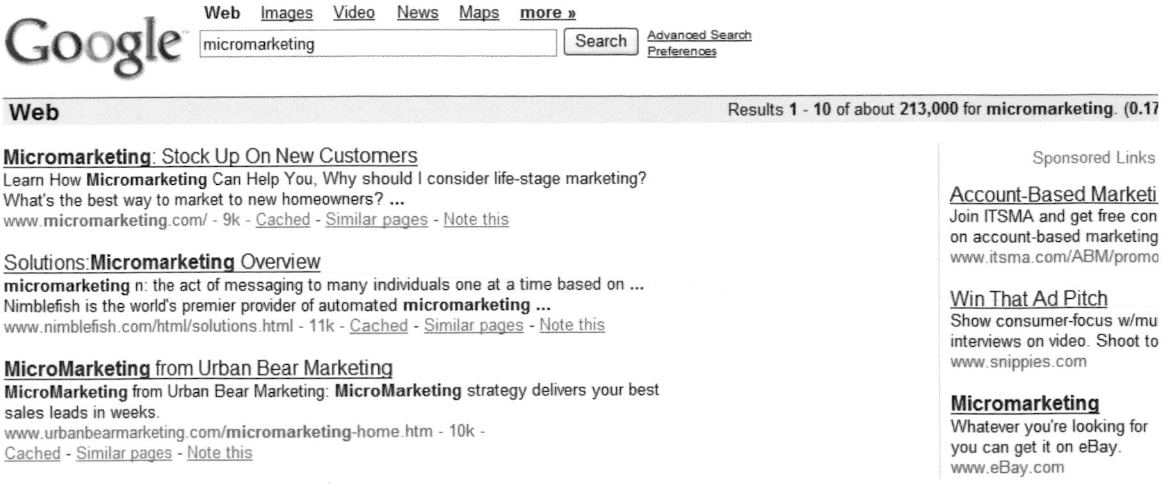

Figure 11.1 Advertisements ("Sponsored Links" at right) returned by Google in response to searching on "micromarketing."

First, desktop search facilities are not new; they have been around for decades.[4] But several features of desktop search are new, including the ongoing shift toward facilities that can perform integrated searches across several forms of information; that are well-behaved in their use of computing resources; and that are low maintenance and work well with, or perhaps are a part of, operating systems. Desktop search facilities can now index and search not only files but also email messages, recently viewed web pages, and, increasingly, the information in our expanded PSI, regardless of where or on which machine this information resides.[5] Search facilities such as Spotlight on the Macintosh[6] or Instant Search in Microsoft Vista[7] are designed to work automatically in the background, making little or no demands on our time or our computing resources.

Second, desktop search facilities do not and cannot work in the same way as web search services like Google with respect to their relevance ranking. There is, for example, no direct translation of Google's PageRank algorithm[8] to the desktop. On the other hand, sophisticated ranking algorithms based on in-link count and authority may not be needed for desktop search. The effective use of data about our patterns of information access and use may be more

---

[4] For example, the SMART system implemented by Michael Lesk and Gerald Salton at Harvard in the early 1960s enabled a kind of search for personal information. SMART was ported to UNIX on DEC systems in the late 1970s by Fox, Buckley, Voorhees, and others working for Salton at Cornell. A system supporting search for personal information was in place on MacIntosh systems running AIX at Brown University in the late 1980s (see also *http://www.thecore.nus.edu. sg/cpace/ht/HTatBrown/IRISbibl.html* and *http://research.sun.com/people/nicoley/pubs.html*).

[5] See Russell and Lawrence (2007) for a discussion on the expanding scope of desktop search facilities.

[6] See *http://en.wikipedia.org/wiki/Spotlight_%28software%29*.

[7] See *http://en.wikipedia.org/wiki/Instant_Search#Search*.

[8] See *http://en.wikipedia.org/wiki/Pagerank*.

important.[9] These patterns can be used in a manner analogous to the PageRank algorithm to favor some documents over others (e.g., based on frequency and recency of access).

Third, as Cutrell, Dumais, and Teevan (2006) explain, search is best viewed as another tool of PIM that may obviate some activities of PIM, such as organizing information in order to ensure its later accessibility, while having minimal impact on other PIM activities, like organizing information in order to make sense of it or as part of planning a project.

If anything, a discussion focused on the magical "genie" ability of search to materialize information on command overlooks the tremendous potential of search and search technologies to support PIM in ways that are wide-ranging but not always visible. These possibilities are explored in the following sections:

- ⊘ *Search-as-interaction* looks at the standard search dialog as a way to find information. At each step of finding, there are opportunities to "get personal" and so improve the search interaction.

- ⊘ *Search-as-technology* examines the tools and structures underlying the search interaction and explores how they could support a wider set of potential applications.

- ⊘ *Making search more personal* reviews the many ways, most still unrealized, that search can be used in support of PIM.

- ⊘ *Wayfinding and search* returns to a central theme of this book: How can we better situate our interactions with our information so that we can get from here to there and back again? If an appointment in our digital calendar prompts us to search the Web for the location of a meeting place, why can't our computers help us to connect the dots so that the search result is readily accessed later on from the appointment?

Throughout this chapter, we look at ways that search can "get personal" (or more personal) by factoring in the personal information available in many PIM situations.

11.2 Search-as-interaction

Search-as-interaction gives attention to the visible parts of search, such as the user interface for specifying a search and for listing results. Search-as-interaction also focuses on search as a dialog between person and computer. Search is initiated by the person who tries to construct a query that describes the item or set of items he wishes to receive. Or sometimes people initiate search simply to explore, without a definite result in mind.[10] In either case, we might hope that, as search improves, people will focus less on the search query as a way to "trick the system into giving me what I want" and more on expressing the need(s) that motivated them to search in the first place.

The computer responds with results judged by the computer to have matched the person's query. This representation is often a simple listing. But variations in representation might group results in different ways or connect items together in a network display. Items represented in a results listing

---

[9] See, for example, Teevan, Dumais, and Horvitz (2005).

[10] See, for example, the April 2006 special issue, "Supporting Exploratory Search," of *Communications of the ACM.*

are generally ordered by some attribute such as date (date received, last modified, last encountered) or relevance. The search interaction may continue through several iterations, possibly either until the person gets what he's after, settles for what he gets, or gives up. In some cases, the search dialog is initiated indirectly; for example, a person may commission a search "agent" to periodically search the Web for and report back on new items that relate to a topic of interest.

Finding (as discussed in Chapter 4) is multistep: we must remember to find in the first place; we engage in a combination of recall and recognition, often through several iterations, in order to find a desired item; we must decide whether to repeat the process in order to assemble a complete set of information. Search (as interaction) is one way to find/re-find information items. Search-assisted finding involves, and can get more personal with respect to, each step of finding, as discussed in the remainder of this section.

11.2.1 Recall

When we use a search service such as Google, Yahoo!, or MSN Search, we are prompted to enter one or a few words into a text box, as depicted in Figure 11.2. The search service returns a listing of web pages that contain (or are associated with) query words ordered by some measure of relevance. Most search services support the creation of more advanced queries which specify additional properties of the desired web pages (such as language and format) and combine search terms using Boolean expressions. However, these advanced options are rarely used.

The situation is different when search is used to re-find information items previously experienced—especially items we know well, such as documents or email messages that we have authored. When we are looking for a specific information item—the last in a string of email messages, for example, or the most current version of a document—we can and may need to recall attributes of the item other than just one or two of its content words. We may specify, for example, item attributes such as date or date range (e.g., based on date sent or date last modified), type (e.g., email message, web page, MS Word document, etc.), folder name (for email or files), and even people involved (e.g., authors, senders, recipients).

The Phlat research prototype (see Figure 11.3) provides an example of a search user interface (UI) designed to support a richer search interaction.[11] The "Query Area" provides support for typing words for the standard content-based search. The "Filter Area" supports the specification of additional

Figure 11.2 Search input into Google.

---

[11] For more on Phlat, see Cutrell and Dumais (2006) and Cutrell et al. (2006).

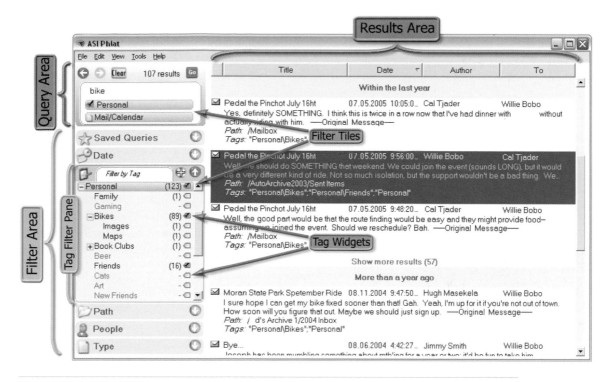

Figure 11.3   The Phlat prototype search user interface.

restrictions on the search. Also, the search UI and results listing are visible simultaneously to support a rapid, iterative refinement of the search query.

In the Phlat prototype, the search for an item can be guided by a number of properties. Several properties, such as the date of a recent encounter or the people involved, are not properties of the item itself, but rather properties of our interactions with the item.

The increasing and increasingly incidental capture of information[12] creates more opportunities to establish meaningful associations to an item based on encounters with the item, which can then be used to support search. Still more useful associations may be inferred. For example, it may be possible to infer the association to the task that motivated a recent encounter with an item.[13] The ability to use these associations to retrieve the item again brings us closer to an ideal expressed by Lansdale (1988)—that anything we're able to recall about an item or our interactions with it can be used to help narrow the search for this item.

---

[12] See, for example, Tan et al. (2007).

[13] See, for example, Shen et al. (2006).

11.2.2 Recognition

After recall comes recognition. We scan the results returned by a search query, and as we do, we try to recognize the items that meet our needs. The attempt to recognize search results representing personal information items should improve with the inclusion of personally relevant information.

Consider efforts to re-find an item such as an email message, a document, or a web page that we've experienced before. In efforts to re-find, Dumais et al. (2003) note that, although most people prefer an ordering of search results by time, the definition of "time" can vary with an item's form in ways that generally correspond to a personally meaningful event—past or anticipated. For example, the meaningful time for an email message is the time it was received in the inbox; for photographs, it's the time the photograph was taken; for web pages, it's the time of last access; for documents, it's the time last modified. A general preference for ordering by time when attempting to re-find information items is reflected in defaults for desktop search facilities such as Google Desktop, Windows Desktop Search, and Yahoo! Desktop Search. By contrast, search services directed toward the Web, such as Google, MSN, and Yahoo!, order search results by an assessment of relevance.

For items less recently encountered, memory is not usually anchored to a specific time but may be connected to memorable events that closely followed or preceded the item's encounter.[14] A memorable event may be the birth of a child, a summer vacation, or a world event such as the tsunami of December 2004. The human tendency to mark time by memorable events might someday be used in support of query formation, as in "Show me the document I worked on before the annual project review meeting."

A representation of memorable events can also be used to give greater meaning to a time-ordered results listing. Cutrell, Dumais, and Teevan (2006) describe the Memory Landmarks interface in the Stuff I've Seen (SIS) prototype (Figure 11.4), in which a time-based ordering of results is bracketed by "landmarks" representing memorable events. Landmark overlays can significantly improve retrieval times and user satisfaction.[15]

There are many other possibilities for personalized ordering and organization of search results. For example, a results listing might be structured according to the people we interact with, our enduring areas of topical interest, or by projects we are currently working on. Alternatively, since people, topics, and projects are often reflected in the folder hierarchies we create,[16] search results might be structured by an abbreviated display of a folder hierarchy.

11.2.3 Help to remember and to "re-collect"

Search can also take a more personal turn by reminding us of items we might otherwise overlook. Personalizing the search experience in support of recall and recognition will only help us if we are able to remember in the first place and can "repeat"—initiate new acts of finding/re-finding until a sufficiently complete set of items is "re-collected" for the task at hand.

---

[14] For more on the importance of context in memory, see Davies and Thomson (1988).

[15] See Ringel et al. (2003).

[16] See, for example, Boardman and Sasse (2004).

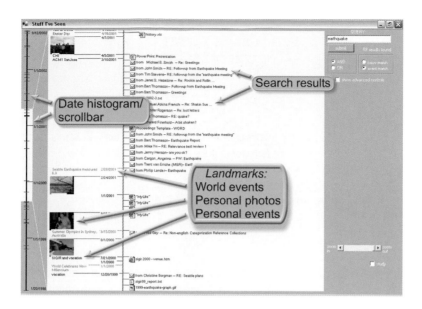

Figure 11.4 **The Memory Landmarks interface in SIS.**

A more personal search might help us both to remember and to re-collect. For example, Dumais and colleagues (2004) describe an Implicit Query (IQ) prototype that analyzes the content of an email message as it is being composed, in order to build a query. Results returned by the query are displayed in a side panel.[17] Such programs walk a fine line between distracting or unnerving a person, versus being mostly ignored.

Search can also help us to repeat finding, as needed, in order to assemble a sufficiently complete set of items for the task at hand. One way to do this is by application, implicitly or explicitly, of relevance feedback techniques.[18] Items to be assembled into a task-relevant set might be related through a consideration not only of overlapping content, but also of access patterns ("What other items do I generally access when I access this item?").

11.3 Search-as-technology

Underlying the user interface of search and the visible aspects of the search interaction is the *technology* of search. Search-as-interaction has obvious application to the finding activities of PIM. Search-as-technology has much broader application across a range of PIM activities.

---

[17] For related efforts to generate search queries from the current informational context, see Budzik, Hammond, and Birnbaum (2001); Czerwinski et al. (1999); Henzinger et al. (2003); and Kraft, Maghoul, and Chang (2005).

[18] The basic idea of relevance feedback, which comes in many variations, is to refine a search query and results returned based on explicit or implicit assessment of the relevance of information items previously returned or of terms salient in these items. See, for example, Salton and Buckley (1990).

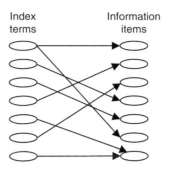

Figure 11.5 **A basic index supports fast look-up of information items that contain or are related to the term.**

The most important aspects of search technology are the processes and structures used to make search fast. Search needs to be fast—slow searching is an entirely different experience, as anyone who has done a full-text search using the standard "puppy dog"[19] file system search of Windows XP can attest.

Fast search depends on an index, sometimes referred to as an "inverted file" or "inverted index." An index is essentially a mapping from *index terms* (content words, property values, tags) to information items (see Figure 11.5). In some instances, the index may also include the section or position within the information item, where the index term can be found. During an index-assisted search, the query is broken into terms matching index terms, and associated information items are retrieved. Without an index, a search must sequentially consider each information item that could potentially match the query. A serial search through all the content of items in even a limited set of items—files under "Documents" or "My Documents," for example—can take hours to complete. An index-assisted search can often complete in a second or two.

Building an index includes the following general steps.

1. *Collect the items to be indexed.* Web search services generate collections from one or more web crawls that operate continuously to locate pages for indexing. On a person's computer, items to be indexed may be located by inspecting local email files for email messages or the web cache for web pages that the person has visited recently, and by collecting files that have changed since the last time the index was updated. Collecting items is easier if the indexing routine can depend on notifications from the operating system concerning newly arrived email messages, newly visited web pages, and files that have recently been deleted, created, or modified.

2. *Extract data for each item to be indexed.* Data extracted includes metadata or property/value pairs that describe the item, text from the item, and possibly other content data as well (e.g., pictures, voice).

---

[19] The search window for file system searching in Windows XP contains a puppy dog animation.

3. *Identify index terms from the extracted data.* Many index terms correspond to item content words.[20] Other index terms may correspond to tags or property/value pairs in the item's metadata. Still other terms may be computed from the available data by the indexing process itself. For example, all email messages from any member of "Taskforce-Blue" might be associated with a "Taskforce-Blue" index term (even though the messages themselves do not contain the string "Taskforce-Blue" or include an association to it).

4. *Create/update the index.* Index terms are associated to information items so that, later, the index provides its essential function—the fast look-up of items that match query terms. Optionally, term/item associations can be differentially weighted. Or term positions within an item might be recorded. Or, for each item indexed, the index might store summary information, including content terms occurring frequently in the item and infrequently elsewhere. As these and other kinds of information are added, the index might be equivalently thought of as a text database with several potential uses.

Certainly the process described above is simplified and idealized. Extraction of data from or about items can be a major challenge—especially for items like music and photographs with little associated text. Segmentation of data into index terms poses its own challenges. Words, for example, are conveniently separated by spaces and other "white space" characters in European languages but are not in Japanese or Chinese.

This short description cannot encompass the indexing process in all its detail and variations; instead, the point is that the indexing process touches and works with an enormous amount of personally relevant data. There are many possible uses for this data aside from its direct use in support of the standard search interaction. The indexing process that is requisite for fast searching could be leveraged to support a kind of personal data mining[21] activity, which might help answer questions like the following:

- What documents are similar to this one? How many duplicates or near-duplicates of this document do I have and where?

- What words do I tend to use (overuse?) in the documents that I write or in the email that I send? Are there other words I might use instead?

- What words do I tend to use interchangeably? Should these equivalence classes of words be included in a personal thesaurus and used, as needed, to expand a search's scope?

- When I use ambiguous terms like "jaguar" in a query, what sense(s) do I generally mean? Should senses be added to a personal dictionary and used, as needed, to narrow the scope of a search?

- What topics do I consistently search for on the Web?

- What topics are reflected in the articles (usually PDF documents) and web references that I keep on my hard drive?

---

[20] In languages that reliably use "white space" characters, words are easily identified. In some languages, such as Chinese and Japanese, identificatoin of content words is less straightforward.

[21] Data mining "mines" a collection of data for useful information that may lie hidden within. For more on data mining, see the Wikipedia "Data Mining" article at *http://en.wikipedia.org/wiki/Datamining*.

- What features do the items in this folder have in common?

- What characterizes the email to which I'm most likely to respond? Least likely to respond?

- Whom do I interact with and in what ways through email, instant messaging, blogs, wikis, and other modes of communication?

- How might I better organize the email messages, documents, and web references that I keep?

- What documents on my hard drive do I never use and, in fact, am I unlikely to ever use given the kinds of terms I use in search?

Note that an item can sometimes serve as a basis for a query (e.g., a query to return similar items). Conversely, a large number of persistent queries can be indexed, by their constituent terms, for faster retrieval in a manner similar to the way items are indexed. Potentially the same index that supports search can also support *information filtering*. In search, the focus begins with the query, and an attempt is made to retrieve information items that match this query. In information filtering, the focus is on an information item, and an attempt is made to identify matching categories (persistent queries).

Belkin and Croft (1992)[22] note that information filtering and retrieval are "two sides of the same coin." The queries returned as matches to an item can be regarded as ways to categorize the item. Queries returned might also map to (classification) suggestions for how to tag an item or where (in which folder) to place an item. The index is then used in support of keeping as well as finding—a topic to be explored in greater detail in the next section.

11.4 Making search more personal

Some ways to personalize search in support of finding, in each of its steps, were reviewed in Section 11.2. But personalized search has something to offer for other PIM activities as well:

Keeping. Search can suggest places to keep an information item under consideration. Segal and Kephart (1999) describe the use of a simple text classifier to suggest folder locations for a current email message. The classifier's suggestions are derived from the frequency of terms in the document (term frequency) compared with the rarity or uniqueness of each term in the set of documents (inverse document frequency). This measure (TF/IDF) is commonly used in term weighting and is factored into similarity judgments for ordering search results. Unfortunately, when the number of folders to consider is large, serial consideration of each takes too long. But again, search technology can help. Folders or tags to be considered can be indexed with respect to sets of defining terms. Then the classifier can generate a query through term analysis of the current item, and an index-facilitated search can quickly produce a set of candidate folders or tags by which to "keep" the item under consideration.

Organizing. Search in support of keeping suggests existing folders. Search in support of organizing might suggest new ways to group a collection of items which can then be realized

---

[22] See also Foltz and Dumais (1992).

through new folders. The data collected during indexing can drive a content-based clustering of items in a collection. If a cluster is found to be useful, the user gives it permanence through the creation and naming of new folders. Clustering based on content alone has a long history, and yet its success is still marginal. An analysis of content may produce a high percentage of clusters that are not useful or make no sense. This is partly explained by the high percentage of "noise" in an item's content. Also, items may overlap in ways that are accidental and not particularly useful. Content-based clustering may improve through application of techniques, such as latent semantic indexing,[23] that attempt to "squeeze out" the noise in content that often leads content-based clustering astray. Content-based clustering may also be supplemented by techniques that factor in patterns of item access and usage.[24]

Maintaining. Search has application to several of the maintenance challenges discussed in Chapter 6. Which information items take up space in the PSI but are never used? Where are copies or near-copies of an item located? If a piece of information such as an email address or reference is wrong, how many items need to be corrected? Which items (think especially of photographs or video recordings) are in older formats and should be updated to a current format? Each of these questions can potentially be phrased as a search query. Search does not do maintenance by itself—we must still decide what to do with the items returned—but search can make locating items requiring maintenance much easier.

Managing the flow of information. Search has potential for the management of both incoming and outgoing information. Some filtering of incoming information—deciding whether an email message is "junk," for example—can be based on content. For other decisions, such as whether to interrupt a person, a search's content analysis may provide input to other analyses that factor in additional information about the person and the current situation.[25] Search also has the potential to monitor the outflow of information. We might like to know, for example, when some or all of a document we've posted to the Web is copied by someone, especially if copying is done without attribution. While content words may not be individually distinguishing, they may become distinguishing in combination with one another. In this way, a copy that's superficially altered from the original may still be identified through searches that key on distinguishing combinations of content words.[26] People may also increasingly search to find out where information about them is "flowing" on the Web, by "googling" themselves, for example.

Making sense of information. Index-enabled search makes grouping and sorting a collection of information items faster and also potentially more meaningful. Activities of grouping and sorting form the bedrock of our attempts to make sense of information (think back to the description of Mendeleev's efforts in Chapter 9). As we perform these activities, patterns and relationships emerge that were not initially apparent. Speed—that is, system performance—matters. With fast, index-enabled searching, we can be more speculative, more adventurous in our efforts to make sense of our information.

---

[23] See Deerwester et al. (1990).

[24] See Shen, Dietterich, and Herlocker (2006).

[25] See, for example, Horvitz and Apacible (2003).

[26] For more on technologies to detect copies and near-copies, see Henzinger (2006); Cooper, Coden, and Brown (2002); and Chowdhury et al. (2002).

The potential for search to impact PIM can also be explored with respect to personal information in each of its several senses, as is illustrated in Table 11.1.

Table 11.1 Search can help to manage personal information in each of its senses

	Relation to "me"	Current search support	Getting more personal
1	Controlled by, owned by me	Desktop search facilities	*Keeping*: Suggest places to keep an item. *Organizing*: Suggest new folders (or tags). *Maintaining*: Suggest items to be archived. Identify versions of the same item or instances of the same piece of information (phone number, email address, etc.) *Making sense*: Fast grouping and sorting make it easier to see useful relationships among information items.
2	About me	"Self-googling" on the Web	Searching the "dark matter" on the Web to locate information about me (medical records, credit history, tax records) Agents alert when information "about me" is modified, accessed, or transferred.
3	Directed toward me	Junk email filters; rules and alerts	Filters on *all* digital input channels—IM, email, phone. Filters learn from usage patterns.
4	Sent (posted, provided) by me		Search to track where sent/published information goes. Track the distribution of email messages sent, reports published, articles posted to blogs, etc.
5	(Already) experienced by me	Integrated desktop and web searches	Re-finding items no matter which device they are on. Support for each step of finding.
6	Potentially relevant (useful) to me; about to be experienced by me	Content web filters block access to personally offensive web pages; agents to send periodic updates on topically relevant information	Automatic queries based on current task, context. Queries expressing persistent interests are derived from and anchored to topic folders.

*A man travels the world over in search of what he needs, and returns
home to find it.*

Irish author, poet, and dramatist George Moore (1852–1933)

11.5 Wayfinding and search

We return to a central theme of this book: PIM is about creating, maintaining, and using a mapping
between need and information. This mapping is realized partly by search interactions that mediate
between us and an underlying structure (represented in the index and methods for its use in
processing a search query). Wayfinding makes more direct use of structure—whether this is the
structure in a menu hierarchy, the collection of hyperlinked interconnecting pages in a web site, or
a conventional folder hierarchy. Key elements of wayfinding, as discussed in Chapter 4, are:

- A sense of starting point
- A sense of destination
- The ability to get from starting point to destination and back again

Wayfinding in the context of PIM involves a collection of interrelated methods for finding and re-finding
information, such as browsing, location-based search, and orienteering.[27] Wayfinding within, out of,
and back into a PSI is focused on the information being sought—the destination—but wayfinding is
also about the journey, the return, and the ability to repeat this journey again later. As we click through
the folder hierarchy of our filing system, for example, in order to retrieve a document, we gain more
than just the document. We also gain a familiarity with the folder organization along the way to the
desired document. We may see other documents or other folders that we would not have noticed had
we jumped directly to the document. Wayfinding gives us a sense of location and context.

The basic search interaction described in this chapter, referred to as logical search by Barreau
and Nari (1995) and *teleporting* by Teevan et al. (2004), is generally discussed as an alternative to and in opposition to wayfinding. This section takes a different approach—we consider
ways of integrating wayfinding and search.

11.5.1 Searches that use the way

You're at a party; it's getting late; maybe you've had a little too much to drink. Sure, you know
the way home, but, oh, wouldn't it be nice to snap your fingers and be transported back home
instantly. Facilities using auto-complete now do something like this in support of our return to documents on our personal computer. By typing a few letters of the file name or the name of a containing folder, we can see a listing of suggested completions (i.e., likely destinations). We can continue
to type letters to make the listing shorter, or we can select the desired completion from the list.
These facilities do a *begins-with* search on a file path, which, in turn, is established by the same
hierarchy that supports a more gradual, stepwise browse through folders to the desired document.
In this example, then, search makes use of the same structures that support wayfinding.

---

[27] For more on various wayfinding techniques, see Barreau and Nardi (1995); Bates (2002); and Teevan et al. (2004).

11.5.2 Folders that predict, folders that learn

In a second example, search supports the maintenance of the folders used in wayfinding. Folders—file folders, in particular—can be regarded as an expression—very limited, selective, and imperfect, to be sure—of a person's internal categories.[28] Of course, not all folders we create have much to do with the categories we keep in our heads or, if they do, the categories are not very good. For example, folders with names like "stuff" and "more stuff" may be nothing more than holding bins with little consistency or coherence among the items within.

But other folders do have internal consistency and coherence. Some folders (see Figure 11.6) reflect enduring areas of interest. Other folders may correspond to goals we would like to achieve (e.g., "lose weight," "get a job," "invest wisely") and may, in fact, correspond to internal goal-directed categories.[29]

Now we have search-enabled virtual folders,[30] also known as *smart folders* on the Macintosh, *search folders* in Microsoft Outlook, or *Saved Searches* in Microsoft Vista. Virtual folders are not really folders at all but are a way to make a search query persist over time. People exert direct control over which items belong in a conventional folder, but we cannot directly control the content of a virtual folder. Conventional folders are defined, and their membership is determined, directly or by *extension*; but a virtual folder is defined, and populated, indirectly, by definition

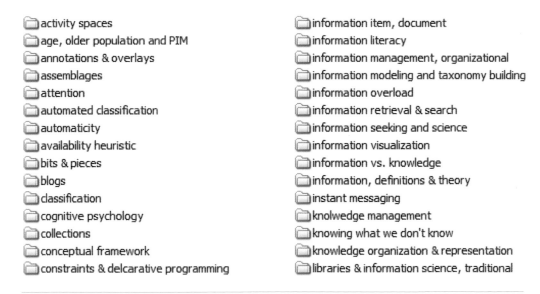

activity spaces
age, older population and PIM
annotations & overlays
assemblages
attention
automated classification
automaticity
availability heuristic
bits & pieces
blogs
classification
cognitive psychology
collections
conceptual framework
constraints & delcarative programming

information item, document
information literacy
information management, organizational
information modeling and taxonomy building
information overload
information retrieval & search
information seeking and science
information visualization
information vs. knowledge
information, definitions & theory
instant messaging
knolwedge management
knowing what we don't know
knowledge organization & representation
libraries & information science, traditional

Figure 11.6 **An example of topically organized folders.**

[28] See Jones and Ross (2006) for a longer discussion of relationships btween folders and tags as external expressions of internal categories.

[29] See Barsalou (1991).

[30] See *http://en.wikipedia.org/wiki/Virtual_folders*.

or *intention*.[31] A virtual folder has an associated definition that can be used as a search query; the items we see listed in the folder are the search results returned by this query.[32]

The trouble is that we are not very good at creating clear definitions.[33] Categories like "documents I looked at yesterday" are easy, but categories like "research relating to my term paper" or "stories my mother might like" are very difficult to define. To paraphrase US Supreme Court Justice Potter Stewart,[34] we may not be able to define what should go into a folder, but we know it when we see it.

An alternate approach is to have the computer "learn" the definition of a folder through the items that we place there. Let people define by extension, and let the computer build a corresponding intentional definition. The MailCat system developed by Segal and Kephart (1999) used the messages in email folders to develop a simple TF/IDF text classifier which could then be applied to suggest folder locations for incoming email messages. User involvement was key, however, since MailCat could not predict the single right folder with 100 percent certainty. Even if perfection were possible, a fully automated system of classification might carry other disadvantages. With no "manual" processing of incoming information, people could feel a loss of control, or they could be completely unaware of information that had entered their PSI. Mail-Cat kept the choice of folder location with the person but made this choice easier to make.

As a variation on the approach taken in MailCat, we might imagine that conventional folders, such as those depicted in Figure 11.6, could be enhanced by the inclusion of a definition/query generated automatically by an analysis of items a person has placed in the folder explicitly. Folder definitions can be based on content analysis alone or might also include an analysis of usage patterns, possibly as part of an ongoing exercise in supervised learning. Folder definitions can be composite, to express the several senses in which an item might belong to the folder. For example, a folder containing "stories my mother might like" could include a definition (query) to retrieve both "silly human stories" and "silly animal stories."

Definitions can be processed automatically as search queries each time the folder is opened, and results could be listed as suggestions in a separate pane of the folder window. Or suggested additions might be generated only at the person's request. In either case, the person decides whether suggested items are placed in the folder. This process can repeat; as new items are placed in the folder or older items are removed, the folder's definition is altered to reflect these changes.

11.5.3 Situated searches

A plan to search, like a plan to send email (see Chapter 10), seldom emerges fully formed from our heads. Instead, the information need and our expression of it in a search query are often guided by the information item currently under consideration. We receive an email from a colleague asking us to send a report we wrote last year that is "somewhere" on our hard

---

[31] See Quine (1969).

[32] Of course people can, if they choose, force an item to go into the folder by, for example, assigning it a keyword that is included in the definitional query associated with the folder.

[33] For a classic treatment of this subject, see Wittgenstein (1953).

[34] See *http://en.wikipedia.org/wiki/Potter_Stewart*.

drive, or an expense report form prompts us to search the intranet for the page that lists per diem rates for travel to different parts of the world. Perhaps there is a page that uses the term "mashups," prompting a search for other web pages to explain what it means. An upcoming appointment in a digital calendar about dinner at a new restaurant prompts searching the Web for information about it: Where is it? What is its phone number? Is it fancy or casual?

And yet our use of search, like our use of email, generally forces us to step away from or outside of our current informational context—to go to a separate search page, for example. As a step toward greater integration, utilities can now be added to most web browsers to send selected text directly into a search query (see, for example, Figure 11.7).

Why stop there? To invoke a guiding principle of tool development in support of PIM: if something is useful in one place, for one form of information, try making it work elsewhere for other forms of information too. Why not select and search on text in email messages, PDF documents, text documents, and calendar appointments? Search, moreover, is only one of several ways to access the information we need—we might also email, IM, or phone a friend or colleague. Chapter 10 described a general "Ask/tell" command accessible from an information item with options to email, IM, phone, or search.[35]

When a search is situated, elements of the information context, such as the text surrounding the insertion point, also have the potential to improve search results.[36] Text might be used, for example, to disambiguate terms such as "bank" or "jaguar."

So far, we've talked about the outbound journey, from where we are now, our current informational context, to information that might be useful in this context. What about the return journey? How do we bring the results back for use in connection with the item prompting our search in the first place? In Chapter 10, situating an email conversation meant access, perhaps via an overlay, to both the message sent and any responses to this message subsequently received. Similarly, the overlay might be used to situate the search dialog— providing access both to the outgoing query and to results returned for this query.

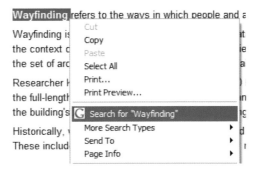

Figure 11.7   An example of an in-context search utility.

---

[35] Alternatively, different forms of search (e.g., one targeting the Web, another targeting information within our PSI) might be combined with language and look-up functions such as those available in MS Word for accessing word definitions, synonyms, and translations.

[36] For more on the uses of surrounding text, see Kraft et al. (2006) and Kraft, Maghoul, and Chang (2005).

11.6 Looking back, looking forward

Search can impact PIM both as an interaction and as an underlying technology.

- ⌀ Search as an interaction most obviously supports finding and re-finding. But variations on interactive search can also support other PIM activities such as keeping, maintenance, and possibly even making sense.

- ⌀ Search-as-technology can potentially be leveraged to support a variety of features not normally associated with search (e.g., "Tell me what words I use (too) often"). Search-as-technology can also be used more broadly in support of search-as-interaction. For example, the indexing process that now supports fast search of information on the desktop might also be used to generate a customized, personalized thesaurus for use in searching—both locally and on the Web.

A consideration of PIM activities and the senses in which information is personal each suggest ways to personalize search:

- ⌀ Search can help with each kind of PIM activity. Search can suggest how to file or tag new items (keeping) and new ways to group items by folders or tags (organizing). Search can help to identify copies or near-copies either for version control (maintenance) or to monitor the uses of our information by others (managing the flow of information). Search can also help with our efforts to identify larger patterns in a collection of information (making sense).

- ⌀ Search can help in the management of personal information in each of its several senses. Search can help us to monitor the ways in which information about us or sent by us is used by others on the Web. Searches are increasingly integrative, enabling us to re-find information we've experienced before, no matter whether this information is on the Web, a network file share, or a local device.

A need prompting a search interaction often arises from our interactions with an information item (e.g., a document, email message, budget, web page, etc.) in an informational context. As with email (and other modes of communication), therefore, there are advantages to situating a search in the current informational context. For example, text in the information item in focus, especially near the insertion point, might be used to disambiguate the search query. Also, situating the search makes it easier for people to return to a search—either to look through current results or possibly to modify and reissue it to search of new results.[37]

But implicit in discussions of the benefits of situating email and search is that the display space in which to view an email or search interaction is large enough to provide some context—at minimum, the resolution of a 1024×768 display screen that is standard today on even smaller notebook computers. What if the screen display is that of a Smartphone or PDA? More generally, how can we remain effective in our practices of PIM when the devices to support PIM must fit into a pocket or a purse? This is the topic of the next chapter.

---

[37] See, for example, Shen, Vemuri, et al. (2006).

PIM *on the go*

Increasingly, tools let us work with our information anytime and anywhere. To the good, this means "having things our way." For example, we can better use those small scraps of time between meetings, in traffic, or during halftime. But what if we don't always know what our way is? What if, in relation to cool new gadgets, we have no more sense of what's good for us than the proverbial "kid in the candy store"?

Chapter *Twelve*

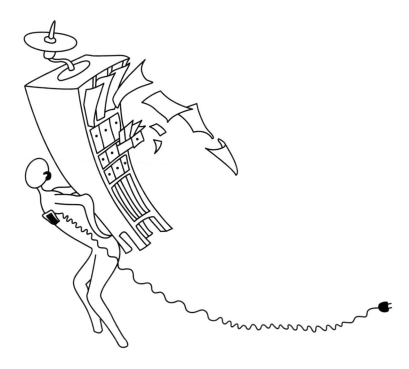

Excuse me, everybody, I have to go to the bathroom. I really have to telephone, but I'm too embarrassed to say so.

U.S. author, poet, journalist, and humorist Dorothy Parker (1893–1967)

12.1 Starting out

Where are you now as you read these lines? Are you at home lying on a living room sofa? . . . at work in a meeting room making use of the few minutes before your meeting begins? . . . on a bus (or train or plane) commuting to work? . . . in a coffee shop? As you read this or any book, you might be in any one of these places or others as well. You might even choose to listen to an aural transcription or voice synthesis of a book's words as you drive a car or jog or walk.

It was not always so. In earlier times, if you read at all, your reading activities were fixed to one or a few set places. Books were large, heavy, precious things to be preserved and used exclusively in special locations such as a library or a study. Technologies of book production dramatically changed our habits of reading even before the advent of the computer and digital information. We have paperback books, for example, that are relatively small, lightweight, and cheap—things we can take with us wherever we go.

The writing of this book was also situated in many places. I wrote some of it as I sat finishing a cappuccino in a coffee shop. I wrote other parts from an easy chair in my living room, the seat of a plane, and the table of a meeting room. I wrote relatively little of the book from either of my offices at home or at the university. The book's writing has been a (nearly) anywhere activity.

To write, we need only something to write with (a pen or a pencil or even an aerosol spray can) and something to write on (a notebook, a scrap of paper, or the side of building). Traditionally though, writing, especially academic writing, was rooted by the need to have the supporting information of journals and reference books nearby.

More recently, writing was rooted by the computer. I first wrote using a computer in 1977 as I worked to finish my master's thesis. I was thrilled by the prospect that I could see, modify, and print out drafts of my thesis. I could rearrange whole sections without having to shuffle and reshuffle scraps of paper. My writing stayed tied down by the computer for more than 20 years.

How much times have changed! My current notebook computer has sufficient processing power and memory to handle multiple applications and even more windows, and its display and keyboard are a reasonable substitute for those of desktop computers. Actually, my notebook is old, underpowered, and falls significantly short of current standards for notebook display resolution and storage capacity. But it's good enough. I do occasionally dock to a larger display when I'm doing serious editing. But the rest of the time, I take the notebook computer with me. I'm free to go where I want. The notebook—mostly—lets me have things my way with respect to the ways I manage and use my information.

But recently I faced a choice between watching my son's soccer match and working on several looming deadlines. Could I somehow do a little of both? Certainly not with a notebook computer! Its use on the sidelines of the soccer game would have been seen—even in this high-tech crowd of parents—as a "geeky" and anti-social thing to do. It would have been uncomfortable, sitting hunched over typing and looking at the display. And I would have had no connectivity to the Web.

I chose the game over work. But another parent did something quite similar to what I had thought of doing. Using a Smartphone during breaks in the action, he was also able to catch up on his work. He was connected. He answered email, did quick searches on the Web, and even quickly skimmed some documents relating to projects he was trying to complete.

Only a few years ago, the story of this father and his actions might have been dismissed as the fancy of an advertising person or a futurist. Not anymore. With respect to many visions of PIM-on-the-go, the future is already here—or nearly so.

Chapter 2 talked about the use of information and tools of information technology to "have it my way" with respect to our precious resources of money, energy, attention, and, above all, time. One reading of the phrase "PIM-on-the-go" is perfectly consistent with this drive to "have it my way": Our tools (PDAs, Smartphones, etc.) let us work with our information anytime, anywhere, and in ways that make the best use of the current circumstances. PIM-on-the-go means making productive use of those small scraps of time between meetings, in traffic, or during halftime breaks that might otherwise be lost making small talk, cursing the traffic, or getting annoyed with a commercial. PIM-on-the-go means making effective, immediate use of those bursts of creative energy we all have but that are so difficult to schedule or predict. PIM-on-the-go means being able to focus our attention fully on one situation with the assurance that our tools will work like an excellent human assistant to alert us to other matters requiring our attention as these arise.

But tools in support of PIM-on-the-go, like all tools, are double-edged: the tools that cut for us can also cut against us. It's nice to think we can have things our way: according to our needs and desires and not according to limitations imposed by current external circumstance. But what if we don't always know what our way is? What if, in relation to cool new tools and gadgets, we have no more sense of what's good for us than the proverbial "kid in the candy store"?

Wireless connectivity through powerful portable devices of computation, can, for example, create a situation in which we're always "on" and always subject to interruption. We go about in a state of perpetual distraction, never fully able to participate in or enjoy the moment (not even when our daughters and sons score goals). PIM-on-the-go creates new (we might say constant) opportunities and temptations to multitask—to alternate our attention and time between two or more activities in the same period of time. But multitasking is sometimes counterproductive or downright rude. The technical ability to manage and use our information anytime and anywhere may greatly outpace our understanding of limitations that apply— limitations in etiquette and more basic limitations in our ability to do two things in the same period of time.

Equally, the complexity of PIM-on-the-go tools and the demands of their maintenance can put us in the position of being tools of our tools. We spend precious time learning how to back up, charge up, synchronize between, and update our various devices and gadgets—time that might have been much better spent with our friends, family, or even alone on a meditative walk.

Dreams and nightmares alike are visions not of what will be, but of what might be. With respect to both PIM-on-the-go and PIM-on-the-Web (the topic of the next chapter), supporting tools are still in their infancy. Unlike the tools of our conventional personal computers (from notebook to tower), the tools in support of mobile and web-based computing are not (yet) set in a rigid pattern around well-established applications. There is time to practice what is being preached for PIM—that, for example, information fragmentation is bad and to be avoided, and that information integration is good and to be promoted. There is a tremendous opportunity to do things right. This chapter and the next will take a few steps on a long journey to explore what doing things "right" with respect to our mobile and web-based computing might mean.

Exploration in this chapter proceeds through the following sections:

☑ *Getting oriented.* This section reviews a few of the large number of technical terms and buzzwords that relate to PIM-on-the-go.

☑ *A foreseeable future.* We look at the PDA in 10 years or so as a possible replacement for wallet, keys, cell phone, and . . . our personal computer. We follow a future soccer dad through a typical day, and then we consider the darkness as well as the light of future visions.

☑ *What to expect from PIM-on-the-go.* We'll think about what to "expect" in two senses of the word: What are we likely to have? What should we demand? The camera/heart-rate-monitor/exercise meter/web-browser/email/IM/SMS/cell phone we routinely carry with us will have a large number of features. Which features really matter? Convergence is not enough. The information on a single gadget can still be deeply fragmented by different tools (software applications) and organizations. How can an understanding of PIM guide us toward a truly integrative use of information and information management tools?

Given the astonishing pace at which technologies and tools are developing, it would make little sense for this chapter to focus on a review of tools and technologies related to PIM-on-the-go. Any such review is certain to be dated even as it's written. Instead, we will focus on considerations of PIM that endure no matter which "cool new tool" has just been released.

We'll make one assumption along the way. We'll assume the existence of a device that we routinely carry along with (and eventually as a replacement for) our wallets and keys. We'll picture this as a single device with accessories like a headset rather than several independent devices. This device will be called a personal digital assistant (PDA).[1]

12.2 Getting oriented

We'll use the following terms in our discussion of PIM-on-the-go. Many of the definitions derive from Webster's, Wikipedia, or Wiktionary.[2]

- *Personal digital assistants (PDAs)* are handheld computers that were originally designed as personal organizers, but became much more versatile over the years. PDAs are also known as *pocket computers* or *palmtop computers*. Most recently released PDAs can function as a telephone.

- *Mobile computing* is "a generic term describing your ability to use technology 'un-tethered,' that is not physically connected, or in remote or mobile (non-static) environments."[3] Mobile computing is what we do today with a PDA or a laptop (notebook) PC.

---

[1] The new convergent PDA also has all the features of a cell or mobile phone.

[2] See *Merriam-Webster's New World Dictionary*, 2nd edition; *www.wikipedia.org*; *en.wiktionary.org/wiki/*.

[3] See *http://en.wikipedia.org/wiki/Mobile_computing*.

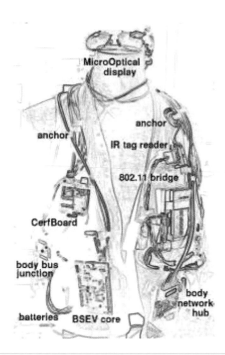

Figure 12.1   A suit we might all be wearing sometime soon? *Source:* From *http://www. media.mit.edu/wearables/mithril/.*

- *Wearable computing.* One definition comes to us from Steve Mann: "A wearable computer is a computer that is subsumed into the personal space of the user, controlled by the user, and has both operational and interactional constancy; i.e., is always on and always accessible. Most notably, it is a device that is always with the user, and into which the user can always enter commands and execute a set of such entered commands, and in which the user can do so while walking around or doing other activities."[4] Figure 12.1 shows one conception of a wearable computing suit.

- *Ubiquitous computing (ubicomp)* "integrates computation into the environment, rather than having computers which are distinct objects. Other terms for ubiquitous computing include pervasive computing, calm technology, things that think, everyware, and, more recently, pervasive Internet."[5] The increasingly common access points that provide us with broadband connections to the Internet (e.g., from houses, coffee shops, and even parks) are an example of ubiquitous computing.

---

[4] See *http://about.eyetap.org/fundamentals/.*

[5] See *http://en.wikipedia.org/wiki/Ubiquitous_computing.*

- "A *notebook (*also *notepad*, writing pad, legal pad, etc.) is a book of paper on which notes may be written. It was invented in 1920 by Australian J. A Birchall, who first stuck paper together and added a cardboard backing, rather than leaving it loose leaf."[6] There are two things noteworthy about this reference. First, it may come as a surprise to some (it did to me) that something so commonplace as a notepad was invented comparatively recently. Second, in all our discussion of high-tech gadgetry, we should not forget the everyday notebook (now in sizes that slip easily into a pocket) as a very useful gadget, in its own right, for PIM-on-the-go.

The human body is a magazine of inventions. . . . All the tools and engines on earth are only extensions of its limbs and senses.

U.S. philosopher, poet, and essayist Ralph Waldo Emerson (1803–1882)

12.3 A foreseeable future

Doormats are now available in Sweden inscribed with a cute but useful listing of things to remember on the way out the door. The listing, roughly translated from bottom to top, includes the following essential items: (1) wallet, (2) keys, and (3) mobile (cell) phone (Figure 12.2).

If we imagine a doormat with similar intent from a hundred, two hundred, even two thousand years ago, we should not be surprised to see two of these items listed. A wallet to carry our money and keys to secure our homes and other possessions have long been standard items to take on-the-go. The cell or mobile phone is a much more recent addition and would not have been included on doormats in any language until the last 15 years or so.

Figure 12.2 **A Swedish doormat reminding its owner to bring along cell phone, keys, and wallet.** *Source:* Excerpted from *www.designtorget.se.*

---

[6] See *http://en.wikipedia.org/wiki/Notebook.*

Consider the possibility that, in another 10 years, doormats may not list any of these items.[7] These items will morph into what is referred to in this chapter as simply the PDA—a little wallet-sized box we can't imagine leaving home or going anywhere without. The PDA may subsume all functions listed on the doormat in Figure 12.2. It will be used to call people, unlock doors, and pay for items.

What else? Oh . . . and it will also replace our personal computers.

In the middle of the 1990s, Microsoft released a major new version of its popular Office productivity suite, called Office 97. It came with recommended minimums for processing speed, random-access memory (RAM), and disk storage. Machines were expected to have, for example, a minimum of 16 MB of RAM.[8] Now, roughly 10 years later, many cell phones far exceed requirements for Office 97. In fact, cell phones exceed capacities for PCs of only a few years back. For example, one of the currently available Smartphones comes equipped with 64 MB of RAM, 128 MB of ROM, and a 2 GB removable mini-SD card storage[9] organized as a Windows file system.

What can we expect in another 10 years or so? The storage capacity at which flash memory—the primary storage of cell phones and PDAs—can be cheaply produced continues to increase exponentially according to Moore's law.[10] In 2006 Samsung announced a flash hard drive with a capacity of 32 GB. Assume that relevant capacities double every two years. If so, then in about 10 years we can expect a flash memory drive with a capacity of about a terabyte—much larger than the capacities of most PC hard drives today. Similar projections apply to processing power.

Certainly, the current use of PDAs is constrained by their input and output (I/O). Keying information into a PDA is cumbersome and time consuming, and displays are small. But support for I/O continues to improve. Touchpads support virtual keyboards and handwritten input. Displays are already good enough to support viewing of documents, web pages, movies, and TV shows.

Over the next 10 years, support for voice recognition may reach a tipping point so that, for many of us in many situations, spoken input will be faster than keyboard input. On the output side, we may see our information through high-resolution images projected on special glasses.[11]

---

[7] Of course, in the spirit of ubiquitous computing, a doormat of the future might flash or beep if we leave without our PDA or other important items (e.g., umbrella if rain is in the forecast). In more radical scenarios of ubiquitous computing, there is no need even to bring the PDA because necessary computing resources are built into the environment through which we move in a typical day.

[8] With thanks to Michael Kelly, director of Engineering Excellence Emerging Practices at the Microsoft Corporation for providing me with this information.

[9] The device's file system is TFAT (Transacted file system), and the file system on expansion cards (SD, CompactFlash, etc.) can be either FAT or FAT32; for a review, see *http://www.mobiletechreview.com/phones/Cingular-8525.htm*.

[10] See the "Moore's Law" Wikipedia article at *http://en.wikipedia.org/wiki/Moore%E2%80%99s_law*.

[11] For example, see *http://www.eyetap.org/*.

But the PDA's displacement of the personal computer does not depend on future scenarios of input and output. The PDA will plug into a laptop-like monitor/keyboard combo for sit-down use in a coffee shop where ambient noise is likely to confuse even a powerful voice recognition facility. In an office, the PDA may dock to a much larger display just as our laptops do today. We'll use these larger displays for tasks involving the manipulation and synthesis of large amounts of information.

Even as it is enhanced through these I/O attachments, the PDA itself will carry all the processing power, memory, and storage we will need in most situations for most activities. Its terabyte of storage will hold all the digital information we've ever generated or ever experienced—all of the web pages we've visited, photographs we've taken, documents we've written or read or want to read. If we make lots of video recordings, even a terabyte will go quickly. But for many of us, the terabyte of storage will be enough—certainly enough to carry with us a working set of all the information we're likely to need for our daily activities—and with an option to access the Web for more.

And our PDA will be a camera too. People who dream of making a full-motion video recording of all the events they experience in their lives will need extra storage.[12] Of potentially greater utility for many of us may be a "SenseCam" setup[13] in which pictures are taken at periodic intervals throughout the day to be used later as reminders of and pictorial landmarks for the various activities of a day. Over time, extra storage may be needed in this case as well. Even so, the PDA, perhaps with wearable attachments for picture taking, will form the nexus of such a recording scheme. External storage devices or the Web will simply attach to supplement storage.

Some people will still prefer the use of a laptop or desktop computer for some activities. Capacities for these machines will continue to grow, and these machines may still be preferred for special-purpose activities such as software development or multimedia editing. Likewise, serious photographers will still carry special-purpose cameras.

But, for many of us, the advantages of the PDA will be irresistible. The PDA will displace the laptop computer in the same way that the laptop has displaced the desktop computer. The PDA is portable—even more so than the laptop computer. All the information we normally need will be in one place, certain to be with us at all times. The functionality of the PDA will be good enough—better than good enough. And the PDA will attach and accessorize to realize still more uses.

Headsets, keyboards, mice, and larger displays are one kind of extension to the PDA. Another kind of extension comes in the form of "wearables" (see the sidebar, "Wearable Computing," later in this chapter) that are fashionable as well as functional. For example, watches we routinely wear can communicate wirelessly with a PDA so that we can "watch" not only the

---

[12] For examples of efforts to "save everything," see Czerwinski et al. (2006); Gemmell et al. (2002); and Gemmell, Lueder, and Bell (2003).

[13] See *http://research.microsoft.com/sendev/projects/sensecam/*.

time, but also sports scores, stock market summaries, eBay auction prices, traffic congestion maps, and so on.

With all this in mind, let's imagine a day in the life of a soccer dad like the one already mentioned, only sometime in the near future.

12.3.1 Someday soon in the life of a soccer dad

Sometime in the next decade or two, our soccer dad, call him Thomas, is married, in his early 40s, has two children ages 7 and 9, and works as a marketing manager for a high-tech consulting firm. Like most of us, Thomas always has more to do than time to do it in (or energy to do it with). He loves his job, but he struggles to preserve a balance that also includes quality time for his family and friends, time to exercise, and time for himself.

7:10 am, wake-up

It's Monday morning, and Thomas's watch is beeping ever more insistently. Time to get up. His watch lets him watch more than just the time. A glance at his watch tells Thomas that he had a good night's sleep with a proper balance between periods of dreaming (rapid eye movement) and deep sleep. The medication he's taking for his mild case of sleep apnea seems to be working. His watch tells him that his blood pressure and pulse are both at low, healthy levels. Maybe the meditation he has been trying recently has been helping.

Thomas showers and dresses. As he does so, he takes his PDA out of its charging bay and places it in his pants pocket. His pants pockets also contain some bills, some loose change, and a few business cards. Otherwise, the pockets are empty. He has no separate wallet and no keys. Instead, he uses his PDA to buy the things he needs and to lock and unlock the doors to his house, car, and office.

8:00 am, breakfast

Thomas shares breakfast with his wife and his children. During breakfast, he takes some time to review the homework of his children. Homework assignments for each child are accessible via special Web wikis to which teachers, parents, and even the students can contribute. Wikis are directly accessed at the breakfast table via Thomas's PDA. Thomas also uses his PDA to scan a headline summary of recent news highly customized for Thomas and the work he does. Thomas can opt to see news articles displayed on a screen in the kitchen or on a foldable, paper-like display he can place next to him as he finishes breakfast, much like a conventional newspaper. Thomas can also use this display to see a combined family calendar on which the day's activities and appointments for all family members are superimposed.

8:20 am, drive to the meeting

Using his PDA, Thomas looks at his schedule for the day and for the week. He'll drive directly to a meeting at a client site. He clicks to see a map showing where the meeting is and how bad the traffic is. The web-based mapping service estimates it will take Thomas between 30 and 40 minutes to reach the client site. Better get going.

As Thomas leaves the house he unlocks his car with a press of his PDA.[14]

Thomas plugs his PDA into his car while he's driving and dons his headset. Now he can take advantage of the larger display capacities of the dashboard (which he takes care to look at only when driving conditions permit) and windshield (on which traffic and directional information can be superimposed). As he drives along, he makes a request by voice for updates on traffic conditions and also for aural directions to the client site.

Thomas is scheduled to give a presentation at the meeting. As he is driving along, he thinks of an additional point to make, and he also thinks of a funny anecdote he might tell to break the ice. Via his headset, he speaks both the point and the anecdote into his PDA to be stored in association with other materials for the meeting.[15]

9:00 am, client meeting presentation

At the client site, Thomas brings his PDA up to the projector in the meeting room to connect the devices, and then controls his slide presentation with the PDA, allowing him to move around as he talks. During the presentation, his watch gently vibrates to alert him to its display of a short "back-channel" message from his boss, also at the meeting, reminding him to mention some marketing data recently collected. The data itself is directly available on his PDA.

Thomas returns to his office from the presentation and decides to walk rather than drive to a lunchtime meeting that is several blocks away. His watch records the motion (sending it to the PDA), and Thomas receives "credit" toward his goal of burning at least 1000 extra calories each day in exercise. On the other hand, as he swipes his PDA over the menu item he orders, a debit is recorded that more than offsets the calories consumed by the walk.[16] His lunch and that of his colleague (his turn to pay) is paid for via his PDA, which can then tell him instantly whether he is sticking to the monthly budget he and his wife agreed to keep.

On the way back from lunch, Thomas notices a rare gap in his schedule and decides to stop by a coffee shop. While he finishes a latte, he finalizes plans for a business trip to Boston later in the week. The coffee shop has free wireless access which Thomas uses to access the Web from his PDA as a faster alternative to the 4G access that is also possible from his PDA. The coffee shop rents laptop-like keyboard/display combos into which PDAs such as Thomas's can

---

[14] Unlocking might be more automatic than this. Some cars, for example, already support a "smart key" so that just touching the door handle unlocks the car.

[15] As it turns out, in the confusion of the meeting, Thomas looks at neither note. Even so, he remembers to make the point and tell the anecdote. For Thomas, the act of taking the note—whether in written or aural form—is often enough to remember the note's content later.

[16] Even though Thomas really wants to lose weight, he abandons the careful bookkeeping of calories a week later as being far too oppressive.

be plugged for better input and output (using a larger display and keyboard).[17] However, Thomas is particular about displays and keyboards and carries his own combo with him in his briefcase.

Yes, Thomas still carries a briefcase—in fact, he feels "naked" without it. Along with the display/keyboard combo, his briefcase contains monthly and weekly magazines and paper printouts of documents that Thomas hopes to find time to read during the trip to Boston. Where possible and when documents do not require modification or markup from Thomas, he still prefers to read documents in paper rather than digital form.

3:30 pm, leave work early for soccer game

Thomas leaves work early in order to make it home in time to take his daughter to her soccer match. At the game, he takes pictures and full-motion video, recording both players and onlookers. Other parents are doing the same. During breaks in the action and after exchanging small talk with other parents, Thomas is able to work through several email messages and also makes one telephone call and receives another—all mediated by his PDA. The incoming call is from his wife. Several other incoming calls are automatically diverted by the PDA, with callers given a message that Thomas is "in a meeting" and options to leave a voice message, send an email, or send a text message.

On the way home from the game, Thomas receives a voice reminder from his PDA via his headset to stop by the grocery store and pick up a few items for the evening's dinner. (It's his turn to cook.) Also, his PDA mentions that now might be a good time to pick up a new set of windshield wipers for his car—the car dealership where wipers can be bought is en route from the soccer field to the grocery store. Thomas skips the dealership but does shop for groceries, using his PDA to recall the list of items needed for dinner.

6:00 pm, dinner with family

At home Thomas cooks dinner, following a recipe he found on the Web. The recipe is viewed in a large font on a display in the kitchen to which his PDA is connected. While cooking, he also listens to music and then an Internet radio news broadcast—transmitted via his PDA to his home audio system. During dinner, he and his wife reminisce about the wonderful vacation they shared on a Greek island before the children were born. As they do so, Thomas is able to use his PDA to quickly bring up pictures of their trip for shared viewing on a picture display in their dining room.[18] After dinner, the whole family retires to the family room to continue to look at pictures and videos from past vacations. Thomas uses his PDA both to control the big-screen TV and to send the pictures and videos that are displayed on the TV.

---

[17] Under scenarios of Universal Plug and Play (UPnP, see *http://en.wikipedia.org/wiki/Universal_Plug_and_Play*) and Ultra wideband (UWB, see *http://en.wikipedia.org/wiki/Ultra-wideband*), Thomas's PDA might be configured to connect easily and wirelessly to available, albeit authorized, peripheral devices.

[18] When not in active use, the picture display is set to sequence through a collection of "paintings by the masters" supplied from a home media server, which can also serve up music and films to meet various enterainment needs and tastes of different family members. Thomas could, if he chose to, transmit pictures of his daughter's soccer game directly from his PDA—both for storage on the home server and for viewing on the house's picture display.

Watching the pictures brings up a lot of great memories, and everyone has fun. But Thomas is also struck by how quickly the time passes. The children have grown so much! And even though he sees the same "Thomas" every morning in the mirror, the pictures make it clear how much he and his wife have aged over the past 10 years. Thomas resolves to spend more time with his wife and children over the coming week. Life is too short.

12.3.2 Notables in the soccer dad scenario

Nothing in the particulars of this scenario is implausible. An actual Thomas of the future may be able to do more:

- Thomas may be able to blink an eye or wiggle an ear to activate taking a picture from an ear piece, glasses, or some other device he wears so that he doesn't have to take his PDA out of his pocket during the soccer game.

- A necklace may capture and support recognition of subvocal speech so that Thomas can use voice input even in public spaces such as a favorite coffee shop.[19] Or perhaps Thomas can "air type" using a projected keyboard.[20]

- Tiny projectors inside the PDA could allow walls, tabletops, or screens made of flexible materials to be used as displays while the PDA owner is on the move. Some firms are developing displays built into eye-glasses, in order to do away with the screen altogether. This approach also supports an augmented reality overlay of information on the real world, which could be useful when giving directions. Thomas's PDA might even label people at a party or conference to remind him of their names.[21]

Thomas is not wired in a body suit of wearable devices. He views information via the display of his PDA much of the time, and he plugs into a larger display in situations where he's able to sit down for longer periods of concentrated work. In our scenario Thomas does use voice recognition, but only as needed in situations like driving a car where his hands and eyes need to be directed elsewhere. At other times, he reverts to finger presses on his PDA, occasionally extended by use of an external keyboard. An actual, future Thomas may have dispensed with the use of paper altogether. However, this scenario makes a more conservative assumption—namely, that predictions for a paperless informational space will continue to be wrong.[22] Information in paper form still figures prominently in Thomas's life in the scenario.

If technical assumptions of the scenario are relatively conservative, the larger practice of PIM so enabled is remarkable in at least two respects. Thomas's practice of PIM is:

- *Radically portable.* The PDA enables Thomas to be an "informational turtle." By carrying his PDA in his pants pocket wherever he goes, Thomas carries nearly all of the information he is likely to need for his current activities. He also carries the means to work with

---

[19] NASA, for example, is experimenting with detection of subvocal speech; see *http://www.nasa.gov/centers/ames/news/releases/2004/subvocal/subvocal.html*.

[20] See, for example, *http://www.alpern.org/weblog/stories/2003/01/09/projectionKeyboards.html*.

[21] From "The Phone of the Future," *The Economist* 381(8506),16, 2006.

[22] See Sellen and Harper (2002).

this information and the means to access still more information as needed (e.g., via web access and various modes of communication).

- *Radically personal.* The PDA is Thomas's constant companion. Thomas takes it wherever he goes—even during exercise workouts. Thomas wears one accessory of the PDA—the "watch" watch—24 hours a day, even as he sleeps through the night. The PDA and its watch accessory redefine what it means for a tool to be "personal." Virtually all interactions Thomas has with digital information are mediated by his PDA. More personal still, accessories such as the watch can measure aspects of Thomas's body such as heart rate, blood pressure, and movement.

The PDA is a constant companion in the same way that wallet, keys, date book, and cell phone are constant companions for someone today.

12.3.3 A darker side to the future

What could possibly be wrong with a companion—the PDA—that is there ready to help us day and night and never leaves? Part of the answer is contained in the question: the PDA never leaves. It remains a constant source of distraction, not only for its owner but for other people nearby as well. We don't need to travel to the future to imagine the problems presented by a PDA that is always there and always on. Think only of what people do now with cell phones or with iPods and other MP3 devices for listening to digitally encoded music. Or think of our children who play with handheld gaming devices. Or, for that matter, think of people who work through email on their laptop computer. These people are straddling two environments—and often doing a poor job of being in either. They are physically present in one environment even as their minds are totally absorbed with another informational environment brought to them via their email, the game they are playing, their music, or their phone conversation.

A PDA that combines the functions of a phone, email, IM, SMS, audio and video entertainment, and games further increases the number of ways in which our attention can be drawn away from the physical environment and into an informational environment.

A camera/phone/music player/heart and blood-pressure monitor/PDA loaded with computing power and large amounts of storage comes with other dark-side risks as well:

The worst of times, not the best of times. Our use of a PDA, even when it does not create an annoyance to others or a danger to ourselves, can compromise our participation in both our physical environment and our informational environment. Consider Thomas again. He carries his PDA to his daughter's soccer game in the hope that he'll be able to realize an ideal of multitasking: in the same period of time he would like to both see the game and give support to his daughter while also getting a little work done. But suppose he does neither very well? Thomas might struggle in a distracted way to read the email messages shown on his PDA display and to key in responses that are poorly considered and poorly expressed and so cause confusion and even offense to intended recipients. Meanwhile, his daughter scores a goal and looks up beaming to see her father's approval, only to see him bent over and totally absorbed by his PDA.

"Smile! You're on candid camera." Thomas is taking pictures at the soccer game. Other people are too. Wearable computing accessories may make picture taking even more seamless and nonobvious than it is for Thomas (who still points and clicks his PDA to take a picture). Wherever we are, certainly in public spaces, we're likely to be on camera. We are already on camera when we visit a bank or shop at a convenience store. Now, with the ubiquity of PDAs capable of taking pictures and full-motion video, we could be on camera whenever we are in a public place. We have met Big Brother. He is us.

"I just wanna make a phone call . . ." A YouTube video spoof provides a send-up of the iPhone as the ultimate "everything" gadget.[23] It's a shaver, a toaster, an aid in sexual performance, and . . . a hard-to-use cell phone. Whether the spoof is accurate for iPhone or not, it raises an issue of general relevance to feature-packed PDAs. As features and functions are crowded together on a small physical device, how can essential functions still be accessible and usable?

"And now to suit our great computer . . ." (as the line from a Moody Blues song goes). Many people I know first carried their mobile phone for outgoing calls only. But now the expectation is that the phone is on for incoming calls as well. The phone rings or beeps; we answer. Suppose Thomas becomes a slave to this PDA? He is constantly on call, day and night. He spends considerable time to synchronize between his PDA and other devices. And then more time to upload backups of his PDA and to download software updates.

What happens if the PDA goes away? Or falls into the wrong hands? Suppose Thomas loses his PDA? Can someone else use it to spend his money, take his car, rob his house, and steal his identity? Even if the PDA works only for Thomas, its loss could be a disaster. No money. No keys to open his car or his house or his office. The PDA's loss means the loss of countless other support functions on which Thomas has become hopelessly dependent.

What happens if the PDA doesn't (ever) go away? After a severe windstorm in December 2006, much of the greater Seattle area was without power for several days to over a week. Those without power—especially for a week or more—were well glad to have it back again. But many of us had a common experience in the first few days. Life without electricity forced us into a simpler way of living that we were happy to have experienced. A common story went like this: Members of a family, normally scattered throughout a large house and beyond, gathered together for warmth and companionship into a single living room lit by candlelight. Children played board games. Parents actually talked to each other. I've heard similar stories relating to the temporary loss of email or Internet connectivity—people expressed an appreciation for a forced period of disengagement during which they did other things—completed chores they'd been putting off, read, reflected, or simply relaxed. But as soon as the electricity comes back on, the connection to the Internet is restored or the email begins to arrive again, and we're back into our normal mode of work and living. What does Thomas lose for the constant presence of his PDA?[24]

---

[23] See *http://www.youtube.com/watch?v=1xXNoB3t8vM* and *http://www.nbc.com/Late_Night_with_Conan_O'Brien/index.shtml.*

[24] It might be said that these are "people problems" rather than problems with the technology per se. But such an argument may overestimate the control we exercise over our bodies ("wired" as we are to respond in certain ways) and over our immediate environment, which is also wired in its own way to support certain patterns of technophilic behavior.

Convergence but no integration. The radical convergences enabled through advances in computing technology leave open the possibility of a devil's irony: Suppose that all of Thomas's information and information tools are "there" on one device, the PDA, and yet more fragmented than ever by different applications? Convergence without integration could also make it much more difficult for Thomas to manage his information.

Lives as a matter of public record. If people's daily lives are recorded with words, pictures, and even data from their own bodies, what about their lives can be kept private? Can Thomas's PDA be subpoenaed if he happens to be in the vicinity of a crime scene? What if his PDA inadvertently captures pictures he never should have taken and never intended to take—who has the right to those pictures?

Men have become the tools of their tools.

U.S. essayist, poet, and naturalist Henry David Thoreau (1817–1862)

Wearable Computing

– Mike Nakahara

The items worn on the body sit on very valuable real estate. These items are, for the most part, with you all the time, are something you want to wear, and typically something you want to keep. Until recently, items were worn for purposes of protection and decoration, but now we have the chance to add PIM to the list of uses for our bodily wear.

Some areas of the body are more valuable than others with respect to access and utility. Take the eyes, for example; they not only provide you with a way to experience the world around you, but they are also a great place for showing off designer sunglasses. The ears are likewise very valuable and have the added benefit of being on both sides of your head. Other key areas are the wrists. Although these do not provide an input or output function, they do have the advantage of being mobile and easily and quickly accessed in view of the eyes and within range of your ears. In the following paragraphs, we will explore some common wearable devices that can help to enhance the user experience when considering the sum of wearable devices as a whole.

In and of themselves, a watch and a phone each have their specific functions. A watch tells time and a mobile phone handles voice calls. But the application of new technology and wireless services has improved the usefulness of these devices in areas outside of their traditional roles. As an example, since the watch is on the wrist, integrating sensors to detect heart rate, blood pressure, or physical activity monitors can collect information continuously and provide invaluable data on one's health in a nonintrusive manner.

So we might ask, How can the usefulness of these devices improve further through integration? Take the example of the heart-rate monitor. If the watch connects to the phone via a wireless link such as Bluetooth, it can use the phone's data link as a connection to the Internet. It would then be able to contact an online personal trainer about a workout that had just occurred. The personal trainer can analyze the data, come up with a new program, and send it back to the person in real time from anywhere in the world. More important, an emergency number might be automatically dialed in the event that the person's heart stops beating or starts beating irregularly.

Now let's look at the phone. Strictly speaking, the phone is not wearable technology; it is typically kept in a pocket or purse. The effort and time needed to access the phone is not a difficult bar to hurdle. But there are times when pulling a phone out of your pocket or purse immediately presents an unwanted awkward moment. One solution to this dilemma is to use a wristwatch as an extension of the phone for call notification and to even provide call control to eliminate the fumbling search for the phone itself. The watch is accessible within a second and is something that is worn and with you while you are awake. The watch is now a secondary display and control surface for your phone.

So what's next? Although there are a plethora of audio headsets available to consumers, the physical integration of eyeglasses as the display surface with audio headset technology not only would keep the phone tucked away securely, but would open the door to a whole new world of applications that are not restricted by the physical dimensions and perceived resolutions of current cell phone displays. As an example, navigation information can be displayed in real time, as you walk around the city, pointing out the workplaces of your friends or the nearest coffee shop in an unfamiliar part of town. Movies in high definition and surround sound could be enjoyed while traveling on a bus to and from work. When seeing a past acquaintance, having her personal information displayed in front of you could take you from an uncomfortable moment to a very useful encounter.

Now that we have a control surface, audio I/O, and a wonderful display surface, what can we add to enhance interaction with our information? Wearing a keyboard and mouse is out of the question, but perhaps voice recognition would be suited for this ecosystem of wearable technology. Voice recognition technology has matured beyond simple command recognition. Natural language, conversational speech, and contextual grammar recognition are only a few of the techniques being utilized in systems today to promote a more human interaction with computer systems. Add this to the growing processing capabilities of a wearable gadget, and you have the makings of a virtual environment that truly enhances your interaction with your very real surroundings.

Technology is constantly being pushed to make these scenarios a near-future reality. But there are also nontechnical preconceptions that must be hurdled to bring consumer acceptance into the picture. Although many consumers are acclimated to charging a phone, the concept of recharging your watch, glasses, or coat is not only unfamiliar but also a very cumbersome proposition. This also brings up the question about multi-gadget dependencies. If the battery charge of a device runs out, the overall usability of the system is degraded (similar to forgetting your wireless headset for your phone).

As the user experiences this and similar scenarios, adjustments will have to be made to make sure the access and opportunity for recharging all their devices are available.

Also, the question of fashion versus function is a very real concern for gadgets. Fashion is a more recent challenge for the electronics industry. As more gadgets become wearable, the need to address the personal style choices of consumers becomes more important. But fashion tends to focus on small volumes with multiple styles, while electronics manufacturers typically deal with high volume in limited variations. Currently the industry deals with this conundrum by producing accessories that are reasonably low cost yet add just enough personal style to turn something black and functional into something personal and precious. The after-market accessory industry for cell phones and MP3 players is simply the tip of the iceberg of the upcoming opportunity for wearable technology and the challenges that they will bring.

Wearable gadgets are indeed a new and exciting area of innovation. Seeing the world through the integration of information with your surroundings and interacting with it in an effortless fashion opens up a whole new way to make our everyday lives easier to navigate. The benefits of making this a reality are probably even greater than we realize today and should be well worth the effort to work through the many challenges that have been discussed.

12.4 What to expect from PIM-on-the-go?

A problem of more immediate relevance to many of us than the drawbacks of an ever-present PDA is how to make sense of all the new PDAs (Smartphones, PocketPCs, iPhones, etc.) with their many features. Even for people who have a strong technical background, the list of features for today's PDAs can seem overwhelming; and it is not clear how to use them together to support our daily PIM activities. We should ask more of our PDAs than what we get today. Features should work much better together to support our activities rather than being a collection of standalone tools that do not work together well, or at all.

Consider the example of a listing of features for one PDA posted on the Web in January 2007 (Figure 12.3). How are we to make sense of such a list of features? Which features really matter? Which features are we not likely to need or use? Worse, which features will later become distractions or impediments to our use of the features we really care about?

Some features listed, such as the ability to "type and edit MS Word/Excel files," seem mostly intended to reassure us that functionality we're already familiar with on our personal computers is also available for the PDA. Other features, such as the camera (with zoom and video capture), are not commonly found on laptop computers.

Features listed in the figure are more elemental than integrative. As consumers, we're left to mentally combine features to determine how we might really use them in order to complete activities in our lives. In the section that follows, we'll use PIM activities to guide us toward more integrative use of PDA functions.

Included Features

Enhanced email, internet, messaging, and organizer all in one
Microsoft® Windows MobileTM 5.0 with MSFP
Slim style with full QWERTY keyboard and internal antenna
Type and edit MS Word/Excel files; view PowerPoint & PDF docs
Global coverage - Tri-band UMTS; quad-band GSM/GPRS/EDGE
Bluetooth® v1.2 wireless technology
Windows Media® Player 10 Mobile for music and video
1.3 MP camera with 2x zoom and video capture
Simultaneous voice and data capabilities
Direct Push Technology - immediate access to email, calendar & contacts
Pocket MSN® - Access Hotmail®, MSN Messenger®, and more
Multimedia Messaging - Send text, photos & video clips
Personal email support - XpressMail, POP3, IMAP4
Enterprise email - Microsoft Direct Push, GoodLink and ActiveSync
Access Microsoft Exchange Server and synchronization with Outlook
Shortcuts to email, the internet and dialing from the Today screen
Improved one-handed user experience and updated GUI
Address book, calendar, memos and task list
Voice command for voice dialing
Speakerphone

Figure 12.3 List of features for one PDA (the Palm Treo 750). *Source:* From *http://www. cingular.com/cell-phone-service/cell-phone-details/?q_list=true&q_phoneName=Palm+Treo+750&q _sku=sku620003.*

12.4.1 Keeping and re-finding

The device described in Figure 12.3 includes a calendar for keeping appointments, a camera to take pictures, and email support (and support for other communication modes as well). Thomas uses these features (in a more advanced version since we are encountering him in the future) to (1) make (and keep) an appointment to attend his daughter's soccer game, (2) take a picture of his daughter celebrating a late-game soccer goal with her teammates, and (3) send an email message to a colleague at work during the soccer game's half-time break.

Each item has value in its own right. The appointment is an important reminder and also includes details concerning the time and place of the soccer game. The picture represents and supports a precious memory of the soccer game. The email message sends necessary information and a request to a colleague.

But each item in this threesome can acquire additional value by helping Thomas to re-find and make sense of the other two items.

1. *The appointment helps to re-find the picture.* Thomas may later return to the appointment in his calendar and want to access "all pictures I took during the soccer game." Also, the appointment has text that might be used to index the picture later so that, for example,

Thomas could search for "all pictures taken during one of Sarah's soccer games" or even "all pictures of Sarah."

2. *The picture helps to re-find the email message.* The picture might be included as a land-mark in the left-hand column of a time-ordered listing of information items (similar to that displayed in Figure 11.4 of Chapter 11). For example, Thomas may want to access the email message he recalls having read during his daughter's soccer game, yet he may be unable to remember on which day the soccer game occurred. Rather than search through his crowded calendar, it may be faster for Thomas simply to scan through a time-ordered listing of email messages recently received, in a two-step process: by first scanning through a listing of pictures he has taken, and then, once the soccer goal picture is located, by scanning through email messages nearby in the listing. Pictures as landmarks can help to bracket and narrow the scope of a person's scan through a list of items in an effort to recognize a desired item.

3. *The email message helps to re-find the picture.* The email message sent and the picture taken have little directly to do with each other except that they occurred in close temporal proximity and are also both associated in Thomas's mind with the larger event of the soc-cer game. Just as Thomas might use the picture as a way to access the email message, he may want to use the email message later as way to access the photograph.

Note that these examples of a re-finding synergy between individual items are best realized when the PDA is plugged into a larger display. But the PDA, especially in its use to send email messages or take pictures anywhere and anytime, enables an initial creation or capture of items which can later be used in mutual support of re-finding.

We should single out the camera in this discussion because most of us would not routinely carry a camera around with us as we move through the activities of our day. And yet many or most of us will do so "for free" as a part of a PDA we do carry around routinely. The camera feature that many of us may have initially dismissed as a "toy" or novelty item can and should become much more than this. Picture quality will continue to improve. The PDA can be inte-grated with accessories such as a headset or some article of clothing or jewelry, so that taking a picture can be more spontaneous or even automatic. We can take pictures without stepping out of the current situation.

Pictures have benefits that often accumulate as the years pass and our memories fade. But pictures can also have a more immediate benefit through their use as landmarks. The integra-tion of pictures with other information items in our lives has the effect of building a fabric of strong, mutually supporting interconnections between various items that might otherwise lie fragmented in separate "information silos."

12.4.2 Maintenance

Creating backups of digital information is an essential and also easily postponed maintenance activity. Our PDAs must also be periodically recharged.[25] And every so often the software

---

[25] Even as other PDA capacities, such as processing power and storage, continue to increase exponentially, battery capacities increase at a much slower, linear rate (Hawkins & Blakeslee, 2006).

on our PDAs must be updated or "patched." Why not combine these activities? All three might happen through a single charge-upload-download device as we sleep through the night.[26]

The recharging and maintenance of accessories to the PDA should also be considered. Support for maintenance will impact the likely adoption of accessories such as the "watch" watch. Today people are not in the habit of charging their watches. Instead, we expect our watches to last for a year or longer on a single replaceable battery. Some people will think that the watch as an accessory to a PDA is more trouble than it's worth. But others may value the features of a "watch" watch—the ability, for example, to get some information without the need to fish a PDA out of a pocket or purse. Some may even have a range of different watches for different occasions, for fashion[27] as well as function, so that even as one watch is being worn, at least one other watch is being charged.

12.4.3 Managing the flow of information

A PIM perspective encourages us not just to think about the management of email or instant messaging or phone calls, but to think more broadly about the management of communication modes and associated channels of information flow. Communication, regardless of mode, involves an exchange of information. But before the intended information is itself exchanged, the parties to this exchange must agree, explicitly or implicitly, on the conditions for the exchange.

Consider this example: Thomas wants to talk with his colleague Sally about the budget for their work on a client project. Using his PDA, Thomas makes a telephone call to Sally and hears by synthetic voice that Sally is currently in a meeting. The voice gives Thomas options to (1) engage Sally in an IM conversation, (2) leave a voice message, or (3) send an email message. Thomas chooses option 1, but then by mutual agreement he and Sally settle for a shorter exchange via IM in which only some essential information is exchanged and in which an agreement is reached to talk over the phone or in person later. (Sally writes, "Your budget is $$$ but I present in 2 min. See u tomorrow morning or call.")

This ordering of options itself reflects a reasonable assumption that Thomas called in the first place because (1) he needs an immediate response, and (2) he needs a more interactive mode of communication (phone or IM rather than voice message or email message). Both assumptions are true. Thomas needs information ASAP, but he needs a more interactive dialog with Sally even to be sure what information he needs. Thomas also wanted the richness

---

[26] We see a variation of this feature today in, for example, the iPod's simultaneous ability to recharge and synchronize its store via a single USB connection.

[27] Certainly "watch" watches need to be designed for fashion as well as function. The high-powered executive who today wears an expensive Rolex to "make a statement" may not buy the "watch" watch unless a similar statement can be made in its wearing. On the other hand, many people—high-powered exectives included—may wear the "watch" watch to make another statement: that they are current on cool new technologies.

of the telephone call for its ability—through pauses and voice intonations—to communicate information "between the lines" concerning the project status and the client reliability.

But both assumptions might have been false. Thomas might have used the phone because he was in traffic and so needed a hands-free mode of communication. And he might have actually been hoping that Sally would *not* answer the phone so that he could quickly leave a kind of "tag—you're it!" voice message establishing his attempt to reach her and transferring to Sally the responsibility to call back.

The good news is that we can select a mode and establish a channel of communication according to our needs (e.g., for interactivity, immediacy, richness of channel) and in ways that make the best use of our limited resources. The bad news, of course, is that we have to select among the several modes and channels of communication. Or, more accurately, the bad news is that modes of communication are frequently managed by separate applications with little in the way of a bridging tool to help us in making an integrative choice among modes. This is changing. Microsoft Office Communicator, for example, provides notification of an incoming call along with options to accept, reroute, or establish an IM conversation instead (Figure 12.4).

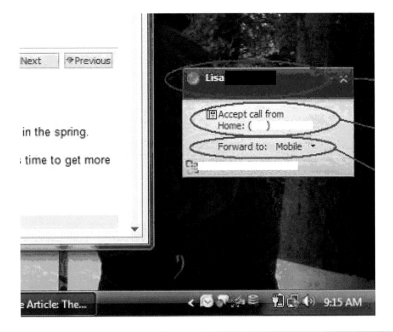

Figure 12.4 The Microsoft Office Communicator can notify you about an incoming phone call and provide options to accept, reroute, or switch to an IM conversation. *Source:* **Courtesy of Mike Kelly, director of Engineering Excellence Emerging Practices, Microsoft Corporation.**

An exchange of information, like other interactions with information, carries both costs and benefits. We exchange information to get things done and to make better decisions and also, over the long run, to build relationships with others. But each exchange consumes limited resources of time, attention, energy, and money. As Table 12.1 illustrates, the calculus of cost and benefit is by no means simple.

12.4.4 Measuring and evaluating

Measuring and evaluating as essential kinds of PIM activity were discussed at length in Chapter 8. The PDA as constant companion for use in a wide range of daily activities greatly increases the opportunities to measure and evaluate our practices of PIM.

We are especially interested in measuring and evaluating our information management activities with respect to their consumption of precious resources in our lives—our money, energy, attention, and, most especially, our time. For each of these resources, we often ask, Where does it go?

Table 12.1   Different modes of communication afford different advantages and make different demands

	Time and place	Interactivity	Acceptable delay in response	Richness of channel
Face-to-face	Same time; same place	High	Seconds	Very high (sight, sound, touch, smell)
Videophone	Same time; same place	High	Seconds	High (sight, sound)
Telephone	Same time; different places	High	Seconds	Medium (sound)
IM	Same time; different places	High	Minutes	
SMS	Near time; different places	Medium	Minutes to hours	
Voice mail	Any time; any place	Low	Hours to days	Medium (sound)
Email	Any time; any place	Medium	Minutes to days	Low; text but also multimedia links and attachments
Surface mail	Any time; any place	Low	Days to weeks	Low to medium
Web	Any time; any place	Medium	No expectations	

The constant and very personal presence of all of this functionality in our PDAs creates new opportunities to track our expenditures of money, energy, attention, and time so that we can understand better how each resource is used.

Time

We already make great efforts to track and manage our time, yet when faced with a basic question like "can you meet me at 1 pm on Friday?" many of us must still say something like, "I think so but let me check my schedule when I get back to the office." People with PDAs or Smartphones are already in the habit of taking their calendar with them so that they can answer right away. PDAs replace the paper-based organizers used for managing time, commitments, and contacts. But calendars in digital form—especially if these are synched with a central server—provide many functions not possible for a paper-based calendar. For example, others with permission can schedule meetings for us without engaging us in the lengthy process of negotiation.

Aside from scheduling meetings, the PDA as constant companion can help us to answer several other time-related questions. For example:

How much time did I spend (or have I so far spent) on this project? This basic question has long been important for people in some professions and in some organizations, but the question is relevant to most of us as we try to manage our time. Accurate answers not only help us to budget our time better, but can also help us to decide whether to take on similar projects or tasks in the future. Good answers depend partly on having a better shared sense, between us and our tools, of what a project or task is and of when we've stopped working on one task and have moved on to another. Our tools can help by getting smarter about tasks and task transitions. Tools can also help by providing better support for the creation and use of plans that situate and implicitly label our interactions with project-related information. The PDA as constant companion can help by providing basic data in the form of informational events—time and location stamped—as these occur throughout the day.

How could I spend my time better? Again the PDA as constant companion can help to provide a more complete set of data needed to answer this question. The PDA can track activities involving the use of an email application, a web browser, a spreadsheet, or a word processor. A PDA will also be a phone and should be able to track the time we spend in telephone conversations. A PDA will be a remote control too, so that we can even track the time we spend watching television.

Attention

Earlier in this section, we considered the PDA as a means of consolidating and managing all the interruptions we might experience, ranging from phone calls to requests for an IM session to reminders of an upcoming meeting. Our PDAs can also alert us to serendipitous opportunities that arise as we move from one place to the next. In the scenario involving Thomas, his PDA combined current location information with an item residing on his to-do list to let Thomas know that he was near the dealership where the wipers he needed might be bought.

Energy

The use of a PDA to better manage our energy and its expenditure throughout a day is more speculative. Some people already attempt to schedule their days and their weeks according to their biorhythms. Can a PDA help us to identify and predict periods of the day when our energy levels are relatively high and relatively low? How would we use this information? Some of us might prefer to schedule routine activities for low-energy periods of the day and reserve high-energy periods for work involving concentration—the planning of a new project, for example.

Money

Many people are already in the habit of making a note of how much they pay out and for what. The note may be made in a paper notebook or calendar, as a memo in a PDA, or perhaps simply on the back of a credit card receipt. But tracking expenses in this way is cumbersome, time consuming, and requires a special effort that is easily forgotten. The use of a PDA as a smart wallet creates the opportunity to track expenses seamlessly and in ways that enable us to quickly assess where our money is going. In the scenario involving Thomas, for example, he is able to approve the payment of a restaurant bill with a few presses on his PDA and can also, as he does so, categorize the bill (e.g., Is it reimbursable? Under what budget? If not, is it tax deductible?). Thomas can also quickly bring up a current status on the month's expenses to determine whether he and his family are sticking to their budget.

12.4.5 Making sense of things

The potential integration afforded by the PDA can also aid in our efforts to make sense of our information. Items that are interconnected enrich the context in ways that do more than simply help us to re-find things. Consider again the photo Thomas takes at the soccer game after his daughter scores a goal. We saw how other items, such as a calendar entry with the text "soccer game" might help to tag the photo so that it could be more easily found later. Likewise, the photo associated with that particular day might help to distinguish that day from many others in Thomas's calendar so that he can more quickly return, as needed, to its listing of appointments and meetings.

But the two items—photograph and calendar entry—in association with each other do potentially more than this. Photos—especially as we return to them years after they've been taken—are more likely to make more sense when they are given a time and location (Where and when did I take this?) and a connection to other events nearby (e.g., the text in a calendar recording an appointment for a daughter's soccer game).

Similarly the meaning of other information items—the calendar appointment, for example, with its short cryptic note—is enriched through their connection (by time and location) to the photograph of the goal celebration. Items woven together by time and location into a single fabric give meaning to each other and to a larger "day in a life" snapshot.

12.5 Looking back, looking forward

A study by Dell claims that users who get notebook computers put in an average of 7.7 hours of additional work each week.[28] Suppose the study is accurate? What are people doing during these extra 7.7 hours? Is this time well used or time spent playing games, sending unnecessary email, or aimlessly browsing the Web? Does this time take away from time spent with family and friends? Is it taken from projects that really matter?

If we take the statistic seriously, we have reason to expect that the number of additional work hours will be even higher for the supercharged PDAs of our future. Indeed, by one way of measuring, the PDA of the future claims all of our time, day and night.

Whether extra time spent with a PDA—or any other information device, for that matter—is good or bad depends on the answers to other questions. What are we doing? Is the PDA used in support of life's important activities, or is the PDA demanding the extra time for its own "care and feeding"? Will the PDA be a powerful attractor for the integration of personal information? Or will it be just a loose packaging of many elemental features all jumbled together in ways that increase our problems of information fragmentation?

Even as we applaud and are sometimes awed by PDAs whose power, potential uses, and features lists double every two years (or sooner), considerations of PIM lead us to ask questions such as these:

- ☑ Which PIM activities are impacted and how? How do features help us to find, keep, organize, re-find, maintain, manage the flow of, measure and evaluate our use of, and make sense of our information? Do PDA features work together in support of these activities?

- ☑ How do PDA features help us to manage precious resources such as our money, energy, limited attention, and, especially, time?

---

[28] See *http://www.dqindia.com/content/Columns/2006/106100301.asp.*

If our daily activities are a kind of elliptical orbit around our information and our informational tools, then certainly one point of focus is our devices—our laptop and cell phone today, but perhaps soon to be replaced by a single powerful PDA as a point of convergence. But there is another, even more powerful focus in this orbit. It's time to talk about PIM on the Web, the topic of Chapter 13.

PIM on the Web

The Web is a place where anything informational can happen. It enriches our lives

Chapter
Thirteen

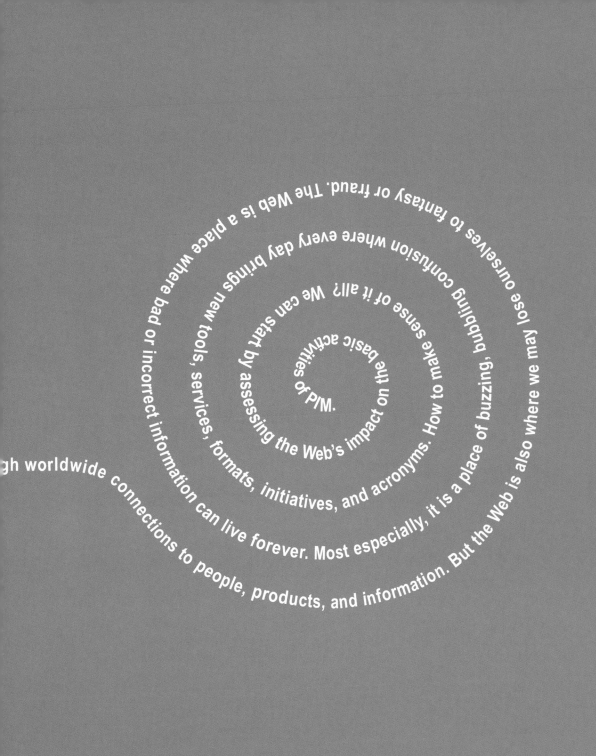

The Web is a place where bad or incorrect information can live forever. Most especially, it is a place of buzzing, bubbling confusion where every day brings new tools, services, formats, initiatives, and acronyms. How to make sense of it all? We can start by assessing the Web's impact on the basic activities of PIM. ...gh worldwide connections to people, products, and information. But the Web is also where we may lose ourselves to fantasy or fraud. The Web is a place where bad or incorrect information can live forever.

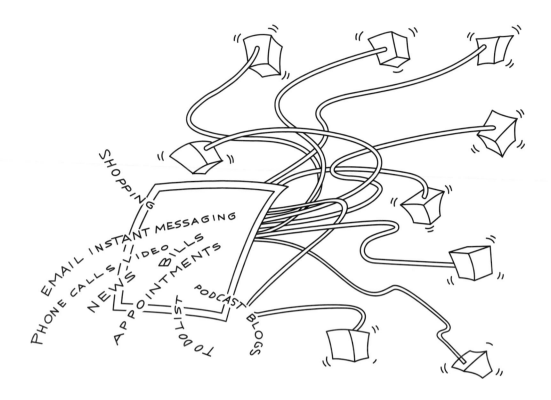

I have an almost religious zeal . . . not for technology per se, but for the Internet which is for me, the nervous system of mother Earth, which I see as a living creature, linking up.

Dan Millman (1946–)

13.1 Starting out

If the gadgets we can carry are one point of convergence for things informational in our lives, the Web is surely the other. The Web or, more generally, the Internet, is the conduit for an increasingly large proportion of the information we use in order to make sense of and effect change in the world around us.

It goes further. A college student stays up through the night playing a MUDD (multi-user dungeons and dragons) game with other gamers from around the world. A teenager leaves the family dinner table to spend the rest of the evening surfing the Web and other (ostensible) teens' pages on MySpace while simultaneously involved in six different IM conversations. The middle-aged man borrows time throughout his workday to work on several different blogs—making additions to his own and posting comments to others.

He gets recognition and affirmation through these interactions that he does not get through interactions in his physical world.

For these people and many others, the Web itself forms a large part of their world, and living means being on the Web. In extreme cases, "web" living is done at the neglect of school, job, friends, and family in the—still present—physical world and at the neglect of other physical considerations such as exercise and good diet. We may know people like this. Are we becoming like these people too?

But the Web is more than this. The Web is also a powerful enabler of the activities we perform in our physical world. If we're looking for a family-friendly hike to take in the early spring, we may go first to the Web to see which hikes are recommended by fellow hikers, how to reach the trail head for a selected hike, and how bad traffic is—right now—along different routes to the trailhead. The Web can give us ratings, contact information, and directions to restaurants to go to after the hike according to our dietary preferences, price range, and level of adventurousness. The Web helps us to keep in touch with our family. We turn to the Web to find and then buy that perfect gift for a friend on her birthday. The Web gives us the information we need to design a healthy plan of exercise and diet.

In short, the Web is the place where anything and everything informational can happen. As with PDAs and other digital gadgets, the pace of change on the Web is breathtaking and sometimes bewildering. Discussions of both gadgetry and the Web are rife with terminology and conflicting predictions of the future. And for both, we're left with the same basic question: How can this help us to manage our information better so that we can get on with our lives and living? To address this key question, sections of this chapter parallel those of Chapter 12.

☑ *Getting oriented.* This section provides working definitions for a few terms that relate to PIM-on-the-Web.

☑ *A foreseeable future?* This section takes current web trends a little further—we look down the road until the crest of the next hill. Going just this far raises some fascinating possibilities and also some serious concerns.

☑ *What to expect from PIM-on-the-Web.* How can the Web help us in our practices of PIM? What can we anticipate? What should we demand?

A variation of the introductory disclaimer for Chapter 12 applies to this chapter as well: It makes little sense to focus on a review of the latest tools and initiatives related to PIM-on-the-Web. Any such review is certain to be dated even as it's written. Instead, this chapter focuses on considerations of PIM that apply to the Web no matter which initiatives, releases, or buzzwords are currently in play.

13.2 Getting oriented

The list that follows is just a sampling of terms relevant to PIM-on-the-Web—it is not exhaustive. The definitions provided are not complete, but they can help us establish a working understanding of each term and its relevance to PIM. Many of the descriptions are from Wikipedia entries.[1]

- The *Internet* is a "worldwide, publicly accessible network of interconnected computer networks that transmit data by packet switching using the standard Internet Protocol (IP). . . . The World Wide Web is accessible via the Internet, as are many other services including e-mail, file sharing, and others."[2]

- The *World Wide Web* "is a system of interlinked, hypertext documents that runs over the Internet. With a Web browser, a user views Web pages that may contain text, images, and other multimedia and navigates between them using hyperlinks."[3] The World Wide Web is often referred to as *WWW* or, simply, the *Web*. Note that the Internet is not the same as the Web—the Internet enables the Web and much more. However, the terms Web and Internet are frequently used interchangeably in informal discussions. Throughout this chapter, the Web will refer both to the World Wide Web and more broadly, to the growing host of applications and services enabled through the underlying technology of the Internet.

- *Web 2.0*, sometimes referred to as the second generation of the Web, refers to a loose collection of Web-based services and initiatives to promote online collaboration and information sharing among users. Commonly mentioned examples of Web 2.0 are social networking sites, wikis, and sites supporting a shared, social tagging of information items.[4]

- The *Semantic Web* is "an evolution of the World Wide Web in which information is machine processable (rather than being only human oriented), thus permitting browsers or other software agents to find, share, and combine information more easily."[5] "The Semantic Web is about two things. It is about common formats for integrating and combining data drawn from diverse sources, whereas the original Web mainly concentrated on the interchange of documents. It is also about language for recording how the data relates to real-world objects."[6]

Note that Web 2.0 and the Semantic Web are not directly related to each other and pursue changes to the Web at two different levels. Web 2.0 is focused on uses of the Web to facilitate social interaction, collaboration, and the "wisdom of the crowds"[7] effect. The Semantic Web is focused on issues of infrastructure needed to transform the Web into a kind of global platform for data processing and exchange.

---

[1] See *www.wikipedia.org*.

[2] Excerpted from the Wikipedia "Internet" entry, February 2007 (*http://en.wikipedia.org/wiki/Internet*).

[3] Excerpted from the Wikipedia "World Wide Web" entry, February 2007 (*http://en.wikipedia.org/wiki/World_Wide_Web*).

[4] See the Wikipedia "Web 2.0" entry at *http://en.wikipedia.org/wiki/Web_2.0*.

[5] Excerpted from the Wikipedia "Semantic Web" entry, February 2007 (*http://en.wikipedia.org/wiki/Semantic_web*).

[6] Excerpted from the W3C web site defintion for "Semantic Web," February 2007 (*http://www.w3.org/2001/sw/*).

[7] In some cases, the average or aggregate estimate from a large sampling of people is better than estimates made by any one person. The effect is sometimes (but not always) demonstrated when contestants "ask the audience" on the television show *Who Wants to Be a Millionaire?* See Surowiecki (2004) and the Wikipedia entry for "The Wisdom of Crowds" (*http://en.wikipedia.org/wiki/Wisdom_of_the_crowds*).

The following futuristic—some might say overly fanciful—scenario helps to illustrate the vision that World Wide Web inventor Tim Berners-Lee and others have for the Semantic Web:

> At the doctor's office, Lucy instructed her Semantic Web agent through her handheld Web browser. The agent promptly retrieved information about Mom's *prescribed treatment* from the doctor's agent, looked up several lists of *providers*, and checked for the ones *in-plan* for Mom's insurance within a *20-mile radius* of her *home* and with a *rating* of *excellent* or *very good* on trusted rating services. It then began trying to find a match between available *appointment times* (supplied by the agents of individual providers through their Web sites) and Pete's and Lucy's busy schedules.[8]

Whether scenarios such as this one are achievable or even desirable, efforts and discussion related to the Semantic Web have already accomplished a shift toward using and thinking of the Web not only as a universal way to exchange documents among people, but also as a universal way of exchanging data among applications.

These terms should be enough to get us started on our journey of exploring the ways in which the Web is impacting our practices of PIM and the ways considerations of PIM should impact developments on the Web. Many other terms relate to a discussion of PIM-on-the-Web. Some, such as *wikis, blogs,* and *podcasts*, were described in Chapter 10 as part of its discussion of email and other modes of communication. The meaning of other terms such as *social tagging, RSS,* and *mashups* will be described later in this chapter as the need arises.

The Internet is so big, so powerful and pointless that for some people it is a complete substitute for life.

Andrew Brown (1938–)

13.3 A foreseeable future?

As with Chapter 12's section of the same name, the focus here is on reasonable extrapolations of current trends. Given these trends, consider the following transition toward a "Web Wide World" over the next few years:

- *Our information goes onto the Web*. Web-based backups continue to get faster, easier, and cheaper. The use of web-based backups raises issues of identification, privacy, and security. Assuming these can be addressed—admittedly a big assumption—then advantages of web-based backups will be compelling. Many of us may choose to take things one step further so that we maintain an image of our information on the Web that is synchronized automatically and opportunistically (when cycles and bandwidth permit) with a local copy as maintained on a personal computer or a PDA.

---

[8] "The Semantic Web," *Scientific American*, May 17, 2001—*http://www.sciam.com/print_version.cfm?articleID=00048144-10D2-1C70-84A9809EC588EF21.*

- *Web-like authoring of information becomes much easier.* The process of hyperlinking information needed for web publication is now a very different activity from the methods we employ to organize our digital information into the files and folders of our desktop computing environment. Why is this so? A long-standing vision of hypertext is that a useful structure—associative trails, for example—can emerge easily, even effortlessly, as a by-product of our efforts to use and make sense of our information. These structures may be useful to others eventually as we decide to share our information, but they should be useful to us immediately.

- *Most of what we do is mediated by the Web.* Shopping, selling, socializing, and working are all increasingly web-based or mediated by the Web.

- *We are "on" the Web.* If our information is on the Web already—organized and hyperlinked for our own needs—then publishing on the Web becomes mostly a matter of deciding what information to share with whom and under what circumstances. We'll have tools to help us set access permissions that determine what information is available to whom in what ways and under what circumstances (see the related discussion on managing privacy in Chapter 7).

This "line of sight" look into the future makes one large, debatable assumption—namely, that issues of privacy, security, and identity verification are resolved to a level of satisfaction that is comparable to our current situation. Identity theft happens now, of course, but news of such thefts does not stop most of us from using surface mail, email, or our credit card. We accept the risks for the rewards and feel some empowerment through the steps we can take to minimize these risks (for example, by shredding paper documents containing account or credit card information or by dealing only with reputable businesses). An assumption here is that we can achieve a comparable point of risk/reward tradeoff with respect to being on the Web with our working information (not just backups of this information).

Certainly other predictions in addition to those listed above can be made as well. For example, by extension to Chapter 12's discussion of device addressability, we might expect that all devices on the electrical grid—potentially all devices with a power cord—can be addressed via technologies that support the Internet over existing power lines.[9] As another example, wikis and web-based software applications such as Google Docs[10] may enable radically new forms of collaboration and may even redefine the document as a means of packaging information for distribution. But the bulleted assumptions listed above are enough to set up the scenario of the next section.

13.3.1 Some life soon on the Web

Imagine a web-enabled life sometime soon as lived by—we'll call her Sally.

Sally is born in about five years' time. Her loving parents begin a web space for Sally that includes an online baby book with pictures, videos, letters, and descriptions of everything Sally does in her first years of life.

---

[9] See, for example, the Wikipedia "Power Line Communication" article (*http://en.wikipedia.org/wiki/Power_line_communication*) and the November 30, 2006, "Shockingly Slow" article in *The Economist* (available for subscribers online at *http://www.economist.com/science/tq/displayStory.cfm?story_id=8312140*).

[10] For more information on Google Docs, see *https://www.google.com/accounts/ServiceLogin?service=writely&passive= true&continue=http%3A%2F%2Fdocs.google.com%2F&ltmpl=homepage&nui=1*.

In elementary school, Sally's web space expands to include all of her homework assignments and even scanned images of everything she writes or draws.

As Sally moves into middle school and then high school, her web space expands to include more homework and also special spaces where Sally interacts with her friends and other teens.[11] Sally also keeps an online diary with her innermost thoughts concerning her friends, the boy she has a crush on, and her parents.

As Sally moves on to college, her web space is her starting point for socialization with a growing circle of friends she meets there. Sally also uses her web space to plan her education and her career beyond college. What courses to take? To accomplish what?

After college, Sally works as a consultant. She rarely works for one company for more than a year or two and sometimes works for several companies at once. Her web space becomes an important repository of information concerning work she has completed, is doing now, or can be shared with prospective clients for marketing purposes.

Sally also uses her web space to identify and plan for lifetime goals. Sally wants to marry and have a family. She loves her career but does not want to wait too long before having children. Sally can easily, but selectively, share some of these goals with other people who have similar goals via services such as 43 Things.[12] However, she chooses to keep much of her information on the Web private, just as her counterpart today does for most of the information kept on a laptop computer. Sally is using the Web as a primary workspace and repository for her practice of PIM. Information she owns—the first sense of "personal information" as described in Chapter 2—is now kept directly on the Web (and is also kept, in synchronized fashion, on her PDA).

Many years later, Sally and her husband use their jointly held web space to plan first for their children, their children's college education, and then their own retirement.

After both Sally and her husband have passed away, their web spaces—separate and jointly held—are bequeathed to their children as a legacy and a record of how life once was.

13.3.2 A darker side to the future

What's wrong with an informational web-based alter ego that never, ever goes away? A similar question was posed in the previous chapter concerning a PDA of the future that never, ever goes away. And the obvious answer is also similar—the answer is right there in the question. Our web presence never goes away:

Information about us on the Web never, ever goes away. Persistence of information is a problem even if we exercise initial control over what information we share and with

---

[11] There is currently no way to be sure that the people Sally is interacting with are really "teens" or that anything they say about themselves is really true.

[12] See *http://www.43things.com/*.

whom. The information we share, perhaps recklessly, in our youth can persist to haunt us many, many years later (see the related discussion in Chapter 7). People in the public eye already know well the problems that can arise when their former selves are resurrected. But what might someone find out about you through a search on Flickr or YouTube?

Complete and total identity theft. A person able to access all of our information online could give a much deeper meaning to the expression "identity theft."

What if all of our information disappears or is corrupted? When all of our information is on the Web (and shadowed by a PDA or personal computer), how can we avoid a night-mare scenario where one day all of our information—all of it—is gone or irretrievably corrupted? Suppose a time-delayed virus infects and destroys not only the current copies of our information, but all backups as well? Do we need to consider a range of lower-fidelity backups more resistant to attack including, even, paper for some portions of our PSI?

We neglect the physical world. Putnam, in his article "Bowling alone" (1995), describes an increasing disengagement of people from traditional means of socialization and community. I still vote at a polling station in the city hall where I live—assisted by volun-teers. I like this connection to my (physical) community. But initiatives call for the gradual phase-out over the next few years of these physical polling places in favor of voting by mail and over the Web. Another point of contact with my physical community is thus taken away.

Everyone seems to be like me—at least the people I've met so far. We have tremendous choices in a web-enabled virtual world. We can pick our friends through sites like MySpace and FaceBook. We can customize the news we see using an RSS reader. We can order everything so that we almost never need to shop again in the physical world. But this choice is also a potential source of problems. First, there is the problem of being overwhelmed and possibly paralyzed by the choices available.[13] Second, and possibly more serious, we may not always know what's good for us. Through our choices we may box ourselves into a self-contained, self-confirming world in which everyone we talk to and everything we see and do acts to confirm and strengthen viewpoints we have already.

13.4 What to expect from PIM-on-the-Web

Leaving aside visions of a web-based future, good and bad, we face a more immediate ques-tion similar to the question presented by PDAs: How to make sense of all the new kinds of web sites (e.g., blogs, wikis), services (e.g., del.icio.us, Flickr), formats (e.g., RSS, Atom), and applications? Most web services cost nothing but are hardly free with respect to other personal resources. Each tool takes time to learn and then to use. Many tools increase our levels of distraction by begging for "just a little" attentional space on the toolbars of browsers that may already be crowded with icons for other tools and features.

---

[13] See Schwartz (2004).

And yet, certainly, web-based tools have the potential to make big improvements in our practices of PIM and, through these practices, in our ability to lead the lives we want to live. But which tools? In what ways?

This section considers the Web in relation to the basic activities of PIM. How might the Web impact our efforts to find, keep, organize, maintain, manage the flow(s), measure and evaluate the use of, and make sense of the information that matters to us in our daily lives? What can we expect—not just what can we anticipate, but also what should we ask for? What should we demand?

13.4.1 Finding

Many ways of using the Web to support the finding activity take advantage of the Web's enormous size in numbers of web pages, hyperlinks between these pages, tags, searches, and page downloads. For example, the PageRank algorithm, which reportedly provides the basis for all of Google's search tools, works by a kind of "wisdom of the crowds"[14] averaging of in-links to different web pages. A page's in-links (from other pages) count as "votes" for this page. An individual vote cast by a page is weighted according to the number of voting pages it receives from other web pages divided by the number of its out-links.[15]

In the same spirit, some social tagging web sites such as del.icio.us[16] work by aggregating tags provided by many different taggers to form a kind of collective description for the web page being tagged.[17] Letting large numbers of untrained people tag also helps to address the vocabulary problem[18] that occurs when the range of terms that different people might use in reference to the same object (web page, yellow page entry, command name) is exceedingly large. The tags that I apply to a web page may not agree at all with the tags you might think of for this same web page and thus may do you little good as a means of accessing the web page. However, as the collective "we" of taggers for a given web page grows, so too does the likelihood that someone else out there has tagged the page in ways that would help you. Again, a number enabled by the scale of the Web—the number of taggers—is used to advantage in support of finding. It matters not that people tagging are not trained to do so—to the contrary, lack of training may increase the likelihood that the judgments of different taggers are independent from each other—a precondition for the "wisdom of the crowds" effect.

Techniques of aggregation and averaging applied to large quantities of data have many other applications in support of finding. Search services are able to support our efforts to recall search

---

[14] See Surowiecki (2004).

[15] With respect to division of voting power among outgoing links and accumulation of votes through in-links, PageRank resembles a spreading activation mechanism elaborated to explain the workings of human memory as originally described by Anderson (1976) and subsequently analytically compared by Jones and Furnas (1987) with other information-retrieval, relevance-ranking algorithms.

[16] See *http://del.icio.us/*.

[17] For more on social tagging, see Golder and Huberman (2006) and Marlow et al. (2006).

[18] See Furnas et al. (1987).

terms, for example, through special web browser add-ins that suggest common search term completions to the characters we have typed so far. Suggestions effectively turn our recall step into an easier step of recognition. Our recall efforts are also aided by "Did you mean . . .?" suggested alternate spellings to the search terms we occasionally misspell. Suggested corrected or alternate spellings do not depend on look-up from a formal dictionary but can be derived instead through a wisdom-of-the-crowds comparison of frequencies for variations in spelling.

Given the scale of the Web, we're certain to find others out there with similar needs and interests to our own and similar ways of viewing (and tagging) the information we see. If we're able to locate these kindred souls, then we might be interested in the pages they have tagged, as well as the tags they have used. And, likewise, our "tagging twins" might be interested in the pages we have tagged. This is an essential motivation for schemes of collaborative filtering.[19]

These applications of the Web in support of finding are surely just the beginning. There are even potential uses of the Web in finding and re-finding private information that we choose not to publish on the Web. Private information items might, for example, be tagged in ways that agree with tags applied by our like-minded "twins" to public information on the Web.

13.4.2 Keeping and organizing

Within the great expanse of the Web, pages relating to a given topic can vary greatly with respect not only to their content but also to their structure. Many pages are mostly self-promotional and offer little content or useful structure. But other pages provide not only good content but also an organizing structure. Structure is often explicitly represented through bullets, numbers, headings, and internal hyperlinks.

The Wikipedia web site,[20] for example, provides short, encyclopedia-style articles on a wide and ever-growing range of topics. Subtopics of a topic area are represented through article headings, and key concepts are often represented through special formatting and hyperlinks (giving people the option to jump to a more detailed description of a concept).

The Web also provides a wide variety of highly structured "how to" sites (how to get into a top college or university; how to buy a house; how to run a marathon; how to get a job; how to get pregnant; and so on). "How to" structures in some web articles can be quite elaborate. The web article "How to Buy a House," for example, lists 20 steps leading to home ownership. Individual steps addressing questions, such as "How much home can you afford?" shown in Figure 13.1, themselves are often structured into steps or areas to consider.

People seek out useful structures as well as content[21] —and for good reason. The structure of a page or site can help a reader to organize and understand not only the topical content on the page itself, but also related information that is found elsewhere.

---

[19] See, for example, Breese, Heckermen, and Kadie (1998); Maltz and Ehrlich (1995); and Udell (2005).

[20] See *http://www.wikipedia.org/*.

[21] See Qu and Furnas (2005).

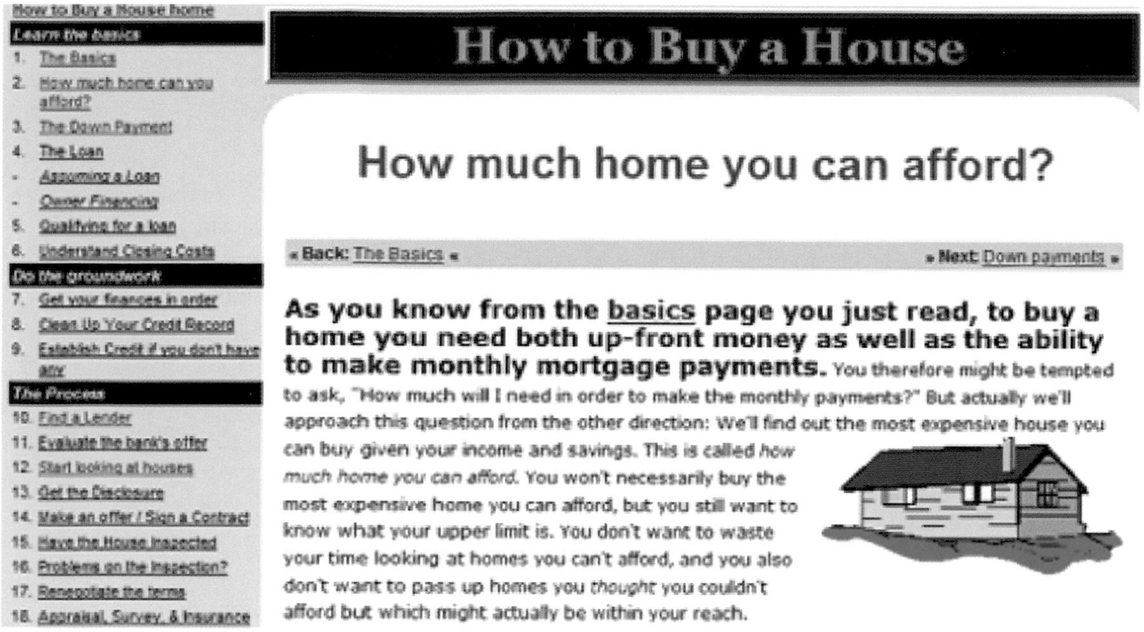

How to Buy a House home
Learn the basics
1. The Basics
2. How much home can you afford?
3. The Down Payment
4. The Loan
  - Assuming a Loan
  - Owner Financing
5. Qualifying for a loan
6. Understand Closing Costs
Do the groundwork
7. Get your finances in order
8. Clean Up Your Credit Record
9. Establish Credit if you don't have any
The Process
10. Find a Lender
11. Evaluate the bank's offer
12. Start looking at houses
13. Get the Disclosure
14. Make an offer / Sign a Contract
15. Have the House Inspected
16. Problems on the Inspection?
17. Renegotiate the terms
18. Appraisal, Survey, & Insurance

How to Buy a House

How much home you can afford?

« Back: The Basics «   » Next: Down payments »

As you know from the <u>basics</u> page you just read, to buy a home you need both up-front money as well as the ability to make monthly mortgage payments. You therefore might be tempted to ask, "How much will I need in order to make the monthly payments?" But actually we'll approach this question from the other direction: We'll find out the most expensive house you can buy given your income and savings. This is called *how much home you can afford*. You won't necessarily buy the most expensive home you can afford, but you still want to know what your upper limit is. You don't want to waste your time looking at homes you can't afford, and you also don't want to pass up homes you *thought* you couldn't afford but which might actually be within your reach.

Figure 13.1 **Example of a web site to help people plan activities and structure content relating to buying a house.** *Source:* **Excerpted from *http://michaelbluejay.com/house/index.html.***

In fieldwork for the Keeping Found Things Found (KFTF) project, we are seeing a similar tendency for people, when starting a new project, to refer to structures already developed for completed projects.[22] Structure can come in a variety of forms, including folder hierarchies, spreadsheets, documents, and document templates.

Of course, the structure in an article, such as the one depicted in Figure 13.1, not only provides a way to think about and organize relevant information, but also offers a plan for completion of the project (in this case buying a house).

But web articles on subjects such as house-buying are static. We can look at them, but we can't change them. We can't reorder steps or delete those that don't apply to our situation. If we want to use the article's structure elsewhere—in a folder hierarchy to organize our own personal information for example—we need to re-create this structure ourselves.

In the KFTF project, we are working on a kit to enable web authors to develop *Life Organizers* (or, simply, *Organizers*) for a variety of personal projects[23], such as buying a house. On the Web,

---

[22] See Jones et al. (2006).

[23] Here, as elsewhere in this book, "personal" in relation to personal project does not mean that the project is private or involves only you or is just for fun. The project is personal in the sense that you are personally responsible for its planning and completion. You may delegate tasks or inspire others to help, but ultimately the project will not happen without you. Projects can be work-related ("finish budget forecast") or not ("plan a surprise birthday party"). Projects described in one KFTF study, for example, included "plan Italy vacation," "set up 529 for kids," "school phone book," and "plan January ski trip."

Organizers will appear as well-formatted web articles such as the one depicted in Figure 13.1. However, users can download a selected Organizer to reside in a region of their PSI that they control (e.g., on their personal computer or PDA). An Organizer, once downloaded, can "inflate" just like other Project Plans as created by the Project Planner (described in Chapter 5; see also Jones, Munat, & Bruce, 2005).

A Plan supported by the Planner has a dual life. It can appear as a structure of folders and files that can be manipulated through conventional file system views (e.g., icon, list, details). Equivalently, the Plan can be viewed, modified, and customized through any of several document-like, rich-text views as supported by the Planner. A Plan is a hierarchy of tasks and subprojects that must be executed in order to complete the project and that can be associated with remind-by and due dates (which appear in the user's Microsoft Outlook calendar). These same elements, as file system folders, can serve as holding areas to contain not only documents but also email messages, web pages, and other information items that are needed to complete an associated task or subproject. The Planner embraces the hypertext ideal in which effective organization of information emerges as a natural by-product of a person's efforts to think about and plan a project.

13.4.3 Maintaining

In our efforts to maintain our information and key elements of the mapping between information and need (such as folder or tagging structures), we face immediate, longer-term, and legacy challenges as described in Chapter 6. The Web can help with each set of maintenance challenges.

The immediate maintenance activity of greatest importance is backup—very important, but easily overlooked or postponed. In the worst case, we don't think about backup until a hard drive fails or our information is seriously corrupted. But the backup done locally using external storage (e.g., an external hard drive or DVD disks) can be cumbersome and time consuming. Many of us may already experience the convenience of online information backup through services provided at our place of work. However, companies discourage the use of backup services for the storage of non-work-related information.

Now many companies are providing web-based storage at rates that are already cheap and getting cheaper. As of February 2007, for example, Amazon offers storage at rates of 15 cents per gigabyte per month.[24] Another company offers unlimited storage for a flat rate of $55 per year.[25]

Web-based backup has a number of advantages to a backup done using external storage at home. A primary benefit for most of us is that it can be conveniently scheduled to take place while we're sleeping or perhaps even as an ongoing, incremental background process that

---

[24] See Amazon Simple Storage Service (Amazon S3) at *www.amazon.com*.

[25] See the Mozy online backup site at *http://mozy.com/*.

works whenever we're connected to the Internet. In Chapter 12's example, a nightly backup of information on the PDA was integrated with battery charging and a download of software updates. Our information, as maintained in a web store, can be periodically copied to newer storage media so that we need never worry about physical decay in a magnetic tape, disk, or hard drive.

As discussed in Chapter 6, our understanding about maintaining personal information leads us to ask for and expect additional features from future web backup services, including:

*   *Format assurance.* As older formats fall into disuse, a future web backup service might convert information items to newer formats that are still supported.

*   *Information assurance.* We need to know that information backed up will really be there later if we need it—especially if we need the information to restore information lost on a local computer or PDA. We need to know that our information is available even if the company providing our backup service is acquired by another company or goes out of business. (See the more detailed discussion about this issue of provider reliability in Chapter 6.) Preferably, our information is copied to two or more separate physical locations so that even in the event of a disaster—natural or manmade—at least one copy of the information is still intact. Some of us might also subscribe to an additional service that can periodically send a complete copy of our information back to us on a stack of DVDs for added backup redundancy.

In addition, we need to know that our information, as stored on the Web, is safe and secure, accessible by us but not by others without our permission. As we consider legacy issues of maintenance, we need a means, through a kind of informational will and testament, for sharing our information with others in the event of our death. This, too, is a matter for web-based backup services to address.

But the Web may be more than merely backup for our personal information. A future Web may be one of two primary places where our information resides, the other location being a personal computer or PDA that we take with us. Such an arrangement gives us two kinds of "anywhere" access to our information: with our PDA, we can access our information no matter where; without our PDA we can still access our information providing we have access to the Web.

In such a world, information must be not only backed up but also synchronized so that changes made on the Web register on the PDA and vice versa. For example, checking for duplicates or close matches to a document (that might cause confusion some months later if returned in response to a search) might be a task better done on the Web side rather than on our side. Likewise, propagating updates and corrections (e.g., an email address or phone number) might be better to do on the Web. Both activities could possibly be done as part of a process to create and update an index to speed search.

13.4.4 Managing the flow of information

On the outflow side, we can expect increasing sophistication in facilities that manage our privacy concerns (e.g., through use of PEP or its successor as described in Chapter 7).

We can also expect services that track the flow of information about us or sent by us as it travels through the Web (as described in Chapter 11). To be sure, some information about us—financial or medical, for example—will remain submerged in databases not visible to the Web or accessible to web search services.

On the inflow side, information and informational events are directed toward us throughout a typical day in the form of newspapers, email messages, requests for an IM session, phone calls, and drop-by visits. Incoming information consumes our time, energy, and attention. Most of us can't simply ignore all incoming information. Some information—an emergency call concerning a friend or loved one—may require our immediate attention. In other cases, failure to respond can mean missed opportunities and annoyed colleagues, bosses, and friends.

Many opportunities to manage incoming information arise as our presence on the Web grows. Chapter 2, for example, told the story of Alice. As Alice's presence on the Web grew, she was able to depend on her web site and a growing collection of web services to handle incoming requests that, in earlier times, she would have needed to take her own time to answer.

Personal web sites or the spaces that can be created through a service such as MySpace or FaceBook provide information such as directions or a resume that might otherwise need to be sent via email or, in earlier times, via a phone call or letter. Other web services such as Evite[26] help to manage responses to invitations that might otherwise clog the inbox.

What information to let in? What information to let out? To whom? Why? What do we stand to gain or lose? The management of information flow depends on the answers to these and other questions. As noted in Chapter 7, operative rules can be complicated and difficult for people to express directly. We can hope for an increasing development in the expressive power of protocols such as P3P and, equally important, in user interfaces that support a mapping from user preference to enforceable XML expressions.

13.4.5 Measuring and evaluating

A Prairie Home Companion, a popular radio program in the United States, depicts a fictional town in Minnesota where all the children are "above average." We can all recognize the yearning that we and, even more so, our children are each above average (even if, for any fixed group, some are above average only if others are below average).

Quizzes and questionnaires in newspapers and magazines are a commonplace invitation to "Test your IQ," "Rate your marriage," and so on—and then to compare scores with those of a collective, mostly undefined "other people" out there somewhere. How many of us do so, if only in secret, just for some indication as to how we measure up?

Now there is the Web with its enormous numbers of users and the potential to collect data and disseminate averages on virtually everything imaginable. Many averages are interesting.

---

[26] See *www.evite.com*.

Others, simply silly. Some, such as average salary according to profession, location, and years of experience, can have real practical value.[27] Several web sites also let users pose their own questions and take their own polls[28] (albeit with responses coming from a mostly undefined population of users).

The PDA of the future, as described in Chapter 12, may serve as an intimate device for taking measurements of a person throughout his or her day—some directly related to a PIM practice (e.g., time spent reading new email messages, time spent on the Web), some not (e.g., miles walked or jogged in a day, average heart rate), and some with perhaps indirect relevance to a PIM practice (e.g., physiological measures that might indicate periods of high and low energy through an average day).

If we choose to share these measures (anonymously) with aggregating web sites, we might get back, in return, data showing how we compare with others (although the "others" who provide their data are likely to be a special population). How much email do we receive each day compared with other people? With similar jobs? With similar educational and technical backgrounds? How much time do we spend in email compared with other people with similar jobs? . . . Per email message received? Do people using one email application spend significantly less time per email message than other people using other email applications?

Interesting comparisons can be qualitative as well as quantitative. How do other people manage their email? Their web information? Their documents—digital and paper-based? If people have a system that works for them, perhaps it will work for us too. In return, perhaps we have strategies and tactics that might be useful to others—albeit as modified to suit their own needs and situations.

To promote an exchange of "problems and solutions" relating to PIM, the KFTF project has launched a "Tales of PIM" (TOP) web site.[29] Anyone can visit to view the problems and solutions posed by others. After a simple registration process, visitors can describe their PIM-related problems and solutions and they can respond to the problems and solutions posed by other visitors. Even if one person's solutions can't be directly applied to our own special circumstances, they may inspire us to consider modified versions of these solutions or to think more broadly about the solutions that might work for us.

We cannot leave the subject of web-supported measurement and evaluation without a brief mention of web-based software applications and the tremendous opportunity they afford software developers and designers (see also the related sidebar in Chapter 8). In the "olden days" (e.g., late 1990s), some users volunteered to use "instrumented versions" of software products such as the Microsoft Office suite. Instrumented versions collected a variety of useful data concerning how often various features were used, for how long, and whether a feature's

---

[27] See, for example, *www.salary.com*.

[28] See, for example, *www.vizu.com* and *www.polldaddy.com*.

[29] The Tales-of-PIM web site (*http://talesofpim.org*) also includes sections for general discussion of PIM-related issues.

use appeared to generate successful outcomes. Data returned some months later could be analyzed to help tweak the product in subsequent releases.

Web-based software applications fielded by companies, such as Google, AOL, and Microsoft, can provide feedback within days or even hours. This makes it possible for them to offer corrective releases within weeks after a product's initial distribution. Products, especially in beta mode (which seems the perpetual state of some products), can even ship in several variations to gauge which versions seem to work best. (Of course, a software provider's measures for which variation works best do not necessarily coincide with our own.)

13.4.6 Making sense

We make sense of information through our hands-on interactions with it. We read, make notes, highlight, and annotate (with margin notes or the digital equivalent), arrange, rearrange, and summarize. As we do so, we seek to identify important relationships and implications—large and small. What does this report tell me about the likely success of a web service planned for next year? Does this start-up company have a workable business plan? If I accept this additional meeting today, will I still have time to meet two deadlines by the end of today? How far away is the meeting, and am I likely to be stuck in rush-hour traffic on the way back?

We make sense of our various appointments and other commitments through their juxtaposed representation in month-at-a-glance, week-at-a-glance, and day-at-a-glance calendars, whether paper-based or digital. Similarly, as we plan some activity such as a surprise birthday party for a friend, we may begin to make sense of things only after we write our thoughts down—on paper or in some digital form. Who should be there? When? Where? Dinner party or afternoon activity? What needs to happen? Who can help out? Both the act of writing and its visible results help us to think through the plans to be made.[30]

The Web can help us to make sense of our information. Web initiatives can help us not only to locate the information we need, but also to juxtapose and combine this information in ways that help us to make sense of it. Two developments are reviewed here: *RSS* as a way to bring together information from several sources, and *mashups* as a further integration of information obtained through RSS and, more generally, through application program interfaces (APIs) that treat web sites as sources of data rather than sources of documents to be displayed.

RSS stands variously for Really Simple Syndication, Rich Site Summary, or RDF Site Summary. The confusion concerning what RSS stands for corresponds to a confusion of standards with version numbers that include .9, .91, .92, 1.0, 1.1, and 2.0. And then there is also Atom, which is meant to address various limitations of each RSS version and their mutual incompatibilities.

Since this chapter won't puzzle over all these variations and their technical differences, the term "RSS" will suffice. From our perspective as web users, RSS gives us the ability to

---

[30] For a longer discussion on the importance of external representations and the externalization process, see Zhang (1997).

receive updates from various feeds, including blogs, wikis, news feeds, or podcasts. Web sites providing RSS feeds often come marked with the logo illustrated in Figure 13.2 or a rectangle with the letters *xml* or *rss*.

With the help of an RSS reader, updates from different sources can be arranged on the same web page for at-a-glance viewing. A common use of RSS readers as provided through web portals such as Yahoo! is to create a kind of customized newspaper front page such as that shown in Figure 13.3 with headline news, updated sports scores for favorite teams, weather reports for travel locations, stock ticker information for selected companies, and so on. But the applications for RSS are much broader. Ray Ozzie, creator of Lotus Notes and now chief technical officer at Microsoft, refers to RSS as the "UNIX pipe of the Internet."[31]

Figure 13.2
Site logo that indicates it provides an RSS feed.

The number of RSS feeds and their diversity continue to grow. The blog "lab.arc90.com,"[32] which itself supports an RSS feed, also lists "25 New Ways to Use RSS." Among them: "Get some knowledge on a regular basis" (by subscribing to feeds provided by sites such as wordsmith.org and brainyquote.com) or "Track eBay" or "Subscribe to recipes from your favorite chefs." The number of available RSS feeds is enormous and still growing. Some web search services focus only on the retrieval of sites offering RSS feeds. For example, a February 2007 search for "recipes" using *www.feedster.com* returned more than 250,000 matches.

Of greater potential relevance to our efforts to make sense of information are "mashups." A *mashup* "is a website or application that combines content from more than one source into

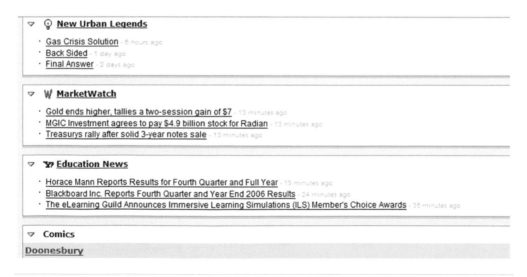

Figure 13.3 **A customized web news page created using the Yahoo! RSS reader.**

---

[31] "A Conversation with Ray Ozzie," *ACM Queue*, November 2005, page 18.

[32] See *http://lab.arc90.com/2006/06/25_new_ways_to_use_rss.php*.

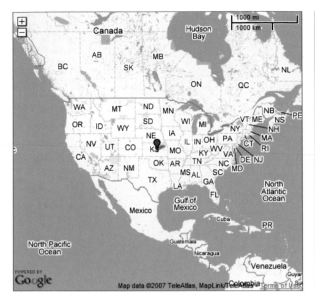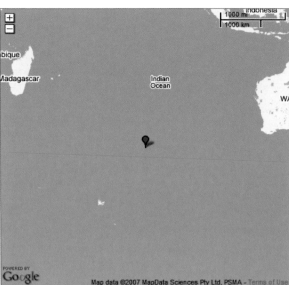

Figure 13.4 **A mashup using Google maps to map any point on the Earth to its opposite on the Earth's other side.** *Source: From http://www.zefrank.com/sandwich/tool.html.*

an integrated experience."[33] Mashups, like the envisioned Semantic Web, use web sites not as a source of pages to display but rather as a source of data to be combined and displayed in new ways. Mashups draw data from other web sites via RSS and other site-supported APIs.

Many mashups apply overlays to geographic maps. For example, the mashup depicted in Figure 13.4 tells me that Kansas, the state where I grew up, is on the opposite side of the world from some place in the middle of nowhere in the Indian ocean. (My coastal friends would tell me this is only fitting.)

Business Week Online describes a less frivolous, potentially much more useful, mashup involving Google Maps: "Chicagocrime.org, for instance, combines two services—a Chicago Police Dept. crime Web site and Google Maps—and lets you type in an address to see recent crimes in specific Chicago locations. The site attracted 1.2 million page viewers in just its first two weeks.[34]

In Figure 13.5, the mashup reveals the concentrations, by location, of first-degree murders committed in Chicago in January 2007. Geographic information can form the basis for any number of useful mashups.[35] A mashup might, for example, map photographs you have taken

---

[33] From the Wikipedia "Mashup" entry, February 10, 2007 (*http://en.wikipedia.org/wiki/Mashup_%28web_application_hybrid%29*).

[34] "Mix, Match, and Mutate," BusinessWeek Online, July 25, 2005, *http://www.businessweek.com/@@76IH*ocQ34AvyQMA/magazine/content/05_30/b3944108_mz063.htm.*

[35] See, for example, *http://googlemapsmania.blogspot.com/2006/12/50-things-to-do-with-google-maps.html.*

Figure 13.5   January 2007 first-degree murders in Chicago by location. *Source:* From *http://www.chicagocrime.org/types/homicide/1/.*

by location.[36] A future mashup might combine map information with information from our PDA to tell us where we tend to go in a typical week.

But mashups are certainly not limited to map overlays. RedMonk analyst Stephen O'Grady compares the potential of mashups and the sharing of data on the Web to the benefits realized with open source: "As creative as your organization may be, the community at large will always be more creative."[37]

The Internet is like alcohol…. It accentuates what you would do anyway. If you want to be a loner, you can be more alone. If you want to connect, it makes it easier to connect.

Esther Dyson (1951–)

---

[36] See *http://www.panoramio.com/.*

[37] Excerpted from "From Web Page to Web Platform," Martin LaMonica, CNET News.com, August 16, 2005.

13.5 Looking back, looking forward

In a foreseeable future, much of what we do in life may be mediated by and recorded on the Web. The Web connects us to products and other people worldwide to enrich our lives. The Web is a revolution in progress.

But on the darker side, the Web is a place where information about us, even incorrect information, may live on forever, resisting all our attempts at control or correction. The Web is a place where someone else might masquerade as us without detection for long periods of time. The Web, or the small space we carve out, can become its own, self-affirming reality in which we "live" even to the neglect of our physical world.

These dystopian visions of the Web may never come to pass for most of us. But for many of us, one problem with the Web is already apparent: the Web is a place of buzzing, uncontrolled confusion. Replace "World Wide" with "Wild West." How to make sense of all the new web-based tools and services (and associated formats, initiatives, and acronyms) that seem to emerge with each new day? One way is to measure and evaluate using basic PIM activities as a yardstick. What impact does a tool or service have on the PIM activities we do? How does it help us to find, keep and organize, maintain, manage information flow, measure and evaluate, and make sense of our information?

The Web has tremendous potential to support every kind of PIM activity:

- *Finding*. Shared, social tagging can make it easier to find publicly available information and possibly also private information as well. The Web provides many ways to create "information collectives" that support the exchange of information between people with similar interests.

- *Keeping and organizing*. Not only content but also structure can be shared on the Web. Someday soon we may see downloadable "organizers" that we can use and modify as a basis for organizing our own information and planning our own projects.

- *Maintaining*. The Web can serve not only as a backup of our information but also as a primary repository for this information—giving us nearly anywhere, any device access to our information.

- *Managing information flow*. Our presence on the Web can serve as an initial point of contact and screening for those who want to reach us in person. We can use our presence there as a kind of alter ego to project ourselves and our thoughts, talents, and opinions.

- *Measuring and evaluating*. The Web provides a global forum for the exchange of various measurements, observations, anecdotes, problems, and solutions of relevance to our practice of PIM. Also, the Web promises to radically shorten the feedback/release cycle of software improvements.

- *Making sense*. Through initiatives, such as RSS, and the development of mashups, information can be juxtaposed and integrated in many new and useful ways that help us to make sense of things.

The Web, like the PDA, will be a point of convergence for our information and our practices of PIM. Thoughts of the Web as a point of convergence are inspired by hardware advances supporting, for example, increases in bandwidth (especially along the "last mile" to our homes) and storage capacity. But equally, the Web is a point of convergence for its basic ability to connect, nearly instantaneously, person to person and person to information, no matter where these are in the real world, no matter what the physical distances. It seems that we, collectively, worldwide, are only beginning to explore the possibilities enabled by this basic ability to connect.

But connecting, whether through the Web or a PDA, is not enough to overcome the pervasive PIM problem of information fragmentation. Some ways of connecting may even make matters worse. Nor do the convergences afforded by developments in the Web and in PDAs necessarily translate to integrations of personal information as an antidote to fragmentation. We can't just sit back and assume the integrations we need will naturally fall out from work frenetically pursued on the Web and in digital gadgets. So what are these integrations anyway? And what does it take to get them? This is the topic of Chapter 14.

Bringing the pieces together

Information fragmentation is "private enemy #1" in our practice of PIM. Fragmentation makes all activities of PIM more difficult and more error-prone. What's the antidote? With integration, pieces fit together to make a more perfect whole but still retain their individual identity. With unification, the pieces lose independence with respect to the focus of unification. A little bit of unification—in the form of an item event log, for example—may go a long way toward enabling several kinds of integration.

Chapter
Fourteen

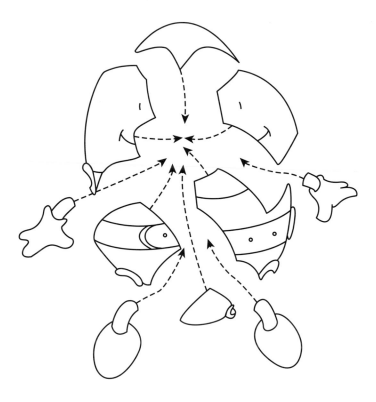

*Humpty Dumpty sat on a wall; Humpty Dumpty had a great fall.
All the king's horses and all the king's men; Couldn't put Humpty
together again!*

Mother Goose nursery rhyme

14.1 Starting out

As we've moved through the chapters of this book, information fragmentation—especially as it results from a proliferation of information forms—has returned repeatedly, in different guises, as "private enemy #1" in our personal practices of PIM. Fragmentation makes all steps of finding and re-finding more difficult. With information scattered, we're less likely to be reminded to use it later in situations where the information is needed. Information transformed—from document to email attachment, for example—may be much more difficult to recognize even when it's "right there" in front of us. And, in our efforts to "re-collect" the scattered set of items needed to make a decision or complete some other task, our very success in retrieving initial items may hamper our ability to retrieve remaining items or prompt us to conclude, too soon, that we already have all the information we need. For example, a person may consult an electronic calendar, a shared paper calendar, a web page, and email correspondence, and then accept a dinner invitation for next Thursday only to discover a fifth item of information—a paper schedule for a daughter's soccer game—that registers a previous commitment for the same evening.

Information fragmentation also further complicates the fundamentally difficult challenge of keeping current information in anticipation of future need. If keeping is like throwing a ball into the future toward an anticipated need, then our throw must be aimed to consider not only the time and place of our future need, but also the relevant information device, organization, and form.

Similarly, information fragmentation complicates the various meta-level activities of PIM. We need to organize and maintain not one but several stores and forms of information. Files may need to be managed on a desktop computer at work, another at home, and on a portable notebook computer too. Email messages may need to be managed in several different accounts. Digital photographs may need to be managed on the flash memory of one or several cameras. Contact and calendar information on our mobile phones needs to be kept in synch with corresponding information on one or more computers.

The antidote to information fragmentation is presumably information integration. The advantages of integration seem evident from definitions such as "To form into one whole; to make entire; to complete; to renew; to restore; to perfect."[1] The whole is greater than the sum of the parts. Synergy. A fabric made stronger for the warp and weft of its separate threads.

But what is information integration, and how is it achieved? "Bringing the pieces together" would seem to be a necessary condition for information integration. If so, we're on our way. Powerful convergences, as enabled by technologies of the Web, our mobile devices, search, and various forms of tagging (author-defined, social, automated) are working to neutralize many of the current sources of information fragmentation. Search can bring together information of several different forms, even if this information is scattered through several different organizations. We can imagine a not-too-distant future where our personal information is seamlessly synchronized between a portable, pluggable (dockable) PDA and the Web, so that all the information we need is immediately available or quickly accessed no matter when or where we need it. Convergence nirvana.

But bringing information together is only the first step and may even be the wrong step if nothing further is done. Remember the "This is your life" party described in Chapter 4? We don't necessarily want to face a roomful of relatives, friends, former lovers, business associates, and neighbors—people who have nothing in common with each other save their association to us at some point in our lives. People in our lives are naturally separated from each other according to physical location, stage in our life, and our various roles and activities. Some advantages of these separations are obvious; others become evident only when separations are removed.

---

[1] *Webster's, http://machaut.uchicago.edu/cgi-bin/WEBSTER.sh?WORD=integrate.*

A similar effect may follow from proposed schemes of information integration and unification. Even as these schemes remove separations that cause us problems, they may inadvertently remove separations that are useful, even essential, to our practices of PIM.

Information integration may, by definition, be a good thing, just as information fragmentation is, by the definition given in this book, a bad thing. But we're left with the task of figuring out more precisely what information integration is and how it is achieved. As we address this challenge, we move through the following sections in this chapter:

☑ *Getting oriented* makes a subtle but important distinction between integration and unification as these terms are applied to PIM.

☑ *Stories of synergy* provide several different examples of the benefits that can result from an integrative approach to personal information and from activities relating to the management and use of personal information.

☑ *Kinds of integration*. There are several. We'll draw on the stories of synergy to explain each.

☑ *Enabling unifications*. We consider the RDF (resource description framework) representational formalism as a basis for a comprehensive unification of personal information. Common, consistent use of an "item event log" places much less demand on software applications and is a useful step toward integration.

14.2 Getting oriented

A subtle, but useful distinction can be drawn between integration and a related term: unification. Consider dictionary definitions for *unification*:

• "The action or process of unifying or uniting; reduction to unity or to a uniform system; the result of this."[2]

• "The act of unifying, or the state of being unified."[3]

• "An act of combining two or more things into one; an instance of uniting."[4]

Now let's consider *integration*:

• "The making up or composition of a whole by adding together or combining the separate parts or elements; combination into an integral whole: a making whole or entire."[5]

• "To form into one whole; to make entire; to complete; to renew; to restore; to perfect.[6]

• "The act or process of making whole or entire."[7]

---

[2] From the *OED, http://dictionary.oed.com/cgi/entry/50267405?single=1&query_type=word&queryword=unification&first= 1&max_to_show=10.*

[3] From *Webster's, http://machaut.uchicago.edu/cgi-bin/WEBSTER.sh?WORD=unification).*

[4] From Wiktionary, *http://www.wiktionary.org/.*

[5] See *http://dictionary.oed.com/cgi/entry/50118573?single=1&query_type=word&queryword=integration&first=1&max_to_ show=10.*

[6] *Webster's, http://machaut.uchicago.edu/cgi-bin/WEBSTER.sh?WORD=integrate.*

[7] See *http://en.wiktionary.org/wiki/Integration.*

The distinction is this: With integration, pieces fit together to make a more perfect whole but still retain their identity as separate pieces, somewhat like a mosaic. With unification, the pieces blend together and, at least with respect to the focus of unification, the pieces lose the ability to act independently of one another.

We have already considered examples of both integration and unification throughout this book. For example, in a sidebar in Chapter 7 ("What Next for Tool Development?"), Mike Kelly describes an integration (coordination) of calendar and cell phone such that the phone's rings can be automatically muted during scheduled meetings. On the other hand, in Chapters 4 through 6, sidebars by the same writer describe advantages that can result from a unified use of structured storage across applications. If different applications surrender autonomy in their ways of storing and using some kinds of information (e.g., contact information) and, instead, make uniform use of a single system-level function for the write and read of this information, then corrections, updates, and the uniform application of an auto-complete feature become much easier. Later in this chapter we'll discuss the Haystack system, which carries this uniformity of storage much further through a proposed uniform use of the RDF representation for all data used by all applications.

It might be argued that while integration is good, unification is even better. The advantages Mike Kelly describes, for example, require unified use of a *single*, *shared* store. Coordinated use of separate stores is not likely to cut it. Imagine, for example, the combinatorial nightmare that could follow from an attempt to communicate and synchronize changes between several different stores. But application developers pay a price for unification. Use of a shared store means a surrender of control (e.g., to the operating system) and possibly a degradation in performance as well. In general, the benefits of unification need to be weighed against its costs. And, as later examples in this chapter illustrate, sometimes a little unification is all that is needed. More is not necessarily better and may be worse.

Why bother with either integration or unification as anything other than a theoretical nicety of interest to academics? In a word, *synergy:* "Increased effectiveness, achievement, etc., produced as a result of combined action or co-operation."[8] The whole is greater than the sum of the parts. Synergy happens when important patterns are apparent in the juxtaposition of items, patterns that would not be apparent (or much less readily so) if the items were separated from one another in time and space. Synergy is what happens when one or both of two activities are made easier or more effective for their coordination. Synergy is stopping off at the drugstore on the way back from the grocery store to save a separate trip. By small extension to include a related notion of leverage, we might also say that synergy is what happens when some new activity is completed more easily or more effectively for its relationships to other activities we've already done.

Which is needed or more important for synergy? Unification or integration? Mostly integration —according to the stories in the next section—but a little unification is needed as well.

---

[8] *http://dictionary.oed.com/cgi/entry/50245388?single=1&query_type=word&queryword=synergy&first=1&max_to_ show=10.*

The whole is more than the sum of its parts.

Aristotle (384–322 B.C.)

14.3 Stories of synergy

Here are some stories of synergy from now and a not-too-distant future.

14.3.1 Sally takes notes

As Sally looks through her notes for a meeting, she sees a hastily written, almost indecipherable message to "check out the wdaiw? site." During a recent talk that Sally attended, the speaker mentioned a web site with some potentially important information for a project Sally is working on, but she was momentarily distracted and did not hear what the speaker said. She wrote down something that now she cannot read. What to do? Fortunately, the note itself can be used to retrieve a recording of the speaker's talk positioned to play the minutes of the talk surrounding the time when the note was made. This integration of notes taken and audio recording is already a feature supported in Microsoft OneNote.

Comment. Sally experiences a synergy that results from an integration between her active note-taking of the speaker's talk and a passive recording of this talk. An indecipherable result of Sally's note-taking activity is used to index and retrieve precisely that portion of the talk that prompted Sally to take the note in the first place. A least one unification is required as well: the recording of the talk and the taking of notes need to be keeping time in the same way.

14.3.2 Neil talks the walk

Neil sometimes likes to walk as he thinks through a problem. He likes the exercise, and walking really helps him to unwind a little so that he can think more clearly. As ideas occurred to Neil, he used to write them down. But stopping to write was cumbersome. Also, this method certainly did not work as a way to record thoughts—ranging from to-do items to big ideas—that often occurred to him as he drove to and from work.

Neil tried making voice notes on his mobile phone using a voice-activated, hands-free head-set. But these audio notes seemed to go into a "black hole"—easy to record, but very difficult to retrieve later on.

Now Neil's new PDA (with cell phone functions) automatically stamps voice notes by location as well as time. Neil can also request a conversion from voice to text. He can even ask that notes be flagged for his attention later (through a beep on his phone or through an "Attention Central" visual display as described in Chapter 10 if a monitor is available).

The ability to retrieve by location has proven especially useful for Neil. If he can't remember the note itself, he can often remember where he was when he made it. Neil can later retrieve these notes either by specifying the place or by actually going back to the place. He recently recalled, for example, that he "said something important" while last in his recreation room downstairs. He had no idea what. But by returning to the recreation room, he was quickly able to retrieve the last "voice note" he made while in that room.

Comment. Neil experiences several kinds of synergy. He is able to combine two useful activities—walking and thinking ("talking") over a problem—in the same period of time. Notice that Neil is not simply multitasking or time-sharing. He is not simply switching back and forth between two different activities (though he does so when he replies to email messages while listening to a football game). The relationship between thinking/talking and walking might best be described as a relationship of *commensalism*.[9] The activity of walking is mostly unaffected by Neil's efforts to think/talk through a problem—except when he slows down momentarily to work through a particularly tough concern or an interesting idea. On the other hand, Neil's attempts to think through a problem are often helped by his walking. It helps to free Neil's mind so that he can think more creatively.

Neil's PDA accomplishes an important integration between a recorded note, as an information item, and the context, including location and time, in which it was written. The circumstances surrounding the note's creation that Neil is able to recall—location in particular but also time—now facilitate its later retrieval.

14.3.3 Edith sees a better way

Edith has been brought in as a consultant to complete a major organizational review for one division of a large manufacturing company seeking to become "leaner and meaner." Over the course of several months, Edith will interview scores of people at various levels and from various groups within the division. She will engage in countless email conversations. She will review several hundred reports. Some are sent as Word or PDF document attachments; others are available only as web pages on the corporate intranet. At the end of this data-gathering and analysis period, Edith is expected to deliver a final report. This is a big project for Edith. If she does well, more opportunities may follow.

In an effort to avoid jumping to conclusions or imposing her own biases, Edith takes a deliberate bottom-up approach in her work. She begins with a careful consideration of the raw information she has collected and then works upward to initial summary observations, interim conclusions, and then final recommendations. She also wants traceability. For each major recommendation she eventually makes, she wants to be able to point "downward" to lower-level conclusions or observations and then back to excerpts from original interviews, email messages, documents, and web pages in support of these observations.

Edith characterizes her job roughly as involving the following overlapping stages:

1. Gather. *Information comes packaged as information items in various forms, including interviews,[10] documents, pointers to web pages, and email messages.*
2. Extract. *Extract one or more "nuggets" from each information item. Nuggets are excerpts of text and sometimes graphics too. Nuggets are placed in a special space for the project*

---

[9] *http://en.wikipedia.org/wiki/Commensalism.*

[10] Interviews produce a special form of information (when interviewees agree)—audio recordings that are automatically transcribed and interspersed with and annotated by the notes Edith takes free-hand (also automatically transformed to digital text).

on Edith's computer through a Drag & link operation. Edith can click on a nugget to return to the source item with the excerpted text of the nugget highlighted. She can add her own comments to a nugget and also add property values or simple tags to a nugget. She can associate a nugget or a grouping of nuggets to tasks and times that then appear in her calendar of events.

3. Analyze. *Edith can sort, name, group, and otherwise work with nuggets through several different views ranging from free-form (tablet) to hierarchical or tabular (with nuggets as rows and properties as columns). As she does so, important patterns begin to emerge. Edith groups nuggets together according to their relevance to summary observations that she can enter free-hand. Edith is even able to extract nuggets from groupings of nuggets to participate in a second (and third) round of analysis.*

4. Draft. *Edith makes a rough draft of the final report. When in draft mode, Edith selects a similarly named mode of her word processor that turns off spell-checking and most format-ting features. Edith finds these features to be mostly a distraction when she is trying to get her ideas down.*

5. Format and finalize. *Edith completes the final report with the aid of an assistant. This final stage also includes several rounds of review, during which key employees in the division have an opportunity to comment.*

Comment. Edith experiences one important synergy:

• Edith is able to see a collection of nuggets in a single view. She can then see patterns and relationships she might otherwise miss. Moreover, nuggets, even though these represent a range of information forms, can all be manipulated in the same ways. A nugget can be clicked to return to its source item. A grouping of nuggets can stand for a grouping of source items.

Also, Edith experiences a kind of synergy from the coordinated, stage-appropriate availability of word processing features:

• Edith's word processor provides her with an integrated assembly of features appropriate to her mode of use. Draft mode has one constellation of features; review mode (not dis-cussed here) has another.

14.3.4 Robert builds a dream

Robert[11] has taken early retirement to build the house that he and his wife have long dreamed of. His wife will help out with comments and suggestions as best she can, but she still has a full-time job to do as well. This is Robert's project to drive to conclusion. Robert has a great many things to think about and decide. Who will be the architect? The contractor? How should the house be laid out to meet the needs that he and his wife have now and the needs they will have as they grow older? Each room of the house represents a design project in its own right. How will the kitchen work? (Both Robert and his wife like to cook, and they like to host dinner parties.) What about the master bedroom? The living room? The media room? What about

---

[11] Robert's story illustrates a vision that directs the KFTF efforts to prototype the Project Planner (see Jones et al., 2006).

flooring, countertops, and wiring? How can the house be built to be as "green" as possible in terms of materials used and energy needed for heating and cooling? Many choices, many decisions.

Robert downloads a "Build your dream house" organizer—one of many "life organizers" available from the Web. The organizer helps Robert to structure his project from major decisions and subprojects (e.g., "Get financing," "Hire an architect," "Plan the kitchen"), all the way down to more basic tasks such as "Decide on kitchen countertops." The organizer comes with suggestions, explanatory graphics, and "See also" links to the Web. The organizer includes tables that Robert can fill in to help in the decisions he and his wife make for various alternatives. For example, a "countertop" table includes columns for "cost," "durability," and "clean-up." The organizer supports several different views, including an outline view, a "mind map" view, a workflow timeline view highlighting major phases of a home-building project, and even a "print layout" view that makes the whole plan appear as one large document.

There are two features about the house-building organizer that Robert especially values:

- Robert can modify his plan as he sees fit. Once downloaded, the organizer "inflates" into a starter plan that is Robert's to modify as he likes. The organizer provides a useful starting point, but the rest is up to Robert. Using the Project Planner (see Chapter 5) as an overlay to the file system, Robert adds, deletes, and rearranges to make the plan his. When he sends an email as prompted by a task in the plan, a reference to this email is inserted in the plan itself. Similar references are made to documents that Robert creates.

  Tasks in the plan can be given property values to represent their relative importance and current status. Tasks can be associated with dates and times in Robert's calendar. Each task organizes and provides access to information needed for its completion. For example, through the "Decide on kitchen countertops" task, Robert can access a decision table, contractor document, and several web references that relate to the choice of countertop styles.

- The plan is a part of Robert's file system. The structure of a house-building plan translates into a structure of folders, subfolders, tags, and properties. Relevant information items of various forms—documents, web pages, email messages, example pictures (of what Robert and his wife want the house to look like)—all of these are represented in the file system either directly as files or as pointers (shortcuts, aliases) to the information items.

Comment. Robert experiences one important synergy from the integration of planning and organizing:

- Information is organized as a by-product of Robert's planning efforts.

Robert may experience additional synergies from an ability to bring together various information items—regardless of their forms—into a single organization of subprojects and tasks, which, in turn, can be associated with key dates and times. Key relationships—key task interdependencies, for example—may be apparent in this organization that might otherwise be overlooked.

Robert experiences synergies of a different kind when activities he is doing now are more effective for being able to leverage previous efforts and experience:

- Subprojects and tasks in the plan correspond to folders in the file system. The files under these folders correspond directly or via reference (e.g., in the case of web pages or email messages) to the information items organized in the plan. Robert can continue to use his file folders as his primary means of actively organizing his digital information. The Planner simply provides another way of viewing and working with his files and folders.

- The project plan supports "outline" and "print layout" views. Robert can work on the project and its information through these views in the same way he works in his word processor through views with the same names. The skills Robert has already developed for use with his word processor readily transfer to the use of the Planner.

- Robert's efforts get a big head start for the ability to download a Life Organizer to use as a starting point. The Life Organizer certainly doesn't anticipate all of Robert's plans, and it includes things that Robert and his wife don't care about (like a playroom for the kids). But it also includes many things that Robert would not have thought about or might have thought about too late to do anything about. In using the Life Organizer, Robert leverages not only his previous efforts and experiences, but also the efforts and experiences of others.

14.3.5 Ginny remembers the way things were

At nearly 90 years of age, Ginny has a lifetime of memories extending back through World War II and the Great Depression and into the "Roaring Twenties." More important, Ginny knows things about the family and its history that no one else does. Her children, grandchildren, and, now, even her great-grandchildren have made sporadic attempts at family gatherings to entice Ginny to say more about the way things once were. But nothing much comes of these attempts. In a typical sequence, Ginny might say, "What do you want to know?" Her grandson Scott might pose a fairly general question like, "What was WWII like?" to which Ginny might make an equally general response.

Then, during one visit to Grandma Ginny, Scott came across a box of old photographs, and as a lark, he scanned them into digital form. Later, at a family gathering, he assembled the digital copies into a slideshow. As pictures were presented, Grandma Ginny talked and was recorded as she did so. Ginny talked not in generalities but in specifics that painted a rich landscape of life as it used to be. "Those were our closest neighbors when we lived on the farm. We would get together with them and other neighbors every month or so for a dance. One time it was snowing so hard. . . ." Digital photos and a digital recording of Ginny's reminiscences could then be interleaved. The photographs brought back a rich set of memories for Ginny. Later, the photos helped to organize and provide entry points into an aural recording of Ginny's reminiscences. In turn, the aural recording brings these photographs alive. Before, the old photographs were "just a bunch of old photographs." Now the photographs integrated with the aural recoding are a rich record of family history.

Comment. In previous stories, desired outcomes large and small might have been achieved without the synergies described—albeit in modified form and with greater difficulty. Sally might still have found a way to get to the web site that sounded interesting during the talk. Neil could have stopped walking (or driving) long enough to jot down a few notes. Edith would still have written her report, and Robert might still have built his dream house (if such a thing is ever possible given the second-guessing of hindsight).

The outcome in Ginny's story is that now the family has a recording of Ginny's reminiscences integrated with a collection of old photographs that otherwise might have been shunted aside in an attic somewhere and forgotten. It's difficult to see how anything approaching this desirable outcome could have been achieved without the integrated application of tools and technology. Scott gets some of the credit, of course, for scanning and creating digital copies of the old photographs. Suppose he had simply passed around the photographs at a family gathering—starting with Ginny so that she could reminisce as others passed the photo around. Imagine how this might work. Ginny sees one photograph, smiles, passes it to the next person and starts talking about the story behind the photo. But then maybe Uncle Bob, unable to see the photograph that is still in someone else's hands, gets restless and starts talking as well. And then Ginny says something like, "Oh, you all don't want to hear me go on about these old pictures."

Chapter 2 talked about ways in which our separate spaces of information can pull us apart even though we are together in physical space. Ginny's story is different. Information—a picture shared through its display for all in the family to see—acts to bring people together. Ginny loves an audience (even though she would never admit it). Without the integrative use and effects of information and information technology, there might have been no story involving Ginny, her memories, and a "bunch of old photographs."

14.4 Kinds of integration

The preceding stories of synergy illustrate several kinds of integration:

- *Visual integration.* For paper documents, the desktop and other flat surfaces of an office traditionally served as a view space. We may move paper documents from filing cabinets to the desktop in order to "see" the information better. Computers provide several alternatives for comparable viewings of digital information, including the computer desktop, a folder listing of files (or email messages or web references), and the window displays of opened documents, email messages, and web sites. Our view of items can act as a powerful extension to our limited internal working memory for information.[12]

- *Feature integration.* Features, within and across applications, should work together according to our activities. Features of a word processor that are needed for the final production of a document can be a time-wasting distraction when people are trying to complete a rough draft. As another example, calendars and cell phones should work together so that our cells won't ring at inappropriate times, such as when we are attending a meeting.

- *Integration of task, time, and information management.* It should be possible to group and tag information according to task and time of anticipated use.

---

[12] See, for example, Larkin and Simon (1987).

- *Integration of activities and experiences (context)*. Activities should be integrated with elements of the context (location, time, sound, sight) in which they occur. The time of our last interaction with a document (email message, web page) is recorded currently. But many other aspects of the interactive context are not. We may recall that, when we last viewed an information item at home, not at work, the weather was warm and sunny. But these recollections provide little help in our interactions with the computer. As we create a new email message or e-document, or as we browse to a web site, we may have a particular task in mind, but there is very little support for communicating this task to the computer. Worse, newly created documents are often placed, by default, in a place like "My Documents." In general, the context we share with the computer in our interactions with information items is very limited.

- *Integration of activities with each other*. Look for ways that one activity might leverage another. For example, we plan projects and we organize project-related information. The to-do list or the outline we create as we plan a project can also provide a basis for the organization of project-related information. Can a good organization emerge as a by-product of planning?

- *Integration of the new and the old*. For example, people may have considerable time and energy invested in existing folder hierarchies and other organizations. Moreover, these organizations and supporting applications are used in many ways that are not well understood. Consequently, a new tool has a better chance of success if it is able to build on these organizations and extend the functionality of existing applications rather than forcing a leap to an entirely new way of doing things.

14.5 Enabling unifications

In support of the kinds of integration just listed are key unifications. For example, the ability to display information from several applications at the same time (i.e., support of visual integration) depends on their shared use of a window manager.[13] Certainly, the Web has been a powerful force of integration through its promotion of underlying unifications in the way information items are addressed (via URLs or, more accurately, URIs)[14] and accessed (via protocols such as HTTP). Using the Web, we can group items together without regard to the physical location of the server on which they are stored. The ability to group items in ways that suit our needs and without regard to physical location is further strengthened by increasingly sophisticated search engines (searching not only on item content, but also on an increasingly comprehensive set of metadata).

Here we consider two potential unifications: the common use of RDF for data representation; and the common, consistent use of what will here be called simply an *item event log* to record all of our interactions with information items.

---

[13] For a more in-depth discussion of unifications that support us in our practice of PIM, see Karger (2007).

[14] A Uniform Resource Identifier (URI) is a string of characters used to identify any resource (e.g., file, web page, or even function that returns a value). A Uniform Resource Locator (URL) is a kind of URI that also supports the resource's location (e.g., on the Web). For more information, see the Wikipedia "URIs" article at *http://en.wikipedia.org/wiki/URI*.

14.5.1 RDF

The digital information items discussed in this chapter—in particular the file—are high level. The operations we can perform at the file level are useful, but limited. We can create, move, rename, and delete files. The data within a file is typically in a "native format" and readable only by a single application—the word processor, spreadsheet, or presentation software used to create the file. In this circumstance, opportunities to share, consolidate, and normalize data (e.g., to avoid problems with updating) are extremely limited. Information concerning the structure and semantics of the data stays behind in the source application. Moreover, the data is copied, not referenced, which can lead to many problems of updating later on.

As a result, data concerning a person we know—say, Jill Johnson—may appear in many, many places in our PSI. This is another variation of fragmentation. Because of this fragmentation, even simple operations, such as correcting for a spelling mistake in Jill's name or updating for a change in her email address, become nearly impossible to complete. We may update some copies but not all. Also, we may experience the frustration of having some operations—name resolution, for example—available in one place (when sending email) but not in another (when working with photographs).

More consistency in operations, such as name resolution and better support for updating, may follow from increasing support for standards associated with the Semantic Web,[15] including XML (eXtensible Markup Language), RDF (Resource Description Framework), and the use of URIs. RDF and XML, for example, can be used to include more semantics with a data interchange. URIs might be used to address data, in place, so that it doesn't need to be copied in the first place. Support for these standards may make it possible, in some future day of PIM, to work with information and data packaged around concepts such as "Jill Johnson" rather than with files. Data for Jill would be mostly referenced, not copied. We could readily add more information about Jill or make a comment like "she's a true friend." And we could group information about Jill together, as needed, with other information.

These and other possibilities are explored in the Haystack project.[16] Haystack represents an effort to provide a unified data environment in which it is possible to group, annotate, and reference or link information at smaller and more meaningful units than the file. In the Haystack data model, a typical file will be disassembled into many individual information objects represented in RDF. Objects can be stored in a database or in XML files. When an object is rendered for display in the user interface, a connection is kept to the object's underlying representation. Consequently, the user can click on "anything" in view and navigate to get more information about the associated object (to get Jill Johnson's birthdate, for example) and also to make additions or corrections to this information.

Haystack creates a potential to explore, group, and work with information in many ways that are not possible when information is "hidden" behind files. However, many issues must be

---

[15] See Berners-Lee (1998).

[16] See Adar, Karger, and Stein (1999); Huynh, Karger, and Quan (2002); Karger et al. (2005); and Quan, Huynh, and Karger (2003).

addressed before the Haystack vision is realized in commercial systems. For example, the use of RDF, whether via XML files or a database, is slow. Beyond performance improvements, a great deal must be done if application developers are eventually to abandon the control they currently have with data in native format in favor of a system where data comes, instead, from an external source as RDF.

14.5.2 An item event log

Certainly one important unification for all of us is a shared notion of what time it is. Time has also been suggested and explored in prototype systems as a way to unify our information items. For example, the MEMOIRS system[17] treated documents and other information items (appointments, for example) as events to be placed in sequence according to time. Each time a document was modified, it was copied to create a new "event." Perhaps best known of the time-based approaches to information integration is LifeStreams.[18] In LifeStreams, documents, other information items, and memorable events in a person's life are all placed in a single, time-ordered stream.

Both MEMOIRS and LifeStreams treat documents and other items as the event. As such, a document can have only one associated time. But what if I want a document to have two times? The first time might reflect the date and time that I last modified the document, and the second might be a future time of anticipated use (e.g., "at the status meeting next Tuesday"). To accomplish this, I must create two copies.

Another approach that might accomplish a unification using not only time but also location is to support the common, unified use of an item event log. Recall from Chapter 2 that items "encapsulate information in a persistent form that can be created, modified, stored, retrieved, given a name, tags, and other properties, moved, copied, distributed, deleted, and otherwise manipulated."

Suppose each of these manipulations was registered as an event. An event is a structured data item that includes, but is not restricted to, the following properties: (1) an operation or manipulation (e.g., create, modify, store, retrieve, name, rename, tag, move, copy, etc.); (2) a reference (e.g., URI) to the information item that is the object of this manipulation; (3) time; and (4) location.

Item event logs, if consistently used by all applications we use to manipulate our information, could form the basis for many of the integrations described in this chapter. Current versions of the Macintosh and Windows operating systems already support logging, although not in ways that are consistently used by all applications. Most notably, our manipulations of information through email and other applications that create their own "file system within a file" (e.g., database applications) are not properly logged in a single item event log.

---

[17] See Lansdale and Edmonds (1992).

[18] See Fertig, Freeman, and Gelernter (1996) and Freeman and Gelernter (1996).

Break a vase, and the love that reassembles the fragments is stronger than that love which took its symmetry for granted when it was whole.

West Indian poet and playwright Derek Walcott (1930–)

PUTting It All Together

One example of "bringing the pieces together" in a useful way was an effort some years ago (2002) by an assistant and her manager (Mike Eisenberg, then dean of the Information School at the University of Washington, and his assistant Danielle Miller). They were experiencing the usual problems of PIM multiplied by the information stores they each maintained separately but jointly needed to access. Each of them separately maintained folder organizations for email and e-documents. The assistant also organized paper documents into the hanging folders of several file cabinets.

Things were not working. None of the folder organizations worked very well by itself, and there was only partial agreement between any of the organizations. They decided to do something. Over the course of several weeks, they met periodically to discuss how their information *should* be organized. The assistant represented her understanding of their discussions in simple sketches illustrating important categories of information for their work and how these categories might be organized together.

In the end, they had a classification scheme—a taxonomy. Included in the top level of this taxonomy were the following categories:

- *Outside:* Organizations/entities not part of the UW

- *UW:* Colleges, schools, departments, programs, etc., at a university-wide level

- *ISchool:* Information School programs, students, proposals, committees, finances, etc.

- *Personal:* The manager's notes, papers, etc.

- *Courses:* Syllabi, overheads, etc., for courses that the manager taught

This taxonomy was imposed, as an organizational scheme, on the various collections of information that the manager and assistant kept separately but needed to share with each other (including collections of email, e-documents, paper documents, and even collections of Favorites pointing to web sites). Even for collections that were not freely shared—email messages, for example—the taxonomy provided a shared language of reference.

In general, a taxonomy need not be a hierarchy and might involve advanced concepts such as *faceted classification* (see, for example, Bates, 1988). But simplicity is often a virtue. A simple hierarchical organizational scheme is supported by existing tools. Its rules of application are easy to learn, easy to communicate (to the new assistant, for example), and can be easily and consistently followed (by both manager and assistant).

More than just schema for organizing the manager's information, the taxonomy establishes the more important divisions among the many activities that the manager pursues. The taxonomy provides a way of understanding these activities and how they relate to one another. The taxonomy also provides a basis for communication between the manager and his assistant.

The taxonomy that the assistant and her manager created to organize the manager's information can be called a *Personal Unifying Taxonomy* or *PUT*. A PUT has the following characteristics:

- A PUT is personal. Each person's PUT is unique and customized to his or her needs.

- A PUT is unifying in its completeness. A PUT can be used as is, or with small extensions, to classify and organize a person's information regardless of form. For example, email, e-documents, and paper documents as shared by the assistant and her manager all had the same top-level structure. Subfolders were used to provide additional, finer-grained organization for e-documents.

- A PUT is a taxonomy. For our purposes, the words "taxonomy" and "classification scheme" are interchangeable. Implicit in the use of either term is the notion that there is an associated external representation and rules for its application which can be consistently followed.

In the KFTF project, we have begun to explore the development and potential utility of PUTs. A PUT reflects various activities, people, and areas of interest in a person's life—past, present, and future.

PUTs are often hierarchical but not necessarily so. For some people, a PUT may be only a single, top level of categories representing the key roles, projects, and areas of interest in the person's life. People develop a PUT with reference to their various organizations for paper documents, e-documents, email messages, web references, and so on. People can then apply the PUT or portions of it to achieve some measure of consistency across different information organizations.

One person who developed only the top-level of a PUT still saw real value in the consistency she was then able to impose across different form-specific organizations:

> I think the value of the PUT is on several levels. One, it makes the "keep" decision so much easier. I don't have to wonder what to do with something—leaving it in a random place until there is so much clutter, it makes me anxious (or worse yet, deleting it because I don't know where to file it). . . . Finally, I've found it very easy to maintain—seldom needing to change the top level after using it for a couple of months. It works!

However, a great deal of work remains to be done to determine a process and principles of PUT development and to determine whether a PUT can be maintained over time to realize benefits that compensate for its costs of creation and maintenance. The larger point is that, in our fascination with the potential of new tools and technology, we should not overlook the potential to improve through changes in our techniques, strategies, and habits of PIM.

14.6 Looking back, looking forward

A distinction has been drawn in this chapter between unification and integration. With integration, pieces fit together to make a more perfect whole but still retain their identity as separate pieces. With unification, the pieces lose independence with respect to the focus of unification (e.g., shared use of a single data-storage facility).

Which do we need—integration or unification? We need both. Integrative uses of information and the features in information tools build on and depend on underlying unifications.

But the stories of synergy related in this chapter suggest that a little bit of unification might go a long way toward enabling several kinds of integration. For example, an item event log could provide a basis for interrelating information of several different forms—to each other, to the contexts in which the information is used, and to the tasks for which the information is needed.

The underlying unifications themselves, whether modest or comprehensive, do not realize the synergies illustrated in the stories. Synergies are at least partially dependent on an integrative mindset that looks for opportunities to "bring the pieces together" in ways that are mutually supporting.

What does our practice of PIM say about the lives we lead? Is the fragmentation we experience symptomatic of a larger fragmentation in our lives? Many of us may drive to the health club to work out—even as we leave our children at home to play video games on the X-box. And then we drive our children to various sports activities. What about getting some exercise and some family time by playing a game of soccer together?

There is another sense in which we need to bring the pieces together. It's time to bring together the pieces of this book. By the time you read this book, technologies will have changed. Nevertheless, the basic challenges of PIM as discussed in this book will remain, and considerations and approaches for dealing with these will endure as well. This is a topic for the next and last chapter of this book.

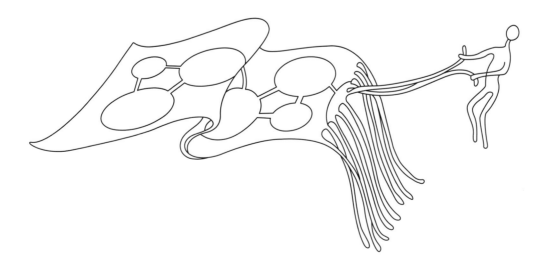

Finding our way in(to) the future

The future is not a place we can go or get into. But we can direct ourselves and our efforts *to* the future by considering the enduring challenges of PIM and related certainties. We can bet on having too much information and too little time to deal with it. We can keep our direction *in* the future through key considerations of PIM: How is personal information, in each of its several senses, managed through PIM activities as a means to manage our resources—money, energy, attention, and most of all, our time?

Chapter Fifteen

I learn by going where I have to go.

Theodore Roethke (1908–1963)
From "The Waking"

15.1 Starting out

One joke has it that the future is a fun place to visit but we wouldn't want to live there.

The joke turns on the notion that the future is a place that we might go into in a similar way that we might take a subway into midtown Manhattan. We can go into a city. We can go into business. We can get into college, or into trouble, or possibly even into heaven. But we cannot go or get into the future. The future is, by definition, "The time ahead; those moments yet to be experienced"[1] or "Of or pertaining to time to come."[2] The future is, always, just ahead of us, just about to begin.

---

[1] See *http://en.wiktionary.org/wiki/future.*

[2] See *http://dictionary.oed.com/cgi/entry/50091311?query_type=word&queryword=future&first=1&max_to_show=10&sort_type=alpha&result_place=1&search_id=0mL9-cj5AcV-11010&hilite=50091311.*

But let's try substituting the "into" with each of its prepositional components.

We can talk about finding our way *to* the future or *in* the future. Finding our way "to the future" implies a sense of direction. We act today according to assumptions we make about tomorrow. If we're optimistic, we buy stocks or even a lottery ticket. If we're pessimistic, maybe we buy bonds or consider joining a survivalist community somewhere in a remote part of Montana.

Finding our way "in the future" also has some connotations. The phrase sometimes carries a sense of resolution or purpose. "In the future, I'll exercise one hour more every week" or "Next time, I won't react so quickly."

This chapter takes a long look back at the journey we've made through this book and looks forward at the journey ahead, both for PIM as a field of study and for each of us in our individual practices of PIM. The chapter has two major sections:

- ☑ *To the future* looks at the future as a direction to maintain as we're tacking back and forth in our sea of personal information. Do we know where we're heading? Many predictions about the future are certain to be completely, hilariously off course.[3] But, as the writers of horoscopes know, some predictions are a sure thing. In the next few days, we are each certain to experience moments of happiness, sadness, frivolity, and frustration. To do so is to be human. Similarly, we are certain to experience basic challenges in our practices of PIM, no matter what the future brings in the way of new tools and technologies.

- ☑ *In the future* takes a more prescriptive approach. What should PIM, as a field of study, encompass? What basic considerations can we use as a compass in our own practices of PIM? How do we stay the course given the many demands (on our time, energy, attention) that we're sure to face and given the temptations of seemingly magical new tools and technologies? If the "To the future" section is about finding the way—the direction—to the future, then the "In the future" section is about keeping it.

Lots of folks confuse bad management with destiny.
U.S. journalist, humorist, and homespun philosopher Kin Hubbard (1868–1930)

15.2 To the future

We begin this section with a consideration of basic, enduring challenges of PIM. The section then considers truisms and "prevailing winds." Finally, we consider an abyss: What happens if the power goes out?

---

[3] See Norman (1993) for a review of past predictions proven wildly wrong.

15.2.1 Enduring challenges of PIM

Tomorrow we will face the same basic challenges of PIM that we face today:

- *Finding* is a multistep process with a possibility of stumbling at each step. First, we must *remember* to look. We must *recall* something about the item we seek to find—such as its approximate location (in a pile or a folder), a property, tag, or content. We must be able to *recognize* the item or its representation from among several alternatives. Finally, in many situations of information need, we must *repeat* the finding activity several times in order to "re-collect" a complete set of information items.

- *Keeping* is multifaceted. Keeping, like finding, can involve several steps. Keeping may even trigger an act of finding—as in re-finding the right folder or pile in which to place an information item. But the essential challenge of keeping (and organizing) stems from the multifaceted nature of our information needs. Is the information useful? Do special actions need to be taken to keep it for later use? Where? When? In what form? On what device? With no crystal ball to see into the future, answering these questions is difficult and error-prone. But the attempt to do so may help us to remember the information item later in appropriate circumstances. Some caution is advised, therefore, against an over-reliance on well-intended attempts to automate these decisions.

- *Meta-level activities* are important but easily overlooked. At the heart of any PIM practice is a mapping between information and need. The mapping is partly in our heads and partly realized in external organizational structures and supporting tools. Critical to the creation, maintenance, and use of this mapping are various kinds of meta-level activities. But there are few events in a typical day to direct our attention to these meta-level activities. As a result, meta-level activities can easily become after-thoughts. Research into meta-level activities and their support also appears to get less attention than, for example, research into finding (which can draw on support from established communities in information seeking and information retrieval). But it is at the meta-level that we may realize some of the most productive synergies between applied research in PIM and basic research in cognitive science.

The following kinds of meta-level activity are critical to a practice of PIM.

- *Maintaining and organizing.* We can hope that actions to back up and safeguard our information become more routine, even automatic. Farther out, we might hope for services and supporting tools to assist in matters of format migration and information updates. But even under optimistic scenarios where these immediate and near-term issues of maintenance are addressed, we're left with more basic issues concerning the maintenance and organization of information that can never be completely automated or outsourced. How does our information reflect, remind, and reinforce our values, goals, hopes, and fears? Our information speaks for us, about us—not only to ourselves but to others and possibly long after we're gone from this world.

- *Managing privacy and the flow of information.* Incoming information—in many forms and through many modes of communication—attracts our attention, our time, and, sometimes, our money. On the outflow, information about us can fall into the wrong hands through trickery or outright theft. Look for help from tools and stronger, more enforceable laws. But the game will continue even so. We, and our resources, are too valuable to be left alone. Becoming an "island fortress" with total shutdown of information channels—incoming and outgoing—is not an option for most of us. We must then decide the who, what, and when of information inflow and outflow.

• *Measuring and evaluating.* Is this working? Should I change? These questions have broad application, of course, but special significance in the context of our practices of PIM. How well do the current elements of our PIM practice—its supporting tools, schemes of organization, overall strategies—work? Can we do better? Is it worth our while to change?

• *Making sense of our information.* The challenges we face in our efforts to make sense of our information are especially likely to endure. Patterns in our information and its uses—large and small—await our discovery. As we better understand our information and its uses, we make better use of the precious resources of our lives—money, energy, attention, and, most especially, time.

15.2.2 As sure as the setting sun

Other verities of PIM will endure as well, including the following.

Information overload will always be with us

Concerns of information overload are not new. Consider the following quote:

> We have reason to fear that the multitude of books which grows every day in a pro-digious fashion will make the following centuries fall into a state as barbarous as that of the centuries that followed the fall of the Roman Empire. Unless we try to prevent this danger by separating those books which we must throw out or leave in oblivion from those which one should save and within the latter between what is useful and what is not.

This was said by one Adrien Baillet in 1685.[4]

But information overload and our reactions to it can vary. In a worst-case reaction to an over-supply of information, our efforts to process the information break down completely—much like the example of Lucy in the candy factory as described in Chapter 7.

Information overload itself can assume a relatively benign or more malignant character. We can't even hope to give a cursory scan to all the information that is potentially useful to us in one or another aspect of our lives. This is a given. But does useless (to us) information prevent us from getting to the information we need? This is a problem. Pirolli (2006) notes that, by some measures, the density of useful, relevant information—its amount as a percentage of the total amount of available information—is declining. Can search facilities, spam filters, social tagging services, and the like, help us to wade through the useless information for the prover-bial needle in the haystack that we seek?

---

[4] As noted by Ann Blair (1961).

Information fragmentation will always be with us

Information fragmentation will always be a problem but, like information overload, can assume forms ranging from relatively benign to purely malignant. Some information fragmentation is the price we pay for continued innovation in our tools. Tool developers must have the freedom to innovate. As they do so, we can look forward to new forms of information, new supporting tools, and new features of information management and use. In an admittedly idealized progression, we can hope that useful features first provided in one tool are copied in other tools and eventually find their way into the operating system for all tools to use and support.

But today we see many examples of seemingly avoidable information fragmentation. Consider iTunes. My version[5] works well enough as a way of organizing the songs I've purchased. I especially like the ability to define any number of playlists as a way of tagging and sequencing songs I want to hear on different occasions (e.g., "party music," "songs of memory lane," "music to work by").

But I would also like to reference some songs elsewhere in my file folder hierarchy. For example, one song was especially appropriate for a presentation I planned to give. I wanted to create a pointer to this song in the same file folder that contained other materials relating to the presentation. I selected the song, then chose the Copy command from a context menu, and then navigated to the presentation folder to see if I could do a "Paste Shortcut." Nothing doing. I faced similar problems in my efforts to create a shortcut to an email message in Outlook and in my efforts to do anything—Paste or Paste Shortcut—with a OneNote page.[6]

We see another kind of fragmentation—call it a fragmentation of features—within applications themselves. As Edith from Chapter 14 worked to complete a rough draft of her report, she was able to use a draft mode of her word processor in which potentially distracting features such as advanced formatting options and automatic spell-checking were turned off. But if I try to achieve a similar effect with my word processor, I need to carry out several separate operations. Worse, turning off an option to "Check spelling as you type" means that this is turned off everywhere across all the documents I'm working on and not just for the rough draft. Suppose I later turn on automatic spell-checking as I work to put finishing touches on another document. If I then go back to the rough draft document, automatic spell-checking is back on again for this document as well.

These examples illustrate a larger point. Some fragmentation is a price we pay for tool innovation. But much of the fragmentation we currently experience can be avoided with a little effort and more awareness of issues of information fragmentation in software design.

---

[5] As I write these lines, I have iTunes 6.0.

[6] Neither email messages in Outlook nor pages in OneNote are directly realized as files in the file system, which adds some complications to the requisite addressing of a shortcut. As managed by iTunes, songs are each in a separate file on my computer, and it would seem that the extensions required to reference songs elsewhere should be straightforward. I can already create shortcuts for songs by going "behind" iTunes to access them directly as files. Of course, I then do so without the iTunes user interface.

Too much to do, too little time to do it, and . . . "new, improved" tools to help

As consumers we hear constantly of new and improved tools to help us manage our information—new services, new utilities, new releases of existing applications or operating systems, new, smaller, more powerful, more feature-rich laptops, PDAs, or other gadgets. Tools can make a big difference. Tools can also be exciting and fun to try out. Tools can help us to meet our PIM challenges, but tools certainly won't eliminate these challenges.

And, no matter how cool the tools, we're likely to have too much to do and too little time to do it in. There are basic reasons why this is so. First, even when our tools really do save us time on our current projects, we invent or are assigned new projects. We may do so on our own. In working environments where we are directly, or indirectly, in competition with our colleagues (e.g., for a fixed number of better positions, or a fixed amount of recognition in the form of awards and pay raises), we take on new projects because if we don't, our rivals will (using the same new tools).

In a larger context, our collective efforts may sometimes result in a profoundly positive-sum game,[7] but the game we play in our daily lives is often zero-sum. Some of us will get promotions and raises; others will not. Moreover, some of us may liken our promotions to the levels in a video game—success means we get to keep playing albeit at a faster, more frenetic pace.

We need to make our own choices. The choice may be to opt out of competition for a prized promotion, or we may choose to be more selective about the projects we take on so that we're able to complete a smaller number but with more visibility and impact. A larger point is that we cannot assume that our tools will save us from ourselves or from naturally competitive work environments.

15.2.3 Prevailing winds

In keeping with a nautical theme, we might also talk about "prevailing winds" to be reckoned with as we steer toward a more distant PIM future. Chapters 12 and 13 described the PDA and the Web, respectively, as powerful points of convergence for our personal information. Desktop computing, as we still know it today, is certain to be transformed in significant ways. Will most of us even be using a desktop computer, or notebook computer for that matter, in a few years (from this book's first printing in 2007)?

Whether or not desktop and notebook computers still have a role to play in our lives, we can expect that the Web and the PDA will continue to transform our lives. Some transformations are already evident. Others may take us by surprise. Chapters 12 and 13 list a number of the activities—ranging from shopping to dating to playing poker—that we can now do online anywhere, as enabled by a connection from us to the Web via our gadgets.

Even the portability of notebook computers has transformed working habits for many people who may now feel comfortable spending an hour or two at a coffee shop or even a baseball

---

[7] See Wright (2000) for more on the "non-zero" nature of life and human activity.

game while they continue to work on their laptops. Some speak of a nomadic style of computing where conventional offices are replaced with meeting spaces into which people come and go. A person may work in several different spaces throughout the course of a workday.

15.2.4 The abyss?

What happens if the lights go out? In December 2006, residents of Seattle experienced a severe windstorm that knocked out the city's power. Nearly everyone was without power for a few days; some were without power for over two weeks. Nothing worked. Traffic lights didn't work, which created enormous traffic jams that stretched on for miles. Gas stations couldn't pump gas. Grocery stores couldn't sell food—not just because coolers didn't work but because electronic cash registers didn't work either.

The experience made an important and unsettling point concerning our uses of digital information and technologies: without power for an extended period of time, our computers, PDAs, cell phones, digital cameras, and various devices of digital storage are as useless as a stack of old eight-track tapes (with no eight-track player).

What to do? Make paper (high-quality acid-free paper) backups of your most treasured information items. Seriously. Obviously, if our lights and our electricity should go out for any extended period of time, then we, our society, our civilization, will have many more immediate problems to deal with than the preservation of information. At that point we keep selected information—documents showing title to our houses, treasured photographs, birth certificates, and the like—as a legacy. We keep these in non-digital form, not just or even necessarily for ourselves, but for those that survive us. A research challenge is to develop higher-density alternatives to paper that are even longer lasting and also share with paper a lack of dependence on electricity for preservation.

Life has a practice of living you, if you don't live it.

English poet, author, and librarian Philip Larkin (1922–1985)

15.3 In the future

Who knows what the future—especially a more distant future 10, 20, or 30 years from now—will bring? With reference to enduring challenges and problems of PIM, the "To the future" section charts a direction to pursue even in the face of this uncertainty. But how do we keep this direction both in the study of PIM as a research area and in our individual practices of PIM? In posing this question, the future is no longer a direction or a distant point on the horizon. The future is right in front of us. This future as our "next now" is explored in the following three subsections:

- *A journey for another day* gives brief mention of several important PIM-related topics that are in special need of greater attention from the research community.

- *Considerations in the practice of PIM* discusses the four resources, six senses of personal information, and seven activities of PIM that should be considered before deciding what and how to improve a practice of PIM.

- *Uncharted waters in the study of PIM* lists some of the major issues facing researchers in the study of PIM.

15.3.1 A journey for another day

Some important PIM-related topics have been discussed only briefly here, both for lack of space in a book already grown large and, in some cases, because there simply isn't enough data yet to report. These topics include:

- *Individual and group differences in PIM.* A point illustrated throughout this book is that each practice of PIM is unique. People also differ in their approach to PIM and their needs for PIM by age group (e.g., teens vs. college students vs. elderly people) and special circumstance (e.g., patients fighting a life-threatening illness such as cancer).[8]

- *Teaching and learning PIM.* In a world where success, at school, at work, and in all aspects of life, depends critically on an ability to manage information effectively, is it time to think of teaching PIM as a basic skill (in much the same way we talk about teaching the "three R's" of reading, writing and arithmetic)? To do so means taking a closer look at practical considerations and techniques of PIM such as those provided in the "What Now for You and Me?" sidebars in Chapters 4 through 9 of this book.

- How do considerations of PIM vary for *different forms of information* such as paper documents, email messages, digital music, photographs, and videos? Emphasis in this book has been mostly on essential commonalities shared by information items regardless of their forms. But certainly form matters too. Paper printouts, for example, can be easily taken where we go, marked up, and then discarded when "used up" (with the assurance that the digital original remains). Email messages carry an expectation of response. Digital photographs and videos representing events in our lives are irreplaceable. Developments in tools and technologies continue to create what are effectively new forms of information. Beyond digital photographs, digital music, and digital videos and films, there may be, some day soon, information forms supporting a complete, three-dimensional, sight, sound, smell, and touch sensory immersion in some alternate reality.[9] How should our practices of PIM change to take advantages of form-specific features? When, for example, is it better to hand someone a paper printout of a report rather than send the same report via email? And what can we do now in anticipation of the new forms that are "coming soon"?

- *PIM in the larger world.* The study of PIM cannot succeed by considering a person in isolation from the various groups in which that person works and lives. How do individual practices of PIM relate to a group's efforts to manage information—sometimes referred to as GIM (group information management)? Transitions from PIM to GIM must be addressed in several

---

[8] Gwizdka and Chignell (2007) provide a useful overview of individual differences in practices of PIM. Both Moen (2007) and Pratt et al. (2006) explore the special PIM needs of people who are trying to manage various goals and roles in their lives even as they assume the new role of "patient" (battling cancer or some other illness requiring long-term treatment).

[9] In some sci-fi visions of the future, even we become forms of information to be disassembled at the departure gate, teleported at light speed to some remote planet, and then reassembled at the arrival gate.

situations, including (1) the informal division of information management responsibilities in a household (Who manages the investments? The bills? Medical information for the children?); (2) the exchange and structuring of information that happens among members of a team working to finish a project; and (3) companywide efforts to determine a set of rules, tools, structures, policies, and procedures that might make best use of company information. The "What Now for IT Departments?" sidebars in this book address some of the issues that emerge at the junctures between PIM and GIM for this third case.[10]

- *Privacy and security.* Of special concern in relation to PIM in a larger world are issues of privacy and security. The ease and cheapness with which personal information can be recorded, saved, and transmitted in digital form creates new problems of privacy protection that did not exist, or were much less severe, when information was kept in paper form only.[11] Better privacy protection also depends on user interfaces that more clearly communicate to people the implications of their privacy preferences and of the privacy policies advertised by organizations with which they interact.[12]

15.3.2 Considerations in the practice of PIM

We improve our practices of PIM by considering elements of our practice—current and possible. Elements include schemes of organization (whether based on tags, properties, folders, or a combination of these), supporting tools, and strategies. For any element under consideration we can ask the same basic questions with respect to four important resources, six senses of personal information, and seven activities of PIM.

Suppose, for example, we're thinking about trying out a new web-based tool available for free download. What demands does this tool make on our four important resources: *money, energy, attention,* and *time*? A tool "for free" may not be free at all if using it means that we're continually distracted by advertisements. Does the tool help manage any of these resources better? Financial planning tools help us manage our money. Filtering tools may help us manage our attention. Calendar tools may help us manage and track our time better. Someday soon we may even see tools that track our energy levels throughout the day so that we can schedule our time and tasks accordingly.

Our next step might be to examine how the tool impacts our use and management of personal information in each of its six senses:

1. *Information controlled and/or owned by us.* Examples include email messages in our email accounts and files on our computer's hard drive.

2. *Information about us that others may have or may want.* Examples include credit or medical history, web-browsing patterns, and records of library books checked out.

3. *Information directed toward us.* Examples include phone calls, drop-ins, TV ads, web ads, and pop-ups.

---

[10] For a discussion of the relationship between PIM and GIM, see Lutters, Ackerman, and Zhou (2007).

[11] See Shamos (2007).

[12] See Karat, Brodie, and Karat (2007).

4. *Information that we send out (post, provide)*. Examples include the information we send in an email, post to a blog or a personal web site, or publish in a report or an article.

5. *Information already experienced by us*. Examples include web pages that remain on the Web, books that remain in a library, and TV and radio programs that remain somewhere in "broadcast ether."

6. *Information potentially relevant (useful) to us*. This sixth sense of personal information includes information "out there" that we would like to see. This sense of personal information also includes information that we do *not* want ourselves (or our family) to see, such as offensive material on the Web.

How does the tool impact each of the seven kinds of PIM activity?

1. *Keeping*. Does the tool (strategy, organizational scheme) help with the initial decision to assess usefulness? Does it support the tagging or filing of an item to reflect the time, place, and form of anticipated use later on?

2. *Finding*. Does the tool (strategy, organizational scheme) help me to remember to look for the item later? Does it make use of what I'm able to recall to help me narrow the scope of my search or support my recognition of an item? Does the tool support the repetition of finding, as needed, to accumulate a complete set of items to meet the current need?

3. *Organizing*. Does the tool (strategy, organizational scheme) consolidate or leverage existing organizations or support the reuse of organizational structures? Will it support the use of organizing templates?

4. *Maintaining*. Does the tool (strategy, organizational scheme) make it easy to move or archive items no longer in active use while making backups easy and automatic? Does it preserve the ability to use (view, edit) an item over time, even as formats migrate?

5. *Managing flow*. Does the tool (strategy, organizational scheme) provide controls for incoming and outgoing information?

6. *Measuring and evaluating*. Does the tool (strategy, organizational scheme) collect useful measures concerning my use of information or elements (tools, schemes of organization, strategies) of my PIM practice?

7. *Making sense*. Does the tool (strategy, organizational scheme) help me to arrange my information in new ways that make useful, new patterns and relationships more apparent?

15.3.3 Uncharted waters in the study of PIM

Even in what we might call the "home waters" of PIM, as a field of study, large regions remain unexplored. Only three of these are listed here.

Methodologies of PIM

The development of methodologies especially suited to PIM is still in its infancy. There is a need for methodologies both in *descriptive* studies—aimed at better understanding how people currently practice personal information management—and in *prescriptive* evaluations—to better understand the efficacy of proposed PIM solutions (usually involving a tool but sometimes focused, instead, on a technique or strategy). The descriptive and the prescriptive can form a complementary and iterative relationship to each other:

1. Descriptive data from fieldwork observations, interviews, and broader-based surveys can suggest directions for exploratory prototyping of supporting tools (and supporting techniques as well).

2. Prototypes are built and evaluated to reach more definite, prescriptive conclusions concerning support that *should* be provided. The development and evaluation of prototypes can frequently suggest specific areas of focus for the next round of fieldwork.

One approach to the descriptive study of PIM is to create ethnographies in which a person and his or her practice of information management are the subject of an exploratory, longitudinal case study.[13] The results of case studies may be very enlightening but do not, by themselves, form a proper basis for generalization. However, these studies can help to identify the focus of a more targeted, single-session study or survey.

One simple expedient can link the descriptive to the prescriptive both in research and in our own personal efforts to improve our practices of PIM: we can look at what people (including ourselves) are taking the trouble to do today, without or in spite of current tool support. How can tools better support these activities? Also, we can look at the creative solutions people have devised and ask, Can these work for the rest of us?

In the study of PIM as a discipline and, certainly, in our own study of other people for ideas that might apply to our PIM practices, we are not necessarily focused on a "representative sample" of people (whatever that might be). We are not just interested in the typical or ordinary person. We're also interested in unusual or even extraordinary people. We're interested in people who may be ahead of the curve in their practices of PIM.

Planning

Not much is formally known concerning how people go about managing projects in their lives. Understanding project planning also has relevance to a number of established disciplines, including cognitive psychology, HCI, information science, and the study of human information behavior. But the study of how people manage a project is not yet well developed in any of these disciplines. Mumford, Shultz, and Van Doorn (2001) note that the study of planning has proceeded in "fits and starts" over the past 50 years and remains underdeveloped.

Of special relevance to the study of PIM is the possibility that better support of planning might also, as a by-product, lead to better organization of the information needed to complete a project. But how can such synergy happen and under what circumstances? There are many examples

---

[13] Design methodologies that commonly share an emphasis on context and situation include *contextual inquiry* (Beyer & Holtzblatt, 1998), *situated activity* (Suchman, 1983), and *situated design* (Greenbaum & Kyng, 1991). These and other methodologies emerged from a participatory design movement that originated in Scandinavia (see Schuler & Namioka, 1993).

where well-intentioned tools to help people plan and structure their information have proven much more of a burden than a benefit.[14] Is there a way to support planning that doesn't get in our way?

Developing a sense of digital space

Spatial metaphors have been used throughout the book to facilitate our exploration of PIM. We each have a *personal space of information.* We may prefer to use one or another form of *wayfinding* (e.g., location-based search, browsing, orienteering) to find and re-find information. This book itself has taken us on a journey now nearing its end. We can hardly avoid the use of spatial metaphors. Our language—any human language—is filled with prepositions that are spatial in their original meanings. We're *under* a tight deadline or *on top* of things, or maybe this is all *beside* the point.

What does it mean to have a digital sense of space? Chapter 4 described the importance that relative position at times has for the items on a menu or in a results list. Well-intentioned efforts to boost more likely choices to the top can sometimes be disorienting.

But Chapter 4 also noted other situations in which space and spatial location are irrelevant. We're happy to select the first item suggested by an auto-complete mechanism. If the item we repeatedly select remains in a lower position, then we're correct in saying that the auto-complete is "stupid"— stupid in the sense that it is unable to learn from our persistently expressed preference—in the way that we would expect any person with average intelligence to learn.

As our computers continue to improve in the speed and sophistication of their graphics and animation, we can well imagine a time sometime soon when we may move in a virtual world of information in ways that directly map to our movements through physical space. The idea to do this is not new[15]—and neither are the reasons not to. The challenge is to emulate the attributes of physical space selectively without inadvertently introducing the many limitations of physical space into our PSI.

Now I won't be back till later on,
if I do come back at all . . .

From Buffalo Springfield's "On the Way Home"
Lyrics by Neil Young (1945–)

15.4 On our way

Related to a sense of space is a sense of place. Where is home? Success in our practice of PIM means being "at home" with our information. But in a larger sense, our information can reflect and sometimes also facilitate our conceptions of what home is or ought to be.

---

[14] See, for example, Shipman and Marshall (1999).

[15] See, for example, Negroponte (1979).

Sometimes the role of information in our sense of home is direct and obvious. We look at an architect's drawings of our dream house and we see ourselves reading a good book by the fireplace in the living room or entertaining guests around a kitchen countertop as we prepare dinner.

But in most cases the reflection of home is indirect. Are we mostly where we want to be in life? If so, then our information should reflect and facilitate our efforts to keep this enviable state of affairs. We should have investment plans, insurance policies, and a calendar of events— business and social—to look at and work with to help us keep what we have attained.

For many of us, we are not yet where we want to be in life. Or we have arrived in some respects but not in others. Perhaps we have a great job but now we need to find ways of working less so that we can have a great family life as well. Or perhaps we're not at home in our current neighborhood or with our current set of friends. If we're serious about making improvements, and purposeful in our activities, then this too is surely reflected in and facilitated by our information. For example, we might have brochures or a web history list that relates to our explorations of alternate neighborhoods. Or our calendar might reference meetings we have scheduled at which we plan to delegate some of our work responsibilities.

"There's no place like home," Dorothy said in the *Wizard of Oz* as she clicked her heels to return to Kansas. But the discussion above makes home more of a destination than a point of return. And for Dorothy too, in a later book by L. Frank Baum, Oz became a new home to which she moved herself and her family. Indeed, popular conceptions of home, reflected in movies, songs, and Norman Rockwell images, are idealized, even dreamlike—more a place to be realized than a certain reality to which we can return.

"You can never go home again" is another oft-repeated phrase. And many of us wouldn't want to if "home" meant returning to our starting point in life. Even so, the places and experiences of our past have defined and shaped us. A look at old family photographs or a high school year-book may be bittersweet—a source of pleasure and pain. The memories these pictures evoke can also be therapeutic. As any therapist might say, knowing where we came from can help us in our lives today and in our efforts to get where we want to be in life.

Our conceptions of home, then, as reflected in and reinforced by our information, might best be thought of as a mix of where we've been, where we are now, and where we want to be—our hopes and dreams for the future.

Consider one last cliché: "Home is where the heart is." One interpretation of this saying is that we're at home if we're with the people or in the place we love most. Another interpretation is that we're at home when we're living our daily lives according to the values and principles we hold most dear. What can information possibly have to do with this sense of home? I'm reminded of the email message I used to send myself at the end of every day to be read at the beginning of the next day. The message contained a list of things I wished to be, not do, in my life. Be kinder, less judgmental, and more tolerant. I think it's time to start sending that message again.

References

Abrams, D., Baecker, R., & Chignell, M. (1998, April). Information archiving with bookmarks: Personal web space construction and organization. Paper presented at the ACM SIGCHI Conference on Human Factors in Computing Systems, *CHI 1998* (pp. 41–48), Los Angeles.

Ackerman, M. S. (2000, April). Developing for privacy: Civility frameworks and technical design. Paper presented at the Conference on Computers, Freedom, and Privacy (pp. 19–23), Toronto, ONT, Canada.

Ackerman, M. S., Cranor, L. F., & Reagle, J. (1999, November 3–5). Privacy in e-commerce: Examining user scenarios and privacy preferences. Paper presented at the 1st ACM Conference on Electronic Commerce (pp. 1–8), Denver, CO.

Adar, E., Karger, D., & Stein, L. A. (1999, November 2–6). Haystack: Per-user information environment. Paper presented at the 8th Conference on Information and Knowledge Management, *CIKM 1999*, Kansas City, MO.

Aftab, O., Cheung, P., Kim, A., Thakkar, S., & Yeddanapudi, N. (2001). *Information Theory and the Digital Age* (No. 6.933). Cambridge, MA: Massachusetts Institute of Technology.

Allen, D. (2001). *Getting Things Done: The Art of Stress-Free Productivity*. New York: Penguin.

Anderson, J. R. (1976). *Language, Memory, and Thought*. Hillsdale, NJ: Erlbaum.

Arms, C. (2000). Keeping memory alive: Practices for preserving digital content at the National Digital Library Program of the Library of Congress. *RLG DigiNews, 4*(3).

Bälter, O. (1997). Strategies for organising email. In H. Thimbleby, B. O'Conaill & P. J. Thomas (Eds.), *Proceedings of the 12th Conference of the British Computer Society Human Computer Interaction Specialist Group—People and Computers XII, Vol. 12* (pp. 21–38), Bristol, UK: Springer.

——. (2000, April). Keystroke level analysis of email message organization. Paper presented at the ACM SIGCHI Conference on Human Factors in Computing Systems, *CHI 2000* (pp. 105–112), The Hague, The Netherlands.

Bälter, O., & Sidner, C. L. (2002, October 19–23). Bifrost inbox organizer: Giving users control over the inbox. Paper presented at the 2nd Nordic Conference on Human–Computer Interaction (pp. 111–118), Aarhus, Denmark.

Bao, X., Herlocker, J. L., & Dietterich, T. G. (2006). Fewer clicks and less frustration: Reducing the cost of reaching the right folder. In *Proceedings of the 11th International Conference on Intelligent User Interfaces* (pp. 178–185), Sydney, Australia (ACM Press).

Note: All the names of the authors in this list do not appear in the index.

Barreau, D. K. (1995). Context as a factor in personal information management systems. *Journal of the American Society for Information Science, 46*(5), 327–339.

Barreau, D. K., & Nardi, B. (1995). Finding and reminding: File organization from the desktop. *SIGCHI Bulletin, 27*(3), 39–43.

Barrett, L. F., & Barrett, D. J. (2001). An introduction to computerized experience sampling in psychology. *Social Science Computer Review, 19*(2), 175–185.

Barsalou, L. W. (1983). Ad hoc categories. *Memory & Cognition, 11*(3), 211–227.

——. (1991). Deriving categories to achieve goals. In G. H. Bower (Ed.), *The Psychology of Learning and Motivation: Advances in Research and Theory* (Vol. 27). New York: Academic Press.

Bates, M. J. (1988). How to use controlled vocabularies more effectively in online searching. *Online, 12*(6), 45–56.

——. (1989). The design of browsing and berrypicking techniques for the online search interface. *Online, 13*(5), 407–424.

——. (2002). Speculations on browsing, directed searching, and linking in relation to the Bradford distribution. In H. Bruce, R. Fidel, P. Ingwersen & P. Vakkari (Eds.), *Emerging Frameworks and Methods: Proceedings of the Fourth International Conference on Conceptions of Library and Information Science, CoLIS 4* (pp. 137–150), Seattle. Greenwood Village, CO: Libraries Unlimited.

Belkin, N. J. (1993). Interaction with texts: Information retrieval as information-seeking behaviour. Paper presented at the Information Retrieval 1993: von der Modellierung zur Anwendung (First Conference of the Gesellschaft fur Informatik Fachgruppe Information Retrieval) (pp. 55–66), Konstanz, Germany.

Belkin, N. J., & Croft, W. B. (1992). Information filtering and information retrieval: Two sides of the same coin? *Communications of the ACM, 35*(12), 29–38.

Belkin, N. J., Oddy, R. N., & Brooks, H. M. (1982). ASK for information retrieval: Parts 1 & 2. *Journal of Documentation, 38*(2/3), 61–71, 145–164.

Belkin, N. J., Seeger, T., & Wersig, G. (1983). Distributed expert problem treatment as a model for information system analysis and design. *Journal of Information Science, 5*(5), 153–167.

Bellotti, V., Dalal, B., Good, N., Flynn, P., Bobrow, D. G., & Ducheneaut, N. (2004, April 24–29). What a to-do: Studies of task management towards the design of a personal task list manager. Paper presented at the Conference on Human Factors in Computing Systems, *CHI 2004* (pp. 735–742), Vienna, Austria.

Bellotti, V., Ducheneaut, N., Howard, M., & Smith, I. (2003). Taking email to task: The design and evaluation of a task management centered email tool. Paper presented at the ACM SIGCHI Conference on Human Factors in Computing Systems, *CHI 2003* (pp. 345–352), Fort Lauderdale, FL.

Bellotti, V., Ducheneaut, N., Howard, M., Neuwirth, C., & Smith, I. (2002, June 25–28). Innovation in extremis: Evolving an application for the critical work of email and information management. Paper presented at the Conference on Designing Interactive Systems, *DIS2002* (pp. 181–192), London.

Bellotti, V., Ducheneaut, N., Howard, M., Smith, I., & Grinter, R. (2005). Quality vs. quantity: Email-centric task-management and its relation with overload. *Human–Computer Interaction, 20*(1–2), 89–138.

Bellotti, V., & Sellen, A. (1993, September 13–17). Design for privacy in ubiquitous computing environments. Paper presented at the 3rd European Conference on Computer Supported Cooperative Work, *ECSCW'93* (pp. 77–92), Milan, Italy.

Bensaude-Vincent, B. (2001). Graphic representations of the periodic system of chemical elements. In U. Klein (Ed.), *Tools and Modes of Representation in the Laboratory Sciences.* Dordrecht, Germany: Kluwer Academic.

Bergman, O., Beyth-Marom, R., and Nachmias, R. (2003). The user-subjective approach to personal information management systems. *Journal of the American Society for Information Science and Technology, 54*(9), 872–878.

Berlin, L. M., Jeffries, R., O'Day, V. L., Paepcke, A., & Wharton, C. (1993, April 24–29). Where did you put it? Issues in the design and use of group memory. Paper presented at the Conference on Human Factors and Computing Systems, *INTERACT 1993* and *CHI 1993* (pp. 23–30), Amsterdam, The Netherlands.

Berndt, E., & Morrison, J. (1981). Capacity utilization measures: Underlying economic theory and an alternative approach. *American Economic Review, 71*(2), 48–52.

Berners-Lee, T. (1998). Semantic Web roadmap: An attempt to give a high-level plan of the architecture of the Semantic Web—*www.w3.org/DesignIssues/Semantic.html.*

Beyer, H., & Holtzblatt, K. (1998). *Contextual Design: Defining Customer-Centered Systems.* San Francisco: Morgan Kaufmann.

Bianco, A. (2004, July 12). The vanishing mass market. *BusinessWeek.*

Blair, A. (1961 [January 2003]). Reading strategies for coping with information overload ca.1550–1700. *Journal of the History of Ideas, 64*(1), 11–28 (University of Pennsylvannia Press).

Blair, D. C., & Maron, M. E. (1985). An evaluation of retrieval effectiveness for a full-text document-retrieval system. *Communications of the ACM, 28*(3), 289–299.

Bliss, H. E. (1933). *The Organization of Knowledge in Libraries.* New York: H. W. Wilson.

Boardman, R. (2004). *Improving Tool Support for Personal Information Management.* London: Imperial College.

Boardman, R., & Sasse, M. A. (2004). "Stuff goes into the computer and doesn't come out": A cross-tool study of personal information management. Paper presented at the ACM SIGCHI Conference on Human Factors in Computing Systems, *CHI 2004* (pp. 583–590), Vienna, Austria.

Bondarenko, O., & Janssen, R. (2005, April). Documents at hand: Learning from paper to improve digital technologies. Paper presented at the ACM SIGCHI Conference on Human Factors in Computing Systems, *CHI 2005* (pp. 121–130), Portland, OR.

Bower, G. H., Clark, M. C., Lesgold, A. M., & Winzenz, D. (1969). Hierarchical retrieval schemes in recall of categorized word lists. *Journal of Verbal Learning and Verbal Behavior, 8*, 323–343.

Braman, S. (1989). Defining Information: An Approach for Policymakers. *Telecommunications Policy, 13*, 233–242.

Breese, J. S., Heckermen, D., & Kadie, C. M. (1998). *Empirical Analysis of Predictive Algorithms for Collaborative Filtering*, No. MSR-TR-98–12, Microsoft Research.

Briet, S. (1951). *Qu'est-ce que la Documentation.* Paris: EDIT.

Broadbent, D. E. (1958). *Perception and Communication*. London: Pergamon Press.

Brooke, J. (1998). Science and religion: Lessons from history? *Science, 282*(5396), 1985–1986.

Bruce, H. (2005). Personal, anticipated information need. *Information Research, 10*(3).

Bruce, H., Jones, W., & Dumais, S. (2004). Information behavior that keeps found things found. *Information Research, 10*(1).

Brush, A.J.B., Bargeron, D., Gupta, A., & Cadiz, J. J. (2001). Robust annotation positioning in digital documents. In *Proceedings of the SIGCHI Conference on Human Factors in Computing Systems* (pp. 285–292), Seattle (ACM Press).

Buckland, M. K. (1991). Information as thing. *Journal of the American Society for Information Science, 42*(5), 351–360.

——. (1997). What is a "document"? *Journal of the American Society of Information Science, 48*(9), 804–809.

Budzik, J., Hammond, K., & Birnbaum, L. (2001). Information access in context. *Knowledge Based Systems, 14*(1–2), 37–53.

Bush, V. (1945, July). As we may think. *The Atlantic Monthly, 176,* 641–649.

Buzan, T., & Buzan, B. (2004). *The Mind Map Book: How to Use Radiant Thinking to Maximize Your Brain's Untapped Potential*. London: BBC.

Capra, R., & Pérez-Quiñones, M. A. (2005). Using Web search engines to find and refind information. *IEEE Computer, 38*(10), 36–42.

Capurro, R., & Hjørland, B. (2003). The concept of information. In B. Cronin (Ed.), *Annual Review of Information Science and Technology (ARIST)*, *37*, 343–411.

Card, S. K., Moran, T. P., & Newell, A. (1983). *The Psychology of Human–Computer Interaction*. Hillsdale, NJ: Erlbaum.

Carmody, S., Gross, W., Nelson, T., Rice, D., & Van Dam, A. (1969). A hypertext editing system for the /360. In M. Faiman & J. Nievergelt (Eds.), *Pertinent Concepts in Computer Graphics* (pp. 291–330). Urbana, IL: University of Illinois Press.

Carstensen, P. H., & Nielsen, M. (2001, September 30–October 3). Characterizing modes of coordination: A comparison between oral and artifact based coordination. In *Proceedings of the 2001 International ACM SIGGROUP Conference on Supporting Group Work* (pp. 81–90), Boulder, CO.

Chowdhury, A., Frieder, O., Grossman, D., & McCabe, M. C. (2002). Collection statistics for fast duplicate document detection. *ACM Transactions on Information Systems*, *20*(2), 171–191.

Churchill, E. F., Trevor, J., Bly, S., Nelson, L., & Cubranic, D. (2000). Anchored conversations: Chatting in the context of a document. In *Proceedings of the SIGCHI Conference on Human Factors in Computing Systems* (pp. 454–461), The Hague, The Netherlands (ACM Press).

Claborne, G., & Jones, W. (2005). Linnaeus, Mendeleev, Dewey and Ranganathan: What can they tell us today about the organization of information? Technical Report No. IS-TR-2005-11-01. Seattle: University of Washington.

Cockburn, A., & McKenzie, B. (2000, September 5–8). An evaluation of cone trees. In *People and Computers XV, Proceedings of the 2000 British Computer Society Conference on Human–Computer Interaction* (pp. 425–436), University of Sunderland (Springer-Verlag).

Cole, I. (1982). Human aspects of office filing: Implications for the electronic office. Paper presented at the Human Factors Society 26th Annual Meeting, Seattle.

Combs, B., & Slovic, P. (1979). Newspaper coverage of causes of death. *Journalism Quarterly, 56*(4), 837–843.

Computer Research Association Conference on Grand Research Challenges in Information Security and Assurance (2003, November 16–19), Warrenton, VA—*www.cra.org/Activities/grand.challenges/security/*.

Consolvo, S., Smith, I. E., Matthews, T., LaMarca, A., Tabert, J., & Powledge, P. (2005). Location disclosure to social relations: Why, when, & what people want to share. In *Proceedings of the SIGCHI Conference on Human Factors in Computing Systems* (pp. 81–90), Portland, OR (ACM Press).

Consolvo, S., & Walker, M. (2003). Using the experience sampling method to evaluate ubicomp applications. *IEEE Pervasive Computing Mobile and Ubiquitous Systems, 2*(2), 24–31.

Cooper, J. W., Coden, A. R., & Brown, E. W. (2002). Detecting similar documents using salient terms. In *Proceedings of the 11th International Conference on Information and Knowledge Management* (pp. 245–251), McLean, VA (ACM Press).

Cornelius, I. (2002). Theorizing information. *Annual Review of Information Science and Technology, 36*, 393–425.

Covey, S. R. (1989). *The Seven Habits of Highly Effective People*. New York: Simon and Schuster.

Cranor, L. F. (2002). *Web Privacy with P3P*. Cambridge, MA: O'Reilly.

——. (2005). Privacy policies and privacy preferences. In L. F. Cranor & S. Garfinkel (Eds.), *Security and Usability: Designing Secure Systems That People Can Use* (pp. 447–471). Sebastopol, CA: O'Reilly Media.

Craik, F.I.M., & Lockhart, R. S. (1972). Levels of processing: A framework for memory research. *Journal of Verbal Learning and Verbal Behavior, 11,* 671–684.

Csikszentmihalyi, M. (1991). *Flow: The Psychology of Optimal Experience*. New York: HarperCollins.

Cutrell, E., & Dumais, S. T. (2006). Exploring personal information. *Communications of the ACM, 49*(4), 50–51.

Cutrell, E., Dumais, S. T., & Teevan, J. (2006). Searching to eliminate personal information management. *Communications of the ACM, 49*(1), 58–64.

Cutrell, E., Robbins, D., Dumais, S., & Sarin, R. (2006). Fast, flexible filtering with phlat. In *Proceedings of the SIGCHI Conference on Human Factors in Computing Systems* (pp. 261–270). Montreal, QUE, Canada (ACM Press).

Czerwinski, M., Dumais, S., Robertson, G., Dziadosz, S., Tiernan, S., & van Dantzich, M. (1999). Visualizing implicit queries for information management and retrieval. In *Proceedings of the ACM SIGCHI Conference on Human Factors in Computing Systems* (pp. 560–567), Pittsburgh (ACM Press).

Czerwinski, M., Gage, D., Gemmel, J., Marshall, C. C., Pérez-Quiñones, M., Skeels, M. M., et al. (2006). Digital memories in an era of ubiquitous computing and abundant storage. *Communications of the ACM, Special Issue on Personal Information Management, 49*(1), 44–50.

Czerwinski, M., Horvitz, E., & Wilhite, S. (2004, April 24–29). A diary study of task switching and interruptions. Paper presented at the ACM SIGCHI Conference on Human Factors in Computing Systems, *CHI 2004* (pp. 175–182), Vienna, Austria.

Davies, G., & Thomson, D., Eds. (1988). *Memory in Context: Context in Memory.* Chichester, England: John Wiley & Sons.

Deerwester, S., Dumais, S., Landauer, T. K., Furnas, G. W., & Harshman, R. A. (1990). Indexing by latent semantic analysis. *Journal of the Society for Information Science, 41*(6), 391–407.

Dervin, B. (1992). From the mind's eye of the user: The sense-making qualitative-quantitative methodology. In J. Glazier & R. Powell (Eds.), *Qualitative Research in Information Management* (pp. 61–84). Englewood, CO: Libraries Unlimited.

Dervin, B., and Frenette, M. (2003). Sense-making methodology: Communicating communicatively with campaign audiences. In B. Dervin and L. Foreman-Wernet (Eds.), *Sense-Making Methodology Reader. Selected Writings of Brenda Dervin* (pp. 233–249). Cresskill, NJ: Hampton Press.

Dillon, A., & Vaughan, M. (1997). It's the journey and the destination: Shape and the emergent property of genre in evaluating digital documents. *New Review of Multimedia and Hypermedia, 3,* 91–106.

Dong, X., & Halevy, A. Y. (2005, January 4–7). A platform for personal information management and integration. Paper presented at the 2nd Biennial Conference on Innovative Data Systems Research (CIDR), Asilomar, CA.

Dourish, P., Edwards, W. K., LaMarca, A., & Salisbury, M. (1999, November 7–10). Using properties for uniform interaction in the Presto Document System. Paper presented at the 12th Annual ACM Symposium on User Interface Software and Technology, *UIST 1999* (pp. 55–64), Asheville, NC.

Dumais, S. T., Cutrell, E., Sarin, R., & Horvitz, R. (2004, July 25–29). Implicit queries (IQ) for contextualized search. In *Proceedings of the 27th Annual International ACM SIGIR Conference on Research and Development in Information Retrieval* (p. 594), Sheffield, UK (ACM Press).

Dumais, S., Cutrell, E., Cadiz, J., Jancke, G., Sarin, R., & Robbins, D. (2003, July). Stuff I've seen: A system for personal information retrieval and re-use. Paper presented at the 26th Annual International ACM SIGIR Conference on Research and Development in Information Retrieval, *SIGIR 2003* (pp. 72–79), Toronto, ONT, Canada.

Durso, F. T., & Gronlund, S. (1999). Situation awareness. In F. T. Durso, R. Nickerson, R. W. Schvaneveldt, S. T. Dumais, D. S. Lindsay, & M. T. H. Chi (Eds.), *The Handbook of Applied Cognition* (pp. 284–314). Chichester, England: John Wiley & Sons.

Eisenberg, M., Lowe, C. A., & Spitzer, K. L. (2004). *Information Literacy: Essential Skills for the Information Age* (2nd ed.). Westport, CT: Libraries Unlimited.

Engelbart, D. C. (1961). Special considerations of the individual as a user, generator and retriever of information. *American Documentation, 12*(2), 121–125.

——. (1963). A conceptual framework for the augmentation of man's intellect. In *Vistas in Information Handling*. London: VI Spartan Books.

Engelbart, D., & English, W. (1994 [video made in 1968]). A Research Center for Augmenting Human Intellect. Reprinted in *ACM SIGGRAPH Video Review, 106.*

Feldman, S. (2004). The high cost of not finding information. *KM World, 13*(3)—*http://www.kmworld.com/Articles/ReadArticle.aspx?ArticleID=9534.*

Fertig, S., Freeman, E., & Gelernter, D. (1996, April 13–18). Lifestreams: An alternative to the desktop metaphor. Paper presented at the ACM SIGCHI Conference on Human Factors in Computing Systems, *CHI 1996* (pp. 410–411), Vancouver, BC, Canada.

Fidel, R., Bruce, H., Pejtersen, A., Dumais, S., Grudin, J., & Poltrock, S. (2000). Collaborative information retrieval. In L. Höglund (Ed.), *The New Review of Information Behavior Research: Studies of Information Seeking in Context.* London: Taylor Graham.

Fidel, R., & Pejtersen, A. M. (2004). From information behaviour research to the design of information systems: The Cognitive Work Analysis framework. *Information Research, 10*(1).

Fiske, S. T., & Taylor, S. E. (1991). *Social Cognition* (2nd ed.). New York: McGraw-Hill.

Flanagan, J. C. (1954). The Critical Incident Technique. *Psychological Bulletin, 51*(4), 327–358.

Folk, C., & Gibson, B. (Eds.). (2001). *Attraction, Distraction and Action: Multiple Perspectives on Attentional Capture* (Vol. 133). Amsterdam: Elsevier Science BV.

Foltz, P. W., & Dumais, S. T. (1992). Personalized information delivery: An analysis of information filtering methods. *Communications of the ACM, 35*(12), 51–60.

Fonseca, F. T., & Martin, J. E. (2004). Toward an alternative notion of information systems ontologies: Information engineering as a hermeneutic enterprise. *Journal of the American Society for Information Science and Technology, 56*(1), 46–57.

Franconeri, S. L., Hollingworth, A., & Simons, D. J. (2005). Do new objects capture attention? *Psychological Science, 16*(4), 275–281.

Freeman, E., & Gelernter, D. (1996). Lifestreams: A storage model for personal data. *ACM SIGMOD Record (ACM Special Interest Group on Management of Data), 25*(1), 80–86.

Freitas, A. L., & Higgins, E. T. (2002). Enjoying goal-directed action: The role of regulatory fit. *Psychological Science, 13*(1), 1–6.

Friedman, B., Kahn, P. H., Jr., Hagman, J., Severson, R. L., & Gill, B. (2006). The watcher and the watched: Social judgments about privacy in a public place. *Human–Computer Interaction Journal, 21*(2), 235–272.

Furnas, G. W., Landauer, T. K., Gomez, L. M., & Dumais, S. T. (1987). The vocabulary problem in human–system communication. *Communications of the ACM 30*(11), 964–971.

Furnas, G. W., & Russell, D. M. (2005). Making sense of sensemaking. In *Extended Abstracts of CHI 2005, Conference on Human Factors in Computing Systems* (pp. 2115–2116), Portland, OR (ACM Press).

Garvin, D. (2000). *Learning in Action.* Boston: Harvard Business School Press.

Gemmell, J., Bell, G., & Lueder, R. (2006). MyLifeBits: A personal database for everything. *Communications of the ACM, 49*(1), 88–95.

Gemmell, J., Bell, G., Lueder, R., Drucker, S., & Wong, C. (2002). Mylifebits: Fulfilling the memex vision. Paper presented at the 2002 ACM Workshops on Multimedia (pp. 235–238), Juan-les-Pins, France.

Gemmell, J., Lueder, R., & Bell, G. (2003, November 7). The MyLifeBits lifetime store. Paper presented at the ACM SIGMM 2003 Workshop on Experiential Telepresence, *ETP 2003* (pp. 565–567), Berkeley, CA.

Gemmell, J., Williams, L., Wood, K., Bell, G., & Lueder, R. (Oct. 15, 2004). Passive capture and ensuing issues for a personal lifetime store. Paper presented at the 1st ACM Workshop on Continuous Archival and Retrieval of Personal Experiences, *CARPE 2004* (pp. 48–55), New York.

Gershon, N. (1995, December). Human information interaction. Paper presented at the 4th International World Wide Web Conference, Boston.

Gibson, J. J. (1977). The theory of affordances. In R. E. Shaw & J. Bransford (Eds.), *Perceiving, Acting, and Knowing: Toward an Ecological Psychology* (pp. 67–82). Hillsdale, NJ: Erlbaum.

——. (1979). *The Ecological Approach to Visual Perception.* Boston: Houghton Mifflin.

Golder, S., & Huberman, B. A. (2006). The structure of collaborative tagging systems. *Journal of Information Science 32*(2), 198–208.

Gonzalez, V. M., & Mark, G. (2004). Constant, constant, multitasking craziness: Managing multiple working spheres. Paper presented at the ACM SIGCHI Conference on Human Factors in Computing Systems, *CHI 2004* (pp. 113–120), Vienna, Austria.

Gordin, M. (2004). *A Well-Ordered Thing: Dmitrii Mendeleev and the Shadow of the Periodic Table.* New York: Basic Books.

Greenbaum, J. M., & Kyng, M. (1991). *Design at Work: Cooperative Design of Computer Systems.* Hillsdale, NJ: Erlbaum.

Grudin, J. (1988). Why CSCW applications fail: Problems in the design and evaluation of organizational interfaces. In *Proceedings of the 1988 ACM Conference on Computer-Supported Cooperative Work* (pp. 85–93), Portland, OR (ACM Press).

——. (1993). Interface: An evolving concept. *Communications of the ACM, 36*(4), 110–119.

——. (2001). Desituating action: Digital representation of context. *Human–Computer Interaction, 16*(2–4), 269–286.

Gwizdka, J. (2002a, April 20–25). Reinventing the inbox: Supporting the management of pending tasks in email. Paper presented at the ACM SIGCHI Conference on Human Factors in Computing Systems, Doctoral Consortium, *CHI 2002* (pp. 550–551), Minneapolis.

——. (2002b, September 30–October 3). TaskView: Design and evaluation of a task-based email interface. Paper presented at the Conference of the Centre for Advanced Studies on Collaborative Research, *CASCON 2002,* Toronto, ONT, Canada.

Gwizdka, J., & Chignell, M. (2007). Individual Differences. In W. Jones & J. Teevan (Eds.), *Personal Information Management.* Seattle: University of Washington Press.

Hackos, J., & Redish, J. (1998). *User and Task Analysis for Interface Design.* New York: John Wiley & Sons.

Hafner, K. (2004, November 10). Even digital memories can fade. *New York Times.*

Hawkins, J., & Blakeslee, S. (2006). *On Intelligence.* New York: Owl Books.

Henzinger, M. (2006). Finding near-duplicate web pages: A large-scale evaluation of algorithms. In *Proceedings of the 29th Annual International ACM SIGIR Conference on Research and Development in Information Retrieval* (pp. 284–291), Seattle (ACM Press).

Henzinger, M., Chang, B.-W., Milch, B., & Brin, S. (2003). Query-free news search. Paper presented at the 12th International World Wide Web Conference, Budapest, Hungary.

Herrmann, D., Brubaker, B., Yoder, C., Sheets, V., & Tio, A. (1999). Devices that remind. In F. T. Durso, R. Nickerson, R. W. Schvaneveldt, S. T. Dumais, D. S. Lindsay, & M. T. H. Chi (Eds.), *Handbook of Applied Cognition* (pp. 377–407). Chichester, England: John Wiley & Sons.

Holtzblatt, K., & Jones, S. (1993). Contextual Inquiry: Principles and Practice. In *Participatory Design: Principles and Practices*. New York: Erlbaum.

Horvitz, E., & Apacible, J. (2003). Learning and reasoning about interruption. In *Proceedings of the 5th International Conference on Multimodal Interfaces* (pp. 20–27), Vancouver, BC, Canada (ACM Press).

Horvitz, E., Apacible, J., & Koch, P. (2004, November). BusyBody: Creating and Fielding Personalized Models of the Cost of Interruption. Paper presented at the CSCW, Conference on Computer Supported Cooperative Work (pp. 507–510), Chicago.

Hunter, J., and Choudhury, S. (2003). A semi-automated digital preservation system based on semantic web services. In *Proceedings of JCDL '04* (pp. 269–278), Tucson, AZ (ACM Press).

Hutchins, E. (1994). *Cognition in the Wild*. Cambridge, MA: MIT Press.

Huynh, D., Karger, D., & Quan, D. (2002). Haystack: A platform for creating, organizing and visualizing information using RDF. Paper presented at the International Workshop for the Semantic Web, Honolulu.

Hyde, T. S., & Jenkins, J. J. (1969). Differential effects of incidental tasks on the organization of recall of a list of highly associated words. *Journal of Experimental Psychology, 82*, 472–481.

Jensen, C., & Potts, C. (2004, April 24–29). Privacy policies as decision-making tools: an evaluation of online privacy notices. In *Proceedings of the SIGCHI Conference on Human Factors in Computing Systems* (pp. 471–478), Vienna, Austria.

Jensen, C., Potts, C., & Jensen, C. (2005). Privacy practices of Internet users: Self-reports versus observed behavior. *International Journal of Human–Computer Studies, 63*(1–2), 203–227.

Johnson, S. B. (2005, January 30). Tool for thought. *New York Times*.

Jones, W. (1986). On the applied use of human memory models: The Memory Extender personal filing system. *International Journal of Man Machine Studies, 25(2)*, 191–228.

——. (2004). Finders, keepers? The present and future perfect in support of personal information management. *First Monday—http://www.firstmonday.dk/issues/issue9_3/jones/index.html*.

——. (2006). Personal information management. *Annual Review of Information Science and Technology (ARIST), 41*, 453–504.

Jones, W., & Anderson, J. R. (1987). Short- vs. long-term memory retrieval: A comparison of the effects of information load and relatedness. *Journal of Experimental Psychology: General, 116*, 137–153.

Jones, W., Bruce, H., & Dumais, S. (2001, November 5–10). Keeping founds things found on the Web. Paper presented at the 10th International Conference on Information and Knowledge Management, *CIKM 2001* (pp. 119–134), Atlanta.

——. (2003, September). How do people get back to information on the Web? How can they do it better? Paper presented at the 9th IFIP TC13 International Conference on Human–Computer Interaction, *INTERACT 2003* (pp. 793–796), Zurich.

Jones, W., Bruce, H., & Foxley, A. (2006). Project contexts to situate personal information. Paper presented at the 29th Annual International ACM SIGIR Conference on Research and Development in Information Retrieval, Seattle.

Jones, W., Bruce, H., Foxley, A., & Munat, C. (2006). Planning personal projects and organizing personal information. Paper presented at the 69th Annual Meeting of the American Society for Information Science and Technology, *ASIST 2006*, Vol. 43, Austin, TX.

Jones, W., & Dumais, S. (1986). The spatial metaphor for user interfaces—Experimental tests of reference by location versus name. *ACM Transactions on Office Information Systems, 4*(1), 42–63.

Jones, W., Dumais, S., & Bruce, H. (2002). Once found, what then?: A study of "keeping" behaviors in the personal use of Web information. In *Proceedings 65th Annual Meeting of the American Society for Information Science and Technology, ASIST 2002*, Vol. 39 (pp. 391–402), Philadelphia.

Jones, W., & Furnas, G. W. (1987). Pictures of relevance: A geometric approach to the analysis of similarity measures. *Journal of the American Society for Information Science, 38*(6), 420–442.

Jones, W., Munat, C., & Bruce, H. (2005). The Universal Labeler: Plan the project and let your information follow. In A. Grove (Ed.), *Proceedings 68th Annual Meeting of the American Society for Information Science and Technology, ASIST 2005*, Vol. 42, Charlotte, NC.

Jones, W., Phuwanartnurak, A. J., Gill, R., & Bruce, H. (2005, April 2–7). Don't take my folders away! Organizing personal information to get things done. Paper presented at the ACM SIGCHI Conference on Human Factors in Computing Systems, *CHI 2005* (pp. 1505–1508), Portland, OR.

Jones, W., & Ross, B. (2006). Human cognition and personal information management. In F. T. Durso, R. S. Nickerson, R. W. Schvaneveldt, S. T. Dumais, D. S. Lindsay, & M.T.H. Chi (Eds.), *Handbook of Applied Cognition*. New York: John Wiley & Sons.

Kahneman, D., & Tversky, A. (1979). Prospect Theory: An analysis of decision under risk. *Econometrica, XLVII,* 263–292.

Kaptelinin, V. (1996, April 11–13). Creating computer-based work environments: An empirical study of Macintosh users. Presented at the SIGCPR/SIGMIS 1996 Annual Meetings of the Association for Computing Machinery Special Interest Group on Computer Personnel Research/Special Interest Group on Management Information Systems (pp. 360–366), Denver, CO.

——. (2003, April). Integrating tools and tasks: UMEA—Translating interaction histories into project contexts. Paper presented at the ACM SIGCHI Conference on Human Factors in Computing Systems, *CHI 2003*, Ft. Lauderdale, FL.

Karat, C.-M., Brodie, C., & Karat, J. (2005). Usability design and evaluation for privacy and security solutions. In L. F. Cranor & S. Garfinkel (Eds.), *Security and Usability: Designing Secure Systems That People Can Use* (pp. 47–74). Sebastopol, CA: O'Reilly Media.

——. (2006). Usable privacy and security for personal information management. *Communications of the ACM, 49*(1), 56–57.

——. (2007). Management of personal information disclosure: The Interdependence of Privacy, Security and Trust. In W. Jones & J. Teevan (Eds.), *Personal Information Management.* Seattle: University of Washington Press.

Karat, J., Karat, C., Brodie, C., & Feng, J. (2005). Privacy in information technology: Designing to enable privacy policy management in organizations. *International Journal of Human Computer Studies, 63*(1), 153–174.

——. (2006, April 22–27). Evaluating interfaces for privacy policy rule authoring. In *Proceedings of the SIGCHI Conference on Human Factors in Computing Systems* (pp. 83–92), Montreal, QUE, Canada (ACM Press).

Karger, D. R. (2007). Unify everything: It's all the same to me. In W. Jones & J. Teevan (Eds.), *Personal Information Management.* Seattle: University of Washington Press.

Karger, D. R., Bakshi, K., Huynh, D., Quan, D., & Sinha, V. (2005, January 4–7*).* Haystack: A general-purpose information management tool for end users based on semistructured data. Paper presented at the Second Biennial Conference on Innovative Data Systems Research, *CIDR 2005*, Asilomar, CA.

Karger, D. R., & Quan, D. (2004). Collections: Flexible, essential tools for information management. In *Extended Abstracts of CHI 2004, Conference on Human factors in Computing Systems* (pp. 1159–1162), Vienna, Austria (ACM Press).

Kaye, J. J., Vertesi, J., Avery, S., Dafoe, A., David, S., Onaga, L., et al. (2006). To have and to hold: Exploring the personal archive. In *Proceedings of the SIGCHI Conference on Human Factors in Computing Systems* (pp. 275–284), Montreal, QUE (ACM Press).

Kelly, D., & Teevan, J. (2007). Understanding what works: Evaluating PIM Tools. In W. Jones & J. Teevan (Eds.), *Personal Information Management.* Seattle: University of Washington Press.

Kidd, A. (1994, April 24–28). The marks are on the knowledge worker. Paper presented at the ACM SIGCHI Conference on Human factors in Computing Systems, *CHI 1994* (pp. 186–191), Boston.

Kim, K.-S., & Allen, B. (2002). Cognitive and task influences on web searching behavior. *Journal of the American Society for Information Science and Technology, 53*(2), 109–119.

Kirsh, D. (2000). A few thoughts on cognitive overload. *Intellectica, 30*(1), 19–51.

Klein, G., Moon, B., & Hoffman, R. R. (2006). Making Sense of Sensemaking 1: Alternative Perspectives. *IEEE Intelligent Systems, 21*(4), 70–73.

Knickerbocker, B. (2002, September 11). A corner still not turned in America's story. *The Christian Science Monitor—http: //www.csmonitor.com/specials/oneyearlater/ livesChanged_corner.html.*

Koolstra, C. M., van Zanten, J., Lucassen, N., & Ishaak, N. (2004). The formal pace of Sesame Street over 26 years. *Perceptual and Motor Skills, 99*(1), 354–360.

Kraft, R., Chang, C. C., Maghoul, F., & Kumar, R. (2006). Searching with context. In *Proceedings of the 15th International Conference on World Wide Web* (pp. 477–486), Edinburgh, Scotland (ACM Press).

Kraft, R., Maghoul, F., & Chang, C. C. (2005). Y!Q: Contextual search at the point of inspiration. In *Proceedings of the 14th ACM International Conference on Information and Knowledge Management* (pp. 816–823). Bremen, Germany (ACM Press).

Kuny, T. (1998). The digital dark ages? Challenges in the preservation of electronic information. *International Preservation News*, 17.

Lang, A., Zhou, S., Shwartz, N., Bolls, P., & Potter, R. (2000, Winter). The effects of edits on arousal, attention, and memory for television messages: When an edit is an edit can an edit be too much? *Journal of Broadcasting & Electronic Media, 44*(1*),* 94–109.

Lansdale, M. (1988). The psychology of personal information management. *Applied Ergonomics, 19*(1), 55–66.

——. (1991). Remembering about documents: Memory for appearance, format, and location. *Ergonomics, 34*(8), 1161–1178.

Lansdale, M., & Edmonds, E. (1992). Using memory for events in the design of personal filing systems. *International Journal of Man–Machine Studies, 36*(1), 97–126.

Larkin, J. H., & Simon, H. A. (1987). Why a diagram is (sometimes) worth ten thousand words. *Cognitive Science, 11*(1), 65–99.

Lashley, K. S. (1950). In search of the engram. *Symposia of the Society for Experimental Biology, 4*, 454–482.

LeFurgy, W. G. (2003). PDF/A: Developing a file format for long-term preservation. *RLG DigiNews, 7*(6).

Levy, D. (2001). *Scrolling Forward: Making Sense of Documents in the Digital Age*. New York: Arcade Publishing.

Licklider, J.C.R. (1960). Man–computer symbiosis. *IRE Transactions on Human Factors in Electronics, HFE-1*, 4–11.

Lorie, R. (2002). A methodology and system for preserving digital data. In *Proceedings of JCDL '02* (pp. 312–319), Portland, OR (ACM Press).

Lucas, P. (2000, April 1–6). Pervasive information access and the rise of human–information interaction. In *Extended Abstracts of CHI 2000, Conference on Human Factors in Computing Systems* (p. 202), The Hague, The Netherlands (ACM Press).

Lutters, W. G., Ackerman, M. S., & Zhou, X. (2007). Group Information Management. In W. Jones & J. Teevan (Eds.), *Personal Information Management*. Seattle: University of Washington Press.

Lynch, K. (1960). *The Image of the City*. Cambridge, MA: MIT Press.

Machlup, F. (1983). Semantic Quirks in Studies of Information. In F. Machlup & U. Mansfield (Eds.), *The Study of Information: Interdisciplinary Messages* (pp. 641–671). New York: Wiley.

Mackay, W. E. (1988, September 26–28). More than just a communication system: Diversity in the use of electronic mail. Paper presented at the Conference on Computer-Supported Cooperative Work, *CCSW 1988* (pp. 344–353), Portland, OR.

MacLachlan, J., & Logan, M. (1993). Camera shot length in TV commercials and their memorability and persuasiveness. *Journal of Advertising Research 33*(2), 57–61.

Malin, B., & Sweeney, L. (2004). How (not) to protect genomic data privacy in a distributed network: Using trail re-identification to evaluate and design anonymity protection systems. *Journal of Biomedical Informatics, 37*(3), 179–192.

Malone, T. W. (1983). How do people organize their desks: Implications for the design of office information systems. *ACM Transactions on Office Information Systems, 1*(1), 99–112.

Maltz, D., & Ehrlich, K. Pointing the way: Active collaborative filtering. Paper presented at the SIGCHI Conference on Human Factors in Computing Systems, *CHI 1995*, Denver, CO.

Mander, R., Salomon, G., & Wong, Y. Y. (1992, May). A "pile" metaphor for supporting casual organization of information. Paper presented at the ACM SIGCHI Conference on Human Factors in Computing Systems, *CHI 1992* (pp. 627–634), Monterey, CA.

Manguel, A. (1996). *A History of Reading*. New York: Viking.

Marchionini, G. (1995). *Information Seeking in Electronic Environments*. Cambridge: Cambridge University Press.

Marchionini, G., & Komlodi, A. (1998). Design of interfaces for information seeking. *Annual Review of Information Science and Technology, 33*, 89–130.

Mark, G., Gonzalez, V. M., & Harris, J. (2005*)*. No task left behind? Examining the nature of fragmented work. Paper presented at the ACM SIGCHI Conference on Human Factors in Computing Systems, *CHI 2005* (pp. 321–330), Portland, OR.

Marlow, C., Naaman, M., Boyd, D., & Davis, M. (2006). HT06, tagging paper, taxonomy, Flickr, academic article, ToRead. In *Proceedings of the 17th Conference on Hypertext and Hypermedia* (pp. 31–40), Odense, Denmark (ACM Press).

Marshall, C. C. (2006). Reading and interactivity in the digital library: Creating an experience that transcends paper. In D. B. Marcum & G. George (Eds.), *Digital Library Development: The View from Kanazawa*. Westport, CT: Libraries Unlimited.

——. (2007). Maintaining personal information: Issues associated with long-term storage, preservation, and access. In W. Jones & J. Teevan (Eds.), *Personal Information Management*. Seattle: University of Washington Press.

Marshall, C. C., & Bly, S. (2005). Saving and using encountered information: Implications for electronic periodicals. In *Proceedings of the ACM SIGCHI Conference on Human Factors in Computing Systems* (pp. 111–120), Portland, OR (ACM Press).

Marshall, C. C., Bly, S., & Brun-Cottan, F. (2006). The long-term fate of our personal digital belongings: Toward a service model for personal archives. In *IS&T's Archiving 2006 Conference*, Ottawa, ONT, Canada (Society for Imaging Science and Technology).

Marshall, C. C., & Jones, W. (2006). Keeping encountered information. *Communications of the ACM, 49*(1): 66–67.

Mitchell, J., & Shneiderman, B. (1989). Dynamic versus static menus: An exploratory comparison. *ACM SIGCHI Bulletin, 20*(4), 33–37.

Moen, A. (2007). Personal health information management. In W. Jones & J. Teevan (Eds.), *Personal Information Management*. Seattle: University of Washington Press.

Morris, R. (2003). *The Last Sorcerers: The Path from Alchemy to the Periodic Table*. Washington, DC: Joseph Henry Press.

Morville, P. (2005). *Ambient Findability*. Sebastopol, CA: O'Reilly.

Mumford, M. D., Schultz, R. A., & Van Doorn, J. R. (2001). Performance in planning: Processes, requirements and errors. *Review of General Psychology, 5*(3), 213–240.

Murnane, K., Phelps, M., & Malmberg, K. (1999). Context-dependent recognition memory: The ICE theory. *Journal of Experimental Psychology: General, 128*(4), 403–415.

Murthy, S., Maier, D., Delcambre, L., & Bowers, S. (2004). Putting integrated information in context: Superimposing conceptual models with SPARCE. In *Proceedings of the First Asian-Pacific Conference on Conceptual modeling,* Vol. 31 (pp. 71–80), Dunedin, New Zealand (Australian Computer Society, Inc.).

Naumer, C. M., & Fisher, K. E. (2007). Naturalistic approaches for understanding PIM. In W. Jones & J. Teevan (Eds.), *Personal Information Management*. Seattle: University of Washington Press.

Negroponte, N. (1979). Books without pages. Paper presented at the International Conference on Communications IV, Boston.

Neisser, U. (1967). *Cognitive Psychology*. New York: Appleton-Century Crofts.

Nelson, T. H. (1965). File structure for the complex, the changing, and the indeterminate. In *Proceedings of the 1965 20th ACM/CSC-ER National Conference* (pp. 84–100), Cleveland, OH.

Newell, A., Shaw, J. C., & Simon, H. A. (1958). Elements of a theory of human problem solving. *Psychological Review, 65*, 151–166.

Norman, D. A. (1988). *The Psychology of Everyday Things*. New York: Basic Books.

——. (1990). *The Design of Everyday Things*. New York: Doubleday.

——. (1992). *Turn Signals Are the Facial Expressions of Automobiles*. Cambridge, MA: Perseus Publishing.

——. (1993). *Things that Make Us Smart: Defending Human Attributes in the Age of the Machine*. Reading, MA: Addison-Wesley.

O'Conaill, B., & Frohlich, D. (1995, April). Timespace in the workplace: Dealing with interruptions. In *Extended Abstracts of CHI 1995, Conference on Human Factors in Computing Systems* (pp. 262–263), Denver, CO (ACM Press).

O'Day, V., & Jeffries, R. (1993, April). Orienteering in an information landscape: How information seekers get from here to there. Paper presented at the ACM SIGCHI Conference on Human Factors in Computing Systems, *CHI 1993* (pp. 438–445), Amsterdam, The Netherlands.

Oddy, R. N. (1977). Information retrieval through man–machine dialogue. *Journal of Documentation, 33*(1), 1–14.

O'Dell, C., Jackson Grayson, C., & Essaides, N. (1998). *If Only We Knew What We Know: The Transfer of Internal Knowledge and Best Practice*. New York: Free Press.

Olson, J. S., Grudin, J., & Horvitz, E. (2005). A study of preferences for sharing and privacy. In *Extended Abstracts of CHI 2005, Conference on Human Factors in Computing Systems* (pp. 1985–1988), Portland, OR (ACM Press).

Otlet, P. (1934). *Traité de Documentation*. Brussels: Editiones Mundaneum.

Palen, L. (1999). Social, individual and technological issues for groupware calendar systems. In *Proceedings of the SIGCHI Conference on Human Factors in Computing Systems: The CHI Is the Limit* (pp. 17–24), Pittsburgh (ACM Press).

Peterson, W. W., Birdsall, T. G., & Fox, W. C. (1954). The theory of signal detectability. *Institute of Radio Engineers Transactions, PGIT-4*, 171–212.

Pirolli, P. (2006). Cognitive models of human–information interaction. In F. T. Durso, R. S. Nickerson, R. W. Schvaneveldt, S. T. Dumais, D. S. Lindsay, & M.T.H. Chi (Eds.), *Handbook of Applied Cognition* (2nd ed.). New York: John Wiley & Sons.

Pirolli, P., & Card, S. (1999). Information foraging. *Psychological Review, 106*(4), 643–675.

Pratt, W., Unruh, K., Civan, A., & Skeels, M. (2006). Personal health information management. *Communications of the ACM, 49*(1), 51–55.

Putnam, R. D. (1995). Bowling alone: America's declining social capital. *Journal of Democracy, 6*, 65–78.

Qu, Y., & Furnas, G. W. (2005). Sources of structure in sensemaking. In *Extended Abstracts of CHI 2005, Conference on Human Factors in Computing Systems* (pp. 1989–1992), Portland, OR (ACM Press).

Quan, D., Huynh, D., & Karger, D. R. (2003, October 20–23). Haystack: A platform for authoring end user Semantic Web applications. Paper presented at the 2nd International Semantic Web Conference, *ISWC 2003* (pp. 738–753), Sanibel Island, FL.

Quine, W. V. (1969). *Ontological Relativity and Other Essays*. New York: Columbia University Press.

Radicati Group, Inc. (2005). Taming the growth of email: An ROI Analysis. White paper—*http://www.radicati.com/uploaded_files/publications/brochure/HP_Whitepaper.pdf*.

Ratneshwar, S., Barsalou, L. W., Pechmann, C., & Moore, M. (2001). Goal-derived categories: The role of personal and situational goals in category representations. *Journal of Consumer Psychology, 10*(3), 147–157.

Ravasio, P., Schär, S. G., & Krueger, H. (2004). In pursuit of desktop evolution: User problems and practices with modern desktop systems. *ACM Transactions on Computer–Human Interaction, 11*(2), 156–180.

Ries, A., & Trout, J. (1986). *Positioning: The Battle for Your Mind*. New York: Warner Books.

Ringel, M., Cutrell, E., Dumais, S. T., & Horvitz, E. (2003). Milestones in time: The value of landmarks in retrieving information from personal stores. In M. Rauterberg et al. (Eds.), *Human–Computer Interaction, INTERACT '03* (pp. 184–191), IOS Press.

Rodden, K., & Wood, K. (2003). How do people manage their digital photographs? Paper presented at the SIGCHI ACM Conference on Human Factors in Computing Systems, *CHI 2003* (pp. 409–416), Ft. Lauderdale, FL.

Ross, B. H. (1999). Postclassification category use: The effects of learning to use categories after learning to classify. *Journal of Experimental Psychology: Learning, Memory, & Cognition, 25*(3), 743–757.

———. (2000). The effects of category use on learned categories. *Memory & Cognition, 28*(1), 51–63.

Ross, B. H., & Murphy, G. L. (1999). Food for thought: Cross-classification and category organization in a complex real-world domain. *Cognitive Psychology, 38*(4), 495–553.

Ross, S. E., and Lin, C.-T. (2003). The effects of promoting patient access to medical records: A review. *Journal of the American Medical Informatics Association, 10*(2), 129–138.

Rothenberg, J. (1999). *Avoiding Technological Quicksand: Finding a Viable Technical Foundation for Digital Preservation*. Washington, DC: Council on Library and Information Resources.

Rouse, W. B., & Rouse, S. H. (1984). Human information seeking and design of information systems. *Information Processing & Management, 20*, 129–138.

Rowley, J. (1994). The controlled versus natural indexing languages debate revisited. *Journal of Information Science, 20*(2), 108–119.

Rundus, D. (1971). Analysis of rehearsal processes in free recall. *Journal of Experimental Psychology, 89*, 63–77.

Russell, D. M., & Lawrence, S. (2007). Search everything. In W. Jones & J. Teevan (Eds.), *Personal Information Management*. Seattle: University of Washington Press.

Russell, D. M., Slaney, M., Qu, Y., & Houston, M. (2006). Being literate with large document collections: Observational studies and cost structure tradeoffs. Paper presented at the 39th Annual Hawaii International Conference on System Sciences, HICSS.

Russell, D. M., Stefik, M. J., Pirolli, P., & Card, S. K. (1993). The cost structure of sensemaking. In *Proceedings of the ACM SIGCHI Conference on Human Factors in Computing Systems* (pp. 269–276), Amsterdam, The Netherlands (ACM Press).

Salton, G., & Buckley, C. (1990). Improving retrieval performance by relevance feedback. *Journal of the American Society for Information Science, 41*(4), 288–297.

Scerri, E. (2001). The Periodic Table: The ultimate paper tool in chemistry. In U. Klein (Ed.), *Tools and Modes of Representation in the Laboratory Sciences.* Dordrecht, Germany: Kluwer Academic.

Schuler, D., & Namioka, A. (Eds.). (1993). *Participatory Design: Principles and Practices.* Hillsdale, NJ: Erlbaum.

Schwartz, B. (2004). *The Paradox of Choice.* New York: HarperCollins.

Segal, R. B., & Kephart, J. O. (1999, May 1–5). MailCat: An intelligent assistant for organizing e-mail. Paper presented at the 3rd Annual Conference on Autonomous Agents (pp. 276–282), Seattle.

Seifert, C. M., & Patalano, A. L. (2001). Opportunism in memory: Preparing for chance encounters. *Current Directions in Psychological Science, 10*(6), 198–201.

Selamat, M. H., & Choudrie, J. (2004). The diffusion of tacit knowledge and its implications on information systems: The role of meta-abilities. *Journal of Knowledge Management, 8*(2), 128–139.

Sellen, A. J., & Harper, R.H.R. (2002). *The Myth of the Paperless Office.* Cambridge, MA: MIT Press.

Shamos, M. (2007). Privacy and public records. In W. Jones & J. Teevan (Eds.), *Personal Information Management.* Seattle: University of Washington Press.

Shannon, C. E. (1948). A mathematical theory of communication. *The Bell System Technical Journal, 27*, 379–423, 623–656.

Shannon, C. E., & Weaver, W. (1949). *The Mathematical Theory of Communication.* Urbana, IL: University of Illinois Press.

Shen, J., Li, L., Dietterich, T. G., & Herlocker, J. L. (2006). A hybrid learning system for recognizing user tasks from desktop activities and email messages. In *Proceedings of the 11th International Conference on Intelligent User Interfaces* (pp. 86–92), Sydney, Australia (ACM Press).

Shen, R., Vemuri, N. S., Fan, W., Torres, R.D.S., & Fox, E. A. (2006, June 11–15). Exploring digital libraries: Integrating browsing, searching, and visualization. In *Proceedings of the 6th ACM/IEEE-CS Joint Conference on Digital Libraries* (pp. 1–10), Chapel Hill, NC (ACM Press).

Shipman, F. M. I., & Marshall, C. C. (1999). Formality considered harmful: Experiences, emerging themes, and directions on the use of formal representations in interactive systems. *Computer Supported Cooperative Work (CSCW), 8*(4), 333–352.

Shneiderman, B. (1992). Tree visualization with tree-maps: 2-d space-filling approach. *ACM Transactions in Graphics, 11*(1), 92–99.

Shneiderman, B., & Bederson, B. B. (2005). Maintaining concentration to achieve task completion. Paper presented at the Proceedings of Designing User Experience, *DUX 2005*, San Francisco.

Silverman, B. G. (1997). Computer reminders and alerts. *Computer, 30*(1), 42–49.

Simon, H. A. (1957). *Models of Man: Social and Rational; Mathematical Essays on Rational Human Behavior in Society Setting.* New York: Wiley.

——. (1969). *The Sciences of the Artificial.* Cambridge, MA: MIT Press.

——. (1971). Designing organizations for an information-rich world. In M. Greenberger (Ed.), *Computers, Communications and the Public Interest* (pp. 40–41). Baltimore: The Johns Hopkins Press.

Simon, H. A., & Newell, A. (1958). Heuristic problem solving: The next advance in operations research. *Operations Research, 6*, 1–10.

Southwell, B. G., & Lee, M. (2004). A pitfall of new media? User controls exacerbate editing effects on memory. *Journalism and Mass Communication Quarterly, 81*(3), 643–656.

Spiekermann, S., Grossklags, J., & Berendt, B. (2001, October 14–17). E-privacy in 2nd generation E-commerce: Privacy preferences versus actual behavior. In *Proceedings 3rd ACM Conference on Electronic Commerce* (pp. 38–47), Tampa, FL (ACM Press).

Springer, P. (1999, January 26). Sun on Privacy: "Get Over It." *Wired News—www.wired.com/politics/law/news/1999/01/17538.*

Streitz, N., & Nixon, P. (2005). Special issue: The disappearing computer. *Communications of the ACM, 48*(3), 32–35.

Suchman, L. (1983). Office procedure as practical action: Models of work and system design. *ACM Transactions on Office Information Systems, 1*(4), 320–328.

——. (1987). *Plans and Situated Actions: The Problem of Human–Machine Communication.* Cambridge: Cambridge University Press.

Surowiecki, J. (2004). *The Wisdom of Crowds: Why the Many Are Smarter Than the Few and How Collective Wisdom Shapes Business, Economies, Societies and Nations.* Boston: Little, Brown.

Sweeney, L. (2002). k-Anonymity: A model for protecting privacy. *International Journal of Uncertainty, Fuzziness and Knowledge-Based Systems, 10*(5), 557–570.

Swets, J. A. (1963). Information retrieval systems. *Science, 141*(3577), 245–250.

——. (1969). Effectiveness of information retrieval methods. *American Documentation, 20*(1), 72–89.

Swire, P. P., & Litan, R. E. (1998). Avoiding a showdown over EU privacy laws. Policy brief. Washington, DC: The Brookings Institution.

Tan, D., Berry, E., Czerwinski, M., Bell, G., Gemmell, J., Hodges, S., et al. (2007). Save everything: Supporting human memory with a personal digital lifetime store. In W. Jones & J. Teevan (Eds.), *Personal Information Management.* Seattle: University of Washington Press.

Tauscher, L. M., & Greenberg, S. (1997a). How people revisit web pages: Empirical findings and implications for the design of history systems. *International Journal of Human–Computer Studies, 47*(1), 97–137.

——. (1997b, April 18–23). Revisitation patterns in World Wide Web navigation. Paper presented at the ACM SIGCHI Conference on Human Factors in Computing Systems, *CHI 1997* (pp. 399–406), Atlanta.

Taylor, A. G. (2004). *The Organization of Information* (2nd ed.). Westport, CT: Libraries Unlimited.

Taylor, H. (2003). Most people are "privacy pragmatists" who, while concerned about privacy, will sometimes trade it off for other benefits. *Harris Interactive,* Harris Poll #17.

Taylor, R. S. (1968). Question negotiation and information seeking in libraries. *College and Research Libraries, 29*, 178–194.

Teevan, J. (2006). *Supporting finding and re-finding through personalization.* Unpublished doctoral thesis, Massachusetts Institute of Technology, Cambridge, MA.

——. (2006, October). The Re: Search engine: Helping people return to information on the Web. Paper presented at the ACM Symposium on User Interface Software and Technology, *UIST 2005*, Seattle.

Teevan, J., Alvarado, C., Ackerman, M. S., & Karger, D. R. (2004, April 24–29). The perfect search engine is not enough: A study of orienteering behavior in directed search. Paper presented at the ACM SIGCHI Conference on Human Factors in Computing Systems, *CHI 2004* (pp. 415–422), Vienna, Austria.

Teevan, J., Capra, R., & Pérez-Quiñones, M. (2007). How people find information. In W. Jones & J. Teevan (Eds.), *Personal Information Management*. Seattle: University of Washington Press.

Teevan, J., Dumais, S. T., & Horvitz, E. (2005, April 15–19). Personalizing search via automated analysis of interests and activities. Paper presented at the 28th Annual International ACM SIGIR Conference on Research and Development in Information Retrieval (pp. 449–456), Salvador, Brazil.

Teltzrow, M., & Kobsa, A. (2004). Impacts of user privacy preferences on personalized systems: A comparative study. In C.-M. Karat, J. O. Blom, & J. Karat (Eds.), *Designing Personalized User Experiences in eCommerce* (pp. 315–332). Norwell, MA: Kluwer.

Thompson, L. L., Levine, J. M., & Messick, D. M. (Eds.). (1999). *Shared Cognition in Organizations: The Management of Knowledge*. Mahwah, NJ: Erlbaum.

Tohidi, M., Buxton, W., Baecker, R., & Sellen, A. (2006). Getting the right design and the design right. In *Proceedings of the SIGCHI Conference on Human Factors in Computing Systems* (pp. 1243–1252), Montreal, QUE, Canada (ACM Press).

Tulving, E. (1983). *Elements of Episodic Memory*. Oxford: Oxford University Press.

Tulving, E., & Thomson, D. M. (1973). Encoding specificity and retrieval processes in episodic memory. *Psychological Review, 80*(5), 352–373.

Tversky, A., & Kahneman, D. (1973). Availability: A heuristic for judging frequency and probability. *Cognitive Psychology, 5*, 207–232.

——. (1974). Judgments under uncertainty: Heuristics and biases. *Science, 185*, 1124–1131.

——. (1981). The framing of decisions and the psychology of choice. *Science, 211*, 453–458.

Udell, J. (2005). Collaborative filtering with del.icio.us—*http://weblog.infoworld.com/udell/2005/06/23.html*.

Van Meter, D., & Middleton, D. (1954). Modern statistical approaches to reception in communication theory. *Institute of Radio Engineers Transactions, PGIT-4*, 119–141.

Voida, A., Grinter, R. E., Ducheneaut, N., Edwards, W. K., & Newman, M. W. (2005). Listening in: Practices surrounding iTunes music sharing. *CHI '05* (pp. 191–200).

Wearden, G. (2002). U.S. tech protests EU privacy laws. *ZDNet News—http://news.zdnet.com/2100-9595_22-960134.html*.

Westin, A. F. (1967). *Privacy and Freedom*. New York: Atheneum.

White, R., Ruthven, I., & Jose, J. M. (2002*)*. Finding relevant documents using top ranking sentences: An evaluation of two alternative schemes. In *Proceedings of the 25th Annual ACM Conference on Research and Development in Information Retrieval* (SIGIR 2002) (pp. 57–64), Tampere, Finland.

Whittaker, S. (2005). Collaborative task management in email. *Human-Computer Interaction, 20*(1–2), 49–88.

Whittaker, S., Bellotti, V., & Gwizdka, J. (2007). Email as PIM. In W. Jones & J. Teevan (Eds.), *Personal Information Management*. Seattle: University of Washington Press.

Whittaker, S., Bellotti, V., & Moody, P. (2005). Introduction to this special issue on revisiting and reinventing e-mail. *Human–Computer Interaction, 20*(1–2), 1–9.

Whittaker, S., & Hirschberg, J. (2001). The character, value and management of personal paper archives. *ACM Transactions on Computer–Human Interaction, 8*(2), 150–170.

Whittaker, S., Jones, Q., & Terveen, L. (2002, Nov. 16–20). Managing communications: Contact management: Identifying contacts to support long-term communication. Presented at ACM 2002 Conference on Computer Supported Cooperative Work, New Orleans.

Whittaker, S., & Sidner, C. (1996). Email overload: Exploring personal information management of email. In *Proceedings of the ACM SIGCHI Conference on Human Factors in Computing Systems* (pp. 276–283), Vancouver, BC, Canada (ACM Press).

Whitten, A., & Tygar, J. D. (1999, August 23–26). Why Johnny can't encrypt: A usability evaluation of PGP 5.0. In *Proceedings of the 8th USENIX Security Symposium* (pp. 169–184), Washington, DC.

Williamson, A., & Bronte-Stewart, M. (1996). Moneypenny: Things to do on the desk. In A. Blandford & H. Thimbleby (Eds.), *Proceedings of the 11th Conference of the British Computer Society Human Computer Interaction Specialist Group—People and Computers XI* (pp. 197–200). London: Springer Verlag.

Wilson, T. D. (1981). On user studies and information needs. *Journal of Documentation, 37*(1), 3–15.

——. (2000). Human information behavior. *Informing Science, 3*(2), 49–55.

——. (2005). Evolution in information behavior modeling. Wilson's model. In K. E. Fisher, S. Erdelez, & L. McKechnie (Eds.), *Theories of Information Behavior* (pp. 31–36). Medford, NJ: Information Today.

Wittgenstein, L. (1953). *Philosophical Investigations*. New York: Macmillan.

Wolverton, M. (1999). Task-based information management. *ACM Computing Surveys (CSUR) Archive, 31*(2).

Wright, R. (2000). *Nonzero: The Logic of Human Destiny*. New York: Pantheon.

Yates, F. A. (1966). *The Art of Memory*. Chicago: University of Chicago Press.

Yates, J. (1989). *Control through Communication: The Rise of Systems in American Management*. Baltimore: Johns Hopkins University Press.

Yiu, K. S. (1997). Time-based Management and Visualization of Personal Electronic Information. Unpublished MSc thesis, University of Toronto.

Zhang, J. (1997). The nature of external representations in problem solving. *Cognitive Science: A Multidisciplinary Journal, 21*(2), 179–217.

Index

Activity integration, 380
Advertisements
    commercials, 196–197
    search for, 301–302
Affinity diagrams, 263–265
Allen, D., 279
Alternatives, framing, 227
Anderson, J. R., 225–226
Apacible, J., 106
App-centeredness, 100
Applications
    collaboration, 221–222
    web-based, 361–362
Archives
    in-place, 164
    legacy, 172
    policies, 166, 168
Artificial intelligence (AI)
        program, 11
Attention capture
    future considerations, 396
    inflow management,
        196–197
    PIM on-the-go, 342–343
Attention Central, 289, 294
Attentional surfaces, 149, 161
Authoring, web-like, 352
Auto, in-place archiving, 164
Auto-completion, 96,
        116–117
Availability heuristic, 197–198

Backups
    for data protection, 161
    web-based, 163–164, 170,
        358–359

Bälter, O., xvi, 294–295
Barreau, D. K., 50, 59, 95,
        102, 313
Bates, M. J., 87, 94, 383
Bederson, B. B., 203–204
Belkin, N. J., 87, 310
Bellotti, V.M.E., 8, 48–49, 59,
        233, 272, 274, 280, 288
Benchmarks, 222
Bensaude-Vincent, B., 252
Berendt, B., 191
Bergman, O., 158
Berners-Lee, T., 351
Berry-picking model of
        search, 87–88
Betty Crocker Foods
        scenario, 136
Beyth-Marom, R., 158
Bias from availability heuristic,
        197–198
Birchall, J. A., 325
Bly, S., 102, 164
Boardman, R., 47, 59, 154,
        159, 226
Boiko, B., xvi, 115, 133,
        165–166, 195,
        221–222, 256–257
Bookmarks
    remembering, 102
    setting, 217–218
Breadth of focus, in making
        sense, 250
Briet, S., 36
Broadbent, D. E., 11
Broadcast communication, 221
Browsing, 94

Bruce, H., 98, 102, 132, 358
Brun-Cottan, F., 164
Buckland, M. K., 28–30,
        36–37
Bush, V., 7, 10, 134
Business cards, 64, 130

Camera cuts, 196–197
Capacity utilization, 205
Capra, R., 106–107
Card, S. K., 11
Carmody, S., 11
Categorization, 68
Cell phones, 163
Challenges, future, 390–391
Change, risk in, 227–228
Channel management,
        200–201
Chemical elements, 252–255
Chicago Crime mashup, 262,
        364–365
Choices, framing, 228–230
Chou Enlai, 216
CIT. See Critical incident
        technique
Cleanup process, 161,
        173–174
Clustering searches, 311
Cognition modes, 249–250
Cognitive psychology, 68–69
Cognitive science, 68–69
Cole, I., 50
Collections, 46–48, 138–139
    project planning, 146–148
    reference vs. project,
        139–146

Commercials, 196–197
Communication
applications, 221
in email messages,
288–292
in finding activities, 92
Concept formation, 68
Contact management, 273
Context
in finding activities,
106–107
In-Context Create feature,
146–147
in integration, 380
in maintaining activities, 167
in searches, 316
Continuous effort, making
sense as, 249
Control issues, in finding
process, 84–85
Convergence, PIM on-the-go,
334
Conversations
email messages, 289–294
as information, 38
Conversion services, 169
Coordination, in finding, 92
Corrections in maintaining,
161–162
Costs
organization and
maintenance, 218
storage, 186
Covey, S. R., 119
Critical incident technique
(CIT), 225
Croft, W. B., 310
Csikszentmihalyi, M.,
202–203
Cutrell, E., 103, 303,
306–307

Data protection, 161
Database management, 71
Decision making, 68
Degradation, in maintaining,
167
Deletion paradox, 158

Depth of focus, in making
sense, 250
Dervin, B., 88, 246
Descriptive studies, 397
Desktop search facilities,
107–108
Diagrams, affinity, 263–265
Difficult-to-replace information,
maintaining, 160, 166
Dillon, A., 110–111
Directed searches, 94
Distributed cognition, 69
Divide-and-conquer, in mind-
mapping, 265
Document management,
email for, 273
Documents, definition, 36–37
Dumais, S. T., 98, 102–103,
132–133, 303,
306–307

Ease of learning, measuring,
219
Effectiveness, measuring,
218
Efficiency, measuring, 219
Egocentric navigation, 112
Eisenberg, M., 383
Email messages, 272–274,
296–297
finding activities, 280–282
future visions, 284–294
information fragmentation,
275–279
information overload,
274–275
keeping activities,
279–280, 284
management guidelines,
294–295
meta-level activities,
282–284
Engelbart, D., 11
English, W., 11
Eudora activity measure-
ments, 230–231
European Union, and privacy
laws, 191

Evaluating activities. See
Measuring and
evaluating activities
Event logs, 382
Everyday activities
finding, 89–93
keeping and organizing,
126–129
Experience sampling method
(ESM), 225–226
Experiential cognition,
249–250
External representations
(ERs)
email messages, 289
problems and projects,
143, 232–233
tasks, 71–72

Faceted classification, 383
False positives
email messages, 280
in keeping and organizing,
131, 149
Feature integration, 379–380
Feldman, S., 91
Fidel, R., 70
File vs. pile keeping
approach, 132–134
Finding and re-finding activities, 80–83, 114–115.
See also Search
activities
email messages, 280–282,
284
evaluating, 219
everyday, 89–93
future challenges and considerations, 390, 397
from need to information,
62–63, 86–89
in public stores vs. private
stores, 83–85
IT departments and, 115
limitations, 105–107
PIM on-the-go, 337–338
recall and recognize step,
93–101

repetition in, 103–104
scenarios, 72–74
tool development, 116–118
visibility of information,
102–103
wayfinding, 107–114
web support for, 355–356
Flow of information, 180–185,
207–209
email messages, 283–284
evaluating, 220
future challenges and considerations, 390–391,
397
inflow management,
195–201
IT departments, 194
outflow management,
186–192
PIM on-the-go, 339–341
scenarios, 72–74
searches, 311
staying "in the flow,"
202–207
tool development, 201–202
web, 359–360
Focus-group studies, 224
Folders
for PIM collections,
140–144
in searches, 314–315
in wayfinding, 110
Format issues
in maintaining process,
167–169
web assurance, 359
Forms of information
in finding activities, 97–98
future, 395
information items, 36–40
in keeping and organizing
activities, 131–132
in PICs, 142
Fragmentation. See Information fragmentation
Framework for PIM, 56–58
activity relationships,
72–73

activity summary, 75–77
cognitive psychology and
cognitive science,
68–69
HCI/HII, 69–70
information management,
70–72
mapping information and
need, 60–67
perspectives, 59–60
Framing decisions and
choices, 227–230
Frohlich, D., 203
Furnas, G. W., 246, 249
Future-proofing policies,
165
Future vision, 388–389
certainties, 391–393
challenges, 390–391
considerations, 396–397
directions, 393–394
disaster handling, 394
email messages,
284–294
PIM on-the-go, 325–334
scenario, 394–396
web, 351–354

Geocentric navigation, 112
Global Positioning Systems
(GPS), 113
Gmail, 236
Goal-derived categories, 68
Goals, 173
Google Earth, 262
Google Finance, 236
Gordin, M., 252
Greenberg, S., 84
Grossklags, J., 191
Grudin, J., 188, 192
Gwizdka, J., 280, 288

Hafner, K., 159
Harper, R.H.R., 27, 50, 82
Haystack project, 100,
381–382
Heuristics, availability,
197–198

Hirschberg, J., 160, 163
Hoffman, R. R., 246
Horvitz, E., 106, 192, 252
Human-computer interaction
(HCI) and human–
information interaction
(HII), 69–70
Human information behavior
(HIB), 70
Human memory, as informa-
tion, 39
Hypertext Editing System, 11

Implicit Query (IQ) prototype,
307
In-Context Create feature,
146–147
In-place archiving, 164
Incidental meta-level
activities, 66
Incoming email guidelines,
295
Incremental meta-level
activities, 66–67
Indexes for searches,
308–309
Inflow management,
195–196
attention capture, 196–197
availability heuristic,
197–198
information overload,
198–201
Information, about-me;
directed-toward-me;
relevant-to-me
examples and issues,
34–35
future considerations, 396
privacy issues, 182–183
search support, 312
Information, action, 50
Information assemblages,
104
Information assurance
in maintaining process,
169–170
web, 359

Information, controlled-by-me; experienced-by-me; owned-by-me; posted-by-me; sent-by-me
  examples and issues, 34–35
  future considerations, 396–397
  privacy issues, 182–184
  search support, 312
Information filtering, 310
Information flow. See Flow of information
Information forms. See Forms of information
Information fragmentation
  email messages, 275–279
  future, 392
  from versions and variations, 98–101
  in maintaining activities, 159
Information friction, 8
Information items, 36–40
Information, maintaining extremely difficult-to-replace, 160, 166
Information management
  integration, 379
  study of, 70–72
Information overload
  email messages, 274–275
  future challenges, 390
  in inflow management, 198–201
Information retrieval field of study, 71
Information warriors and worriers, 13
InfoSelect tool, 218
Input-store-output perspective, 59–60
Integration
  in Project Planner, 148
  PIM on-the-go, 334
  unification. See Unification
Integrative meta-level activities, 67
Intellectual property, 165

Interaction, search activities as, 303–307
Internet, 350. See also Web
Interruptions, 203–244
Irreplaceable information, maintaining, 160, 166
IT departments
  finding and re-finding activities, 115
  keeping and organizing activities, 133
  maintaining activities, 165–166
  making sense activities, 256–257
  measuring and evaluating activities, 221–222
  privacy issues, 194
Item event logs, 382

Jeffries, R., 94–95
Jensen, C., 191
Johnson, S. B., 7
Jones, W., 84, 98, 102, 105, 113, 132–133, 154, 358
Jose, J. M., 106
Junk email, 274–275

Kahneman, D., 197, 228
Karat, C., 191–192
Karger, D. R., 46, 87
Kawasaki, G., 294–295
Kaye, J. J., 159, 172, 174
Keep everything approach, 134–135
Keep nothing approach, 135
Keeping and organizing activities, 122–129, 150–151
  email messages, 279–280, 284
  evaluating, 219–220
  file and pile approaches, 131–134
  from information to need, 63–64
  future challenges and considerations, 390, 397

IT departments, 133
  limitations, 134–138
  multifaceted process, 129–134
  PICs, 138–148
  PIM on-the-go, 337–338
  project planning, 146–148
  scenarios, 72–74
  searches, 310–311
  tool development, 137–138
  web support for, 356–358
Keeping Found Things Found (KFTF) project
  articles on, 139
  external representation support, 232
  folder use, 138
  Project Planner prototype, 146
  PUTs, 384
  shared study approach, 238
  TOP site, 361
  web page access, 128
Kelly, D., 219
Kelly, M., xvi, 116–119, 137–138, 170–171, 200–201, 261–262
Kephart, J. O., 310, 315
Kepler, J., 261
Key properties for collections, 140
Kirkland, Washington, planning, 251–253
Kirsh, D., 199
Klein, G., 246, 249
Knowledge acquisition/elicitation study area, 71
Knowledge management, 70–72
Kobsa, A., 191
Koolstra, C. M., 196
Kuny, T., 169

Landmarks in wayfinding, 109–111
Lang, A., 197

Language-Integrated Query (LINQ), 138
Language use groups, 256–257
Lansdale, M., 11, 59, 93, 305
Learning folders, 314
Lee, M., 196
Legacy archives, 172
Legacy data, 165
Legal privacy restrictions, 191
Levy, D., 36
Librarian-assisted searching, 94–95
Licklider, J.C.R., 8
Life Organizers, 357–358
LifeStreams system, 382
Lin, C. T., 162
Linking, in finding process, 94
Liquidity, personal, 204–205
Location-based finding, 95, 107
Logan, M., 196–197
Logic Theorist program, 11
Logical searches, 107, 313
Logs, item event, 382
Lynch, K., 109–110

MacLachlan, J., 196–197
Mail. *See* Email messages
MailCat system, 315
Maintaining activities, 154–157, 176–177
and life views, 171–173
email messages, 282–284
evaluating, 220
for now, 160–164
for later, 166–171
future challenges and considerations, 390, 397
IT departments, 165–166
mansion scenarios, 157–160
PIM on-the-go, 338–339
scenarios, 72–74
searches, 311
tool development, 170–171
web, 358–359

Making sense activities, 244–251, 267–269
affinity diagrams for, 263–265
as outcome vs. activity, 251–255
email messages, 283–284
evaluating, 220
future challenges and considerations, 391, 397
IT departments, 256–257
meta-level activities, 257–260
mind-mapping for, 265–266
PIM on-the-go, 343–344
PSI, 45–50
scenarios, 72–74
tool development, 261–262
web, 362–365
Malone, T. W., 128, 131–132
Manipulation, in making sense activities, 250
Mann, S., 324
Mapping information and need, 60–61
benefits, 65–67
finding and keeping activities, 62–64
meta-level activities, 64–65
Marshall, C. C., 102, 159, 164, 168, 174
Mashups, 262, 363–365
McNealy, S., 187
Measuring and evaluating activities, 212–216, 239–241
considerations, 218–220
costs, 218
email messages, 283–284
future challenges and considerations, 391, 397
IT department, 221–222
PIM on-the-go, 340–342
real life, 230–235
reminders, 217–218

research on, 222–230
scenarios, 72–74
self-study, 236–238
suggestions, 226–230
tool development, 235–236
web, 360–362
MEMOIRS system, 382
Memory Landmarks interface, 306–307
Mendeleev, D., 252–255, 263
Meta-level activities
email messages, 282–284
flow of information, 182–183, 312
future challenges, 390
making sense, 257–260
mapping between need and information, 64–65
Micromarketing, 301
Miller, D., 383
Mind-mapping, 265–266
Misses
email messages, 280
in keeping and organizing, 131, 149
Mitchell, J., 106
Mobile computing, 323. *See also* PIM on-the-go
Monitors, body, 334–335
Moody, P., 272, 274
Moon, B., 246
Moore's Law, 326
Moran, T. P., 11
Morris, R., 255
Morville, P., xvi, 109, 112–113
Multistep finding process
recall and recognize step, 93–101
repetition, 103–104
visibility of information, 102–103
Mumford, M. D., 398
Munat, C., 358
Musser, J., 261

Nachmias, R., 158
Nakahara, M., xvii, 334–336
Nardi, B., 50, 95, 102, 313
Natural language recognition,
    335
Need for information, and
    mapping, 60–67,
    87–89
Neisser, U., 11
Nelson, T., 11
Newell, A., 11
NLS system, 11
Norman, D. A., 249–250, 268
Notebook invention, 325

O'Conaill, B., 203
O'Day, V. L., 94–95
Office Communicator, 340
O'Grady, S., 365
Olson, J. S., 192
OneCare service, 169
OneNote tool, 218
Open ID standard, 171
Organizers, 357–358
Organizing activities. See
    Keeping and organiz-
    ing activities
Orienteering searches, 94,
    107–108
Otlet, P., 36
Out-of-office email feature,
    283
Outdated information,
    170–171
Outflow management,
    186–192
Outgoing email guidelines,
    295
Output facilitation, 104
Output interference, 103–104

P3P. See Platform for Privacy
    Preferences Project
PageRank algorithm,
    302–303, 355
Paper-based information, 10,
    174–175
Passwords, 167

Paths, in wayfinding,
    109–111
Pejtersen, A. M., 70
Pérez-Quiñones, M.,
    106–107
Periodic table of elements,
    252–255
Persistence of information,
    32
Personal digital assistants
    (PDAs), 323,
    326–327
Personal information and
    privacy. See Flow of
    information
Personal information collec-
    tions (PICs), 46–48,
    138–139
  project planning,
    146–148
  properties for, 140
  reference vs. project,
    139–146
Personal information man-
    agement (PIM), 4–6
  benefits, 13–14
  history, 10–12
  ideal vs. reality, 7–10
  on-the-go. See PIM on-
    the-go
  study and practice, 14
Personal knowledge man-
    agement (PKM), 71
Personal liquidity, 204–205
Personal Project Planner
  external representations
    in, 232–233
  hypertext in, 358
Personal searches, 310–312
Personal space of informa-
    tion (PSI), 25–28,
    40–45, 50–53
  evaluating, 226
  forms of information in,
    36–40
  frequency of information
    access, 50
  information types in, 28–33

making sense of, and
    tasks and projects,
    45–50
  wayfinding through,
    107–114
Personal Unifying Taxonomy
    (PUT), 384
Phishing, 189–190
Phlat research interface,
    304–305
Pile vs. file keeping
    approach, 132–134
PICs. See Personal informa-
    tion collections
PIM on-the-go, 320–325,
    344–345
  features, 336–337
  flow of information activi-
    ties, 339–341
  future, 325–334
  keeping and re-finding
    activities, 337–338
  maintaining and mak-
    ing sense activities,
    338–344
  measuring and evaluating
    activities, 340–342
  wearable computing,
    334–336
Pirolli, P., 391
Planning, future of, 398–399
Platform for Privacy Prefer-
    ences Project (P3P),
    192–194
Point-to-point communica-
    tion, 221
Polls, web, 360–361
Portable hard drives, 163
Prescriptive evaluations, 397
Privacy. See Flow of
    information
Privacy Bird add-in, 193
Private stores, finding activi-
    ties in, 83–85
Problem decomposition, 68
Problem solving, 68
Productivity, 13, 222
Project collections, 139–146

Project management,
48–50
Project Planner prototype,
146–148
Properties for PICs, 140
Prospect theory, 229
PSI. *See* Personal space for
information
Public stores, finding activi-
ties in, 83–85
PUT. *See* Personal Unifying
Taxonomy

Qu, Y., 246
Quan, D., 46

Ranking algorithms,
302–303, 355
RDF. *See* Resource Description Framework
Real-life measuring and
evaluating activities,
230–235
Really Simple Syndication
(RSS), 362–363
Recall, recognition, and
repetition techniques
email messages, 281–282
finding and re-finding
activities, 93–104
keeping and organizing
activities, 149
search activities, 304–307
Reference collections
maintaining, 160
vs. project, 139–146
Re-finding activities. *See*
Finding and re-finding
activities
Reflective cognition,
249–250
Reminders
keeping and organizing
activities, 148–149
search activities, 306–307
setting, 217–218
Resource Description Framework (RDF), 381–382

Ries, A., 196
Risk evaluation, 227–228
Ross, B. H., 162
RSS. *See* Really Simple
Syndication
Rundus, D., 104
Russell, D. M., xvii, 235–236,
246, 249–250
Ruthven, I., 106

Sample and optimize
approach, 200
Sasse, M. A., 154, 159, 226
Satisfice approach, 200
Scerri, E., 252
Scrub process, 173–174
Search activities, 300–303,
316. *See also* Finding
and re-finding
activities
and wayfinding, 313–317
as interaction, 303–307
as technology, 307–310
folders in, 314–315
personal, 310–312
recall, 304–305
recognition and recollec-
tion, 306–307
situated, 315–317
Security and privacy. *See*
Flow of information
Segal, R. B., 310, 315
Self-directed email mes-
sages, 273
Self-observation, 233–235
Sellen, A. J., 27, 50, 82
Semantic Web, 350–351
Semi-spam, 275
Sense-making activities.
See Making sense
activities
Sense of digital space, 399
Senses, in navigation, 112
Serendipity, 258–259
Server Privacy Architec-
ture and Capability
Enabler (SPARCLE),
192

Shamos, M., 186–187, 191
Shannon, C. E., 10–11, 28
Shared study approach, 238
Shaw, J. C., 11
Shneiderman, B., 106,
203–204
Short Message Service
(SMS), 285
Shultz, R. A., 398
Sidner, C. L., 102, 281
Signal-detection tasks, 68
Simon, H. A., 9, 11, 52, 134,
200
SIS. *See* Stuff I've Seen
Situated cognition, 69
Situated searches, 315–317
Smart folders, 314
Social cognition, 69
Social tagging systems, 256
Software, web-based,
361–362
Southwell, B. G., 196
Spam, 274–275
Speech recognition, 331,
335
Spiekermann, S., 191
Stewart, P., 315
Storage degradation, 167
Structure, web, 356–357
Stuff I've Seen (SIS) desktop
search prototype,
108, 306–307
Subject lines, in email
messages, 276
Synchronization, 161–162
Synergy, 373–379

Tagging support, 96
Tales of PIM (TOP) site,
361
Targeted advertisements,
301
TaskMaster, 233, 288
Tasks and task management
email for, 273
external representations,
71–72
integration, 379

Tasks and task management (*cont.*)
  interrupted, 203–244
  in Project Planner, 148
  PSI, 48–50
  reminders for, 217–218
Tauscher, L. M., 84
Teaching and learning, future of, 395
Technology, search as, 307–310
Teevan, J., 94, 103, 106–107, 113, 157, 219, 303, 306, 313
Teleporting, 94, 313
Teltzrow, M., 191
Theory of signal detectability (TSD), 228
Things, information as, 30, 37, 40
Thrasks, 233, 287
Thumb drives, 163
Time and time management, 71–72
  future considerations, 396
  for information, 33
  in Project Planner, 148
  integration, 379
  PIM on-the-go, 342
Tool development
  finding and re-finding activities, 116–118
  flow of information, 201–202
  keeping and organizing activities, 137–138
  maintaining activities, 170–171
  making sense activities, 261–262
  measuring and evaluating activities, 235–236
TOP. *See* Tales of PIM site
Treemap algorithm, 164
Triage approach, 200

Trout, J., 196
Trust issues, in outflow management, 190–192
Tversky, A., 197, 228
Twitter Vision, 262
Tygar, J. D., 192

Ubiquitous computing (ubicomp), 324
Unification, 370–373, 384
  enabling, 380
  feature integration, 379–380
  item event logs, 382
  RDF, 381–382
  scenario, 383–384
  synergy, 373–379
Uniform Resource Identifiers (URIs), 380
Updating issues, 161–162
Usability studies, 224

Van Dam, A., 11
Van Doorn, J. R., 398
Vaughan, M., 110–111
Versions and variations
  information fragmentation from, 98–101
  in maintaining process, 167
Virtual folders
  in PICs, 139
  in searches, 314–315
Visibility of information, 102–103
Visual integration, 379
Visualization, in maintaining activities, 164
Voice recognition, 331, 335
Voida, A., 172

Watches, 334–335
Wayfinding, 107, 112–113
  and searches, 313–317

as round trip, 109–114
desktop search, facilities for, 107–108
Wearable computing, 324, 334–336
Weaver, W., 10–11, 28
Web, 348–351, 366–367
  expectations, 354–355
  finding information on, 84
  finding support for, 355–356
  flow of information activities, 359–360
  future, 351–354
  keeping and organizing activities, 356–358
  maintaining and making sense activities, 358–359
  measuring and evaluating activities, 360–362
Web 2.0, 350
Web-based backups, 163–164, 170
Web-like authoring, 352
Westin, A., 188
White, R., 106
Whittaker, S., 102, 157, 160, 163, 272, 274, 280–281, 288
Whitten, A., 192
Wikis, 39, 289–291, 294
Wilson, T. D., 82, 88
Wireless connectivity, 322
"Wisdom of the crowds" effect, 350, 355–356
Working information, 50, 160–161
World representation, 31
World Wide Web (WWW), 350
Writing pad invention, 325

Zillow site, 262